*To Hilary + Tim.
a new generation,*

MORNING SHOWS THE DAY

living + teaching the

The Making of a Priest

*Gospel in a new world
but in to the same Faith.*

Stanley Hoffman

*With the prayers
+ best wishes of*

Stanley Hoffman

10. 10. 95

MINERVA PRESS
MONTREUX LONDON WASHINGTON

MORNING SHOWS THE DAY

ISBN 1 85863 480 6

First Published 1995 by
MINERVA PRESS
10 Cromwell Place,
London SW7 2JN

Printed in Great Britain by
B.W.D. Ltd., Northolt, Middlesex

MORNING SHOWS THE DAY

Stanley Hoffman

CANON EMERITUS OF ROCHESTER
M.A. OXON. HON. M.A. KENT

SOMETIME DIOCESAN DIRECTOR OF
EDUCATION (1965-1980) AND WARDEN OF
READERS, ROCHESTER (1973-1980)

PROCTOR IN CONVOCATION (1969-1970)

EXAMINING CHAPLAIN TO THE BISHOP OF
ROCHESTER (1973-1980)

CHAPLAIN TO THE QUEEN (1976-1987)

FOR MYFANWY (PAT) MY WIFE, WHO NEEDS NO
EXPLANATIONS

FOR PETER AND JILL FOR WHOM IT MAY EXPLAIN MUCH

AND FOR MY FRIENDS.

"A well-written life is almost as rare as a well spent one."
Thomas Carlyle. (d. 1881)

"I have been asked to write an autobiography and I've said I can't.
It's one of the lowest forms of art there is."
Dennis Potter. TV Writer. (1935-1994)

CONTENTS

PREFACE

A famous man, for many years at the centre stage of national life, called his autobiography *Retrospect of an Unimportant Life.* Considering his fame and remembering the controversies in which he had been involved, I always considered this to be the ultimate in false humility. Why, I asked myself, should anyone be interested in the recollections of one who has only been heard on the radio a few times, and that on *local* radio, and had only appeared on television once, and that on *local* TV, in a dispute with John Betjeman on the rival merits of a Victorian Church and an Edwardian Church, nearly forty years ago? On that occasion Betjeman was backing not his beloved Victoriana, but the red brick daughter Church in Haslemere.

So, why have I troubled to write down all these trivialities and all these superficialities, as they may well appear to be to most of my readers?

There are a variety of answers. Firstly I suppose, to amuse myself. It is true that as we get older, and approach decades even beyond our three score years and ten, events and peoples of the past are etched more clearly and distinctly on the tablet of the mind and memory. Living alone now, I have found entertainment and diversion (and I have chuckled more than once) in recalling them to mind. Then I am responding to those who have said to me when we have been sharing remembrances of past days: "Why don't you put it all down on paper?"

Most of all, I have a positive hope, and a confidence indeed, that the experiences and lessons of a bygone age, and of a ministry covering more than half a century on the part of a Curate, a Vicar, a Director of Education, a Warden of Readers, a Lay Training officer, a Diocesan functionary, writer and peripatetic preacher, may be of some help to a modern priest and his congregation.

It seems to me that human beings are almost totally incapable of learning lessons from the past. Why else do we continually make the same mistakes in Church and State? Why is the Church of England still debating those subjects which we debated in theological college more than 50 years ago? Why do we not take the adventurous line and adopt any of the proposals which our forefathers made in past reports to a waiting Church? One has only to read my letter to parents in 1959 to see how little the world and the Church have changed (see Appendix).

But of course times *have* changed and we must change with them. Many of the exciting things we did in parishes in past days are not possible now. We have to "rethink" our attitudes. As I write this preface I recall the great "Mothering Sunday" services we used to hold, with their emphasis on the normal family of mother and father and two children. Today one third of adults attending worship are single, many are single parents. Many of the children in our schools, and what is left of our Sunday Schools, come from divided homes and have divided loyalties. Two out of five people who come to Church today are not even married. Thirteen per cent are separated or divorced, twenty-four per cent have lost their married partner. I am painfully aware that I would not know how to organise a parish today; that money raising is far more of a problem than it ever was; that the laity cannot be treated as they once were; and that they are more than mere helpers in the parish. They are the leaders and the innovators. At last they, and not just the clergy, are seen to be "the Church", the "blessed company of all faithful people".

However, I believe that to read of some of the things we did in the past to extend the bounds of the kingdom of God may stimulate thought, and perhaps experimentation, on similar lines. We do not use our opportunities today. We have "prime sites" in our Churches and churchyards and we do not make use of them. So many of our notice boards are tatty, bearing torn and out-of-date posters. Our parish magazines are too often poor little typescripts with no challenge in them and no teaching. Some of the sermons I hear now from the pew are a poor substitute for the true proclamation of the Gospel. Some are so ill-prepared and so ill-delivered that one would have thought that the "College of Preachers" is unknown, and that the great communicators, A.J. Gossip, J.S. Stewart, Harry Fosdick, Leslie Weatherhead, W.E. Sangster, William Barclay, George Reindorp, Donald Goggan, and Cleverley Ford, had never lived.

If we have a message to give to the world then it must be spread abroad. I am aware of the difficulties of informing every house in a parish of ten thousand people what the local Church is doing, but it can be done, and sometimes the seed sown by a paper pushed through a letter box will bear fruit. I know it. God does use the weak things of the world to confound the wise, and to change lives.

In the first part of this book, my reminiscences are often trivial. My life has been unimportant (except perhaps to those who have loved me and helped me and whom I may in some small way have helped) but isn't life made up of trivialities? Aren't the things we remember with most pleasure the little things? The inconsiderable events and little people whose names we have forgotten, are they not the ones who have actually re-directed our energies and re-vitalised our mundane existence?

I would add this, however, that as I write this preface the Church (and not just the Church of England) is said to be "in crisis". But the Church has always been in crisis, for the word means judgement. We are forever under the loving judgement of God. Very little of what I write about the life of a Diocese between 1965 and 1980 when I was "at the centre" of its affairs would be true today, but can we not learn from the past in a diocese as I am sure we can learn from the past life of a parish? Manpower must be slimmed down, yes; savings must be made because we are in financial straits. Forms of training must change, not just because the Priestly Ministry has been opened to women, but also because the world in which we minister has changed. But the power of God does not change. It is as available and as immediate as it ever was. We need more faith, we need to be much more assured that the Church still has the same message with which the early disciples changed the world. I hope that some of the strictures that I have passed upon the Church as I knew it, and served it, will be taken to heart. I believe that Christians will be persecuted in the 21st century (though in much more subtle ways) just as much as they were in earlier centuries, but we must believe not only that the Church is an anvil which has worn out many hammers, but also that "the gates of hell" will never prevail against it. It was Peter's rock-like faith that Christ built his Church upon, not the man himself.

In the course of any man's life the problems of pain and death will arise to test him. At the moment there is a fierce debate proceeding among our leaders, among the doctors, and in the Church, as well as among ordinary thinking people, about voluntary euthanasia, and because euthanasia is illegal, the inevitable suicides that result. I hope that what I have written about my beloved wife's pain over twelve years, and her ultimate suicide may help to clarify the thinking of those who may read these pages. In revealing our deepest thoughts and feelings, in telling of our reactions to pain and death, my dearest wish has been to turn the reader's thoughts not only to the inevitability of death, but also to the Christian hope.

Much of my story has been written from memory, for foolishly (wisely?) when we left our vast Queen Anne house in Rochester for a tiny wooden bungalow, I destroyed sackfuls of documents and papers. Memory can be faulty. For mistakes made I offer my regrets and if I have hurt anyone by what I have written I am sorry. Forgiveness is something we can expect if we are truly sorry!

In the book I have expressed my gratitude to David Say, Bishop and friend, for sixteen years of help and understanding. It remains only to thank him for his generous words of support and commendation.

Stanley Hoffman
Trevone, Padstow,
Cornwall.

FOREWORD

By the Right Reverend Dr. R.D. Say, KCVO,
(Bishop of Rochester, 1961 - 1988)

The story of the twentieth century, whether it is told by historians, statesmen or churchmen is a story told on a moving escalator with a rapidly changing scene and exciting discoveries and developments at every stage. It has been a century of transition for both Church and State which has left some bewildered and bemused, but others spellbound and expectant. Canon Stanley Hoffman's personal story begins during the first World War and moves through seven decades of changes in home and family life, in the life and worship of English parishes, and in the educational and social policies of successive Governments.

The historian Professor Maitland wrote that "We study the day before yesterday that yesterday may not paralyse today and today may not paralyse tomorrow." Stanley Hoffman makes it clear in his Preface that he has not only written this book for his own amusement and for the satisfaction of his friends, but also that, "the experiences and lessons of a bygone age, and of a ministry covering more than half a century... may be of some help to a modern priest and his congregation."

For all his distinction as a Director of Education, as a Cathedral dignitary and as a Royal Chaplain, Stanley has remained at heart a parish priest. The story of his twenty-four years of parochial ministry is the essential background to his work as an educationalist, a trainer and a preacher. The success of his innumerable papers on belief and practice which both clergy and laity read with enthusiasm was that they were grounded in down-to-earth experience in parochial life and that they avoided the jargon beloved by those more remote from 'the front line'.

Pat Hoffman, Stanley's lively and very brave wife, is the heroine of his story and all who knew her will rejoice that this is so. Until her last long and agonising illness she was as vital and energetic as her husband. Both of them had very busy and demanding jobs and they shared the routines of domestic life and were generous hosts. The chapter on 'Marriage' is described as a 'digression'. It is in fact the heart of a book which it is a delight to commend to those who love the Church of England and who have faith in its future as well as thanksgiving for its past.

David Say

CHAPTER 1

FATHER

"The childhood shows the man
As morning shows the day."
Milton. (d. 1674)

"The Child is Father of the Man;
And I could wish my days to be
Bound each to each by natural piety."
Wordsworth. (d. 1850)

"Honour Thy Father And Thy Mother."
The Fifth Commandment

My father rarely went to Church. There was a time when this fact worried me. Not in his lifetime though. He died in 1934 when I was nearly seventeen and I don't remember his non-practising of the Christian faith as a problem until I was made to think seriously about what theology calls the "Last Things", death and judgement, heaven and hell, while I was at theological college. What is the final destiny of the good people who don't go to Church, don't have a "Prayer Life" and just live by the golden rule of do as you would be done by? If my father had helped to feed the hungry (as he had), had cared for the poor (as he had) given of his money for good causes (as he had) and quietly assisted many folk in his life without publicity or a blowing of trumpets, would not this be enough to ensure for him a place in Heaven? Then I remembered that my father used to swear a great deal, and enjoyed his whisky and cigars more than somewhat. The two things often went together. I can recall one particular occasion when I was driving home with him from one of his rent-collecting forays during which we had stopped at half a dozen assorted pubs, and he tried to pass a tram-car on the left, as one was allowed to do, without noticing that the single line was about to become a double line and the tram suddenly swayed to the left and all but crushed us between its yellow sides and a gas lamp post. My father was a master of the art of cursing, and if ears burn when tram drivers are cursed, then that tram driver would have been earless in a very short time. But there was no malice or real venom in my father's anathemas, and no profanity either. A boy of eight would have noted such. No, it was real old fashioned stuff, good English blasting, not religious blasphemy nor the four letter words of modern sexual pollution. And I remembered it when I was worrying over my father's eternal destiny years later.

As to his drinking, he was never incapable of driving either a horse or a car. I marvel now at his capacity, but in the days when I accompanied him in his retirement on his rounds of his properties in Middlesex during my school holidays, it did not occur to me that his increasing exasperation with other drivers had anything to do with the fact that we had stopped first at the Falcon in Denham, then at the Falcon in Uxbridge, next at the Red Lion in Hillingdon and yet another Inn further up the street whose name I cannot remember, and that on our return we had not passed either the Angel at Hayes nor the French Horn at Gerrards Cross (with one or two others in between) without paying a friendly call. For my father was a friendly man who liked the conviviality of the public house (private bar) and the down-to-earth converse with former business associates and companions. I must not give the impression that he was a tippler or a drunkard, or that he was ever other than sober. It was only on Mondays, rent day, that he had the opportunity of going the rounds, and when a countryman has retired from a very full and active life he misses the society of his old cronies; he misses the talk about the price of hay and the poor potato crop, and the government's current iniquities.

Charles Hoffmann was born in 1865 in Hemel Hempstead, so it is said, though the fact has never been verified. There were two 'n's on this common German name at that time, though one was taken off during the Great War as a concession to the anti-German feeling that was strong at the time. How that could have made any difference it is hard to see. It is intriguing to ponder on the fact that when he was born, one hundred and twenty nine years ago, the second Reform Act had not yet been passed, the first Education Act of 1870 which set up the elementary School Boards was yet to come, the American Civil War was just coming to an end, Charles Dickens was still alive, and neither Disraeli nor Gladstone had yet formed their first administration.

It is even more startling to remember that the first gas cooker had been put into use less than thirty years before his birth, a really effective electric dynamo had still to be invented, the first workable electric lamp was still thirteen years off, there were no motorcars on the streets, the first Underground Railway in London would not appear for thirty three years, that babies born in that year would have to wait until they were fifty seven years old before they could listen to the radio. My father was forty four when Bleriot flew the channel, and he had received all his schooling and was at work (at the age of ten) before Alexander Graham Bell had invented the first workable telephone. It pleases me too to think that if my father was one of the youngest of a large family, as I believe he was, my grandfather on his side was living at the same time as Napoleon.

I have a great respect and a profound veneration for my father. He was a self-made man, as men say, and he had done a good job in the making. To have received all your schooling from an old "dame" at a penny a week and to have finished formal education at a time when the equivalent child of today has not even taken the 11-plus, is a mean and poor preparation for the contests of life. To be driving a cart full of hay the twenty five miles from Hemel Hempstead to London at twelve years old and then to be responsible for selling it on the open market is an almost incredible accomplishment. To have survived the attention of the footpads and gentlemen of the road and to have returned home with horse and cart and money intact is an even more praiseworthy exploit. No doubt he had learned quickly and well from the old Schoolma'am of Hemel Hempstead, then a smallish country village, now a vast, sprawling "New Town", for I remember that his writing was clear and well formed and of considerable character. His father was a "journeyman tailor", a respected profession that died out many years ago.

The journeyman tailor had no shop of his own, but he would travel the countryside with his bundles of cloth, and when he had persuaded his customer, an up and coming tradesman it may be, to have a new suit made, he would install himself in a room in the tradesman's house and set to work on his broadcloth, sitting cross-legged on a cushion or low stool, or even on the floor, until the suit was completed. It was not a very well paid profession, but it brought in enough for the family to live above the poverty line. My grandfather's family is shrouded in the mystery of a hundred and fifty years, and I do not know how large it was. I have two vivid memories of meeting an uncle, an elder brother of my father, in a house at Egham which had a quince tree in the garden. He was a large man with a gouty leg which fascinated me as it lay, huge and swollen, upon a hassock in the overcrowded front room; and two sisters of his, one of whom was unbelievably called Princess, who visited us in our house at Gerrards Cross in their long skirts and picture hats. Of their conversation I remember only that one would say to everything that was being discussed, "Absolutely!" and the other would reply, "Too true!" For years my sister and I would echo these sisters on every pertinent occasion.

"Absolutely!" I would declare. "Too true!" my sister would reply and we would dissolve into uncontrollable mirth.

Of my father's early life after leaving school I was told little. He was a superb craftsman. The kitchen table he had made as a young lad was still in use sixty years after. The long cart he had made with his own hands, wheels and all, in 1886, was still in perfect condition and daily use when we gave up our home and business in 1928. Part farmer, part dealer, part coal merchant, he was a respected business man in our village of Denham in Buckinghamshire when we were born, my two sisters and I. I can only guess that he had worked for various farmers in Hertfordshire and Bucks before setting up on his own. He had married his first wife and settled down in the village before the turn of the century, and by her he had six children, two boys and four girls (including the "one who died" - so common a happening in most families of a former generation) who became my half-brothers and sisters when as a widower he married my mother. It was a normal-sized family for the period, though it would be considered a very large one today, if you add my two sisters and myself. There were adequate means available to keep us all in considerable comfort and when my father died he was able to leave something to each one of us, as well as leave my mother enough to live on.

In appearance he was of more than average height for his generation, though such has been the increase in male height over the years covered by two world wars that he would have been considered below average height today, very upright and rather stocky. The photographic portrait of him which hung for many years side by side with a portrait of my mother shows steady piercing grey eyes, a commanding head, rather round, with a beautifully brushed quiff fashionable eighty years ago, rather heavy cheeks, a slightly too long nose with broad nostrils, and a fine moustache, waxed to a point at each end. He wore good clothes, sometimes even a brightly flowered waistcoat, and across his strong chest there was the gold watch chain popular in his day, hung with various seals including several of the Masonic order. About him there always hung the aroma of a good cigar. I loved to sit on his knee and smell the Erasmic shaving soap which he used every morning (I used the same soap myself - perhaps out of filial piety - until electric shavers came in) and when mixed with the cigar fragrance it was an irresistible combination. He was not naturally a demonstrative man, but on rare occasions he did his best to show that he cared for us. He would take me with him sometimes on his business jaunts and I would hold his hand and listen to his conversation with his intimates. He would let me ride with him in the horse-drawn open carriage which we had before our first motor car, a model "T" Ford. He would let me watch him while he shaved. On one occasion this led to near disaster. He always used an open "cut-throat razor", to the day he died, and on one particular day I was watching, fascinated, through the open bathroom door when I must have done something to distract his attention. The razor slipped, and for ever afterwards he carried a deep scar on his right cheek as large as a half-crown.

He taught me to play "tip-cat" with a short piece of wood, pointed at each end, which is laid on the ground and struck sharply with another piece, three or four feet long and about an inch and a half in diameter. If the "cat" is hit smartly enough and in the right place it will fly many yards, and the one who can cover a measured distance in the fewest number of strokes on the cat is the winner. A dangerous game!

As I was born in the year that he reached the age of fifty-two, he must have been sixty when these events took place and there must inevitably be a yawning gulf between a father of sixty and a boy of eight. Especially as there had been seven other children to love and care for before I arrived on the scene. So my father always seemed rather a remote person who found it difficult to enter into the fears and fantasies of childhood. He was sometimes distant and brusque in his speech towards us, and as a firm believer in filial obedience, would brook no nonsense from his children. It would not have occurred to any of us to be impertinent or insolent towards him. It would not have occurred to us to disobey an order from him. At mealtimes we were taught that "children are meant to be seen and not heard" and woe to any who did not eat everything that was put in front of him, or who attempted to leave the table without asking permission first. It seems to me, looking back over the years, that my father did not like children as a race. This may be because he was the child of his own time, and was applying to us the same methods of upbringing which had been applied to him in his own childhood. He was a Victorian and had had a Victorian upbringing. It was not very many years before his birth that Mr. Barrett was lording it over his family in Wimpole Street to such effect that Elizabeth had to descend to deceit and artifice in order to meet her lover, Robert Browning. Such tyranny may not have been universal in Victorian households, but something like it must have been commonplace. Children had their proper place and it was a lowly place. One did not discuss things with one's children, one told them "what's what". One did not ask one's children where they would like to go for their holidays, or even what they would like for their birthdays. That must be decided for them. There was at least a residue of this attitude in my father's dealings with his children. It was a world of "cautionary tales" of the Hilaire Belloc kind, and my father would probably have approved of R.L. Stevenson's *Child's Garden of Verses* if he had known of it, particularly of the little piece called *System*:

"Every night my prayers I say and get my dinner every day
And every day that I've been good, I get an orange after food.
The child that is not clean and neat with lots of toys and things to eat
He is a naughty child I'm sure, or else his dear papa is poor."

Cleanliness and neatness are rare virtues in some quarters today, but they were essential ingredients of respectability sixty years ago. My father was always neatly turned out. He wore a clean winged collar every day, and his tie was always neatly tied, often with a jewelled tie-pin to keep the knot in place. He wore the then fashionable and middle-class bowler hat on most occasions, and a soft hat for less formal wear. In summer his stocky figure was always topped with a straw boater, fastened to his coat lapel with a silver clip and fine black cord. He had a coat with an astrakhan collar and he wore spats.

We children were not spared corporal punishment whenever it was deemed necessary for the creation of strong and honest character, but our beatings seem to have been confined to those times and incidents when we transgressed the rules of neatness and cleanliness. Two in particular stand out in my memory, both on a Sunday afternoon. On the first occasion my elder sister Enid and I discovered that the granary door had been left open and we had a wonderful time playing in the dusty oats with which our carthorses were fed. We emerged, and I can see the image of us now, white from head to foot in a floury dust. And flour is very difficult to remove, especially if it gets wet. I had ruined a dark suit and my sister had ruined, however temporarily, a velvet dress. We were thrashed with a long, thin, lady's walking stick, and retired weeping to our separate rooms to hug our bruises

On the second occasion that the Devil found work for unoccupied Sunday hands I was alone. The outbuildings in which the horses and carts were kept were periodically painted with pure tar, and down by the piggeries was a very large tar barrel, on a wooden stand about three feet high. I knew what was in the barrel, and I knew how the tar was tapped out of it by the removal of a large wooden pin which plugged the outlet hole in the bottom of the barrel as it lay upon its side on its frame. On this occasion I was curious as to whether there was any tar left in the barrel. Curiosity can be a dangerous instinct in a small boy aged six. I struck the top of the plug a hefty blow from the front. If I had smitten it from the side all would have been well, except for the loss of tar, but there was a fatal inevitability about this episode - it was a lesson in non-interference to end all lessons. The tar barrel was full. My cries were no doubt heard up at the house thirty yards away. My mother came out of the kitchen as I ran, dripping tar from hands and feet, clothes and face. But my screams of surprise and fear were elementary compared with the screams of pain as she belaboured me with the walking stick. I did not put my finger into any unauthorised pie from that day onwards. After the lengthy cleaning up process I spent the rest of the day sitting on the seat in the earth closet outside the back door.

Sir Compton Mackenzie claimed to remember events in his early childhood from the age of two, and one questions whether there is not

a great deal of hindsight in most of our early memories. My
memories do not go back that far, but I do have vivid recollections of
being bathed by my youngest half-sister May in front of the kitchen
fire when I was about three, and I remember where I sat when we had
meals in the kitchen, in a sort of recess behind the table, as it lay up
against the wall, which could only be got into by crawling underneath
the table. It was a wonderfully cosy place to be, and that kitchen table
will always stay in my memory - it was the one my father made when
he was a lad, because I was sat upon it when I got the sharp prongs of
my braces through my tongue, while a neighbour helped my mother to
unclip the braces and remove the prongs and poured Condy's fluid on
to the bleeding member.

My father rarely went to Church. In the years of my conscious
knowledge of him he entered a Church only once, for my half-sister
May's wedding. I have often wondered since why this was. He was
born in a Church-going era. Most of the villagers of Hemel
Hempstead would have been regular Church-goers and I have no
doubt that my father had attended Sunday School, which was such a
valuable supplement to the inadequate schooling which most children
received before state education was made compulsory. There is a
story current in our family that my father *had* been a keen Churchman
in his early manhood, but that he had a quarrel with the Rector and
had given up his duties as a sideman in disgust. I have often
wondered if this was true - it is a common excuse for non-attendance
at public worship. The Church was never mentioned in our family,
except when it was time for the children to be sent to Church.
Perhaps there was a gulf between the classes who went to Church in
our village - the very rich and the very poor, and as my father came
somewhere in between he may have felt that there was no place for
him. Perhaps he felt, as a self-made-man, that he had no need for
God, and that to express such a need would be hypocritical in him.
We did not have family prayers, though grace was always said before
and after meals, and my father would have felt that a meal without
grace was somehow lacking in an essential part.

I have frequently mused on the question of how my father came to
make his money. Farming after the Great War was not a lucrative
business, and I cannot think that he was able to make very much
money during that War. He was forty-nine when it started in 1914,
and because of his age, he was never called up. He saw no war

service, either overseas or at home. He was on more than one occasion arrested in London and made to explain why he was not in uniform. Moreover he was made to explain why his name was a German one, and to prove that he was not a spy. The authorities were very naïve in those days, but the anti-German feeling was running high after the stories of atrocities in Belgium and France. My half-brother Edward had to change his name to Harrison and go to another school because of the antagonism to anyone with a German name. But the War had little effect upon the life of a small Buckinghamshire village except that many of the men were called up.

Those were days when taxes were low. When the Great War began income tax was only 1/8d in the pound, and though it steadily rose to a new peak of 6/- in the pound in 1921/22, living was comparatively cheap if you owned your own pigs and poultry and tilled your own garden. I suspect that it was by judicious buying and selling of house property and by the exercise of a wise economy that he was able to save enough money for retirement at the age of sixty three. The line between meanness and moderation is hard to draw, but my father would have approved the principle (indeed he enunciated it to us on many occasions) that, if you look after the pence, the pounds will look after themselves. To him it was a sin to cut a piece of string. One reason why the biting of nails was frowned upon in our house was that it made untying knots extremely difficult. In the day of the aggravating sellotape this admonition presumably has no force. I think that even as a child I felt that turning envelopes inside out and using them again was carrying economy rather far, but I am grateful now that he did do this, for without it perhaps I should not have received the education which, by my good fortune and his frugality, has been mine.

His own business acumen made him hard with us children in the matter of pocket money. Admittedly 2/- a week was not niggardly in the late twenties and early thirties when many men were on the dole at starvation level but with it we had to do all that was necessary, buying our sweets and our pencils and pens, and paying our school subs. My sister received half a crown. I recall being deeply incensed at the injustice of being paid only a penny a pound for fourteen pounds of blackberries which a friend, Edward Dickinson, and I had laboriously picked from the hedgerows, but with that one and twopence we were both able to go to the pictures, and have sweets to eat as well, in

1929. It may have been frugality, or perhaps a sense that young people do not stand enough upon their own feet that caused one of the incidents in my life when I was deeply ashamed of my father. We were living at Gerrards Cross at the time, and my blackberrying friend had come from the village of Denham where we had lived until 1928 to spend a Saturday afternoon with me. It may well have been the same day. When the time came for him to go home, we found that he had missed the last bus and I appealed to my father to take my friend home by car. He would not. In spite of the pouring rain, Edward Dickinson had to walk the three miles home. Not a very great distance for a man who in his own youth had walked much farther than that seeking work, but I was humiliated and embarrassed at the hardness of it. This is perchance one example of my father's dislike of children. He could be a very stubborn, unyielding man. There was no intentional cruelty in his severity, but it did often create a barrier between us to add to the barrier that already existed because of his age.

And yet he had times of softness and even sweetness. When he forgot his role of stern father he would regale us with the popular songs of his own early manhood - the songs of Charles Coburn, *The Man Who Broke The Bank At Monte Carlo* was a firm favourite; of Harry Lauder and Will Fyfe; of George Robey, his favourite comedian, and Harry Champion. *My Grandfather's Clock* was a song we asked for time and again. He would take me to the cinema too, from time to time, where we would enjoy together the antics of Harold Lloyd and Charlie Chaplin. A visit to the Great Exhibition at Wembley in 1924 when I was seven years old stands out in my recollection because I fell down and cut my knee while looking in one direction and walking in another, as children do, and was given a fountain pen with a special syringe filler as a small consolation.

My father was a true countryman. He loved the sights and sounds of the rural scene. He knew the names of all the wild flowers, he could identify the calls of all the birds and he was full of country lore. I regret now that I took so little notice of what he was telling us on our country walks of a Sunday evening, but I too have a love of the country, its sights and sounds. My father would have avoided modern cities as plague spots. He would have hated the noise and the lights and the "night life". If he had been a reader of anything but the Westminster Gazette he would have enjoyed immensely the

Candleford books, because they lie so close to his own childhood and our life in the village before it was made sophisticated and a dormitory of London.

My father tended his large garden with infinite care and also worked an allotment beyond the stream that gurgled its shallow way across the end of our garden. His leeks were the finest in the village, his potatoes, usually such tasteless growths, the most tasty in the land. His cauliflowers were truly magnificent, and his celery, bleached in the black soft soil, was famous. We always had celery for tea on Sunday when it was in season and I can still taste it now - celery and new brown bread with plenty of butter. My father rarely went to Church, but he would probably have agreed with the poet who wrote: "One is nearer to God in a Garden". Like all real countrymen he was a weather prophet, not always accurate, but usually so. I recall him quoting the well known ditty which is supposed to have originated on the border of a Wilton carpet many decades ago:

Whether the weather be cold or whether the weather be hot,
We have to weather the weather, whether we like it or not.

There is a fatalism which is near to religion in the countryman, and it is reflected in his weather prophecies which are of course perfectly scientific - "Red sky at night, 'tis the shepherd's delight, red sky at morning, 'tis the shepherd's warning". He could tell from the wind changes when and from where the rain would come and, from the flight of the birds, how cold it would be. The flying of the partridges and pheasants had to him some intimations of early or late spring. It was from my father that I learned to read the weather lessons in a cow pasture. If the cows are huddled together the weather is likely to be bad, if they disperse freely and unconcernedly about the meadow, it will be fine. The buzzing of the bees, the flight of the dragonfly, the murmur of the gnats, even the behaviour of the horses in their stalls seemed to speak to my father of things to come "weatherwise". And his prognostications were not less accurate than the forecasts of the thousands of people employed in various ways by the meteorological office.

Wooding was a favourite pastime of ours in the country, and there is nothing quite like the smell of a bonfire in the woods or of a log upon a wide, open fire in the hearth. Wood chopping was a chore that my father imposed upon me and he had a clever phrase to ensure that I cleared up after me - "Pick up every piece with two ends," he would say. And if you do that you don't leave even a tiny splinter behind! I suppose that the village flower and vegetable show will one day die out as we depend more and more for our food upon the products of the quick freezing firms, but to my father the Flower Show was an event of great importance. I believe there is still a "Hoffman Cup" in existence to be awarded to the grower of the largest vegetable marrow or the finest crop of carrots or turnips. Thus passes the glory of the world. To be remembered only for a silver mug bestowed upon the lucky grower of an uneatable mass of vegetable matter. Or is my father remembered in his village for any more worthy reason?

My relationship with my father must have been very superficial. What do I know of him? Though I had turned sixteen when he died I know nothing of his innermost thoughts. Was he a happy man? Was he content with his lot? What elements had been fused together in his life since 1865 to make him the man he was? Had he had a happy childhood? I did not know. Had he suffered from the sternness of a Victorian father in his infancy and adolescence? I do not even know how he felt towards his first wife - whether he missed her when she died. I do not think he was always at ease with the children of his first marriage, as will appear later in my story. What did he think of war? What were his politics? Conservative, I assume. What were his true relations with my mother? Did he love her, or did he marry her to provide a source of maternal care for his five children and someone to cook his roast beef on Sundays? What were his views on art? Did he have any views? On religion? On human progress? In the National Strike of 1926 which all but paralysed the country, which side did he favour? It certainly affected our lives, for coal we were selling at that time at 1/10d a cwt, rose to the unprecedented price of 7/6d per hundredweight. What were his moral standards? Did he lie and cheat in his business dealings or was he utterly and completely honest? The latter, I like to think.

What of his mother, the wife of the journeyman tailor? What sort of woman was she - a dominating personality, who imparted to her son some of his fearsome sternness, or a soft pliable woman, working her fingers to the bone for a too large family on a too small wage? What sports had he indulged in as a lad and young man? Bowls was his favourite occupation in his later years, and shooting in the days when I was a young child. He had a good eye. Had he been a cricketer on the village green at Hemel? Had he played for the village football team in his stripling days? Had he been a popular lad with the village maidens or had he married his first and only love? All I knew of my father was his sternness, his impatience, his code of conduct imposed upon us children, his love of nature and his fatherly care for his family. I feel that sometimes I hated him, sometimes I loved him. Always I slightly feared him, feared letting him down, feared to appear a witless fool, incompetent at games and outdoor activities. It may be that I need not have feared him, that his impatience and austere severity were products of his own covert fears, or even of a deep love which he dared not allow himself to exhibit for reasons which only a psychologist could give. When he was cutting my hair, which he always did in the approved pudding basin style, until I rebelled at about the age of twelve, he would exclaim sharply, "Keep still or I shall cut your ear off!" I always took it as a threat. Now I like to think it was just a statement of fact.

"It is a wise father that knows his own child" declares Launcelot Gobbo to Old Gobbo in *The Merchant Of Venice* and Shakespeare could have added (he probably did, somewhere) "it is a wise child that knows its own father." For we are very much what we are because of what our fathers make us. There is a school of psychiatry which tends to ascribe every dominant trait in our character to the influence of the mother, markedly in the first few months of life. Much more investigation should be made into the influence of the father. Edmund Gosse had done this admirably in literary form in his book *Father and Son* (1907), and Winston Churchill has told us of the influence of his father, Lord Randolph Churchill. The Shakespearean experts have analysed Hamlet's character in relation to his father, and it is a tantalising exercise to try and discover influences which have affected the lives of public figures and made them what they were. In our Royal family, was Edward VII the man he was more because of his mother or the Prince Consort? Were his mischievous and perverse activities indulged in as a reaction to his father's strait-laced Germanic opinions and habits? And was his son George V the rather dull and worthy man that he was in reaction to his father's naughtiness? And did George VI stutter as a result of his stern upbringing at the hands of George V?

All this is much too simple and neat. The truth is of course that we are all very complicated characters, and what we are is not to be ascribed wholly to what our parents were. For in addition to heredity there is not only environment and education but also our own inborn characters which we owe to no-one but God. We are individuals. The Christian faith assures us that we are responsible for our own characters, that we have a free will which we can exercise within the limits imposed upon us by our heredity and our environment, but which is strong enough to overcome the pull of them both. The Christian faith does not deny the fact of heredity. It enshrines it in that most disputed of doctrines, original sin. It does not deny the power that we have to make our children's characters in our own mould. Indeed one of the speculations which has most teased Christians is the effect that the foster father of our Lord, Joseph the Carpenter, had upon the growing child Jesus, though there was no filial and paternal relationship between them. There is no doubt of the influence of the Virgin Mary upon her child, though it is instructive to note that in the Gospel story, the only relationships which stand out between Jesus and his mother are relationships of separation - in the Temple when Jesus was a child, at the wedding in Cana; when he was speaking to the crowd and someone interrupted him to tell him his mother was there - "Who is my mother?" and pointing to the crowd "Here is my mother and my brethren", and at the Cross.

Sentimentalists as well as psychiatrists like to emphasise a mother's spell over her children. I wondered, in my own case, could the emphasis be sustained?

CHAPTER 2

MOTHER

"Honour Thy Father And Thy Mother."
The Fifth Commandment

"A mother is a mother still,
the holiest thing alive."
S.T. Coleridge (d. 1834)

"Who ran to help me when I fell
and would some pretty story tell,
and kiss the place to make it well?"
Jane Taylor, "My Mother" (d. 1824)

My mother must have been a very attractive woman when she was young. The picture of her that hung for a long time in our house alongside my father's showed her as having a lovely complexion which she kept till the day of her death, clear cut features with rather high cheek bones, a straight and well-carved nose with slender nostrils and fine grey-blue eyes. In the fashion of the early years of the century her hair is piled up in tidy profusion, and she is very erect. Posture was important to people in every stratum of society in our grandparents' day, and my mother would tell us how they used boards and braces to attain the ramrod effect. My mother had a great respect and affection for Queen Alexandra, wife of Edward VII, a most beautiful woman with fine dark hair. I suppose that her hair style was in fact modelled on the Queen's to whom she was very like, except that my mother's hair was not so dark. The English felt a deep pity for the beautiful Queen, who was stone deaf and who had such a difficult time with her roaming husband. When she died in 1925 the wave of affection for her, and the reverence for her memory, penetrated even to the consciousness of small school children. I can clearly recall the time of her death, but this may have been because we all had to wear a black armband for a fortnight as a mark of our childish respect. How times change! How the habits of the people change! Affection for the members of the Royal Family is much less today than it was in the hearts of the majority of the people, and when it does exist it takes a different form. It would be impossible to imagine all the children in Great Britain sporting a two inch black armband for the death of Elizabeth the Queen Mother, though the nation's sorrow would not be less than it was in 1925.

My mother's maiden name was Ellen Gertrude Weaser. The Christian names date her birth towards the end of the Victorian era, and they were a common combination, like Sarah Anne, or Mary Jane (or Carol Ann today). She was born on March 9th, 1888 and until recently I had the Bible with this date in it given to her by her godmother with whom she corresponded twice a year until the day of the godmother's death, a true sign of god-daughterly and god-motherly affection. We children looked forward to godmother's letters which always enclosed ten shillings - a sum that produced the tidy wealth of five shillings each for Enid and myself, but which had to be reduced to three shillings and fourpence when my sister June arrived on the scene. The surname Weaser was an unusual one, German in origin, like my father's. I have no idea when either of their families appeared in this country, but as our Royal Family has similar origins I imagine that it was in the early days of the Hanoverian invasion when the German princes would have brought with them their lackeys and servants, maids and valets from their own homeland. In Germany, various forms of both names are still common. Many "Hoffmann"s appear in the Register of Hemel Hempstead residents from the mid-eighteenth century onwards.

Mother had two brothers and two sisters, and she came fourth in the line of the five children born to the keeper of the Falcon Hotel in Denham village. It has been one of my sorrows that I did not know any one of my four grandparents. My father's parents must have died long before he married my mother in 1913, while my mother's father died on the same night I was born in 1917. I know nothing of my mother's inheritance therefore, except what I could glean as a child from the photographs of her parents which hung in the dining room of our house in Denham - grandfather Weaser standing strong and upright in frock coat with braided edges, wing collar and patterned cravat with jewelled pin at his throat, and a smartly trimmed dark grey beard of the same cut as that of King Edward VII. Grandmother

Weaser is seated in a high backed chair, looking a little like the early portraits of Queen Victoria in her black bombazine dress and velvet throat-band with a sort of lace Dutch cap on her head. Grandmother Weaser was much taller than the Queen however, and between them she and grandfather gave my mother both her height and her good looks.

My father was twenty-three years older than my mother, and this was a key factor in our family life. It influenced the person my mother was, it affected their relationship to each other and of each of them to their children. When my sister June was born in 1926 father was over sixty. As a middle-aged man with five children, three of them married when he wed my mother, he could hardly have been thought of as a marriage possibility, though no doubt the status of an established tradesman of reasonable financial solidarity was enough to outweigh the disadvantages of his age and his widowerhood. I have often wondered if my good-looking mother had other opportunities of marriage but the truth will always be shrouded in mystery. To have discussed such a thing with her, to have asked her outright about such a thing, even when I was grown up, would have been thought unmannerly, ungentlemanly and impertinent. On my father's side there was no doubt that he was immensely proud of his young wife, and he protected her in a defensive way against the possibility of contamination by the new movements and attitudes of the post Great War period.

London was of course the centre of the new movements, but as the years went by and particularly as wireless became common in ordinary homes, and the cinema came to neighbouring towns, even country villages in Buckinghamshire could no longer ignore the social trends of the city. There was the new fashion movement in clothes - originating like most movements in this century in America. American influence began when she entered the war and has continued ever since. Until 1914 women wore long skirts but as many of them had begun to work on the land and in industry and nursing during hostilities, it was natural that they should want to retain their freedom after it. My mother began her married life in long dresses, but was allowed by my father to follow the fashion to the extent that her ankles could be seen, and by the middle of the 1920's had abandoned the "hobble skirt" for the "tubular"look, and sack-like dresses and blouses which were current in some fashion circles again in the mid 1960's.

But the post war period was also the "Jazz" period, and it is impossible to dance to jazz music in long skirts, so as the years went by they got shorter and shorter and women's legs began to appear, first in their thick cotton or woollen stockings and then in rayon or silk ones. My mother no doubt was allowed to follow fashion that far, but not high heels! These had always been associated with the less respectable members of society - those who spent weekends in Paris or acted on the stage or had doubtful morals. Nor was she allowed at any point in her married life, not even when she was over forty, to use cosmetics. It was an accepted thing in our home that my father would have no hesitation in carrying out his threat to black my mother's face with soot if she so much as touched a powder puff. And a lipstick would have sent him into paroxysms of rage. I know that this was a sore burden to her, but she need not have worried. Her complexion was always perfect, and she had no need to be labelled by her husband as a "painted hussy".

In hair styles too my father demanded conformity with established social custom up to and well beyond the period when it *was* custom. He would not allow my mother to have her hair cut off, shingled or bobbed or otherwise dealt with, until she was over forty. Short skirts, powder and paint, and short hair were the external signs of the new freedom of which my father disapproved. He was ever a social conservative, and why should he be otherwise, as a man born within the first half of the Victorian era? For a middle-aged man to be accompanied by a wife more than twenty years his junior looking like a "flapper" would have caused a stir in the village and much wagging of tongues there would have been behind the low cottage doors.

My mother was allowed to go to the village dances. After the war dancing became a passion with young and not so young folk. There were victory dances, tea dances, and subscription dances - dances for the relief of sufferers from war, dances to win the peace, at which tangos, fox-trots, waltzes and such replaced the old valetas and barn dances. I would love to have accompanied my parents in spirit to these dances to see how they got on. It would have been a sight to see the stocky moustached gentleman waltzing with the lady who was slightly taller than her husband. One dance I do remember taking place - it was a fancy dress ball in some hall unknown to me now, probably in Uxbridge, our nearest town, and my mother was dressed as a potato. I can see her now clothed from head to foot in a kind of sacking, with potatoes, real ones from father's garden, sown all over it. She won first prize. I remember her putting me to bed that night and the rough and bumpy texture of her costume, before they set out. I am sure that the dances to which they went were very decorous affairs, with none of the abandon and shamelessness of the close embraces which were described by a clergyman critic of them in 1919 - "If these up-to-date dances are within a hundred miles of all I hear about them, I should say that the morals of a pig-sty would be respectable in comparison."

All this makes it harder for me to understand why, when I got the urge to learn to dance after my father's death, my mother would not let me, saying plaintively, in a way I can only describe as distinctly unfair, "Your father would not have wished you to."

Two other habits were becoming very popular among women in the years when my mother was a young married woman - smoking and drinking. Mother was not allowed to smoke, and did not do so until after my father had died, and though she was the daughter of a licensed victualler (even in those days the word publican had something "not quite nice" about it, and was never used by those actually in the trade) it was not until the late 20's that my father would have allowed her to go with him into a public house and then only into the "private" or "lounge" bars. Only the "lower classes" would allow their women folk into the bars of the inns, the "lower middle classes" would be quite content for their women folk to go into a lounge bar, but above that level of society it was "not done". There was a compromise possible when the family was travelling - in fine weather the children and the women folk were allowed to sit outside the public house and drink their lemonade or glass of port at a garden table.

My mother was very conscious of what she called her "lack of education", especially when her children found their way to grammar schools, college and university. The licensed victualler of her childhood days considered himself "a cut above" the lower classes. He was not a member of the "labouring class". He was "in trade", and as H.G. Wells has told us in his novels, this was a stratum of society very conscious of its position somewhere between the ranks of the rich or the professional classes (doctor, lawyer, clergyman) and the lower strata of the "working class". A shopkeeper was in a similar state to the keeper of a hostelry. This consciousness always led men like my grandfather to send their children to "private schools". To one such private school my mother was sent, and there she learned a little more than the children at the local Church "elementary" school of things like deportment, and a little less than they of reading, writing and arithmetic. No doubt she was given a smattering of French though she did not know any in her later years, and art and music and embroidery would have played a larger part in her education than at the local school. But there were immense gaps in the teaching in these private schools - current affairs would have been a closed book, modern history would not have been mentioned, domestic science (or as it is called today housecraft - perhaps the name has changed again under the national curriculum! - "Cookery" as it was called then) would have been considered beneath the dignity of the school to teach. Their libraries would have been poorly equipped, and opportunities for "further reading" would be limited. But all in all, her "education" was certainly no worse than that received by the average girl of her age and generation.

It was too early for her to have been touched by the methods of Madame Montessori or Froebel, so remembering that in her own schooling she had not been encouraged to express her natural feelings, she thought it wrong of us to want to do so. Having received the usual punishments in her own childhood she thought it right that we should be punished whenever necessary. Having had to wear constricting clothes in her own childhood she saw no reason why we should not wear similar garments. My elder sister Enid was made to wear boots long after they had become extremely unfashionable for the young, and so was I, for the perfectly good reason, in my mother's view, that shoes tended to create weak ankles and flat feet.

There were many tears and battles before any concession was made to modernity for either of us. I suppose I was the last boy in my class at school to wear boots as normal footwear, until I was thirteen. How I hated them, and hated more the shame of wearing them when everyone else could wear shoes. Each of us reflects the pressures and prejudices of the age in which we live, and my mother was no exception. The H.A.L. Fisher Act of 1918 which tried, not very successfully, to fill in the gaps in ordinary education was yet to come, and my mother had completed her inadequate schooling by the age of fourteen. Her frequent complaint was: "I never had the advantages you are having", and "I left school too soon to learn anything about that." With her this was a "complex" that lasted throughout life and her ridiculous and unnecessary sense of educational inferiority, would make her ill at ease with the "educated" even when she could have held her own in most conversations by means of her own native intelligence and wit. When she was getting past fifty she was slightly deaf, but in company with clergy and others at Vicarage tea parties at Windsor, she would pretend to be stone deaf so as not to be embroiled in discussion which she felt to be above her head and in which her supposed inferiority would show.

I have often mused on the question of physical activities in the schools of the period at the turn of the century, for though my mother claimed an intellectual imperfection, she could not claim it for sport, and I have wondered if in her "private school" there had been some amateur Suzanne Lenglen or Elizabeth Ryan, for she was an expert tennis player and won the local tennis championship on more than one occasion. In her later years she was an adept at bowls and took part successfully in many tournaments, as the silver spoons she won witness. She was also a great cyclist and one of my earliest memories is of being carried in a seat on the back of her bicycle while she rode up the hill from the village to play tennis at the recreation ground, her long white skirts being kept from the back wheel by a fine network of threads. My mother plainly had a "good eye" for ball games: a physical attribute she did not pass on to her children, for though my sisters were competent at most games, they were not outstanding, and I was a positive dunce. I think my mother and my father both turned a blind eye to my inability to play games well and were probably ignorant, as most parents are, of the damage done to the constitutional sporting duffer by continual admonitions of "butter fingers". They seemed to be unaware that my right eye had little or no sight in it.

My parents' relationship within marriage was one of toleration and material concern on the part of my father, and subordination and obedience on the part of my mother. At no time did I observe any demonstrations of affection between them - but this is not to say that they had no love for each other, only that they would have thought it wrong to display such emotions in public, or parade any tendernesses and endearments in front of the children. My mother lacked nothing for her essential comfort, or material well-being, and in fact she was very generously treated in the matter of clothes; and the same man who turned his envelopes inside out to save half a farthing was the man who gave his wife one of the first "Baby Austin's" as a birthday present. Its official name was "Austin Seven", though I discovered many years later that the irreverent called it the "Bed Pan" and in 1924 when it was first produced it cost £165, the equivalent of at least four or five thousand pounds today, a generous present from the son of the journeyman tailor to the daughter of the local innkeeper. This little car was a gem, and it fascinated me as a boy of seven or eight. When no one was looking I would go down to the outbuilding where it was garaged and sit in the front driving seat, occasionally giving a nervous peep on the tiny horn button. Grey and black in colour, though minute even by modern mini standards, my pride and joy, and I loved it even more than my father's Ford, though until the Austin arrived I had sat often and surreptitiously in that too. A "two-car" family in the non-professional classes must have been a rare thing in the mid 1920's, though the "upper classes" had their carriages and pairs and their Daimler Benzes and their Rolls, and the middle classes had their large Austins and Humbers, Fords and Hillmans.

I would say that my mother had all the clothes a woman in her position could need, but too great adornment of her person was certainly frowned upon. My father would have said that fine birds do not need false feathers, though he occasionally gave her a small piece of jewellery, a golden bracelet or a string of pearls. Then he would sometimes come home with a new oak clock or a new chair or rug as a non-official present. His greatest gifts to my mother were in property which he bought and wisely put into her name so that when he died, as he knew he must, many years before she did, she would be provided for, without crippling estate duties. But he continued to draw the income from them himself and gave her what she needed. When my elder sister was eighteen she too received a pair of semi-detached houses though they were a great burden to her when tenants gave trouble and lived in filth and squalor in them.

My mother always had any help she needed in the house, though in spite of her "lack of education" she was very domesticated, was a good cook and an excellent housewife. Her relationship with my father must have been very happy on that score, and he had no cause for complaint that she was not an excellent wife to him, feeding him well and caring for his material wants with admirable industry. Her relationships with us children are not so easy to define. Looking back to the years when we lived at Denham, very little stands out in my mind as indicative of her attitude to me. There were the occasional beatings because of tar spilling and other naughtiness, but little else worthy of recall. This may indicate, I hope it does, that our relationships were good, since I cannot remember times of prolonged strain or fear of my mother. Nor can I remember periods of affection. Like my father she was not a demonstrative person, and I cannot remember being kissed or hugged by her. It was very different with my youngest half sister May, who was living at home for some years before her marriage, and she showered kisses and tenderness upon me. It was she who mostly looked after me in my pre-school days, pushed me in the pram, took me for walks, took me visiting her friends and relations. I can remember playing gooseberry when she was "walking out" with George Bowden whom she later married, and I must have been a considerable embarrassment to them always to have been on hand. As in the cartoons of the day I was offered and gratefully accepted, sixpence, to make myself scarce when I was not wanted.

Like most of her generation my mother was very competent as a pianist, and again, like most of her generation she would sit at the piano of a Sunday evening and play hymns. Later I would badger her to play some of the sentimental pieces of the day - *In a Monastery Garden*, *Wedgwood Blue*, both by Albert Ketelbey, *The Lost Chord* by Sullivan and the simpler Chopin valses and mazurkas. I think these were my happiest moments, sitting on a stool by the piano while she played. Until a few years ago we still had the heavy old piano stool with its cavernous cupboard for sheet music on which she sat. My love for music and perhaps my first singing lesson must date from these days, for we had no radio worthy of the name until 1927, and no gramophone at all - my first introduction to this instrument was in the poor home of one of our tenants who had a vast machine with a wide horn which played cylindrical records - the type of machine portrayed in the adverts for HMV still. It was on this that I first heard the voice of the idol of the early years of the century, Dame Nellie Melba, and first learned to be stirred by the strains of Elgar's *Pomp and Circumstance* marches. Neither my father nor my mother attempted to give us any kind of a musical education, though I was allowed for a brief while to learn to play the violin. This was a disaster.

I am hoping by the recall of these memories, to discover the influences that make me the person I am. There is as I have said, a school of modern psychiatry which traces a major part of character to the influence of the mother, and in particular where there has been an emotional abandonment. Anxiety states, says this school, can be traced to "the loss of the dynamic cycle of living relatedness to the source of personal being in the early months". Panic, dread and the "death wish" are all traced back to times when the child has called for its mother and mother has not come, or when it has longed to be fed at the breast and the breast has not been there or has been prematurely removed. Inversions and perversions can be traced to "infantile separation anxiety, and they often cross the margin of tolerance into paradoxical states in which the mother who was desired but did not come, is written off as a destroyer." Maternal deprivation and paternal irresponsibility are held to be the causes of much juvenile delinquency and behaviour patterns of a violent nature, as well as of the psychological disorders of paranoia, hysteria, hypochondria, anxiety, depression and many more. It would be foolish to reject the mass of evidence that this is so, especially, the evidence given by the analysis of patients who some years ago were made to relive their experiences under what is called LSD25, now regarded as a dangerous drug. But such influences form only a tiny part of the total influence that makes up a personality.

In my own case I am sure that my father's influence was greater than my mother's and it would seem to me that this school of psychiatry takes too little note of other early influences, some of which I shall attempt to assess in subsequent chapters. It is too simple to ask the sort of question that is asked by the psychiatrist - "Did you get on with your mother? Did she like your sisters better than she liked you? Was she house proud (my mother was)? Or did she not mind a mess as long as everybody was happy? What was her relationship with the neighbours? Was she affectionate? Unfeeling? Over-possessive?" Unless you also ask similar questions about the child's early relationship with the boy next door, about his relationships at school, at Sunday school, in the street at play. And it is not enough to believe that early influences are all. Character is made by a continuing process. This of course the psychiatrists would not deny. My point here is to show that though childhood and early days have a powerful effect, they are not the only controlling factors.

Every single human being has elements of most of these psychological states in his makeup - each one of us has known panic or dread at some time, each one of us has had moments of hysteria and rage, has known alternations of depression and exaltation, each of us has felt a sense of abandonment by those we love at some time, has known what it means to be possessed by some compulsive desire or hatred. And in the creation of these elements many people may have had a hand, other than father and mother.

"Morning shows the day." When a writer starts to analyse the influences of his childhood he finds that he knows little other than what he has been told unless his memory is a good one. The memories that stand out are likely to be few and exceptional, but of the first influence beloved of the psychiatrist I cannot speak - did my mother have a long and difficult labour? The traumatic experiences of being born can have an influence upon later claustrophobic and agoraphobic reactions. I have never felt either of these emotions - neither the desire to escape from a closed room, nor the oppressive weight of open spaces, so it may be that my birth was normal. "Were you wanted?" is likely to be the next question asked by the analyst - "Did your mother look forward to your coming with unabashed joy, or were you an unfortunate accident?", though I hope no analyst would phrase his question so! It is my belief that these questions did not occur to those themselves born in the Victorian era. Children, it was taught, come from God, and it is irrelevant whether you want them or not. It is your duty to have them, to care for them when they come and "do your best by them." This, I would guess, was my mother's belief.

It used to be said in the family that I was a good-looking baby, and that probably helped a great deal to make my mother love me in her own quiet fashion. At an early age I even won first prize in a baby show - three half crowns in a white satin bag, and it was a matter of dispute in the family as to whether the three half crowns belonged to me as the actual winner, or to mother as the one who had produced this beautiful specimen. Certainly my mother was right when she was asked by me about their whereabouts "Oh, you have had them ten times over." I do not know what kind of a baby I was - whether I was placid and contented, or whether I spent my time screaming for attention in the pram - an old fashioned, high wheeled contraption with a huge hood. I can only believe that my first two years at any rate were normal, but when I was two I developed measles very badly. In 1919 measles was not thought to be more than a childish ailment, and the effect upon the eyesight was often underrated. The measles left me with permanently impaired sight in my right eye. This has been one of the most formative factors in my whole life not only from the physical point of view but also from the psychological, because with the muscular atrophy caused by the disease came the squint which I suffered until I was 20 years old, and which was only partially corrected by an operation at Moorfields.

I cannot say whether many of the fears and worries of my childhood do in fact date from that time, but I had the normal complement of them - the occasional night terrors (too much cheese or undigested milk too late at night - or a sense of deprivation from the mother's breast in infancy?) the sleep walking and the nail biting, the thumb-sucking and the temper tantrums that most normal children have. What is normality - does it exist? Is a person who does not suffer from some of these things in childhood just an insensitive animal? Like the man in the street, the normal child does not exist. Perhaps it would be truer to say that the normal child is one who has his normal quota of abnormalities.

Nor do the psychiatrists, unless they are also Christians, take enough account of human sin. Does a child scream when it is thwarted in its desires because of some traumatic experience in infancy or does it scream because of original sin? Does an adolescent get into trouble because his father loved his sister more than him, or because the Devil finds work for idle hands to do? While we reject the over-simplifications of the psychiatrist we must not replace them with equivalent theological over-simplifications. The freewill with which humanity has been endowed is a much more satisfactory explanation of human behaviour patterns than some of the expositions of the mental experts. When I kicked and fought my mother and cried with hot tears at some piece of injustice (as I thought) I prefer to think it was the bad old pride coming out in me, the pride that is at the root of self-regard and selfishness.

When on my seventh birthday I was sent to bed screaming because I would not share my new cricket set with the boys and girls who had been invited to share my birthday tea-party, I cannot trace it back to some stress syndrome of my first nine months of life. I can see in it a perfectly normal reluctance to share a prized possession, a reluctance basic to humanity and rooted in the sin of self-regard. And the spanking I received from my mother was a perfectly normal human reaction of annoyance and shame and exasperation. In an ideal world in which human beings of all ages were conscious of their temptations and knew the way in which to fight off the Devil, the child of seven would have happily shared his cricket set and if he didn't, at least the mother of the child would have contained her annoyance and not given physical expression to it! This is in fact the kingdom of God for which Christians work and pray.

I wish I knew my mother's religious attitudes at this time. She sent us to Church, certainly, and I have a vague memory that she accompanied us on several occasions throughout the year. Whether her religious activity was greater than this I cannot say. Whether she prayed or read her Bible is also a mystery to me. Some religious influence there must have been on my life, because it is confidently affirmed in the family that I had decided to be a clergyman by the age of ten, though this is not my own memory. Much stronger in her life, I would guess, was the power of superstition in which she differed little from most of her contemporaries. All the popular beliefs about black cats, dropped pins, the number thirteen, crossed knives, shoes on the table, were hers, and it was my own later scorn of these superstitions that led me to make a study of them. She was an avid reader of what the stars foretell in *Old Moore's Almanac* until some small sense of shame overtook her that the mother of a priest ought not to have faith in such things. Then we heard no more of them. Most superstitions have an origin in religion, and it is one of the marks of the failure of organised religion through the centuries that more often than not the superstition has been stronger than the faith that gave it birth. There are still millions who like my mother will not sit down thirteen to a table, but who have forgotten the significance of the first New Testament supper party at which there were thirteen participants. My mother really believed in the power of these superstitions. If anyone, even in fun, opened an umbrella in the house, she would be cross and irritated, and would ascribe some coincidental accident to the malignant power that watched for such follies. This particular superstition cannot be very old, for though the sunshade is an ancient invention, the umbrella is not. The sight of crossed knives at the dinner table would "set her teeth on edge" as she would say, and dark forebodings would come into her mind as a result.

It must have penetrated my mind that certain things were lucky and certain other things unlucky, because one of our most consistent childish occupations was the search of the four-leaf clover - only one of which have I ever discovered in my life. We were always encouraged to crack empty eggshells after breakfast, though my mother probably did not know that the original reason for this was even believed by Dean Wren, the father of Christopher Wren, to prevent the witches using them as boats! Even as I write there are pictures in the newspapers, and articles about the English sisterhood of witches! And witches are being interviewed on television! It is strange that ideas from the Stone Age can exist alongside the most complicated knowledge of the space age. If superstition can be defined as something that "stands over" from the past, for this is the meaning of the Latin word, then certainly in my mother's mind there were multitudes of things standing over from her own past and the past of her forbears. When our first child was about to be born my mother seriously took me aside and said, "You won't let Pat eat strawberries, will you? Or the child will surely be born with a strawberry mark on it somewhere." "Turn your money over," she would say, at the time of the new moon, "And don't dare to look at the moon through glass." And if anyone should be so careless as to spill salt at table there was a fine flurry - further salt must be thrown over the left shoulder to ensure that impending disaster was averted.

I wonder if my mother would have been superstitious - would anyone be - if the reasons and origins of these strange beliefs were known? Salt was always a precious commodity in the middle east, and it was a sign of friendship "to eat salt" with a guest. An interesting point about Leonardo da Vinci's painting of the Last Supper is the spilt salt-cellar. Broken mirrors would send my mother into a frenzy of worry and any idea that hawthorn blooms might be brought into the house would make her extremely ill-humoured. I am sure that my mother would never have turned a mattress on a Friday or started a journey, or have changed her clothes, if she had by chance put them on inside out.

On the other side she was a firm believer in the effectiveness of white heather, and of the blessings to be bestowed on the bride who was lucky enough to be met at the Church door after the ceremony by a chimney sweep. She would have tried her hardest to eat a mince pie in a different house on each of the days between Christmas and the Epiphany and to have dreamed of the Devil would have given her great joy. "Touch wood" she would say, for a happy event, not knowing the origin of the superstition in the relics of the Cross of Christ. "Bless you" she would say, when someone sneezed, quite ignorant of the fact that the words were a solemn invocation of blessing on the suspected plague sufferers of the 17th century. Never in her life would my mother have passed willingly under a ladder, and not for any practical reason of having paint dropped upon her. If she had known that this superstition has its origins either in the ladder which was used to take Christ down from the Cross, or in the primitive practice of hanging a murderer by pushing him off a ladder, I doubt if it would have made any difference to her belief that it was unlucky.

There was a story in our house that my mother had once been poisoned by eating mackerel, and I am sure that she ascribed this to the popular belief that mackerel exposed to the rays of the sun will become poisonous. More likely this particular mackerel had been exposed to the attentions of the common fly. A sty on the eye can be cured by rubbing with a piece of gold, she would declare, and we were not allowed to wash our hands in water already used in case we "fell out" with the person who had previously used it. A very hygienic superstition.

It is strange indeed that four hundred years of scientific advance have done so little to eliminate such beliefs. It is stranger still that they should have replaced the simple faith in God of the earlier generation of Christians. Strange too that so many people cling to convictions which are so plainly against reason and common sense as well as against scientific truth and religious teaching. Religion is the search for truth, and superstition is the opposite of truth, it stems not from faith but from fear. Superstition is fear of the unknown, religion is worship of the known. Superstition is based upon ignorance, religion is based upon knowledge. Superstition centres upon self, religion centres upon God and our neighbour. I think my mother would have been a much happier woman if she had known the consolations of faith and a true religion rather than depended so much upon the insecure support of her superstitions. This is regrettably the truth, however, that my "religious" memories of her are more concerned with her superstition than with Church-going or prayer and Communion. Until we moved away from Denham that is, and a new relationship with the Church developed.

CHAPTER 3

HOME

"There's no place like home."
John Howard Payne (d. 1852)

"Half to forget the wandering and the pain,
half to remember days that have gone by,
and dream and dream that I am home again."
James Elroy Flecker (d. 1915)

"Home-keeping hearts are happiest."
Longfellow (d. 1882)

Our house in Denham in Buckinghamshire was styled "The Homestead", a very attractive old English name which described exactly what it was - a home with outbuildings, ham meaning home, and stead meaning place or farm, or so the dictionary says. The house was not as attractive as its name. It was of uncertain date, probably late 18th or early 19th century from the quality of its bricks, with sash windows, but not of a size or character good enough to be called Georgian. Though not large, it rambled, with two narrow staircases, and innumerable steps up and down into the many rooms. My favourite room was the front hall into which the front door opened, and whose window looked out upon the lovely old High Street. All the guidebooks used to call Denham, "an old world village", the sort of village conjured up in the pages of Mrs. Gaskell's "Cranford".

From the window in that room I would gaze across at the charming old inn called The Swan, with the daughter of whose proprietor I was in love at the age of seven or eight. She was a pretty dark girl called Vera Johnson, and we used to play "mothers and fathers" in the tap room of the inn between opening hours. She married someone from the film studios which had descended upon Denham in the 20's. From that window too I would watch the funeral processions - the curtain discreetly drawn, but just enough of a tiny crack left for me to see all I wanted to see. All the curtains in the street would be drawn on the day of a village funeral, and the spectacle of it will never be forgotten by those who saw one before the days of motor hearses. The horses drawing the glass fronted and glass sided coffin carriage were topped with waving black plumes, their bright brass on black leather harness glittering and tinkling as they pranced slowly along. The black hearse was a sombrely glittering vehicle with its brass fittings. The mourners' carriages were horse-drawn, and the undertaker's men all wore top hats with wide mourning bands of black nun's veiling hanging from them.

From the same front window I would watch the antics of the Saturday and Sunday night revellers at "The Swan" and the humbler "Green Man" next door. There was a kilted Scot who came to the village regularly for some years each Sunday night in summer to entertain the customers of the two pubs with the skirl of his pipes. He looked a very romantic figure to a small boy, but he was probably an ex-serviceman out of a job, his only source of income the pennies dropped into his Glengarry bonnet at the end of each performance. His playing was no doubt amateurish, his kilt patched, his white stockings dirty and his fur-trimmed sporran moth-eaten, but I loved him and watched, fascinated, as he marched up and down the High Street with his pipes wailing mournfully to the traditional Scottish tunes. I was never allowed to leave the house and get near to the piper and see for myself the mysteries of his strange music, or his stranger uniform. No doubt my parents were afraid that I might be contaminated by the drinking revellers - for in those days the brewer's ale was cheap and potent, and it was imbibed with greater abandon by ordinary folk than it is now.

There was a great deal of drunkenness which I could observe, and did observe, captivated by the extraordinary capers and singular gait of those who had swallowed more than enough strong brown ale. From this window too I loved to look at the rain, and watch the people battling against the driving sheets of water with their huge black umbrellas. I have always loved the sight and feel of the rain and no doubt the psychiatrist has a deep dark explanation for it and even as a child I delighted in the touch of the tender raindrops on my cheeks. Dressed in the warm dryness of gumboots, mackintosh and sou'wester I loved to splash through the puddles on my way to school and they were real puddles unknown on present day roads, because our village roads were not tarmacadamed for many years. To a child there is nothing more delightful than the taste of rain dropping into his open mouth as he lifts his head to the grey and weeping sky. To this day I enjoy walking in the rain, and find a kind of ecstatic delight in the roll of the thunder and in the glare and glint of the lightning, when others find storms frightening and oppressive. I have never had any fear of the elements, in spite of the fact that in my childhood we were taught solemnly that the thunder was the sound of God walking up and down the heavens in angry mood. Who taught me this I cannot recollect, but it was a fixed belief in my childish mind for many years, though unaccountably it does not seem to have frightened me.

For many years God was to me an ogre, a monster, a spiritual giant who inhabited dark cupboards and cellars in our house. This did not cause me to have nightmares or dismay me unless I had been more than usually naughty. Then the large eye of the text above my bed would seem to glint with more than usual fire and the words "Thou God seest me" would have a rather delicious significance. God was taking note of me, and that at least was a good thing. Whether God was made for me in the image of my father or of the Rector standing above me in the pulpit on Sunday afternoons, representative of the all powerful Creator, and bending his disapproving eye upon me when I was inattentive, I cannot say. The idea of God held by us all is a medley of confused and jumbled associations - father, priest. schoolmaster, shepherd. Framed and illustrated texts were much in vogue in my childhood days - in addition to the "all-seeing eye" on the wall over my bed there was a sickly representation of the Good Shepherd, and a mystical representation of the words "Abide in me and I in you." It was not until, very many years later, after I had read a sermon by one of my Oxford professors, Dr. H.L. Goudge, "debunking" the idea of the poor little lost sheep, warm and pathetic, that I understood the significance of the parable of the rescue of the sinner - dirty, greasy and totally unpleasant animal that a "lost sheep" is.

As a house, ours ranked somewhere between the great houses, Denham Place, Denham Court, the Lea (home of the Gilbey family of whisky fame), Wrango Hall, the Fishery, the Priory and the Moor House; and the hovels in which the poorest villagers lived, in the High Street and in Cheapside some of them I regret to say, owned by my father. "The Homestead" had been a public house at one stage in its history, called "The Black Donkey", and this must have given it part of its attraction to us children - the deep cool cellars in which the barrels of powerful beer had been stored, the office used by my father for his business affairs which still had a "counter" in it, at which generations of hobnailed and gaitered villagers must have leaned, the steps up and down into rooms which would trap the unwary foot, the loft over the outhouses in which one day I discovered the cobweb-shrouded inn sign of former days, unfortunately not illustrated by the black donkey.

The house was sandwiched between the Post Office and a general store, with a passage-way running down one side, just wide enough for a horse and cart and later on for a motor car. But the rooms were not large and my memories of them are dark memories for it was the day of chocolate brown paint and dark patterned wallpaper, dull cretonne chair coverings and black imitation leather seats for the dining chairs. It was the day of the oil lamp and in most houses there seemed to me, even as a child, to be an all pervading odour of paraffin. Each week there was an energetic polishing of brass lamp bowls and brass ornaments and a mixing up of Goddard's Plate Powder to refurbish the odd bits of silver on the mantelpiece, draped of course in green velvet or baize with bobbles pendant from the edge. Some of the better houses had gas lamps, but until the electrical power was installed in our house we depended on oil and candles for lighting and the nasty black kitchen range for cooking. Later on my mother transferred her affections to oil cookers and even when we moved into a house with gas she continued to maintain that there was nothing like her "Rippingille" for the perfect cooking of the sponge sandwiches for which she was justly famous.

The *kitchen* was the best room in the house for comfort - it was in front of the kitchen range that I was bathed from the earliest days and my earliest memory is of being washed and bathed, screaming with too much soap in my eyes, by my half sister, May, who used to call me "model back", a term to which I have long since lost all claim. It was in the kitchen too that we had most of our meals and my place was in the dark cupboard beyond the kitchen table, approached in only one way, by crawling under the table, which I have described earlier. It was on the kitchen table, as I have told, that I was sat at the age of four to have the prongs of my braces removed from my tongue by my mother and a neighbour, and where the Condy's fluid was liberally applied to stop the flow of blood. This was my earliest and greatest fright - even at that age there passed through my mind a series of pictures of myself going through life with my braces permanently attached to my tongue. It was on the stone-flagged kitchen floor, on newspapers, that I was cleaned up after pulling out the bung from the tar barrel in the garden and covering myself with that disgusting semi-liquid. It was outside the kitchen door that I received my beating when we had ruined our best clothes in the granary. It was at the kitchen sink that I would watch with wide eyes while my half brothers Ted and Charles washed away the grime and dust of the coal yard. It was while playing soldiers in the kitchen that I fell serenely in love with my beautiful golden-ringletted cousin Irene long before Vera Johnson took her place in my affections. The kitchen too saw most of my tears and my tantrums, for we were not allowed into the "parlour" or the dining room except on Sundays. The kitchen heard my screams on the famous seventh birthday when I refused to allow the other children invited to the rare birthday party to share my new cricket set, and I was duly deprived of both it and their company for the next twenty-four hours. In the kitchen in 1926 I would watch the "nurse" who looked after my sister June as a baby of a few days old, drink her Guinness which I had to fetch for her from the Green Man, being rewarded with a penny for my pains. This "nurse" has been indelibly mirrored in my mind as a sort of Sarah Gamp - I am quite sure she had no nursing qualifications - because of the Guinness drinking; and also because my mother had too much milk for her baby, some of which had to be drawn off, and the woman tried to persuade me that it was good to drink. I had no reason to be horrified at the suggestion since I had drunk the same milk as a baby myself at my mother's breast. But the impression that the suggestion made upon me was terrifying; I shuddered at the thought of drinking my mother's milk from a glass and, for a small boy of eight and a half, the woman began to have a horrifying fascination as some kind of female monster.

The *parlour* was the room where we had our Sunday night sing songs: a room crowded with overlarge furniture, a rosewood upright piano with a stool full of sheet music, a glass fronted cabinet full of Victorian bric-a-brac and the "crest china", collected from all the seaside towns visited by my parents, and suitably inscribed, which was so beloved of the post-1918 war generation. The parlour was kept for use on Sundays only and smelt like it, musty and airless. The horse-hair stuffed chairs in it were sadly uncomfortable, but the room remains for me a memory of Sunday evenings because it was one of the few rooms in which I remember my father sitting with us as a family, and joining in the singing at the piano after I had returned from singing Evensong in the Church choir.

The *dining room* imprinted itself on my mind too for many reasons, some pleasant, some disagreeable, some dreadful, some ecstatically happy. My happiest moments in this room were on those frequent occasions when my aunts and uncles were invited to Sunday lunch - always an ample meal, for my father believed in eating well, with a huge round of roast beef for which I was allowed to dig, wash, scrub and shred the horse radish from the garden, with tasty vegetables also from our own growing, followed by a real trifle with lots of sherry in it.

When my mother had cleared away the dishes and my father had handed round the little glass tube of "Carter's Little Liver Pills" which he always carried in his waistcoat pocket, the men settled down to reminisce on their war experiences. My uncles, Harry and Bertie and Fred (my mother's brother-in-law), had all seen much action in the war and as this took place in the early twenties, their memories must have been vividly fresh. I sat enthralled at the tales they told, vying with each other. I could smell the smells and see the mud of Flanders, sense the excitement as each side mounted its attack - feel the blood rushing through my veins as we prepared to "go over the top", my pulses beating as we fixed bayonets and charged the enemy trenches. There must have been death and sadness in their stories too but the listening child did not note such things - only the glory of war and the patriotic thrill of it.

My father took no part in the story-telling, since he had seen no active service, being too old, a fact which I always felt to be a reproach to him and to my family when other boys told their hair-raising and exaggerated stories of their own fathers' prowess in battle. So for me the dining room spelt the ecstasy of war.

It also marked for me a sad occasion of a great family row in which, as a small boy in the corner, I was an unnoticed spectator. My half-sister May had been kept at home when my father married for the second time, but naturally was not content merely to look after my sister Enid and myself. She needed a life of her own, and on one of her holiday visits to Torquay, she had met and fallen in love with a young piano tuner called George Bowden. They had music, but it seems from later events, little else in common for May had received some professional training as a soprano. She longed to go and get a job in Torquay but my father was adamant. She must remain at home. The row was long and tearful - my father red-faced and stern, his waxed moustache bristling at the rebellion in his family, May red-eyed and emotionally exhausted. The child in the corner watched entranced with a guilty delight. May won her freedom and soon was leaving the house for ever. She returned only to get married - the only time my father went to Church within my own knowledge - in the old Norman Church at Denham though by that time we had removed to Gerrards Cross.

I remember the row, I remember also the family discussion as to what the wedding present should be, though how I came to be allowed to stay in the room is a mystery. My father had decided to give them a house in Torquay, but he was unyielding in his determination that it should be held in May's name only. He did not trust George. I have an immense respect, at this distance in time, for my father's judgement, for the marriage was not happy, and after a few years George decamped and it was a broken marriage but thanks to father's foresight, May had a safe home of her own.

It was in this room that we had installed our first wireless set. I did not know at that time the exciting history of wireless telegraphy, of the courageous wireless operator on board the Titanic as she sank, of the arrest with the aid of the wireless of the murderer Dr. Crippen and his accomplice Miss Le Neve, nor of its value to the Allies in the Great War. But the possession of a "Crystal" receiving set was in itself a dramatic adventure for the ordinary family, twiddling the "cat's whisker" around the surface of the crystal, hoping to hear the latest offering from London 2LO and Daventry 5XX. Whistles and crackles interspersed every programme and a heavy-footed visitor coming into the room would shift the cat's whisker off its effective spot on the crystal, requiring much fiddling to get it back on again.

My father always gave the impression of wishing to resist progress, but in fact he must have been a very progressive man, for our household was one of the first in the village to install the wireless, the first to have electric light, and he was certainly the first of the ordinary villagers to own a motor car.

It was while I was listening to a programme on our crystal set, the headphones glued to my ears, that I had one of the most disturbing and formative experiences of my life. I was about seven years old at the time. My mother and father were both out of the house, my sister Enid was at a Brownie or Guide meeting, and I was alone for what seemed like an eternity of time. As I listened to the wireless another sound broke in upon my consciousness, the barking of a dog. I knew which dog it was - a Pekinese belonging to a neighbour, Mrs. George Sanders. She had three of the breed and I disliked them intensely. Though my parents and the Sanders were friends, and though I was always borrowing flowers from Mrs. George's garden to take to my school teacher, I hated her dogs.

My hearing must have been sharpened by the experience of being alone, for it seemed to me that the dog was inside the house, just beyond the open doorway of the dining room. I did not know why it did not come into the room. It continued to bark and I was literally transfixed. I could not move my head. I could not move my hands, my feet were fastened to the floor, my sweaty bottom was rooted to the chair. My mouth was dry and I could not utter the scream that I wanted to release through my riveted teeth. I did not analyse my fear. I do not know exactly what it was that I feared - being attacked, being bitten perhaps, a physical fear. Perhaps it was not a physical fear so much as a mental one - anything might happen to a little boy when he was left alone by cruel and unloving parents, he might even die of fright. So I must have subconsciously reasoned. The passage of time was no doubt very short, but it seemed to be unending and timeless. When my parents returned, the spell which held me fast in body and mind was broken, and I sobbed my heart out for what seemed like hours on end until I fell asleep exhausted. This was the most frightening trial that I have ever undergone in my life. From it may be traced perhaps my dislike of dogs, especially of the Pekinese variety, from it too came perhaps a succession of terrifying dreams and nightmares which occasionally haunted my sleeping hours for some years to come. But strangely, the experience did not make me want to seek more the companionship of my fellows, it drove me more into myself and made me more of a lonesome boy than I had been before.

As a home? My view of our house as a home must be coloured by my experience in building a home of my own, but looking back upon those days up to the year 1928 when we lived in "The Homestead", I can recognise very few of the things which I would regard as essential to a true home life today. I can remember few occasions when we lived as a family, sharing secrets, exchanging views, even childish views, laughing together at jokes against one another and against the outside world. We rarely took a holiday together. My parents went off to Cliftonville or Scarborough or other fashionable resorts, and we children were either left at home in the charge of a stranger or sent to Torquay to holiday with my sister's godmother in a tiny house in the backstreets of the town.

To this there were two exceptions - on Sundays in the summer, my father would get his hat and stick and would take us for a walk round the village, and in the winter we would go into the parlour and while my mother played - and she played exceedingly well - we would sing. I cannot remember many birthday parties except in other people's houses - I envied particularly the parties held in the Falcon, where my mother's half brother was the landlord. Tom and John Briggs were thought of as cousins and a merry time we had in the back parts of the pub on their birthdays, but we rarely seemed to welcome other children into our house - my father must have been old before his time to resent children so much - or was it because he had eight of them, and longed to be relieved of the burden of them?

There seems to have been an unnatural division in our family - my father took me on outings, and my mother took my sister. With my father I went sometimes to the cinema to see the latest extravaganza of Charlie Chaplin or Buster Keaton or the war films which had just been made - one called *Verdun* and another, *Mons*, I recall. With my father I would go to the Lyceum pantomime each year. One outing we did have together as a family - I think the only one - to the great Wembley Exhibition of 1924 and 1925. This event stamped itself upon my mind - I can still see the great statues made in New Zealand butter, the coats of arms five feet high in the same strange material - the Prince of Wales feathers comes to mind. I remember the fun fair and the great whirling dragon on its switchback. When I cried, I was given a fountain pen with a special filler from one of the side-shows. But I was always a tearful child and my memory of Wembley is marred by tears, as most of my memories are, in childhood. I can see now that my tears must have exasperated my father who would not have understood the cause of them, nor would he have put himself out to get rid of them in a kindly way. The solution to childish tears in those days - in these days too in some quarters - was to take the tearful child to the nearest eating place and fill it full of cream cakes. It was a most effective solution.

The exhibition had been opened by King George V in a surge of patriotic fervour and in an attempt to lessen some of the worst effects of the Great War by expanding British Trade within the Empire and outside it. The word Empire was put into the title, the "British Empire Exhibition", and the mud-soaked roads between the great pavilions were given appropriately imperial names - "Anson Way", "Drake's Way". One of the star exhibits was the famous "Queen's Doll's House", now to be seen in Windsor Castle, full of the most exquisite and minutely detailed workmanship even down to a tiny tin of Colman's mustard on the pantry shelf which is said to have caused the king himself to roar with laughter. There was a complete African village, I recall, and the pageants depicting life in the Empire used to attract 25,000 people at a time. Such are the things that impress the childish mind. The Exhibition itself was a financial failure.

It is strange that we were not encouraged to bring other children home. I cannot recall having more than one friend in the whole time I lived in our village, though my sister had friends at school and in the various organisations to which she belonged. I had an *enemy* however. He was the boy from the Grocer's shop next door, an aggressive child of the same Christian name as myself, and though he was stronger than I and always won our fights - with myself retiring in tears once more, the humiliating thing is that he was younger than I. Because I was so afraid of him, I was too scared even to go into the garden when he was about, in case he should climb over our wall and persecute me yet again. I am sure he was a harmless child and no doubt he has become a friendly chap, a loving husband and father, but this other Stanley plagued my waking thoughts and haunted my dreams. I cannot recall the form of his persecution very clearly. Sometimes no doubt it was physical - the "Chinese burn" was a popular torture among children in those days, and itching powder culled from the rose hips in the hedges and kept in matchboxes, to be put down the necks of the unwary.

How lacking in elementary psychology my parents were! If only they had invited Stanley to a party at our house! For they must have known how much I hated and feared him. And how cruel children can be to each other. Part of the trouble was that I was chubby faced and wore steel rimmed spectacles and this was always a sign of weakness to the enemy - who would call out "Here comes old four eyes", or "Hello granny", or even more hurting - "Yah, boss-eyed". This form of harassment left its mark upon my mind for many years to come, and in my school days later I found it hard to stop myself bursting into tears whenever a boy or a master looked at me with contempt, even though he said not a word nor raised his hand against me. Stanley was a past-master at all the arts of molestation, of teasing and embarrassing, of tormenting and hunting. I hated him. I wished he would die.

Though we were the first to have the radio and a motor car, we did not rise to such amenities as a bathroom or a water closet. My father had been born in 1865, remember, so he would have regarded such things as superfluous, and in a village the standards of hygiene and sanitation were still very low compared with the standards then being demanded in the new housing estates which were rising everywhere. Not that we were a dirty family - far from it. My mother was a martinet where washing was concerned. The nightly wash - all over, standing up in a bowl on the kitchen floor, was a heavy burden to me, particularly the meticulous cleaning out of the ears and the combing of the hair with a scurf comb, a fine toothed comb as sharp as a razor.

My mother had a horror of not keeping "the bowels open". So each week, on Saturday night with clock-like regularity we would be given a dose of syrup of figs, or to vary the taste a little, a lump of Solazzi. Only those who grew up seventy years ago will have met this noxious thing - a crude form of licorice which was quite pleasant to take but which had a devastating effect upon the internal workings - if you had too much of it, you could have diarrhoea for weeks. There was yet a third remedy much prized in our family which was supposed to have the same effect - powdered sulphur mixed in treacle - delicious to the child, fatal to his health. My mother had her own cure for constipation - senna pods, soaked each night in boiling water. If these things did not "work", then it was the bottle of cascara tablets. No wonder she suffered in her later years from the worst forms of intestinal seizures! How ignorant our fathers were about the elementary facts of diet. Two out of every three bottles and boxes in the "medicine cabinets" of those days, contained an aperient.

As I have said, my father was a dapper man and my mother was always well-dressed - his clothes were in keeping with his age, hers too. But *we* were dressed in a rather old-fashioned style. Boots and not shoes were insisted upon to strengthen the ankles - though the opposite effect was obtained. I had for many years to be dressed in a sailor suit, complete with lanyard and whistle, which I was not allowed to blow, and my sister suffered in silence in rather old-fashioned low-waisted, long-skirted dresses. We all wore hats of course, mine the usual school cap, sitting, as mother used to say, "like a pimple on an elephant", on my rather round head. Lace was still fashionable, both for clothes and for curtains. But even I was not made to wear as some of my school fellows were, the hated knickerbockers. Wellington boots seems to have been part of my childhood life - I don't know whether it rained more in our village than elsewhere, or whether the roads and lanes were muddier than most, but we seemed to have to wear gumboots an awful lot - together with the black mackintoshes which seemed to be the child's common rainwear of the day. The modern psychiatrists are telling us that many of the problems which assail us in the sphere of mental disturbance today are due to the clothes which we were made to wear as children - this seems to be nonsense, especially as the wheel has come full circle and things which we hated to wear, like the shiny raincoat and the girls' black stockings became the height of fashion in the 60's and 70's. One wonders how the psychiatrists of 40 years hence will regard their patients, and whether they will trace back many of their mental upsets to Beatle haircuts and leather jackets, to the too tight jeans and pointed Italian shoes of the sixties, or the loose untidy garb of the 80's and 90's.

As a child I loved going to bed. This may well have been because so many of the hours of my waking day seem to have been unhappy - or am I exaggerating? But in bed I would curl up and indulge in my childish fantasies. I would be a racing driver; I would be Harold Lloyd, doing some daring act on top of a New York skyscraper, I would be an aeroplane pilot, pulling the pillow up close round my ears and the sheet up round my chin and making a tiny cockpit for myself. In bed I was at peace. In my own room I could not be annoyed or persecuted or tormented. I am quite sure that the feather beds which we all slept in in those days were very unhealthy, bad for the spine and all the rest, but they were very cosy. Some of my happiest memories are of sitting up in bed after a "bilious attack" - that malady must surely have been removed from the medical dictionary by now - eating bread and milk with golden syrup in it and looking through huge albums full of picture postcards.

These bilious attacks seem to have been frequent in most children in my generation. Whether they were symptoms of some real internal weakness or wrong dieting, and ignorant feeding, it is hard to say - or whether they were the result of trying to make oneself sick because one did not want to go to school, which seems more likely, certainly the food we ate could not have helped much. The milk was delivered to the door by the local farmer still in his filthy corduroys and leather gaiters. He brought with him a two or three gallon can, and ladled out the milk into a jug which may have been sitting on the front doorstep for hours before his arrival, sometimes covered with a saucer, sometimes not. In summer the flies would congregate round the milk jug, and it was common practice to remove cow's hairs before using the milk. Fish was sold in the open market, often after it had been covered with flies. Conditions in the butchers' shops were atrocious. There were no refrigerators in the ordinary home and no food was wrapped. The bread man drove a horse and van, often open at front and back - in wet weather the mud would splash up onto his wares, and the rain would often soak the loaves.

Children have no sense of time and because of this I was in trouble more than once and all because of that same baker's van and, somewhat less frequently Mr. Bronsdon's milk float - what an expressive word "float" is - that two wheeled vehicle seemed literally to float on air as it rolled behind a spanking chestnut horse, young and mettlesome. When the baker's van came down the village street we children would ask for a ride and the kindly baker would lift us in on to the front step of his van and we would do some of his delivering for him. If the round was a long one we might well be home at six o'clock instead of half past four, the time that our mothers had expected us back from school. In the days before the second world war milk was delivered twice a day - I suppose because the morning's untreated milk might well have gone sour by the evening under the conditions I have described, and so it was on one of his afternoon rounds that we would plague the farmer to let us ride on his float.

And if his round ended far from our home as it often did there was the long walk back - kicking the odd conker along the road or the smooth round stone, and a slow progress it was.

One of the outstanding days of the month for a small boy at "The Homestead" was the day of the pig-killing. It seems to me now as I picture it, that this happened frequently, but it cannot have been as frequent as my memory seems to say, as pigs take a long time to grow. When the old sow had done well - and a litter of ten piglets was not uncommon - and the grunting, snorting, squalling porkers had grown to a respectable size, my mother would heat up gallons of water in the scullery copper; the great wooden tubs would be got out, the scrapers and the butcher's knives sharpened and the gruesome rite would begin. My childish ears seemed always to be full of the sound of the pigs as the sharp knives went home - this was the time before the licensing of public slaughter houses and the tightening of the laws governing the killing of animals for human consumption. It was an entrancing sight for me to see the pigs plunged into the boiling water after they had been killed and the men with the scrapers got to work, and soon, in the winking of an eye, or so it appeared to my childish fancy, there was a row of shining white carcasses hanging on the bright, cruel steel hooks under the long porch that overhung the rear portion of our house. My mother would then "do down" the lard, and soon bladders of the stuff were hanging in the huge stone-flagged scullery, like grotesque and bizarrely misshapen white balloons.

I felt no compassion for the animals as I saw them killed before my eyes. But I was not conscious of any cruelty either - I am sure there was none. This was a natural function of the countryman, and my father transgressed no law of humane behaviour towards the animal kingdom. Pigs were given by God to man for his food and it was in the course of nature's normal processes that they grew to maturity and were ready for the knife. To my mother also this was a natural thing, and she felt no revulsion either. These were days when life was not easy for the majority of villagers and to appease hunger was a necessity which knew no reason for squeamishness.

Pig-sticking time was a time when my father's care and generosity towards the poor people of the village showed itself. When the carcasses had been dealt with and the various parts of the pig had been removed, the liver, the lights, the chitterlings, and other, more obscure portions, were wrapped up in sheets of new grease-proof paper and laded into a wide, shallow, scrupulously cleaned wicker basket and I was made to set off on a round of the village, knocking at the doors of the widows and the aged, and handing over a parcel with my father's compliments. I do not remember any shyness at this time - knocking at doors seems to have been my lot from that day until this, but I have always hated knocking unless I had a reason for doing so. To call on a house because they have asked you to call, this is easy, to call on a family because you have something to give them, this too is a simple pleasure, but to knock at a door when you know you will not be welcomed, to knock when you know in fact that you will be unwanted, this is difficult, as every parish priest knows. Though it must be said in all truth that the number of occasions on which I have found my call resented is very small indeed.

I suppose that this was in a sense my initiation into pastoral visitation - it was usually an old lady who came to the door, more often than not with a grimy apron round her waist, and a greasy man's cloth cap upon her head - the women of seventy years ago and more all seem to have liked to wear something on their heads all day. One old dame I recall visiting - with a cloth cap on her head, wearing voluminous black skirts and smoking a pipe. "Hallo, dearie," she would say, her wrinkled old face creasing in a toothless smile - that sounds almost too hackneyed to be true. In fact her smile wasn't quite toothless - there were three or four widely-spaced, yellowing fangs in her mouth! "What have you got for me today?" And she would take the clay pipe out of her mouth and wave it at me. I would hand over the packet of liver or whatever it was, "With my father's compliments," I would say, though I doubt if I knew then what a compliment was. "Come in and have a bit of cake," she would say, and always obedient, I would go into the dark little front room about seven feet by nine, crowded with old furniture and faded Victoriana and reeking of stale tobacco smoke, kippers and dirt. But the cakes were delicious. After a few minutes I would resume my rounds. I don't know how much difference these gifts of meat made to the recipients, but a widow's pension was only 10/- a week then, and for the rest they depended upon the charity of the Church (a blanket and a hundred weight of coal or a half crown at Christmas) and of individuals like my father.

A child's eye view is, quite naturally, distorted and exaggerated in terms of size and space. To me as a child *our garden* seemed to be huge. Now I know that though it was long, nearly a hundred yards from the back door to the stream which marked its southern boundary, it was narrow, not more than twenty yards across. But it was a paradise for childhood's play. In addition to the outhouses, where the carthorses and carts were kept, there were the piggeries and a small orchard where the tar barrel rested on its cradle, and in one of the trees, a Worcester apple tree, I would often sit and dream after school in summer time. There were pear trees and plum trees, raspberry canes and black currant and red currant bushes. All for a child's delight and all out of sight of the house so that I could gorge myself without discovery. My favourite fruit was from a loganberry bush and it is no doubt that it was over indulgence in loganberries, black, shiny, and luscious when ripe, quite unbelievably unpleasant when unripe, bitter and harsh, that caused some of the "bilious attacks" from which I seem frequently to have suffered. The tastes as well as the sights and sounds of childhood remain with me to this day and my favourite apple is still the Worcester, my favourite fruit still the ripe Victoria plum and the mild sweet raspberry. My father was also an expert strawberry grower, but so many dire threats must have been uttered against those who dared to steal strawberries, that I never hazarded a foray into the strawberry bed in one of my raids on the garden.

Some of my most blissful hours were spent leaning over the rickety gate of the piggeries poking at the unfortunate beasts with a long stick, until one day I over-balanced and landed head first in a mass of evil smelling and sticky straw. For a few weeks I kept clear of the pigsties, not willing to risk yet again the punishment meted out for spoiling another set of clothes. The place kept its fascination in spite of its consequent painful associations and I returned in due course to the game of pig poking. The sight and the sound of these animals eating remains with me still, and the sweet-sour smell of the swill they were given, and in that connection a visit I paid in company with my father to a pig swill factory, I think at West Drayton. The overpowering odour of the huge boiling vats of waste foods, the sight of the fat old women with scarves round their heads, stirring the vats with huge sticks, persists and does not disgust me as it would I suppose, if I had come to it as a grown up. Some folk say that they cannot eat pork because the pig is such a filthy animal. Each to his taste, and it does seem strange that a creature of such gross habits (seen from the human angle) should provide such succulent meat.

When I came to study Lamb's essays at school I discovered with joy the delightful dissertation "On the origin of roast pig" and often pictured the events of his tale happening in my own back garden. Mankind, said an old Chinese manuscript (according to Lamb), for seventy generations used to eat its meat raw. Until it discovered the art of roasting in this way: A Chinese swineherd by the name of Ho-ti, had gone off into the woods one day leaving his lubberly son Bo-bo in charge of his cottage and a fine sow with a newly farrowed litter of nine piglets. Bo-bo, being fond of playing with fire, like all boys, accidentally set fire to the cottage and the pigsty, with the result that all the pigs perished. While he was thinking what he should say to his father a delicious aroma penetrated his nostrils and a "premonitory moistening at the same time overflowed his nether lip". Stooping down to feel a pig to see if there were still life in it, he burned his fingers and to cool them he applied them to his mouth. Some scorched crumbs had come away on his fingers, and for the first time in the history of mankind a human being tasted crackling! On his father's return Bo-bo persuaded Ho-ti to taste the roast pig and he too was enchanted, forgave his son and from that time onwards whenever they wanted roast pig they set fire to the house and piggeries. This caused great suspicion among the neighbours and the two were hailed before the judge in Peking. But when judge and jury had all tasted the delicious meat they were given a verdict of "Not Guilty". The judge, a shrewd fellow, winked at the obvious iniquity of this decision and went and bought up all the pigs in the district - soon his Lordship's house was seen to be on fire. The thing took wing and there were fires to be seen in every direction. Insurance houses shut up shop, and houses began to be built slighter and slighter until a sage arose who demonstrated that one did not need to burn down a whole house to roast a pig. Thus was invented the gridiron. "By such slow degrees do the most useful and seemingly the most obvious arts make their way among mankind," concludes Lamb.

The natural processes of birth seem to have been something to be ashamed of in my parents' generation. Perhaps we have allowed the pendulum to swing too far the other way today, when the whole performance can be seen in fullest detail on television, and when half a dozen fictional programmes make us familiar with the inside of hospitals and operating theatres and maternity words. There is an instinctive reticence about the deepest mysteries which to my mind is appropriate and proper. Not prurience, as so much of the modern interest in sex and reproduction appears to be, but reverence for life, seems to me to be the right attitude.

When my sister June was born in 1926 my whole life was changed. I was eight and a half years old at the time. The birth was shrouded in mysterious planning - my sister was to be sent away to one set of friends, I was to be sent away to another set - the Warringtons who lived at the Station house (Mr. Warrington was the Denham Station Master and Jack the son was thought to be one of my friends.). I had no inkling at this time about the reason for this strange happening. I did not question it, rather regarded it as an exciting adventure - to stay for a few days in someone else's house, to play for a few days with someone else's toys. I suppose that I had noticed my mother's increasing size, but it had made no impression upon me. Indeed, I often surprise my family today because I have not noticed that so and so is pregnant. If there had been talk in our house about the approaching birth it had been kept from me. I should not have been greatly interested anyway.

The day of the birth arrived and I was sent to school as usual that afternoon, with instructions that I was not to come back to "The Homestead", but to go back with Jack to the Station House. "You must give this to Jack," I was told as a half pound packet of chocolate was pressed into my hand, "You are not to eat any of it - I expect he will share it with you when you get to his house." Oh the ignorance of my father about the processes of a small boy's mind! What temptation to throw in the path of a child still tainted in spite of baptism, with original sin! As I wandered to school that afternoon I peeped inside the wrappings and saw the chocolate, dark, brown, rich smelling, mouth-watering. I thought to myself, "No one will know if I take a piece off the end and fold the silver paper over." This I did. It was very choice. I put the packet in my pocket again. Half a mile further on I took it out and looked at it again. "Supposing," I said to myself, "I tell Jack that my father gave us this to share. I could eat half of it and no one would know." Soon there was only half a packet left.

The rest needs no telling. Conscience made its last feeble effort to save me from the jaws of hell. When afternoon school was ended I handed Jack two small squares of chocolate. I don't think my parents ever knew the awful character of my deceit. It has haunted me ever since! This could be the place to discuss the implanting of feelings of guilt in the childish mind, but I must resist the temptation to do that. Or it could be the place to berate parents for placing temptations in the path of their children as in ignorance they so often do. I must return to my theme, the influence upon me of having a baby sister.

I enjoyed my few days stay at the Station House. Jack had an air gun - he was a year or two older than me, and we took pot shots at passing railway trains - luckily without hitting any of them. We played his portable toy gramophone, we played at trains, we collected train numbers. It was a happy period. I enjoyed Mrs. Warrington's cooking, especially a thick, rich sweet sauce which I have never come across since, which she used to pour over the Yorkshire pudding we had with our roast beef. Then, on the day of my return home, I was taken into my mother's bedroom to see my baby sister. I was eight and a half years old. If they had prepared me for this in some way I should not have been so shocked. I don't know what it was that I expected as I came fearfully into my mother's room, certainly not the pink baby with closed eyes that lay in my mother's arms in traditional fashion, ugly and wrinkled. "Well, what do you think of her?" I was asked. What a question to put to a child of eight about a sister whom he had known nothing about and not seen until that moment. I did not think anything, and so said nothing. It was not a happy visit, and for a while I brooded on the injustice of grown ups. Injustice which had made them keep this thing from me, injustice which somehow, I sensed it already, would transfer what little affection they showed me, to a third member of the family. From that moment on I was saddled with an unwanted burden - my sister. Again I find it extraordinary, unaccountable and very odd, that my parents should have expected me to look after my small sister as much as they did. A young girl from the village was engaged to help my mother look after June, a sweet girl called Mabel Stone, but she wasn't there all the time and after school I was expected to look after the baby, push her out in her pram, take her with me wherever I was going. I was very proud of her of course, and particularly proud of the shiny new pram, buff coloured I remember, and much more up-to-date than the old prams we had been pushed out in. The derisory cries of my fellows echo still in my ears - it was considered an unmanly thing for a boy to push a pram, or a man for that matter. I wonder now that I did not tip the pram and its contents into the river in my shame!

This use of me as an unpaid nursemaid continued for several years, and the most miserable holiday I ever spent was taken one year at Bognor when I was twelve years old. My parents, June and I, were in a boarding house near the promenade (Enid was away at Guide camp) and each morning I had to take June on to the beach and amuse her as best I could. Each afternoon the same thing happened, though then at least there was a Punch and Judy man to watch. We watched until I knew all his patter by heart. At the end of each show he would sell picture postcards of himself with lucky numbers on - the holder of the lucky number was to win a small camera which could be seen in the window of one of the chemist's shops in town. Each day I would spend my hard-earned pocket money on a set of these postcards and I would then go and gaze at the camera (it probably was not worth more than a few shillings) longing for the day when the number on one of my cards tallied with the lucky number in the window. It never did. I am not a lucky person. I have never in my life won anything in a raffle. Only at guessing the number of sweets in a jar am I any good.

When June had her first bicycle - another cause of resentment, for I was fourteen before I had mine and June was only five or six, I was always in charge of her when she was riding it. Until the day that her wheel got caught in mine, and she was thrown off and broke her collar bone. I was always blamed for this incident. It may well have been my fault, but the injustice of the blame attaching to a young boy who should not have been expected to be in charge of a tiny girl rankled for many years. I am quite sure that no unfairness or injustice was intended on the part of my parents, certainly they were not conscious of any, but injustices there were, as I fear that there always will be in families where a "late child" has arrived to put the noses of the elder children out of joint! As I grew older I realised the folly of resentment, and though at times June and I were very close, at times I was very cruel to her as some kind of compensation for the fact that I could not get rid of her.

The position that Enid held in the family at this time is a bit unclear to me. She was two and a half years my elder and always appeared to be my father's favourite. She was a keen Guide and seems always to have been at a Guide meeting or Guide camp in the summer when to my mind she should have been looking after her sister. The only time when I felt very close to her was one Christmas when we discovered our joint Christmas present under the spare room bed, some weeks before the festival. It was a small pedal car, old fashioned and crude by modern standards but immensely exciting to us in our anticipation. After the discovery we went about like conspirators, whispering in corners, giggling behind our hands and putting on solemn faces whenever our parents were near. Realisation is never as satisfying as expectation though, and in fact that pedal car was a constant source of strife between us once Christmas day had dawned and the present was ours. What a silly thing to do anyway - to give brother and sister such a joint present. There was bound to be a battle as to who should ride in it. In this instance I was the overall winner and after mighty arguments and many tears Enid gave up the struggle and I was left in almost undisputed possession of this precious toy.

Another Christmas I recall with happier memories - we spent it at the farm in High Wycombe owned by my godfather, and old friend of the family, Joe Chalk. It was a cold winter with mountains of snow (1925 I think) and we had made our way along the Oxford road in the old Ford car between mountainous snowdrifts on either side, with room for only one vehicle at a time. Their house was warm and exciting, and the farm buildings were a constant source of delightful discovery. They too had a large garden with a stream in which the milk churns were cooled, but at Christmas time this was a blanket of pure snow. They made us very welcome and gave us children delightful presents. In the evening they played cards with my parents and we watched. Many of my evenings as a child were spent watching my parents playing whist, or half-penny nap with their friends, and when I had been put to bed I would often creep down stairs and listen to their conversation through the closed door. Though Joe was my godfather, I never received a birthday present from him, nor any suggestion that I might keep the promises made by him for me at my baptism. He was not even, I suspect, a member of the Church of England, for when he got older and was retired and started to go to Church as many older people do, it was to the Congregational Church that he went. I was very fond of old Joe, who was a bluff, red faced man with a waxed moustache, like my father's, and a real countryman's accent. He too always smelt pleasantly of the pomade with which his whiskers were made to stand out, he too had an ample stomach crossed by a large golden watch chain hung with many seals. His wife who lived to a good old age always wore the velvet neck band of her era and the black lace dresses of Victorian women. A cameo brooch at her throat, she was a handsome woman of great affection for us children, for she had none of her own. We loved going to High Wycombe to see them, and we loved their frequent visits to our house in Denham, firstly in horse and trap, later in an early bullnosed Morris motor car, open to all the rigours of the English climate.

I suspect that the influence of my first home upon me is greater than I had realised, partly because it was a home of character, as our house at Gerrards Cross was not, for that was built in the worst jerry-building period between the wars; partly because it was in a village which still retained a community identity, but also because I was a lonely child who found his happiness in the house and garden and buildings surrounding him, and not in personal relationships with family or friends.

CHAPTER 4

VILLAGE

"If you would be known and not know,
vegetate in a village.
If you would know and not be known,
live in a city."
Charles Caleb Colton (d. 1832)

Caesar... made no scruple to confess
"That he had rather be first in a village
than second in Rome."
Francis Bacon (d. 1626)

Buckinghamshire is noted for its beech trees, which some believe have given it its name, and certainly "Leafy Bucks" used to be a good description of a large part of a once unspoiled strip of rural England. But now more than one new town, Milton Keynes for example, has been built, and the industrial centres of Slough (now in Berkshire - why?!) and High Wycombe have grown enormously. Though much cleaner and better planned than the industrial cities and towns of the midlands and the north, these three places have completely changed the atmosphere of Bucks in this century. I suppose one always has a nostalgic feeling of affection for the county in which one is born, and my love for the woods and lanes of my native county persists. There is no finer broad high street in England than the one at Beaconsfield, no more delightful village greens than the ones at Penn and Jordans, no village street more beautiful than the one at Denham, still largely unspoiled though the main Oxford to London road runs roaringly on its way only a few hundred yards away. We left the village when I was just eleven years old, so I was not, I imagine, consciously aware of the glory of my county. I did not know then that the Prime Minister had his country home there at "Chequers", that Benjamin Disraeli had lived at Hughenden near High Wycombe; though later, when I went to school there and took part in OTC exercises in the grounds of Hughenden Manor, we were always entertained by a descendant of the great Victorian, a Major Disraeli, who was chairman of the school governors and, I remember, like George V, creased his trousers at the side. I did not know then that the county had been the home of many of our finest poets - Thomas Gray at Stoke Poges writing his famous Elegy in its country Churchyard, William Cowper (I once had a lively argument with our English master as to the pronunciation of his name) at Olney, John Milton lived for a while at Chalfont St. Giles, and Edmund Waller at Beaconsfield. While I was a child the brilliant G.K. Chesterton lived at Beaconsfield and school friends who lived in the same town would often have tales to tell of the doings of the great man, great in body, great in faith, great in humour. Bucks has had its share of political martyrs too, John Hampden who defied Charles I, the most noteworthy of them.

In our house at Denham there was a very large, white, leather-bound volume of the history of Denham with hand-cut paper, and large old fashioned print. It was a history of the village by a former Rector and I wish I had it now, but in one of our moves it was thrown away. I remember reading bits of it as a child, and I retain a memory which I hope is accurate, that Denham is mentioned in William the Conqueror's Domesday Book. Certainly the name of the village is Anglo-Saxon, and the Church of St. Mary where I was a choirboy is circa 14th century, and many of the older houses belong to the 16th and 17th centuries. Some experts put the lancet windows of the Church as early as 13th century and the lovely, flint-faced, Norman tower under its canopy of trees faces the visitor as he walks eastward down the mellow street lined with old brick houses and inns.

The bare bones of architectural detail given in the guide books cannot possibly convey the influence that the village Church had upon the inhabitants of a place like Denham in the earlier years of this century, and one would like to believe, still has, upon villagers who have somehow escaped urbanisation. The Church was not only the centre of worship for the majority of the population who would be baptised, married and buried there and who would put in an appearance at least at Harvest, Christmas and Easter; but it was also the source of education, both spiritual and secular, for most of the children born within its borders. This, for us children, was not an overt influence, as it might be in an Irish village, where the power of the Church and of the parish priest is supreme. Rather it was a hidden control which was quite unrelated to the personality or popularity of the Rector for the time being.

The Rector of our village during my eleven years in Denham was a George Christopher Battiscombe, a Cambridge graduate who had been priested in 1892. He had been a curate in parishes in County Durham, Sussex and Kent before he became Vicar of St. Michael and All Angels, Bromley, Middlesex in 1900. After four years there he had been Vicar of Uxbridge, our shopping town just across the border into Middlesex, for eleven years before going to his last incumbency of Denham, which he held from 1915 to 1939. If he was ordained priest at the usual age of twenty-four, he would have been born in 1868 and would have been about forty seven when he became Rector of this village of a few hundred souls. Today a priest would normally be moving to a larger sphere at that age.

My memories of the Rector are few but very clear. He was to me a very old man when I was a choirboy at the age of seven (he would have been fifty-six) but he had a fine voice and a great reputation as a preacher. He was white-haired and my impression of-him is that he stooped, as many clergy do, and that he did so to avoid meeting the eye of his parishioners. This may have been a completely false impression received by a young child, but assuredly it is true that in the four years in which I met him at least twice a Sunday I cannot remember him ever addressing a word to me, either of kindness or rebuke, and though I must have passed him many times in the street, I cannot recall giving or receiving the sort of greeting that seems to me to be normal between parson and choirboy today.

From the dim conversations about him which were heard in my parents' household, I gathered that he was a taciturn man, and that his concern for his parishioners did not involve him in much visiting, or if it did, it was to the more affluent among them. As this sort of thing is frequently said without a grain of truth about the clergy, I do not record it as a fact but as hearsay. I seem to remember that he always wore deep black and a very clerical black hat, and that the village went in awe, if not in fear, of him. He would appear from time to time in the village school to which I went, and occasionally in the morning Sunday School held in the Day School building. He conducted a Sunday afternoon children's service which I attended, along with most of the children in the village, but I remember nothing of what he taught us. In fact the only sermon of his from which I remember a single sentence was one which he preached on his return from convalescence in Jamaica, after an illness, and in which he spoke of fields of tall waving sugar canes. Why this alone of all the words he uttered in my hearing should remain I do not know. It is a salutary experience for a parish priest to learn that very little of what he says is ever remembered by his people, but he can take comfort from the fact that sermons are spiritual diet of the staple food variety and not exotic dishes to be recalled with nostalgic longing. Some years ago there appeared a letter in a Church newspaper:

"Dear Sir,
I have been a regular worshipper for over thirty years and must have heard over three thousand sermons. I can honestly say that I cannot now remember a single one of those sermons. Should I have lost much if those sermons had never been preached?"

Another letter the next week read:

"Dear Sir,
I have been married for over thirty years. Every night my wife has prepared for me a nicely cooked meal. I can honestly say that I cannot now remember a single one of those meals. But I am sure that if I had not had them I should not be the healthy and happy man I am today."

In former days the village Church did dominate the village - often by its sheer size. Usually, it was the largest building in the parish - often by the fact that it alone provided the social activities necessary to village life. The incumbent was Chairman, by virtue of his office, of the Fête Committee, the Flower Show Committee, the Village Hall Committee, and the managers of the Church School. He and the Churchwardens administered the local village charities, dispensed the Christmas coal, and the blankets for the poor, bought boots and books for Jimmy Brown when he won a scholarship to the local Grammar School. His wife visited the sick and the lonely and the aged, arranged for the nurse to call, and ran the sewing parties and embroiderers guild. The Church ran the Whist Drives and all the clubs for young and old. Even the uniformed organisations of Cubs (I was one) and Brownies, Scouts and Guides, had close links with their parish Church and appeared regularly at worship. In all this there was no dictatorship, no fear of the priest. It was a willing co-operation between Church and people in the creation of a happy, well-knit community, the sort of community which is becoming rarer as the years pass.

Is it possible to estimate the influence of a centuries-old building upon the lives of succeeding generations of those who live beneath its walls or within its shadow? When a Church has stood upon the same hallowed spot for six or seven hundred years, when twenty generations of villagers have been buried in its Churchyard, have sung in its choir, received the Sacrament at its altars, been cared for in body and soul by its Rectors, have been joined in wedlock and had their babies baptised at its font, have had the Church *there* all that time, if only to stay away from, it cannot fail to have cast its spell for good over the whole body of village people, cannot fail to have been potent in guiding the thoughts and actions of folk in whole periods of their history. Such must have been the influence of St. Mary's.

If I try to analyse its influence upon myself, I find that influence not so much in the worship which I took part in, as in the building itself and the Churchyard surrounding it. The building always impressed me as a place of quiet and holiness. Perhaps it was the manner in which we were taught, but it would have been thought blasphemous to raise one's voice above a whisper in that holy house of God. I don't know who taught me, but it was my custom, even as a child, to kneel in a back pew as soon as I entered the Church, to say my prayers, and this with no sense of precious piety but as the natural thing to do.

The building itself was full of excitement even to a child. There was a much defaced 15th century painting of the Judgement over the South doorway by which we always entered the Church, with what I believe is an unusual scene of the sea giving up its dead. At the bottom left the donor has had herself painted into the picture. The picture was restored by Mr. Clive Rouse in 1933. In the sanctuary, on the north side of the altar there was a 16th century monument to Sir Edmund Peckham and his wife. As a child I regarded this monument with awe and wondered if the bodies were still inside the stone plinth, or perhaps even encased in the recumbent stone figures. We were taught (by whom I do not know) that it was sacrilegious to walk over the graves of the dead, and this made life particularly difficult with regard to the brasses and inscriptions in the floor of the Church which my childish fancy placed only an inch or two above the imagined skeletons lying close under the flagstones. This did not worry me when we walked in choir procession, but at other times I can remember hopping and skipping over the inscriptions in order to avoid the desecration of the dead!

The brasses are considered to be very good, and visitors were perpetually in the Church taking rubbings of old Dame Agnes Johnson, last Abbess of Syon, Middlesex (one of two remaining brasses to an abbess in England, the other being at Elstow in Bedfordshire). An incised stone slab with the figure of a man in a gown, Philip Edelen, of the 17th century which is set in the south wall of the chancel, used to fascinate me too. Other Denham families, the Hills, the Bowyers, the Peckhams, the Micklows, abound in a building full of historical and architectural interest.

It was the Churchyard that enchanted me even more than the Church. The yew trees from which (we had always been told, though this is denied today) the English bowmen of the Middle Ages got their bows, the ancient tombs and monuments surrounded by their forbidding spiked iron railings, the excitement of taking a dare to pass through the graveyard after dark, and wondering if the souls of the damned would seep out of the cracks in the archaic and broken down tombs and carry me off to hell. There was nothing morbid in this macabre occupation. It was sheer bravado. It was the sheer joy of challenging the powers of darkness to do their worst.

The children of the village often used the graveyard as a playground, but their play was not irreverent. It was also a public pathway from one part of the village to another, and on the way one would pass the monument which told the fantastic and pathetic story of the "Denham murders", when a stranger killed a whole family of seven one Sunday morning with an axe. The inscription on the stone reads:

> "Beneath this stone lie the remains of Emanuel Marshall and Charlotte his wife. Also Mary Ann his sister, and Mary, Thirza and Gertrude his children who, together with his mother Mary Marshall were all barbarously murdered on Sunday morning May 22nd

1870 by John Owens a travelling blacksmith who was executed in the County gaol at Aylesbury August 8th 1870.
Mary aged 8 years. Emanuel aged 35 years. Thirza aged 6 years, Charlotte aged 34 years, Mary Ann aged 32 years, Gertrude aged 4 years."

This dreadful deed was one of the legends of the village which every child knew by the time he went to school, and every time I passed the house in which the heinous crime was done - it was a farmhouse in my day- I used to shudder inwardly at the thought of it.

Also in the Churchyard there were some of the most hideous marble monuments I have ever seen, angels and the like. Contrasted with them were the simple wooden crosses made in the shape of aeroplane propellers which marked the graves of flyers lost in the first world war.

One might hope that from this constant use of both Church and graveyard we children took into ourselves a profound belief in things spiritual, especially in the reality of some kind of life after death! My own visits to the graveyard became less frequent after one frightening experience in which a man suddenly appeared from behind a great yew tree and exposed himself to me. He was a tall, stooping, untidy man, with straggling moustache and dirty hands, in torn and tattered clothes. I fled in a great fright and never came into the grounds of the Church again unaccompanied. I was about nine years old at the time I suppose, and knew nothing then of the motives that drive these unfortunate souls to bare their sexual organs to small children. It is hard to say if the encounter had any lasting effect upon me - perhaps it did make me more prudish in later years about the uncovering of the human body than I might otherwise have been. At school and on holiday with camping clubs I was always conscious of a reluctance to undress if other boys were about.

Next to the Church in influence upon village life is the "big house" as it is still often called, the home of the squire, who may be the patron of the living, or of some other well-to-do or noble family. In our village there were many "big houses", the chief of them being Denham Place the home of the Hill and Way families, and later in the possession of Lord Vansittart. Hidden away behind its high brick wall, this 17th century house still dominated the life of the village. A very handsome house (villagers used to claim that it had three hundred and sixty-five windows, one for each day of the year) built in what the architectural experts call a "good but conservative" style in 1688-1701 for Sir Roger Hill, it stands in magnificent grounds, with beautiful smooth green lawns, and a formal garden laid out in the 18th century by the famous Capability Brown. There was a lake at the southern end of the house and a fine pair of wrought iron gates of the 1690's at the western end. My best memories of the house however are of the Sunday School parties which were held in the great Hall. I have a lucid recollection of one such occasion when for some reason I had burst into tears and could not be persuaded to stop crying - I cried much as a child - even by the gift of a toy in the shape of a Punch and Judy show. In the end I was dragged ignominiously from the Hall by my sister Enid, who was very annoyed at being made to leave the party so soon.

At the other end of the village, to the east of the Church lay another mansion, Denham Court, along a straight and beautiful avenue of lime trees. A large house, predominantly 18th century, it belonged then to a Commander Swithinbank, who had married a Miss Eno of "Fruit Salt" fame, and its grounds - as far away from the house as possible, was a popular playground for the village children. Parish Fêtes were often held there and one of its great attractions was an ornamental lake with a wooden footbridge in the Chinese style. A large orangery fascinated me as a child, with its warm, rather overpowering scent, and the sight of oranges and grapes growing in profusion in our cold climate impressed the childish mind which had no doubt been told at school that oranges were sub-tropical fruits grown in Spain or Palestine, and grapes found only in Mediterranean countries. It was a sad day for yet another family when Denham Court was sold to the London County Council as a home for girls. When the film industry came to the village it made use of all the local amenities and the Oxford University running track at Iffley Road was reproduced in the grounds of the Court for the film *A Yank At Oxford* which starred Robert Taylor and Vivien Leigh.

Films had come to the village long before the days of J. Arthur Rank and Alexander Korda (who made *Things to Come*, *Fire over England*, and many other famous films at the Denham Film Studios) for as a child of six in 1923 I had taken part along with many other village children in a film about gypsies. One shot especially comes to my mind - of a crowd of children being made to run along in front of an old fashioned gypsy caravan as it crossed over the little stone bridge which spanned the Misbourne at the South Western end of the village. There was a story in the family that this silent film had actually been seen by my half sister in Australia, who recognised the village in which she had been brought up, but as she had never seen me I doubt if she recognised any of the children in that primitive piece. When the studios were first erected on the A412 road - a grossly ugly group of hangar-like buildings of corrugated iron and brickwork, the villagers got used to seeing the stars of the day walking the streets - Anna May Wong, the Chinese star, was a favourite, in a variety of costumes, and they were soon used to the false fronts which appeared for a few weeks along the High Street.

So the village changed. Until the advent of the railway in the early years of the century, Denham was truly an unspoiled beauty of a village. Many are the tales my mother would tell of her days and evenings behind the bar of the Falcon, when the men from the railway, the gangers and plate-layers, the labourers and the navvies, would pour down the Pyghtle (what a strange name - its meaning is lost, and its pronunciation rhymes with cycle) - a narrow lane, dead straight and about a mile long from the station to the village - and crowd into the Green Man, the Swan, and the Falcon in the village; and then no doubt they would pass through and up Cheapside to the Plough for a further wetting of their thirsty, dry throats. The influence of the village pub has declined greatly over the years. But in the first thirty years of the century before the universal advent of the motor car, the radio and the television, when beer was strong and cheap, the pub was a meeting place for the poor, and the lower middle classes. That a village of a few hundred inhabitants could have supported four public houses still amazes me, and that may not be the whole tally, for as I have told, our house was once a public house too, called The Black Donkey.

Most of the working men had very inadequate housing, badly lit with smelly oil lamps, and there were often large families of children crowded into the small cottage rooms. No wonder a man longed to get out into the night and visit the pubs with their bright gaslight, their good fellowship and laughter and when beer, good strong stuff, was only a few pence a pint, one could have a wonderful evening for sixpence. The railway workers of course were far away from their homes and no doubt tongues were loosened and restraints lifted when they had finished a hard day's grind - there was much drunkenness and for a while my mother was not allowed to serve in the bars. But my grandfather was capable of dealing with any trouble or threatening incidents and his pub had a reputation as a good house. No doubt there were a few unwanted or unlooked-for babies in the village during those years too, for life was not so full of innocence as some have imagined.

Church, big house and pub have all played their part in history, but they were not the only influences. The village school, often a Church School, has had its warm chroniclers, and in our age of monstrous glass educational factories it is tempting to forget how new these phenomena are. Most of my generation went to school first in a building raised by voluntary subscription in the mid or late 19th century. The Church was almost entirely responsible for education at the infant and primary level, and in all range schools for much of what later came to be known as secondary education. The first Education Act was not passed until 1870, less than a hundred and thirty years ago, and all it did was to make a grant of a few thousand pounds for the National Schools. Denham School was an all range school - founded by the Church, and managed by the Church, where "Gaffer" Sanders was monarch of all he surveyed on the boys' side, and his wife, "Governess", was mistress of life on the girls' side. A generation of village children had been taught by these two - and in some ways very well taught they were. The girls came to school in button boots, black woollen stockings and white pinafores, the older boys in knee breeches and long stockings and boots. The village schoolmaster had an assured and respected position in village society. He was often feared by the boys and girls under his care because in the early days of this century - until the 1939 war in fact, his right to inflict corporal punishment was never questioned. He was revered by the parents of the village children because he had a smattering of education and culture (sometimes it was not much more) while they themselves often had none. He also had power, power to recommend a good boy as an apprentice, a good girl as a maid in the big house or Rectory, and power to damn too. More about the school and its influence upon me later.

Summoning these recollections from the limbo of the lost years has uncovered for me a hundred sights I had long forgotten, a dozen images I had long since covered with other, mental etchings. Now I see once more the "Tall trees in the greenwood, the meadows where we play, the rushes by the water we gather every day". Mrs. Alexander's hymn is much despised today for its declaration of the status quo as pleasing to God, indeed arranged by God. For us it was a true representation of things as they actually were in a village. It is easy to misinterpret what the author felt when she wrote - "the rich man in his castle, the poor man at his gate, God made them, high or lowly, and ordered their estate," but this is what men felt a hundred years ago, when she wrote, felt it in their bones and believed it with their minds. Felt it, moreover, to be right. Felt it still, seventy years ago. The Hills and the Ways and the Swithinbanks lived in their Denham castles, the Kedges and the Stones and the Clarkes lived in their hovels. Certainly God had made them all - was it a far cry to believe that He wanted it so also? And there was no condescension on the part of the rich to the poor in those days, though there was a false fawning upon the rich by the poor in certain quarters. My father regarded himself as quite as good as the Gilbeys or the Goodlakes, though the Hills of 1924 would have been very surprised to know that there were Kedges living in the village in 1604, as records show!

Now we know that all men are equal, and "some are more equal than others". Now we know, in that unfortunate phrase of Lord Shawcross when the Labour Party won its electoral victory in 1951 - "We are the masters now", that the roles have been reversed. The poor man is in the castle of power and the rich man is collecting half crowns (or, more likely £2) at the gate. It wasn't so much the social significance of that hymn by Mrs. Alexander, who died in 1895, that I find so accurately portraying my childhood, as the simple description of village life. My childhood was bounded by all things bright and beautiful. Flowers meant a great deal to us, for one of the competitions at the annual flower show was for the best and largest selection of wild flowers from the hedgerows. Though I am ashamed to admit now that I have forgotten most of the real names of these flowers, and could not today identify more than half of them, I do remember the "old man's beard", the "Billy's shirt buttons", the "cuckoo pint" (wild arum lily), the "creeping jenny" and the honeysuckle. I can still differentiate between the buttercup ("hold it under your chin - if you see a golden reflection, that means you like butter" we would say - who doesn't like butter?) and the celandine. I still love to walk in the bluebell woods and pick the primroses to make gay and bright the Easter garden in the Church, though in these over-regulated days even that is forbidden by law. The dog daisies abounded in the fields of my childhood, as did the convolvulus and the white briony in the hedgerows. The thistle grew in profusion in one field where someone kept a braying donkey; the groundsel and the mayweed appealed to me because I was told (probably quite wrongly) that canaries like them.

My sister and I spent hours of hot summer days weaving daisy chains and sucking the sweet nectar from the tips of the summer clover. Perhaps these weeds would not be allowed to grow in modern clinical farming days, but they added so much to the beauty of the village fields and hedges. Fungi proliferated in the woodlands which surrounded our village in those days - now it is surrounded by motor ways and monstrous buildings - and we soon learned to distinguish the true mushroom from the poisonous toadstool; the mushroom with its black gills was known to be good to eat, but all kinds of dire results were expected if you foolishly ate a puffball - you would die in agony, your face purple and your stomach eaten with pain. The same results were prophesied by the knowledgeable if you ate deadly nightshade.

All the villagers would collect the berries from the hedges - the blackberries to make jam or jelly, the crab-apples, bitter in their raw state, but delectable when jellied; the elder berries from which wine was made; the sloes from which my father used to make sloe gin, not always successfully, and if the time of fermentation had been misjudged there would be a great bang in the night and another stone jar was split from top to bottom.

We would know all the trees in the village on which the mistletoe grew, all the hedges where the hips and haws shone in winter time. We knew better than to eat the yew berries from the great trees in the Churchyard or the cluster of orange berries on the tip of the arum stalk. We loved the trees, especially, those in which you could make a hideyhole or a tree house. There was one such in Cheapside and in its fork we made a house, stocked with tiny jars of rice and jam, tea and nuts, filched from our larders at home. Rival gangs made rival houses and you were very clever if you could find a tree in which to build a house which none might discover and raid and ruin. The oak was our favourite with its acorns in little cups shaped like clay pipes, and the willows that bordered our stream seemed to be very romantic.

Though we had no "purple headed mountain" anywhere near Denham, we did have a "river running by" and Mrs. Alexander would have been glad to know that we *did* gather rushes, though certainly not every day! The river was the Misbourne, tributary of the unattractive Colne which flows into the Thames. The little stream ran through the village, at one point alongside the village street, and under a charming and ancient bridge just wide enough for a horse drawn vehicle, the same bridge over which we children trooped when the gypsy film was being made and which appears in many of the early Miss Marple films of Agatha Christie.

It was a shallow, clear little stream, abounding in small fish. Many hours did I spend with a bent pin for a hook, hoping to land one of these tiny fish. I was never successful. Not even when my half brother Ted taught me to make a loop of green covered wire on the end of a stick, and lean over the plank that spanned the stream at the bottom of the garden - "when the fish goes through the loop, give it a good pull up and the noose will tighten round the fish's belly and there you are," he said. I don't know whether he believed it himself. It didn't work anyway. I cannot count the number of occasions on which I fell into this stream - it was too shallow to be dangerous along most of its length as it passed through the village, but the legend has it in our family that my father was so tired of fishing me out of the stream that he determined to cure me of the habit once and for all by throwing me in deliberately. This I do not, mercifully, remember! We children were very jealous of our little river where it marched alongside our land and we would warn off any intruders who dared to paddle in it without our permission. We were jealous for the large meadow which my father owned to grow grass for hay for the horse's winter feed. Human pride is a basic emotion, and within that emotion pride of possession is one of the strongest elements among children - possession of property sometimes, possession of a famous or clever parent, possession of past glories.

We gloried in this meadow which ran alongside the Misbourne and which we would cross in summer time as a short cut to school, though this was forbidden by my father. The greatest pride of all was to allow the other children of the village to walk across it with us, or to come and play with us in the haystack. The hay-making was an event of real portent in our lives - in June the crop of grass and clover would be cut - that is why my father forbade us to use it as a footpath

- the ruination of any meadow grass destined for hay. I do remember it being cut by hand scythe, though not for long. The horse drawn cutters soon took the place of the manual cutter. Pick-up balers were of course unknown in the 20's. Horse drawn machines cut it, turned it, raked it, and swept it to the elevator which was turned by one of our horses going round in a circle at the end of a long pole.

It was during one hay-making season that my sister Enid was playing near the gears of this machine when she got her foot caught in the cogs, losing the whole of one toe and the half of another. If someone had not heard her screams and stopped old Jack, the slow and kindly carthorse then turning the wheel, she would have lost her foot altogether. This event greatly impressed itself on my childish mind, and coupled with the fact that in his own youth my father had lost a thumb in a chaff-cutter, I had learned a lesson to keep clear of the working parts of all machinery, a lesson which stays with me today.

For weeks my sister was "laid up" on a couch in the dining room, receiving her visitors like a queen, and I suspect, enjoying herself immensely and the attention being paid to her. She too avoided the farm machinery in future. (The toes had been dealt with in the dining room by our own doctor, who also removed our tonsils at home. No NHS specialisations in those days!)

The multitudinous activities of the village at every season of the year made life intensely interesting to the child. The village child was not so dumb as he may have seemed - he has quick and observant eyes. He knows how a rick should be thatched so that the rain may be kept out of the hay because he has watched the thatcher at work. Sadly there are no ricks now! He knows the various processes necessary to the preparation of the soil for sowing in the spring because he has seen the plough and the discs, the harrows and the rollers at work. Today he can see the combine harvester doing the whole operation of cutting, threshing, bagging corn and baling straw at walking pace, but seventy years ago harvesting took weeks, and the sheaves had to be stooked and dried before they could be gathered and thrashed. June strips the hayfields, August strips the corn fields. The green haulm of the potatoes dies down to a blackish brown and all growth is ending as winter comes. September brings the farm sales and October the falling leaves. Machinery is brought in and painted and repaired before the winter rains come to rust it.

In winter there was often a pond of rain upon a low part of our meadow and when the cold snap came, this would ice over and after school all the children of the village would slip and slide on it, some of the adults would get their skates out of the junk room, polish them and venture a few uncertain steps. When this happened it was useless for my sister and myself to complain that the meadow was *our* meadow - it became the possession of the whole village, and we forgot to lay claim to it in the general delight of skating and sliding. I did not even cry when I fell down on the ice - there were too many people about to notice my tears.

My friend Edward Dickinson and I would walk miles of a Sunday afternoon along the lanes and hedges of our village, whipping at dandelion heads with our walking sticks, talking of this and that, observing the birds and the flowers and the seasons as they came and went. None of this was conscious, but unconsciously, we took into our system an attitude of mind to the things of nature which I have not lost and which can be summed up in the words of Albert Schweitzer's philosophy - "reverence for all life."

At this distance of time it would be cant to claim that we had a rational belief in the necessity of reverence for all life. The philosophy itself is hard to sustain, for though you may believe it is wrong to hurt a fly, is it wrong to kill the germ that causes the boil on the back of your neck? For there too life undoubtedly flourishes! We had no qualms when we caught frogs from the stream, though some of us did draw the line at blowing them up with a hollow straw. We happily went birds' nesting, though we had been told at school never to take more than one egg; we collected moths and butterflies, we put frog's spawn into jars and watched the fascinating process by which the tadpole grew into the frog.

On hot summer afternoons we would laze on the bank of the stream and watch the lovely dragonflies and the little water insects as they hopped along the surface at incredible speed. Here it was that we discovered nature's provision for its creatures in camouflage as we learned to distinguish the insects against their background, the hawk moths and the red admirals, the painted ladies and the common whites, the brimstone yellows (one of the loveliest of all the butterflies), the speckled woods and the meadow browns. At school we were taught to distinguish the house martin from the sand martin, the whitethroat from the chiff chaff, the wicked cuckoo from the spotted flycatcher, though I doubt if I could tell one from the other now. The difference between the swallow and the swift in flight was pointed out to me by my father and I was taught to know the different members of the crow family - the rook, the jackdaw, the magpie and the carrion crow. The harsh cry of the rooks and crows was always with me, as there was a huge rookery in the grounds of Denham Place which we passed on the way to school.

In the churchyard were several owls whose cry we learned to imitate with passable accuracy. Tawny owls and barn yard owls abounded in the woods, and on the stream lived colonies of water wagtails and moorhens and kingfishers. I would accompany my father when he went shooting in the woods with his cronies and we children would have a wonderful time getting in the way and being sworn at. It was on one of these occasions that the headmaster of the local school who succeeded "Gaffer" Sanders, one Captain Thompson, shot his own dog by mistake. This was regarded as a great joke by the village, as he was a newcomer and had not yet won his way into village life, and I fear he never lived it down. Rabbits were their quarry, though in season the pheasant was considered a tasty catch. My father would use some of the village men as beaters, and reward them with some of the shoot, a thing I am sure they were glad at, as food was always scarce and always welcomed in the village homes. This of course is why so many villagers became poachers. They waged a constant war against the gamekeepers of the big estates and very rarely did they come off worse and have to appear before the "beak" in the County Court.

One village event stands out in my mind above all others - the Old English Fair which was held in Denham in 1924, when I was seven years old. Today if it were held it would be called an Olde Englishe Fayre, which shows how far we have come in desecrating our own past history. Unhappily most of these fairs have died out - the war helped their decline and the general unwillingness of anybody to organise anything on any basis but a commercial one.

Fairs were religious in origin. It was always the policy of the Christian Church to baptise pagan rites into Christ, and many of the ancient pagan festivals were turned into Christian feasts. Some fairs like that at Helston in my beloved Cornwall, have been traced back to Roman times, but most owe their origin to the patronal festivals of the Middle Ages. It would be customary to hear mass and then to patronise the booths and stalls which had been set up in the main street of the town. Then would follow games, dancing, athletic contests and other amusements. When fairs had been in existence for several years a charter could be asked for and was often granted, though some of the larger fairs, like that in St. Giles', Oxford, grew to great importance even without a charter from the King. Widecombe fair has passed into history with the song "Old Uncle Tom Cobley", and other famous fairs were held at Sherborne and Market Drayton. Horse fairs were common on Exmoor, Nottingham and Tavistock had their celebrated goose fairs, Stratford had its "Mop" or hiring fair, and sheep fairs abounded in the downland country.

Some of this must have been in the mind of an inspired resident of Denham when the Fair was planned. I do not know who organised it, or how many there were on the committee. I do not know if the preparations all went smoothly, though I doubt it. My mother played the piano in the village hall for all the rehearsals of the dancing. Every child in the village was dressed in an old fashioned smock. Every woman in the village wore an early Victorian dress with a large poke bonnet mostly in blue and white check gingham. All the men were dressed as country yokels of the same period and behaved accordingly.

All along the high street were set up the booths and stalls at which everything under the sun could be bought. The children gathered outside the Church gate and following a village band (largely imported from Uxbridge, I suspect); we danced along the streets to the tune of *The Floral Dance*. Two characters particularly impressed me - the town crier with his many caped overcoat and wide three-cornered hat, swinging his hand-bell at intervals throughout the day to make announcements on behalf of the committee - no amplifiers to ruin the day in 1924; and no doubt his thirst was slaked many times during the day by his friends in the Green Man; and the ancient character "Jack o' the Green" or more accurately Jack in the green, for that describes the tall framework of laurel and other green leaves which was made large enough to enclose completely the man playing the part, leaving only a hole near the top through which his face could be seen. Jack's true origin has been lost in the obscurity of antiquity, and even Christina Hole in her informative book *English Custom and Usage* only mentions him, but no doubt he was associated with some pagan fertility cult. Our Jack was an entertaining fellow and in his all embracing greenery he danced ahead and around the column of capering children as we wended our way down the village street. It was a lovely day - fine and warm, and the crowds had come in their hundreds from the neighbouring villages and towns, by bus and train, by horse carriage and motor car. The day seemed to go on for ever. True happiness is always timeless.

On this day too I had my first penknife. I bought it for a shilling at one of the booths. It did not cut very well, but it was my very own knife, bought with my very own pocket money. It did not last for very long; penknives never do, but no doubt it did much damage in its short life. There was a man on a hobby horse too, I recall, and a court jester complete with cap and bells, but they did not impress me half as much as the magnificently dressed town crier and the rather awesome figure all covered in green leaves. When bedtime came for me I was reluctant to obey, but with many protestations I was put to bed, only to lie awake for what seemed hours to listen to the revellers across the road at the two inns, enjoying their last pints and wending their several ways home, some of them doubtless in need of the support of their less unsteady friends.

On these occasions my father was always the "coconut shy" man. He would exchange his bowler hat for a soft felt one, and stand by his box of wooden balls calling "Roll up, roll up", while I rescued the spent balls from the base of the large tarpaulin backcloth. His calls were interspersed with sharp imprecations called upon my own head for getting in the way of the throwers. When I was nine or so I was thought to be old enough to take charge of the side-show and after a brief spell my father would go off to the beer tent with one of his cronies, leaving me to lose most of what he had taken by my softness. I could not bear to see anybody pay sixpence for three balls and not win a coconut, so I would always let them have three more balls for nothing. I suppose it was all very good preparation for the parish Fêtes and Fairs which later became my lot for so many years.

I returned to the village thirty years ago for the first time for many years. Externally little seemed to have changed - our house was there still, now called by another name. The Swan is still an inn, though most of the old wisteria tree has gone. There are wrought iron gates alongside our house, and the passage is much narrower than I remember it. The son of my father's best friend was still there, Walter Baker of "The Garage", once the forge. The willow trees are still drooping over the stream and the little bridge is untouched. What a come-down for the old Forge to have to be called "The Garage"! Where old Charley Baker used to stand in his leather apron, blowing the bellows to keep the forge fire alight, stood the village taxi. In place of the delicious scent of smoking horse's hoof which arose in a cloud of steam when the red hot iron was applied to the horny surface, there was the stale smell of petrol and oil.

The old forge was a centre of attraction for all the village children seventy years ago, and Charley Baker never minded us standing and staring as long as we did not get in the way. He was a craftsman, a smith, capable of working in any metal, of wrought iron work, of bonding an iron tyre to a wooden cartwheel so that it never came off in the twenty years of its life, of fashioning the different designs of the horse brasses that used to enliven the sound of a passing wagon, and which are now relics of a bygone age, fit only for the pseudo-Tudor fireplaces of pseudo old-world inns. It was from the Baker's garden which marched alongside ours that I used to steal the hazel nuts. It was Mrs. Charley's new baked cakes that I most enjoyed. It was Charley's ragged black moustache and smiling eyes that I remembered as I sat in the parlour of the Garage and talked with Walter his son, and I was touched when he offered to lend me his most precious possession *The History of Denham*, and even more touched when he wrote to ask me to return it, addressing me as "Dear Sir", when all my childhood life he had known me as "Stan".

I wandered down the village street and paid a nostalgic call at the Church, meeting the lady verger, whose aunt had been verger before her for half a lifetime, and who had been a friend of my half-sister May. In forty years she did not seem to have changed but there were no playing children in the Churchyard - I don't think Denham has many children now! There were no bats flying in and out of the yew trees - perhaps they have been banished too. Certainly no one will tell the modern child the awful tales told to me of what happens to you when a bat gets entwined in your hair - "you have to have it all cut off and it will never grow again". In the ground floor belfry of the Church my mind went back to the exciting evening when we first had cassocks and surplices doled out. Till that time we wore our ordinary clothes, but one evening a huge wicker basket lay upon the floor of the belfry where we used to practise and the excitement of finding a garment the right size was intense.

The wooden propellers marking the graves of flyers from World War I had gone, but the awesome slab recording the Denham Murders was still there. I looked for and found the casement window on the ground floor of one of the houses in the High Street through which I had put my head when wandering to choir practice with my eyes turned to the ground, kicking a stone, as was my custom - the window opened right out onto the street and there were no pathways.

What a row there was over that - how cruel I thought my father was to make me go and apologise again for breaking it - and to dock my pocket money of the cost of repairing it. A hard, impatient man, my father!

Even the Church seemed smaller than I had known it. Denham Place was still there, behind its high walls, and Denham Court at the end of the still flourishing avenue of limes. But most of the iron railings had been taken from around the graves and monuments - though the cracks in the stonework still gaped and I did not wonder that I had once upon a time felt that the spirits of the dead might ooze their way through and grab at me. Old Granny Sanders was no longer sitting outside her rose covered cottage - she must have been eighty when I was a child, always in a black bonnet. George her son, whose dogs so frightened me once, was no longer riding his old tricycle down the street, with his rubber tipped walking stick slung beneath the cross bar. His house and the house next door had been given a false front I noticed, but it was still called "Fuschia Cottage", and there was still a tub outside with a fuschia plant in it, surely the same one!

The village looked much the same, but somehow it was not the same. Forgive me, modern residents of Denham, but where is the life of the village? Does the ghost of the Scotsman still march up and down in front of the Swan of a Saturday night? Does my father's ghost still sit in his office doing his accounts and turning envelopes inside out to save money to buy houses for my mother when he dies? Does the spirit of Charley Baker still strike sparks from the anvil with his heavy hammer? Do your children still buy halfpenny sherbets at the village shop, or steal pennies from their mother's purses as I used to do, to buy liquorice bootlaces, and Woodbines at the Plough in Cheapside, which made me sick as I sat behind the haystack in our meadow? Does nobody fish in the stream with a bent pin any more? The village is not neglected, it has had its share in modern affluence, all the houses are painted, and no one lives on doles from the local

Rector or Coal merchant any more but the spirit seems to have departed.

It was Oliver Goldsmith, author of *The Deserted Village* who wrote a little poem on the pains of memory:

O Memory thou fond deceiver,
Still importunate and vain,
To former joys returning ever
And turning all the past to pain.

Thou like the world, th'oppressed oppressing
Thy smiles increase the wretches woe
And he who wants each other blessing
In thee must ever find a foe.

My father died early in 1934 of pernicious anaemia after a short illness and a time in the Royal Northern Hospital. Shortly before his death he was asked if he would like the Vicar to visit him. "If he wishes to come, he may do so," father replied. The Vicar came. I hope his visit was helpful.

My mother died in the tiny bungalow in Shoreham, to which she had moved on the death of John Cross. It was 1955 and she was only 67. She was tired, physically and mentally, worn-out from caring for him in the last three years of his terrible illness, lung cancer, caused by his years of heavy smoking. He had refused to go to a hospital so his final years had been a strain on her.

CHAPTER 5

SCHOOL

"There is now less flogging in our great schools,
but then less is learned there;
so that what the boys get at one end they lose at the other."
Dr. Samuel Johnson (d. 1784)
from Boswell's "Life"

"Alexander at the head of the world never tasted the true
pleasure that boys of his own age have enjoyed
at the head of a school."
Horace Walpole (d. 1797) Letters,
Letter to Montagu. 1736 (aged 19)

"But, good gracious, you've got to educate him first.
You can't expect a boy to be vicious until he's been to a good school."
"Saki" (Hector Munro) (d. 1960)
"The Baker's Dozen"

Statistics have always fascinated me. From the day that I first discovered *Whitaker's Almanac* it has been my constant companion. "Do you know how many houses were demolished in slum clearance schemes last year?" I would ask my unwary friends, and they would murmur polite sounds of incredulity when I told them "64,841", though whether they were surprised at the smallness or greatness of the number was not clear.

"Do you know that in 1990 "only" £7 billions was spent on education whereas Social Security payments cost £66 billions?" (rising to £88 billions in 1994). This surprises most people, and horrifies only a few. "Did you know that of all books published in 1963 the section dealing with religion and theology stands next only to fiction and educational and children's books? A small sign that religion was not such a dead issue as some would like to think!" That list does not appear in Whitaker today.

Do you know how many hours you spent in school?

I went to school a few weeks after my fifth birthday and I left school a few weeks before my nineteenth birthday. Fourteen years, forty-two terms, five hundred and forty-six weeks, two thousand seven hundred and thirty days (not including eight years of Saturday mornings) and counting school from nine o'clock a.m. to four o'clock p.m. nineteen thousand one hundred and ten hours. Adding homework at an average of two hours a night, for eight of the fourteen years, another two thousand eight hundred and twenty hours. And all to what purpose? A cynical question perhaps. In speaking of matters educational it is almost impossible not to say the trite thing - that the time spent outside the classroom is more important than the time spent inside; that true education only begins when one leaves school; that no school really educates for the business of living in the harsh world of reality outside the school gates; that the time spent on Latin verbs would be better applied to mending electric fuses and learning how to lay a stair carpet, for boys, and in learning how to bath a baby and keep a husband happy for girls, (or vice versa in 1994).

My first taste of school was in September 1922, and I did not like the taste at all. The infant department of the village school in Cheapside Lane was a single storey building, long and narrow, heated by an aged Victorian coke stove. Close to the stove in winter our eyebrows were nearly singed. A few feet away from it we were frozen. The windows were placed high up in the walls so that little children would not be tempted to look out upon the world. This building came into my mind's eye many years later when I was responsible as Director of Education in the Diocese of Rochester for overseeing the rebuilding of Church Schools. I was at a meeting of parents in Chislehurst, trying to persuade them that their ancient Victorian Church school should be scrapped and replaced.

I rehearsed all the arguments - educational, practical, financial - they would not be asked for a penny, the Ministry, the Diocese and the County would foot the bill - and then I said "Look at those high windows. The children cannot even see out of them!" Parent after parent got up in high dudgeon - "We do not send our children to school to look out of windows!" they declared indignantly. I tried to reason with them. To no avail. That was the only time in my life that I have been booed at a public meeting.

It seems to me, looking back to 1922, that there were few books in the village school, even fewer pictures, and very little in the way of equipment. When facts were learned by rote, when the basis of teaching was "chalk and talk", there would have been no need, in the eyes of the teachers at any rate, for such things as are seen in profusion in the modern infant school: books, cards, models, paints, toy weighing machines; and the walls covered with gloriously coloured charts and diagrams; when such exciting things can be made out of egg boxes and tubes from toilet rolls. On a visit to Ireland not many years ago I recall jumping up to look through the similarly high windows of their Victorian village schools and seeing only two adornments - a picture of the Pope and a montage of photographs of the heroes of the Irish revolution.

In 1922 we learned our tables by chanting - "two two's are four, three two's are six, four two's are eight" and so on, right up to "twelve twelves". We had no graphite pencils in the infant school, only slates and slate pencils which had to be sharpened on the outside brick walls. The deep cuts made by sharpening these horrid instruments can still be seen outside many old schools. They made an excruciatingly painful sound when they were being used, something between a banshee screech and a squeal of old fashioned brakes on a hay cart. I suppose there must have been some books, rag books, and books of pictures of animals, "A" for Ant, "B" for Baby, "C" for Cat, "D" for Dog, for we all learned our alphabet and somehow, we learned to read. It remains a mystery why so many children passing from the primary to the secondary stage of education in the 1990's cannot read fluently, some not at all, whereas I am quite sure that no child could have passed from the infant to the primary stage of Denham school without the ability to read. It may have been beaten into us, for physical punishment was common, but we could read. We learned to add, subtract and divide, we learned to draw, we learned to sing, we learned to recite, often being made to stand out in front of the class to say our piece.

There were at least 50 "Infants" in this room, presided over by a war widow, Mrs. Husbands. She had children of her own - I remember the name of her son, Bobby, and I think she must have been a very good teacher. We were taught to use our hands in simple creative tasks. One of these tasks was to stuff "Sunny Jim's". The wheat flakes in the "Force" packets are still on sale today, and back in the 1920's it was possible to write away to the makers and obtain the Sunny Jim dolls (unstuffed) presumably at a few pence each. Mrs. Husbands would bring her old cardigans to school - I can still smell the odorous, sweaty wool, for deodorants had not been invented yet, which we would unravel and cut and push into the brightly coloured cotton shapes of the strange creature called "Sunny Jim", and Mrs. Husbands would sew them up. I think I must have been fairly happy in the infants school because apart from the first day there when my mother left me at the gate - mothers were not allowed inside the school boundaries - when I cried piteously, I don't remember the tears falling, as they did later, copiously, when I went "up" into the "big" school.

The basis of all education in the Church School of seventy years ago was the Church Catechism, which we learned by heart and had to repeat after assembly each day of the week. From time to time the "Inspector" would come and test us on our knowledge of it, and of our tables. A "Catechism" is a way of learning facts and doctrines by means of questions and answers. I feel I must explain this because I am sure that many today do not know what a Catechism is!

Q. What is your name?
A. N or M (name or names)
Q. Who gave you this name?
A. My godfathers and godmothers in my Baptism wherein I was made a member of Christ, *the* child of God, (always an accented "the"!) and an inheritor of the Kingdom of Heaven.
Q. What did your godfathers and godmothers then for you?
A. They did promise and vow three things in my name... etc.

The Catechism then went on, for several pages, to outline the promises of the Baptism Service; the Creed and what as a result we believe about God, Father, Son and Holy Spirit. Then the Ten Commandments and how we learn from them our duty to God and our neighbour. The answers to the questions about God and neighbour are incomparable in their directness and challenge, except perhaps for those sections which declare that: I must "order myself lowly and reverently to all my betters." Shades of the yokel pulling his forelock to the squire as he passes by in his carriage! But what could be more defiantly brave than the assertion that I must: "do to all men as I would that they should do unto me; that I should hurt nobody by word or deed; that I must be true and just in all my dealings; bear no malice or hatred in my heart; keep my hands from picking and stealing and my tongue from evil speaking, lying and slandering; that I must keep my body in temperance, soberness and chastity; not to covet nor desire other men's goods, but to learn and labour truly to get my own living, and to do my duty in that state of life unto which it shall please God to call me."?

The Catechism goes on to expound the meaning of the Lord's Prayer and the two Sacraments of Baptism and Holy Communion. It was the duty of the clergyman, declares the Book of Common Prayer of 1662, "openly in the Church to instruct and examine so many children of the Parish sent unto him as he shall think convenient, in some part of this Catechism". It adds: "All fathers, (note that!) mothers, masters and dames, shall cause their children, servants and prentices (which have not learned their Catechism) to come to Church at the time appointed, and obediently to hear, and be ordered by the Curate, until such time as they have learned all that is here appointed for them to learn."

That is why the parish clergy spent so much time in their village schools, though many of them had no clue as to how to teach. No one today would advocate learning by rote as the sole method, but am I naïve in believing that we have missed a great deal, and our children have missed much, not only by *not* learning the basics of the Christian faith and the kind of behaviour that stems from it, but also by *not* learning by heart, as we did, whole poems and passages from Shakespeare? For is it not true that what we learn by heart stays in the mind and bears fruit in the life? When I was taught the Ten Commandments, social rules for a primitive nomadic society though they may have been in origin, they were so implanted in my brain and in my imagination that I *knew it was wrong* to lie, though I did; that it was wrong to *cheat and steal,* though I did; that it was wrong to misuse the Lord's day, and to commit adultery. I had no idea at the time what that word meant. I knew I must not envy other boys for the toys and books they had. To my mind there is a causal connection between the decline of moral standards and the failure of school and Church to teach basic patterns of acceptable behaviour. Of course the teaching must be brought up-to-date. Of course the old social attitudes enshrined in 17th century religious teaching must be abandoned, but the tragedy in schools today, even in Church schools as an Inspectors' Report of December 1992 declares, is that religious education has been well nigh totally abandoned.

Nursery Rhymes must have been the staple of learning by heart and I have identified no less than seventy-one Rhymes that I learned as a child. From them too, with their memorable rhythms, my generation will have learned many of its moral precepts and attitudes, some good, some not so good, for as in Grimm's Fairy Tales, there is a great deal of implied cruelty in some of the Rhymes - the man going to St. Ives had three hundred and forty three cats and kittens in sacks! "Cry baby cry," calls another, "put your finger in your eye, and tell your mother it wasn't I." There was the "old man who wouldn't say his prayers" who was taken by the left leg and thrown down the stairs. There was Polly Flinders sitting among the cinders whose mother whipped her for spoiling her nice new clothes (reminiscent of the time my mother thrashed my sister and myself for covering our Sunday bests with corn dust from the granary!). And what nightmares have been caused by visions of the farmer's wife chasing the blind mice and cutting off their tails with a carving-knife? And what blatant prejudice and sexism is displayed in "What are little boys made of? Frogs and snails and puppy-dog tails, that's what little boys are made of." "What are little girls made of? Sugar and spice and all that's nice, that's what little girls are made of." My sister would chant that to me when we had had one of our many arguments.

Today the psychologists would derive dark implications from the fact that schools were decorated in black, brown or dark green paint; that our wet coats were hung in the same room that we sat at our desks in; that we learned our letters from tracing them in sand on a metal tray; that we were made to go outside, rain or shine, to the stinking urinals and toilets; that corporal punishment was meted out for *ignorance* as well as insubordination and ordinary childish pranks; that it was thought wrong to praise children for their work in case they got to be "above themselves"; and that although boys and girls might sit side by side in their double desks, they were segregated into different playgrounds at "break".

St. Mary's Church School in Denham was an "all range school". It took children from five to fourteen years, so that when I moved from "the infants" into the "big school" I was with other children of wide age ranges, perhaps seven to fourteen. Most of us were in one large room, probably a hundred of us, and though there was a dividing partition which could be drawn across, I guess it had some mechanical defect for it was drawn across only rarely. Two staff taught two groups of people, vying one with the other for the attention of their group.

The girl I sat next to for two years was two or three years older than me, which shows that the idea of mixed ages and mixed ability was no new thing when it came to be promoted in the sixties! We shared a desk, a heavy iron monstrosity with a wooden flap and two inkwells. If you were "teacher's pet" one of the privileges was to fill the inkwells, a difficult and messy business, which is why half of the children had fingers permanently stained with blue-black ink. The method of teaching was chalk and talk, but we were given pens, pencils and exercise books, protractors and compasses, paintbooks and drawing books.

From this period, especially when I was taught "perspective", I date my love of drawing, and I learned some facility at it and not infrequently was awarded "ten out of ten" for my efforts. There were a few pictures on the walls and a small bust of Beethoven. But did anyone play us any Beethoven, either on the piano or on the cylindrical gramophone records then popular? Of course not.

My teacher for a large part of the time was a Miss Tomkins - the archetypal teacher of the cartoons of the day - tall, flat-chested, hair tied up in a bun, pince-nez glasses. She was a good teacher, but we were afraid of her, as I suppose in those days, most children were afraid of their teachers. I frequently wet my trousers because I was afraid to hold up my hand and say, "Please may I be excused?" The first French master we had at the age of eleven in Grammar School, one J.M. McQueen, must have been a better psychologist (he had children of his own) because the first phrase he ever taught us, on our first day at school, was "Puis-je sortir?", may I be excused?

Roseanna Newell who sat next to me was a fair girl with long pale plaits anchored at the bottom with pieces of dirty blue ribbon. She was the eldest of several children and her mother had died, so she was housewife and mother. No doubt she lived in poverty for she was not clean and the odour that emanated from her ragged clothes was sour and rancid. Like all the girls she wore black buttoned boots, grubby stockings, and attached to her pinafore with a safety pin was the "snot-rag" yes, that was its name - on which all through the day she blew her runny nose. Like me she wore those terrible steel-framed spectacles.

After two years I had another desk and another companion, a boy whose name I forget, dark and untidy, who smelt of paraffin. He too came from a poor family and spent his spare time earning pennies by taking round cans of oil for heating and lighting. Gaslight and electricity were unknown luxuries in most homes in the 1920's. With this boy too, who was also about two years older than I was, I worked the patch of garden behind the school allotted in sections to pairs of boys. There we learned to dig and clean the soil, to plant seeds and water them, to distinguish plant from weed. Each patch had its fruit bush and its rose bush. There I learned the art of grafting roses, the careful cutting of the bark and the gentle insertion of the new bud on the old stem, and the binding up with raffia. It was a sore point with me that when we two won the prize one year for the best kept patch it was my partner who received the prize - a beautiful ivory-handled pruning knife. I received nothing, not even thanks from my partner for doing most of the hard work.

As I write, in the last decade of the twentieth century, a great educational debate is proceeding. A Conservative government is attempting to redress what it sees as the mistakes of the past twenty and more years. It is advocating more frequent testing at several stages in a child's school life; it is laying down a national curriculum; it is asking for a return to more formal teaching, especially in Grammar. This last I would heartily approve of because I have always been grateful that the learning of parts of speech and the proper construction of subject, predicate and object were dinned into me: adjectival and adverbial clauses; nouns and prepositions; the nominative, accusative and ablative. All these parts of speech were taught, even drummed into our heads, and though the "parsing" sessions caused tears and nightmares, we learned the basics of our own native language. Today, both in speech and writing, the lack of this teaching is evident in those who write for newspapers and speak on radio and television. Split infinitives; arguing from the particular to the general; logical fallacies; plural nouns with singular verbs; solecisms and mistakes of grammar abound, due to slipshod and careless construction of the simplest sentences. Education in the 1920's lacked much. This element it did not lack at Denham school,

and for this I am greatly indebted, though I have no doubt that I too
have erred often in these writings.

There are certain school occasions which stand out in a child's
memory. For me one of the great occasions was Empire Day, May
24th, Queen Victoria's birthday, when we had games on the
recreation field behind the school and a large tin of boiled sweets was
shared out among us. We went home early too and that was always a
relief. What a lot our successors miss. Empire Day has become the
dull sounding "Commonwealth Day". Instead of being held in lovely
sunny Maytime it is now observed on the second Monday in March.
That may be fine in the Commonwealth of the southern hemisphere,
but who in Britain is going to observe it in the coldest, windiest,
wettest month of the year? The union flag was flown from the mast in
the school playground and we sang patriotic songs. "Gentle reader,"
as the old writers used to say, "did you ever observe a joyful
Commonwealth day when you were at school? Can you still taste the
acid drops from the big sweet tin?"

I recall too, the school plays, though I was never allowed to play a
part in one. A shepherd or St. Joseph in steel-rimmed spectacles -
which I was always breaking, to my father's ill-concealed annoyance -
would not look quite right. But of all the particular days I remember,
the day of the great public punishment stands out. The boy whom I
sat next to had performed some distressing misdemeanour or perhaps
it was a "felony", something more heinous, and worthy of a public
flogging. In the yard at the back of the school the forms had been set
up in serried rows, rising two or three stages, and we were all called
out at break time to witness this boy's humiliation. The Headmaster,
Gaffer Sanders, stood there with a long thin cane in his hand. The
boy was called to the front and his crime was rehearsed and
expounded at length, no doubt all sorts of morals being drawn on the
way. It was explained that to save us from the same fate, and as an
example never to be forgotten, this criminal was to be beaten. A desk
had been taken outside and the boy was told to bend over it.

All at once there was a scream and a girl shot out from the front
row and flew at the headmaster, banging at his chest with one closed
fist, clawing at his face with the fingers of the other. It was the boy's
sister. When at home brother and sister probably fought each other.
Now they had a common enemy. The boy joined in and the cane was
torn from the Head's grasp. I wish I could say what the end of the

96

story was. The whole school broke up in pandemonium. I guess we were taken back to our classrooms. I suspect that the boy never did receive his beating and that the Head was careful ever after not to take too drastic measures to control his pupils. Sanders was an old man by then and he soon left. We had a gentle temporary Head who always spent break time and dinner time (sandwiches, eaten in class) with us boys, and became our friend. He even played flicking cigarette cards with us. We were not afraid to go to him and ask him questions. We were sorry when he left and the permanent appointment of Captain Thompson, war veteran, was made.

Thompson was a good Head, strict but fair. He tried to widen our horizons and I particularly remember his attempt to put on a "Nigger Minstrel Show". We had lots of rehearsals - I was only in the chorus, and we even got to the stage of blacking our faces, but the show was never publicly performed. The use of the word "nigger" was normal at that time. It would cause a lawsuit these days and rightly so. But we had no racial prejudice. I fancy indeed that few of us had ever seen a black man except on the cinema screen or at Bertram Mills' Circus at Olympia, to which we were taken later.

Somehow before I was eleven I seem to have been prepared for the scholarship examination for entry into the local Royal Grammar School at High Wycombe. All that I can summon up from my memory about it is the train journey to Wycombe on the day of the examination, accompanied by Miss Tomkins or Mrs. Dickinson, (mother of my friend Edward) who was on the staff and presided in the other classroom. On that journey, the four of us who were entering were quizzed by her about what little we knew of history, the names of the great poets and composers, and whatever else she thought we might be asked. The exam was held in a primary school in the town and I recollect nothing at all of it. But I passed. The others did not. The RGS was, I think, a controlled Church School in law, grant aided, but allowed to charge fees, as was the local girls High School in the same town to which my sister Enid had gone two years earlier. At the RGS the fees were five guineas a term with books provided. At the High School they were three guineas a term with parents buying books. So my father paid out some £30 a year for our education. Today the equivalent would be about £560. He also paid our train fares which were about £1.10/- a term for a season ticket from Gerrards Cross (where we moved to in the summer before

I started at the Grammar School) to High Wycombe. So that was another £9 a year. School meals were not provided until the 1930's.

If it was a scholarship, why fees? Because fees were paid by all parents whose income exceeded £1,000 a year. I was very proud of the framed certificate in my bedroom which told how I had been awarded the scholarship but was not free to take it for financial reasons. An income of £1,000 a year does not sound very much, but in today's values it would be about £18,000 a year, or more.

The Royal Grammar School, rebuilt on a new site some years before, was a foundation of Edward VI, dated 1562, and pupils were expected to be proud of it and behave accordingly. We were to wear our caps at all times. Punishment for not wearing the cap was a hundred lines, or if preferred, six strokes with the gym slipper. We were not allowed to talk to girls on the way to or from school, not even to our own sisters. House shoes were to be worn while inside the school on pain of slippering. No talking in the corridors! In 1928 it was not a big School, a two form entry, that is to say about sixty-four new pupils each year. One could leave at sixteen and parents had to sign a paper saying that they would allow their children to stay until they were that age. This was felt necessary because so many fathers had been killed in the Great War that there was always a temptation to make the boys leave at fourteen or fifteen so that they could start work and earn money badly needed by the family. It is only recently that I have realised why so many of my companions at school had no fathers. It was only on Armistice Day, November 11th, when the OTC paraded in uniform and members of staff wore their campaign medals, that the fact of war was realised, and the results of war became evident. Our PE master was cruelly called "Soapy" Sumpter because part of his mouth had been shot away and saliva was perpetually dribbling from it. How unfeeling and brutal the young can be!

The staff all had University degrees but only the PE master who came when Sumpter left had been trained to teach. So the quality of teaching was not of the highest. A local Vicar called Bickle came in to take religious education. He liked the boys with plump knees to sit in the front desks so that he could slap them and I remember not one word of what he was supposed to "teach". The strange thing is that one remembers their names and initials at this distance. H.G. Brand who drove a three wheeled "Morgan" car taught Maths; J.E. John, a

Welshman, taught English; P.L. Jones, another Welshman, also taught Maths, as did P. Bartle. J.C. Milner taught History, and Sam Morgan Geography. R. Hutchinson, killed in the Hitler War, taught Latin. He was very kind to me when my Father died. E.C. Millington taught Chemistry and S. Watts, Physics. Watts could not keep order and tortured us by rubbing our short hairs at the side of the head with his knuckles. French was in the hands of J.M. McQueen in the lower forms, and M. Marti, a Swiss, in the upper forms. Art and Woodwork were taught by G.A. Grant who also organised the remarkable "Hobbies Club" which held monthly meetings on all sorts of hobby subjects and also the annual camp to which up to a hundred of us looked forward for months. We camped in old army bell tents in various places, Belgium, Devon, Jersey, Guernsey, the Isle of Wight, and in that way got to know our fellows and the masters better.

The Headmaster was George Arnison, a dapper little man with a short clipped ginger moustache who had been at Giggleswick in Yorkshire and who always smelt strongly of whisky. The School day began with assembly, with all the masters, gowned and hooded on the stage. We went to School on Saturday mornings and had games every Tuesday and Thursday afternoons on the huge field behind the school. A regular punishment was to take a bucket and fill it with stones from the playing fields. We had PE outside until it was too cold, then in the Hall, and later in a purpose-built gymnasium. I hated games and PE and the boxing that we all had to endure. My nose was broken in one encounter and caused great sinus trouble until I was twenty four and had to have it corrected. The gym master, C.E.C. Eastman was a martinet and no crying off games or PE was allowed except for real illness. He was a great apparatus man and devised all sorts of cruel tortures on it. One trick was to jump over the box, then over the buck, bounce high to hang on to a beam, and then over another obstacle. On one occasion the boy in front of me, Johnson by name, failed to release his hands from the beam in time and broke both his wrists.

In my early years at the RGS I was ceaselessly bullied, tied to trees out of sight of the school, and shot at with water pistols. More than once I had my shoes taken away and had to go home in football boots; my case of homework was taken, and my outdoor clothes hidden. I suppose it was good for me. I had to learn to take pain without complaint, but I determined that when I attained power in the School, as I was resolved to do, I would see that all bullying was stopped and if need be the bullies punished. When later I became a prefect and later still the Head Prefect, alone able to administer corporal punishment in the 6th form library on Saturday mornings, I instituted a strict regime applied by all the other prefects, with a simple "court of justice" to examine breaches of the rules! It amazes me that a boy of seventeen or eighteen was allowed such power. It was not good for him (me) or the school, especially as none of the masters had a similar power. They of course had other sanctions!

There has been a revolution in the curriculum taught in schools in the last ten years as well as a revolution in the organisation of schools, and education has suffered at the hands of politicians of different persuasions as well as the hands of the theoreticians and armchair "experts". As a result of Circular 10/65 (the tenth administrative circular put out by the Ministry of Education, now called the Department of Education and Science in the year 1965, and never specifically debated in Parliament) we had the movement to make all schools "Comprehensive", doing away with the selective Grammar and Technical Schools. Then we had the argument about "all ability groups" and "streaming" - should children of all abilities be taught together or should they only be taught with pupils of a similar level of intellectual and academic attainment? Under the Tory governments in power since 1979 there has been a stream of Education Acts, no less than seven in eight years!, and a succession of Inspectors' Reports, many of them contradictory.

At the Royal Grammar School, staff and Governors were not troubled by these divisive and potentially destructive controversies. Though the Grammar schools were in theory "selective", the scope of ability in the yearly intake was very wide, ranging from boys who would be capable in the final year of their schooling of obtaining University scholarships, to boys who would fail a number of "School Certificate" subjects, later called "O" (ordinary) levels and now GCSE's. But as I have already indicated in a critical assessment of the masters, as many had no training in the art and science of actual teaching, the standards were low.

Geography was a matter of learning the names of the rivers and mountains and cities from a map drawn in outline on the blackboard. The master, Sam Morgan, would indicate with a pointer a particular dot on his map and say "what town is that?" or a line representing a river: "what river is that?" then we would try to reproduce the facts in our exercise books! The fatuous incompetence of such teaching is illustrated by the occasion when, on a map of the USA in my book, I had outlined the rivers Missouri and Mississippi running out into the Gulf of Mexico, but across them I had written in large capitals "DESERT", I was presumably trying to indicate where the Arizona desert was. Boys who failed in this sort of exercise were called out to the front of the class and Morgan would point to them with scorn and say: "Look at the intelligentsia!" No wonder some of us failed school certificate in Geography.

Music was taught by a visiting master, F.N. Crute, who ran the school choir, to which I belonged. He did this very well and we were in demand at Christmas time in local churches and we gave a yearly concert in the Hall for parents and friends, but teaching in class was pathetic. The blackboard was used to teach us the tonic solfa and other basics, and gramophone records of classical music were used to help us pick out the distinctive sounds of the instruments of the orchestra, but we played no instruments, we were taught nothing about opera, nothing about the great instrumental and vocal soloists of the day, nothing of the lives of the great composers. We were not taken to concerts as children are today. We were not even given a list of musical terms so that we might know what "allegro" or "lento" meant, though I do remember his efforts to teach us about breves and semi-breves, minims and crotchets, quavers and semi-quavers. The idea of a "hemidemisemiquaver" appealed to me, as one sixty-fourth of a semi-breve! I can still remember how badly behaved and unruly poor Mr. Crute's classes were. Yet, like so many masters who could not keep order or interest us in their subjects, he was a very pleasant and friendly man who had not been taught how to teach.

Shakespeare makes Hamlet say, early in his play:-

"Yea, from the table of my memory
I'll wipe away all trivial fond record
all saws of books, all forms, all pressures past,
that youth and observation copied there."

Which is admonition enough to make all writers abandon their memoirs. In the same play he makes Polonius declare:

"Brevity is the soul of wit."

It is difficult not to record all the minutiae of one's youth, and it is difficult for any writer who is also a preacher and whose sermons are confined to ten or fifteen minutes and who gets into the habit of pruning and cutting, honing and shaping his words, not to expand and indulge himself in words when he has not the constraints of the preacher's time. For the rest of my comments on masters and subjects I will be as brief as I can.

We were taught English by W. Bicknell who was well versed in his subject and later became a Headmaster. With him we studied Shakespeare - *Macbeth* in full, and bits of *Twelfth Night*, *A Mid-Summer Night's Dream*, *As You Like It*, *Much Ado About Nothing*, *Anthony And Cleopatra*, *Henry 4th Part 1*, and *King Lear*. This was an unusual and heavy programme and it did not make me "hate" Shakespeare. In fact I enjoyed learning long passages by heart, which was part of the method of teaching English, and can still recite much of *Macbeth*, the School Certificate play - "When shall we three meet again?", "Fillet of a fenny snake, in the cauldron boil and bake", "If it were done when 'tis done, then 'twere well it were done quickly", "But screw your courage to the sticking place and we'll not fail!", "We have scotched the snake not killed it", and my favourite: "Is this a dagger that I see before me, the handle towards my hand? Come, let me clutch thee. I have thee not and yet I see thee still!" I learned all these passages and many more by proclaiming them out loud, and striding up and down the kitchen in our house at Gerrards Cross.

I am convinced that Shakespeare should still be taught at an early age, eleven or twelve, but that the plays should be taught as plays, not as reading exercises. That was the weakness of our education in drama - we read plays round the class, but we never acted them. We were never taken to see them, as my wife and I took our children to see Shakespeare at the Old Vic when they were studying his plays for examinations. I myself learned more about *A Midsummer Night's Dream* from watching a production of it at my grand-daughter's prep school than from a year's study of it in form 5A. There is one boy among my contemporaries who I am certain became a hater of

Shakespeare. He was the one who in a class reading had to say: "Hark, I hear horses!" It came out as "'Ark, I 'ear 'orses!" Poor fellow. A Grammar School boy who dropped his aspirates? Yes indeed. Many did. He was teased unmercifully for years afterwards. The earliest text we studied was Chaucer's *Nun's Priests Tale*, then we did Wordsworth's *Sonnets* and Milton's *Odes*, and Keats and Shelley and the other classic poets. We all hated Spenser's *Faerie Queen*. Of moderns we were introduced to Masefield, but surprisingly not to T.S. Eliot. He had written *The Waste Land* in 1922 and *The Hollow Men* in 1925, and in 1930 *Ash Wednesday* which marked his conversion to high Anglicanism. He had been, for a brief period, a master at the school, so we should have been introduced to his work.

Among the pre-Victorian and Victorian novelists (no others were studied!) we were introduced to Jane Austen, Thackeray, Dickens and the Brontës, George Eliot, and Stevenson, whose *Travels With A Donkey In The Pyrenees* was a delight. But why were we not introduced to Hardy, Kipling, Wells, Galsworthy, or those who began writing in the twenties? - Priestley, Hughes, Huxley, Greene, all men, or the women of the same era - Bowen, Macaulay, Lehmann? And again, why no other dramatists of the modern age? Our dramatic education was incomplete, though in the later years we were made to study Thomas Dekker's *Shoemaker's Holiday*, Dryden's *All For Love* (an essay question was "Compare Dryden's *All For Love* with Shakespeare's *Anthony And Cleopatra*" - of which it was a reworking published in 1678) and Sheridan's *The Rivals*, Mrs. Malaprop's misuse of words amused us and stays in the mind, and his *School For Scandal*! We were told about the Restoration comedies of Congreve, Wycherley and Farquhar but did not study them.

All in all, looking at the list of names which I have mentioned in the last paragraph or two I have come to believe that in English our education was not as limited and imperfect as I had thought, so W.N. Bicknell must be absolved from some of my earlier strictures.

History has been one of my abiding interests and it was covered by Captain J.C. Milner TD. He was in charge of the Officer's Training Corps. but had been too young, I think, to see active service in the Great War. He was a big man with heavy jowls and was nicknamed, not very originally, "Tiny". History then was a matter of dates and battles, Empires and statesmen. Just as Geography today is concerned with people and environments and the influence of climate and movements of people, as well as rivers and deserts, so history today is seen as the development of ideas and the influence of books and philosophies and national aspirations. For us in the twenties and thirties it was chopped into blocks of dates, 1603-1649, 1789-1815, and was centred on great generals, politicians and prime ministers, Wars and treaties. Benn's *Sixpennies* were popular "cribs" or handbooks because they summarised in a few pages all one needed to know about battles and prime ministers. Arthur Mee's *Children's Encyclopaedia* was a much maligned source of invaluable additional information. I used to claim that I got through English and History from reading and re-reading its articles.

There has been a return to the old ways in some areas of education and the idea of "comprehensiveness" is now discredited, though selection and streaming are in effect returning, much as the Government's education spokesman would deny it. It's a matter of playing with words and calling those doctrines and policies by another name. A new anthology of prose and poetry to be studied by every 14 year old, published in January 1993 includes Chaucer, Blake, Johnson, Shakespeare, Keats, Browning and Dickens as well as writers not revealed to us - Oscar Wilde, Osbert Sitwell and modern poets and writers - Larkin, Thomas, Lessing, Walcott. The list, which could have been drawn up in the fifties, has been much criticised, but writer for writer it is better than the one we had.

At some time it must have become known that I was intending to take Holy Orders, because if there was a clergyman in the yearly school play I always had to take the part. In one of them, by John Galsworthy - *Escape*, I had to smoke a pipe. I thought that if I crumbled cigarettes into the bowl of the pipe the resulting smoke would be milder than proper pipe tobacco. Not a bit of it. Practising at home with my home made brew I was violently sick.

In reaction to the treatment I had received early in my time at RGS I enjoyed membership of the Officers Training Corps. It enabled me to order about and shout at boys who in earlier days had plagued my life. I applied myself to the training and rose through the ranks as Lance Corporal, Corporal, Sergeant, Quartermaster Sergeant and Company Sergeant Major, and enjoyed the annual camps at Strensall, Tidworth and other army centres. The only cups I won at school were for the "Most Efficient Recruit" and the "Most Efficient Cadet".

Owing to the weakness in my right eye which had little or no sight in it I was hopeless at all games, except Eton Fives, but I could shoot. That only needs one eye! My friends were on the whole those who hated PE and games as much as I did. Two of them became priests, one of them, a priest teacher, came back to the old school after war service. Another became a distinguished local politician. As I rose through the school I was academically neck and neck with a boy called James Neil Robinson. He came second when I came first. He came first when I came second. He was one of those who had to leave early to go and serve in his mother's shop for she was a struggling war widow. What a waste of a good academic brain.

It was a very small sixth form in those days, not more than seventeen of us, of whom only four went to University. In the year before me, Frank Essex went to Reading University, and I was the first for many years to go to Oxford. When a new Headmaster succeeded George Arnison, E.R. Tucker of Jesus College Oxford, the school expanded and improved greatly academically. Unhappily he died a young man, but today this same school has a thousand pupils and a hundred and fifty in the sixth form with at least a hundred going into University or Higher Education each year. Tucker made me learn Greek which was useful later in my Theological Course, but I found it extremely difficult to learn. In most other subjects I did well. The school only taught ten basic subjects and I passed School Certificate in seven of them. The only one I failed was geography. I disliked the master who taught it, Sam Morgan, as I have already recorded, because he used cruel sarcasm as a teaching instrument. It doesn't work. If you hate the teacher you will not do well in his subject. But I loved French and English and History, and these were the subjects which I passed in for the Higher Schools Certificate. I hated Latin but I managed to pass higher level in that too. Today I should be judged to have seven "O" levels and four "A" levels. I enjoyed Art and Scripture as well but they were not "A" level subjects. I have often wondered how I would have fared in a modern school and whether I would have understood how to work and use the computer and other pieces of high technology.

When I left High Wycombe to go to Oxford the Headmaster gave me a glowing written testimonial. He said "You may read what I have said, but don't believe it!" I guessed what he meant. Humility has never been one of my virtues.

During the years that I spent at the Royal Grammar School we lived at Gerrards Cross in a four bedroomed semi-detached house which my father had bought for £1,300 from an allegedly bankrupt fishmonger, who, such are the strange quirks of the law of bankruptcy, was able to move into a much larger detached house further along the road. I missed the rambling old "Homestead" with its large garden and stream, with its outside earth closet and water drawn from a well. I missed the piggeries and the horses, and I missed my Sundays in the choir of the village church. I did not miss my persecutor, Stanley Rance, nor having to wear my Eton collar all through Sunday. My mother soon got me into the choir of St. James Church in Gerrards Cross. It was a Victorian monstrosity, built with money provided by two sisters who could not agree whether it should have a tower or a dome, so it possessed both. It was a well known evangelical Church, attended by some of the villagers and many of the well-to-do who abounded in the area. The Vicar was a dull, short-statured man named G.E. Watton. He had succeeded a retired Bishop Hope Gill who rode round the parish in the back of a large open car driven by a chauffeur, and I suspect that he was always well-received in the big houses of the parish. George Watton, who drove a dilapidated Austin 10, was dominated by his formidable wife. He was a diligent visitor, as most clergy were in those days, but his wife offended many, including my mother who had become a member of the Mother's Union but ceased to be very soon after our move from Denham. The men who most influenced me along the road to ordination were the Curates, and the organist who gave me a love of music and who made me, reluctantly on my part, sing my first tenor solo in a Harvest Anthem *Ye Shall Dwell In The Land*.

It has always been part of Catholic teaching that the Sacraments have a validity which is independent of the minister of the sacrament, that for example a Baptism taken by a priest who cannot control his appetite for alcohol, is still a true Baptism. God can and does use frail human beings (are there any others?) to convey His grace.

Fred Crosby had served as a Sergeant in the Army and became one of the many candidates for the priesthood who came out of that terrible 1914-1918 war with a strengthened faith and a desire to serve God and their fellows. He was trained at Knutsford, then a special college for candidates from the Forces, and he it was who most influenced my growth in religion. He prepared me for Confirmation, where I was one of only two boys in 1931, carefully and methodically. He was an interesting preacher and he guided my reading of "religious" books. At one stage he had many months off parish life when he contracted tuberculosis as a result of his war experiences, and spent a long convalescence among the pines in Bournemouth. From there, he and I conducted a lengthy correspondence which widened my horizons and deepened my understanding of what it would mean to be a clergyman. He would not, from his evangelical standpoint, have used the word "priest".

On his recovery in 1935 he was presented to the living of a small parish in north Buckinghamshire where he was very popular. I would visit him there from time to time. At Gerrards Cross he had been the Scoutmaster of the parish troop, and he continued this activity in Loughton. He had, sadly, no children of his own, but he was "good with" boys. It was a shock to all his friends when he was sent to prison for what was then called "interfering with small boys". My conscience still pricks me that I did nothing about him, did not visit him in prison, or seek to comfort his wife. By that time I was living the busy life of an undergraduate. Prison life can have done his health no good and he died soon after. God *does* use fools and sinners to implement his will and I give thanks for all that this unfortunate priest gave me and taught me.

But the case of Fred Crosby raises a problem which has been much in my mind in the fifty and more years of my own priesthood. I have known so many priests who have given way to what used to be called the sins of the flesh, men who have done such good work in their parishes. What was lacking in their training, in the pastoral care and advice that they should have received from Bishop, Archdeacon, and Rural Dean, that allowed them to become alcoholics, adulterers, breakers of their own and other people's families?

Such men are not sent to prison today. They are offered psychiatric help and many of them are happily rehabilitated and can resume some kind of ministry, but their numbers do not lessen, indeed they increase alarmingly. Is it that self-discipline is no longer taught and advocated in the theological colleges? Is it that we have abandoned absolutes? Is it that principles of right and wrong are no longer accepted? That promises are always made with a proviso that if we find keeping them to be too difficult we can abandon them? Is it that we have discarded the idea that we should expect a higher standard of behaviour from our clergy than from our congregations? That of course is a reprehensible idea, since the Christian ideal is for clergy and laity alike to aim at. I am reminded that when my sister and I had a row or we disapproved of what the other was doing, she would say to me "That's not the way someone who is going to be a clergyman should behave!" and I would reply "Nor is that the way a leading light in the Guides should behave!"

Dear Fred Crosby was succeeded by Aubrey Lionel Evan Hopkins, one of the famous evangelical Hopkins family. One of his ancestors was E.J. Hopkins, composer of many popular hymn tunes of the Victorian era *Saviour Again, Brightest And Best, Jesu Lord Of Life And Glory*, and very many Anglican chants. Hopkins had been a scholar of Jesus College Cambridge, had a first class in the Maths tripos, and a second class in Theology. It was he who ran the boys Bible Class on Sunday afternoon which introduced me to the whole question of how to regard the Bible. I even remember one memorable session, when I was about seventeen, in which he detailed the reasons for believing that St. Paul was not the author of the epistle to the Hebrews. Are there any boys' Bible Classes today, and would they be studying the epistle to the Hebrews? Hopkins was a great CSSM man (Children's Special Service Mission) where the emphasis was on having a personal faith and enjoying it. He took us out into the woods around Gerrards Cross and we lit bonfires, with permission, I presume, and had yarns round the fire at our "Sardine Suppers" and "Sausage Sizzles". I owe him much and was able to tell him so about thirty years later when we met at a Moral Welfare (now called Social Work) committee in Maidstone and he was a Vicar in Folkestone.

Hopkins was succeeded by Fergus Edward Harcourt Trevor. I can't say why I remember all their names so clearly! He too was an evangelical and an excellent preacher. We were great friends and I would mow his lawn and look after his tiny children. I was at that stage "into" the pop music of the day which he rather disapproved of but I managed to persuade him otherwise, and also that on his day off he should enjoy himself so I borrowed my mother's car and took him regularly to the Cinema in Uxbridge. I think he must have had some inkling of approaching war for in 1937 he became a Chaplain in the RAF where he served with distinction in many dangerous theatres of war, including Iraq and Singapore, and left the service in 1959 having attained the rank of Assistant Chaplain in Chief. All through the

1939-1945 war we kept in touch and I "kept an eye" on his wife and children for him. He had a deep rich singing voice and an infectious laugh. I owe him much, for it was he who taught me how to teach a Sunday School class.

John Pain had become Vicar of Gerrards Cross in 1938 and the Curate who succeeded Trevor was Rowland Oakes, a Welshman with an evangelical moustache. Also a fine preacher and a highly qualified musician. It was he who wrote to the Bishop of Oxford and asked permission for me to preach at my own parish Church. This was an ordeal, for the congregation had known me as a choirboy and choirman since I was eleven, but I managed it, with a whole crowd of friends and relations present. I had been taking a Sunday School class for some years and with the help of lesson books by G.R. Balleine which are mines of illustrations and stories, I had managed to keep groups of boys, some of whom were not much younger than myself, both interested and well behaved. So creating an immediate interest and sustaining it through a fifteen minute sermon was not as difficult as I had feared. One thing that first sermon fifty-five years ago did achieve was to make me aware of the importance of *teaching*, not waffling, linking religion to life, and not just quoting from the biblical commentaries, and this I have tried to teach to others in theological colleges and as Warden of Readers in the diocese of Rochester.

During this time I became Vice Captain of my House, House House of all the absurd names! The School had only three houses for most of my time, East, West and House. Later, more sense prevailed, and names were given - Arnison, Disraeli and such like. Later, to the chagrin of two of my fellows who had come up through the School with me, Tucker made me Head Boy. I had no prowess at Games but I suppose I had been an efficient and loyal prefect and had a respectable examination record. Family who remember me at this time remark how ridiculous the school cap looked upon my head - we still had to wear school uniform and the cap, even at eighteen. The school had no proper Library in the 1930's and the sixth form met in what was called "the Library". Because of its connections with the Disraeli family, the most prominent books were large leather bound copies, dozens of them it seemed, of Benjamin Disraeli's novels, *Vivian Grey, Sybil, Coningsby, Tancred* and the rest. I always took comfort from the fact that Disraeli made four unsuccessful attempts to enter Parliament, that he was laughed at as a dandy and his maiden speech was shouted down. "The time will come," he asserted, "when you *will* hear me," and they did, for another forty and more years.

The Headmaster, E.R. Tucker, and I probably saw more of each other than most of my contemporaries because he tried in individual sessions in his study, to teach me Greek. He would also, surely an unprecedented thing for a Head in those days, consult me about people and happenings in the School. He would not at that time have been more than twelve years older than I, and he spent a large part of his time out of the school at various educational committees and meetings. I have two certificates still which declare:

> "At a meeting of the Governors held on the twelfth day of March, 1919 the Headmaster was authorised to mention in his Annual Report the names of any boys who in his judgement were worthy of praise having regard both to general proficiency and conduct. And at the same Meeting it was resolved that Certificates in lieu of prizes be awarded to the boys so mentioned..."

I was Head Boy for two years and received two such certificates, in June 1935 and July 1936, the term I left school for good. I would have preferred a prize, if only a book token! I did win two other prizes, I forget what for, but they introduced me to G.K. Chesterton's *Poems* and *The Plays of John Galsworthy*.

It was only in 1933 or 1934 that a "Careers Master" was appointed - he was P.L. Jones, not one of my favourite masters, and I judge that having been a schoolmaster all his life he knew little about careers. My career had been vaguely mapped out for some years - I would one day become a clergyman, but how to achieve that end was a mystery. So few boys had gone to University from High Wycombe RGS that no one had told me that this was the first step, until I wrote to the Bishop of Oxford for advice when I was seventeen. I was sent to see the then secretary of CACTM (the Church's Advisory Council for Training for the Ministry) now ABM, the Advisory Board for Ministry, and I was interviewed by a Canon Woolnough, high in a tiny room in Dean's Yard, Westminster. All I remember of that meeting was the long ginger hairs on the back of his hands, and the fact that he said I must gain entry to University and that the central bodies of the Church could not make any contribution to my education at university and theological college. Which they never did.

Accordingly, using my own initiative, I bought copies of the Oxford and Cambridge Handbooks and looked for small colleges where life would be inexpensive and where Theology was one of the subjects taught. I also investigated the possibility of going to King's College London, but when I discovered that Hebrew was a compulsory subject in the theological course there, I abandoned that idea. I had had enough trouble with Latin and Greek! Selwyn College, Cambridge appealed to me because of its association with the missionary Bishop Selwyn but in the end I chose to apply to St. Edmund Hall, Oxford. My friend Frank Essex had applied there. He told me something about it and I liked what he said. It was the smallest college in Oxford as far as buildings were concerned. It was the oldest college to take undergraduates and dated from the 13th century. It was a "Hall", something unique as the sole survivor of the medieval halls of residence for students. He had also gathered that many of its students would have come from Grammar schools, and so would not be subject to the exclusivity of colleges who took their pupils primarily from the more prestigious "public" schools. I had met many of the products of some of these schools at OTC camps and some of them had treated us with undisguised contempt and superciliousness because we came from mere Grammar Schools. It would not be true to say that the public school boys who did go to "Teddy Hall" treated us with disdain but there was in my three years at the Hall a visible and tangible divide in accent and attitude between the two "types". Frank Essex did not in fact go to Oxford. He went instead to Reading and landed up in Africa as a District Commissioner, so I knew no one when I arrived one Friday in October 1936 in lodgings with Mrs. Mills in Minster Road, off the Cowley Road, Oxford, almost totally unprepared for the academic life that I had been committed to.

Some Comparisons and a Digression

Looking back on one's early life and in particular, one's education, a comparison between "then and now" is inevitable. Sixteen years in professional contact with teachers and schools of all kinds has given me an insight into the remarkable advances in education that have taken place since the 1920's and 1930's. There is first of all the environment. In our "Art Room" there were one or two old sculptures and a faded painting or two. In the modern art room every single "art" is represented - sculpture, painting, drawing, pottery, design, ornament, photography, and not just these, which are the "visual" arts, but the related disciplines and the other arts, music, literature, drama. We were not encouraged to use our artistic imagination in drawing or painting. Our efforts were just copying what we saw. Happily that is not so today. Our art room doubled as a music room and nothing musical was visible except a piano. Today children can see and play almost every instrument of the orchestra; on the walls are posters depicting the history of the development of music, pictures of the composers, the instruments, the types of composition, songs, concertos, symphonies, choral works.

Our science rooms were bare benches with Bunsen burners, sinks and a few glass containers. Our first introduction to science was the making of iron filings and handling a magnet; and constructing a centimetre cube out of paper, long before metrication! We were allowed to demonstrate what happened when phosphorus met water and when sulphurretted hydrogen was released into the air. The theory was just equations containing symbols such as HCl, H_2SO_4, CO_2. All I remember from this is the composition of water, of the air, and the fact that sugar has two different chemical compositions according to whether it is cane sugar or sugar beet. There must have been more to it than this, for I passed "O" level exams in both chemistry and physics. Today the average eleven year old is into atomic physics and new discoveries in chemistry. His leisure time is spent in devising complicated video games and operating his computers and high tech equipment. He knows ten times more about these subjects than we did. There is no doubt that educationally the modern school child is far advanced beyond the standard we attained.

Then it must be said that there has been a great advance in understanding what education is about. To our masters it was largely just the imparting of knowledge, and if we were lucky in our mentors, the widening of horizons. Education then was the attainment of literacy and numeracy, the ability to add up and read; and the imparting of a generally accepted body of knowledge. We were given so little help in what we were expected to learn. I recall J.C. Milner giving me an essay in the sixth form on the Oxford *Movement*, the

Catholic revival in the Church of England which began with John Keble's sermon in the University Church in 1833. Milner gave me no background information, no guidance. My method in those days, and it still is, when I know nothing about a subject, is to find a book on it. I went to my local W.H. Smith's and asked for a book. I was given a history of the Oxford *Group* and wrote a long essay on it. Agreed, it was a display of ignorance hardly believable in a sixth former, but, admitting my own lack of intelligence, was it not an indictment of the method of teaching history in the 1930's?

Education at its best is the development of a person's whole being, intellectual, manual, spiritual, social. It also ought to embody, as it did in ancient Greece, politics, philosophy and public speaking. A large part of it should be in the realm of communication between people, especially people of different cultures and language. It is a total reproach to English education that so few of us can speak another language. In view of the large place which religion, or the perversion of religion, holds in national life throughout the world, an understanding of what religion is and what people believe and why they believe it, would seem to me to be essential. How can we understand what is going on in Ireland, in the Middle East, in India, in South America, without a background knowledge of why Catholics are suspicious of Protestants, why Moslems and Hindus kill each other, why Jews and Arabs cannot live in peace? None of this was available to us at RGS High Wycombe.

In addition to the changes that have taken place in the last fifty and more years in the approach to education, the width of its content and the equipment available to impart it, one difference between "then and now" stands out with intense clarity - behaviour in school

At a 1000 pupil school on Merseyside, Bebington High, an American inspired experiment is proceeding called Assertive Discipline. It is being studied for use elsewhere by ministers and the Department of Education. Discipline was very strict and easily imposed when I was at school. Today it is the one area of education policy on which teachers and Ministers are on the same side. They are all for it, but are in despair about implementing it. Teachers complain that their training has not equipped them to deal with indiscipline, whether it is in the extreme form of physical attacks on them, or the lesser forms of chatter in class, petty disobedience, lost books or homework not done.

In Bedington the experiment is based on a set of simple rules with rewards in the form of bronze, silver and gold "certificates" for every pupil obeying them, and punishments or "consequences" for those who do not. The rules are displayed in every classroom and are expected to be enforced by every teacher without differentiation and not by those only who are considered to be "strict". The rules are:

Arrive for lessons on time with all necessary books and equipment.
Enter quietly.
Remain in seats unless asked to move.
Follow instructions the first time given.
Raise the hand before speaking.
Treat others, their work and belongings, with respect.

Sixty years ago, these were the criteria of behaviour *expected of us!* They were unwritten rules. They did not have to be displayed on notice boards. They did not have attached to them the rewards of a "bronze letter of commendation" noting "high standards of behaviour" to be taken home to parents when they had earned six "R"s (rewards) from each teacher in his subject; or a silver letter for twelve "R"s, a gold letter for eighteen and a diploma for twenty four "R"s. The diploma is presented by the Head at Assembly.

Children breaking the rules have their names displayed "so that the teacher conveys awareness of the misdemeanour without disrupting the flow and atmosphere of the lesson with a rebuke." Repeated offences, registered silently by the teacher with ticks against the transgressor's name, mean automatic lunch time detentions of five, fifteen or thirty minutes. Further disobedience results in ejection from the classroom. This is also the penalty for swearing or violence. Offenders are sent to a "remove" room in supervised isolation for the rest of the day. Parents are immediately alerted and expected to come to the school at the end of the day.

These methods appear after one term's experiment, to be effective. In the first week eighteen were sent to the "remove". Now the weekly average is down to three. The onus is no longer on the teachers to punish. It is on the pupils to choose the consequence of their actions. Both teachers and pupils approve the experiment because it makes the process of learning easier and quicker. Whether it will remain so only time will show.

My object in describing this experiment is to ask why we have come full circle and why it is necessary. These rules and rewards were in essence applied in my primary school in 1922. The rules certainly were unwritten and largely obeyed in my Grammar School in 1928. There were disruptive boys, there were masters who had difficulties, there was some bullying which I have described, but there was no swearing and no violence against teachers. The family is often blamed for indiscipline in schools today - "Lack of parental control" we say. But many boys had no fathers in the post Great War period to control them. My own father had died when I was sixteen. Then we blame "society", with some justice, for "society" has largely abandoned the moral standards which were accepted and obeyed by the majority in my school days. Some would blame the hours spent by children watching violence, cheating, stealing, immorality and the rest, on television screens. There is a well authenticated correlation between such violence on screen and the violence perpetrated in real life. Currently in New York a man is on trial for re-enacting the torture on a ten year old child which he saw on a video of "Silence of the Lambs" a cult film of horror and violence, which was found in his possession. TV is here to stay. The question is how to use it.

Many would argue that the gradual disappearance from the curriculum of any kind of Church-or-community-related religious and moral education can only have resulted in the disappearance of accepted ideals of good behaviour and accepted ideas of right and wrong from family life and from the individual's code of conduct. Of course there is that in human nature which is the source of evil as well as that which is the source of good. We call those elements "original sin" and "original righteousness", and we know that a battle goes on between them - Paul writes: "the good that I would, that I do not. The evil that I would not that I do," but if no moral and religious directions are given in early childhood why should we expect them to appear in later life? Of course there were bad schools as well as good schools in my childhood, as there are good and bad today. RGS was no worse than many in the education it conveyed. It was better than some. It gave me much, but it did not prepare me for the educational shocks I was to receive when I went to an institution of "higher" education and was in competition with boys from schools with a broader and deeper concept of what education is for and how it is to be obtained.

CHAPTER 6

OXFORD

"Oxford is wonderful. All you're required to do is read
books and be cynical about them."
Imogen Stubbs, actress (first class degree in English) 1993

"Whenever philosophical insight is combined with literary genius and
personal charm, one says instinctively, 'That man is, or ought to be,
an Oxford man.'"
G.W. Russell. Irish poet and essayist (1867-1935)

"I spend all my mornings in the Bodleian. If only one could smoke
and if only there were upholstered chairs, this would be one of the
most delightful places in the world. Positively the only drawback is
that beauty, antiquity and overheating weave a spell much more suited
to dreaming than working."
C.S. Lewis, academic and writer (1898-1963)

St. Edmund Hall was founded in the 13th century, but in 1936 was
very short of residential accommodation and as a consequence, in his
three years there, an undergraduate passed two years in digs or
lodgings and only one in Hall. This was a distinct disadvantage, as
the incentive to study is greater if you are close to where the work is
to be done, in your own college library, in your own college room,
near to the University libraries, near to the colleges where you will
attend lectures, and surrounded by your fellow students. Living some
miles out of Oxford city centre the temptations to go to the cinema at
the bottom of the road, to cycle out into the country, to walk up the
hill over Shotover towards Headington were often too strong for me.
In October 1936, I took lodgings in Mrs. Mills' house in Minster
Road, Cowley. It was small and stuffy. I had the downstairs back
room and soon after my arrival from Gerrards Cross - my mother had
driven me the thirty-five miles - I met my fellow Hall man who had
the front room. He was Edward Hinson, a small bright lad from

Stamford School, who never tired of telling us that if certain conditions had been fulfilled, the University would have been sited there, in Stamford, and not in Oxford. Edward was to study French and I, Theology. We became firm friends from the first moment we met.

He had a gramophone and a radio, luxuries to which I had not yet aspired. We also shared a suspicion of our landlady. Our rooms were heated by open coal fires and we each paid a shilling (five new pence) a bucket for the coal. We were convinced that when we were out and the coal buckets were low, Mrs. Mills would fill them up, leaving two or three knobs at the bottom of each bucket for which we paid over and over again. But we did have a room to study in and a bedroom, and all for 30/- a week (£1.50) for bed and breakfast. Evening meals we had either in Hall where in our first year we had to "make" four dinners a week, in other words appear properly dressed in our commoners' or Scholars' gowns, and partake of whatever the Hall Chef (called a Manciple) had laid on; or in the city. Our favourite eating place in the city was the Cadena cafe in Cornmarket Street where, for one shilling and sixpence (7½ new pence) a three course meal could be enjoyed.

Oxford and its environs have changed much since 1936, as I suppose it had changed much since Matthew Arnold, who died in 1888 wrote:

"And that sweet city with her dreaming spires
She needs not June for beauty's heightening."

William Camden three hundred years earlier, and writing in 1586 declared:

"Where the Cherwell flows along the Isis... is seated on a rising vale the most famous University of Oxford, in Saxon, Oxenford, our most noble Athens, the seat of English Muses, the prop and pillar, nay the sun, the eye, the very soul of the nation; the most celebrated fount of wisdom and learning from whence Religion, Letters, and Good Manners are happily diffused through the whole Kingdom. A delicate and most beautiful City where we respect the neatness of private buildings, or the stateliness of public structures or the healthy and pleasant situation."

The dreaming spires are still there, but they are surrounded by tall modern blocks of students' rooms, new laboratories and libraries. The Cherwell is still there and undergraduates still punt lazily along its waters as we did all those years ago. The Isis, the ancient name for the Thames, still flows under Folly Bridge and through Christ Church meadows. The College barges which used to be moored along its banks by Folly Bridge have gone. They were pleasant old tubs, the headquarters of the College boat clubs from which the eights would make their way down river to the spot where the "Torpids" and summer races would begin. What an eccentric name for races which demanded months of hard training and practice and then the application of energy and brute strength for their fulfilment! Torpid means lethargic, sluggish, lifeless, apathetic, adjectives not applicable to dedicated and fanatical oarsmen.

I hope that the rest of Camden's eulogy could still be said of the Oxford I knew. What he meant by "the soul of the nation" can only be conjectured, but Oxford men were then, and to an extent still are, to be found in the Government, Parliament, the Church, the Arts; today they are found also in the Sciences, Drama, Industry, the Diplomatic Corps, heading Universities and Colleges and Schools; they have won more than their fair share of Nobel Prizes and Oxford still leads research in many fields of Science, Medicine and Technology. No boy arriving in this wonderful city from a country Grammar School could fail to be impressed by the "neatness of private buildings" and the "stateliness of public structures", though it is not in my opinion in a "healthy" situation. Lying low in the Thames Valley it suffers from floods and mists and fogs. Head colds, chest colds and flu were the common lot of many of us in the Oxford winters. "Religion" flourished then in many forms and the various professors of Theology were leaders in their field, and some of them were nationally known figures. Churches were well-attended, college chapels had many participating in worship, and the choirs of many Colleges, such as New, Magdalen and Christ Church, had world-wide reputations. "Letters" have continued to flourish through the centuries, but I am not so sure about "Good Manners".

"It is easy to be idealistic about Oxford." Elaine Wilson wrote in January 1987:

> "Oxford is more than the physical beauty of spires,
> towers and bells. It embodies an ideal, the striving of
> Man for intellectual and spiritual truths."

Certainly that has always been the ideal. The reality is different, and much of Oxford today would seem to scorn that ideal. Drugs and drunkenness abound, if reports are true, in almost every College. As I write, a man from my own College is being fined £240 for possessing LSD, Lysergic Acid Diethylamide, a hallucinogenic drug called "acid" by the addicts. He gave himself up to the police after a fellow student fell to his death from a window in New College. Another student, a woman law graduate, was in court, facing charges of supplying various types of drugs to other students in Oxford.

Which leads me on to the observation that there appears to be one other great difference between Oxford life in 1936 and Oxford life today. It is called in general terms "pastoral care". I shall refer later on to one of my closer Hall friends, Hugh Durham, son of a Liverpool clergyman and a fellow ordinand with whom I used to play chess each lunch time and who, half way through his time at the Hall faced a crisis of identity and vocation and of religious belief. In the solving of his doubts and uncertainties to whom could he turn? Not to any of his contemporaries, for our knowledge of life and of the solving of its riddles was negligible. He ought to have been able to discuss his difficulties with the one who later became known as a "moral tutor", but there were no tutors trained as such in the nineteen thirties. Perhaps they were not necessary because most of us didn't have problems of identity or vocation, or if we did, and assuredly some of us had uncertainties, we discussed them with the Chaplain, our confessor, or the local parish priest at home.

Today the press, stimulated perhaps by the publicity that Oxford has received through the TV series *Inspector Morse*, carries a spate of articles about student suicides and drug-taking, mostly implying that the authorities do little or nothing to help students oppressed by the demands which Oxford makes upon them. Some have even implied that so remote are the academics from the students in their charge "in loco parentis", that they do not know what is going on, that they ignore the constraints and pressures caused by the fact that everything in Oxford depends upon the examination system. Everything is geared to it, the books, the essays, the tutorials. Added to this pressure are the facts that the years eighteen to twenty-one are notoriously difficult growing up years; that most students are away from all the constraints and compulsions of home and school, free for the first time in their lives to behave exactly as they wish; and that they are in an environment where the once "big fish in a little pond" has become a "little fish in a big pond." There are nearly 15,000 students at work in Oxford and some are very high fliers indeed. Marianne Talbot, a philosophy tutor, writes: "I have yet to meet the student who does not feel that he or she is the "admissions mistake", that although everyone else is brilliant and coping admirably, they alone are likely to prove inadequate."

What can be done about this increasing problem? And should not the school staffs have warned prospective undergraduates that they were going to be members of one of the greatest centres of academic excellence in the world? And that would mean becoming part of a highly intelligent community of very bright and clever and competitive contemporaries, mostly self-assured and intolerant?

Compared with what was available to us in the thirties, Oxford offers pastoral care of a high order. There is a University Counselling Service which has a budget of £140,000 a year, two full time members and three part-time members who attempt to help and counsel about one hundred students a week. No doubt also the colleges now have their own systems of pastoral care, and the student body itself has its own system of self-help groups and telephone help lines.

Perhaps the problem (what a pity we have no other word for it - dilemma, enigma, puzzle, perhaps?) is not as acute as it is made out to be. Oxford has more than twice the number of students it had in the thirties, and many more women students. The presence of women should surely make life better balanced and normal for the men than it was in my time! A recent report on the situation by Dr. Keith Hawton, a psychiatrist, states that between the years 1976 and 1990 (fourteen years) sixteen men students and five women students were recorded by inquests to have killed themselves. This was thirty percent above the national average for the 18-25 age group, but the difference "virtually disappeared" when open verdicts were taken into account. Only one verdict on an Oxford student in those fourteen years was "open". Further, a total of 214 students made 254 unsuccessful attempts at suicide in the same period, a figure significantly below that for young people as a whole in the City. It is interesting that academic worries were cited by only one third of the students who tried to take their own lives. By far the most common factors were difficulties with personal relationships.

So the predicament of Oxford undergraduates may be just a reflection of the predicament that faces society as a whole in which one third of marriages break down each year. No doubt a high proportion of students have families where divorce, separation, bankruptcy, redundancy, are traumatic experiences which have had to be faced. Ours is also a society where the contraceptive aid has made promiscuity and what used to be called "moral laxity" possible and easy. There may even be feelings of guilt left over from a former age which believed in right and wrong, in divine retribution and eternal punishment. The example of our modern leaders, politicians, "captains of industry" and of our academic mentors has not always been helpful. The late Alfred Jules Ayer, Wykeham Professor of Logic at Oxford from 1959, professed atheist and expounder of the theory of "logical positivism", claimed to have made love to no less than one hundred and fifty women. We are all bound up within this fragmented, uncertain and rudderless society, so there should be no surprise that young people find life difficult to cope with.

Life was more stable, society was more constant, in those few years before Hitler unleashed his viciousness and corruption upon the world. We had recovered from the recession and unemployment of the late twenties and early thirties. The solid Stanley Baldwin was in Downing Street and the dull but worthy George the Sixth was on the throne from 1936. True, we all read Hitler's "Mein Kampf" and were sympathetic to a Germany where there was no unemployment and the motorways were a miracle. We had seen pictures of the Jews being persecuted, their shop windows smashed, but the young Germans who came over on exchange were such charming people. Oswald Mosley and his blackshirts held their meetings in St. Giles and we went along to hear him. Many students attended to barrack and object, but they were no match for his minders. Some undergraduates even belonged to the British Union of Fascists. Some also belonged to the Communist Party and fought during the long vacations on the

Republican side of the Spanish Civil War of 1936-1939. After all, Mosley had been an independent or labour member of Parliament since 1918, so many must have supported his ideas. All the student political parties had a large membership, and the peace movement was strong. Members of the Oxford Union, that cradle of future politicians, had even voted that they "would not fight for King and Country." But from 1939-1945 thousands of them did, and hundreds of them died out of love and service to their fellows.

Again, if reports are true, promiscuous sex is common. In 1936 the College gates were all locked at 9 p.m. and a fine had to be paid for coming in after that hour without permission. Women were not allowed in men's rooms after 6 p.m. and my only contact with students from the women's colleges was in lectures and the Debating Society of which I came to be President. It was not until 1972 that five men's colleges were allowed to take one hundred women students between them as an experiment. The experiment was successful and in 1976 the majority of men's colleges began to admit women. Since that time all but two of the women's colleges have become mixed. It is proposed that Somerville, the leading womens' college, should take in men students in 1994. This has had both its good and its bad side and it may be left to the reader to judge the end results.

"Good Manners" in Camden's 16th century would have included dress, deportment, treatment of the opposite sex, as well as the hiding away of anything to bring shame and disgrace upon a college or a family. Correct speech would have been part of the "manner". In 1936 almost every male undergraduate wore the accepted uniform of sports jacket and grey flannel trousers, with a tie, and brown shoes, preferably "brogues". We were required to wear our gowns at lectures, and when in public in the streets of the city. Dark suits, called "subfusc" had to be worn at all examinations. At dinner in Hall anyone offending good manners, for example by swearing or mentioning the name of a woman, would suffer a "sconce", which meant that he had to provide and pay for a large tankard of beer to be consumed by all those at his table. Few of us swore in those days, certainly not in public, and one student who did, using the word "bloody" in almost every sentence was called by that nickname: "here comes Bloody Strong". Some control was exercised by College academic staff over our behaviour. John Kelly, who was Chaplain and my tutor, later to become an outstanding Principal under whom the Hall expanded both in buildings and in population (from 146 in 1936 to 400 today), wrote in his book "St Edmund Hall":

> "As in previous generations, the hall offered its members and deliberately sought to maintain, a more economical, if also more frugal, life than the colleges. High spending was discouraged: on Mondays for example, the butteryman brought his book to the Vice-Principal, and students who were found to have exceeded the accepted norm of beer consumption were warned, rebuked or penalised. Its comparative cheapness made the Hall attractive to many, especially to the ordinands and prospective school-teachers who still formed a higher than average proportion of its members."

The number of ordinands in my time was about forty. Today I suspect there is not one. Nor has the strict Anglicanism of Oxford survived. There always were nonconformist societies but in the thirties they did not have official "college status". Mansfield College where I took lectures from a leading Congregationalist theologian and which was founded in 1886, is only now (in 1994) attaining a recognised full status as a college of the university through the archaic procedures of a petition to the Privy Council from College and University jointly, approval by the Charity Commission and a revision of its Statutes.

The statutes of the Hall had once laid it down that the Principal and other senior academic staff should be priests of the Church of England. With the coming of a layman, A.B. Emden, as Principal in 1929 ("the Abe") this was no longer true. New statutes promulgated in 1974 stipulated that the College should have a Chaplain, but studiously omitted that he should be a priest of the Church of England and that he should conduct services according to the book of Common Prayer, as the old statutes had done. This of course reflects the loosening of the tensions between the Churches and an acceptance by the established Church that it could no longer demand the exclusive position it once had.

The Principal, A.B. Emden, was an austere man, an autocrat and a much respected historian, especially of the mediaeval period. He was a graduate of Lincoln College who had served in the Great War as an Able Seaman. In this period, and indeed until 1957 when the Hall received its Charter as a full independent College, the government of the Hall was in the hands of Queen's College, next door, and Emden was the last Principal to be nominated and appointed by the governing body of Queen's to a post in St. Edmund Hall. He enjoyed his power and exercised it over the fellows and students, and no doubt he relished hearing the Fellows and Tutors declaring on appointment that they would "obey the Principal in all things lawful and honourable". This clause was only removed in 1951. At this time Fellows had statutory rights but tutors had none. Tutors' salaries were low and they had no pension rights. They were appointed, and could be dismissed by the Principal who also settled with them their terms of employment. They had no Common Room of their own.

But they were an able group of men. G.R. Brewis was Senior Tutor and taught us Logic with a rare humour and in terms which those of us who sat under him have never forgotten. His son, J.S. Brewis, a priest, was Vice-Principal, and J.N.D. Kelly, a graduate of Glasgow University and Queen's (hence his appointment) was Chaplain, and tutor in theology and philosophy. H.J. Hunt was an outstanding French scholar and there were other tutors in Latin & Greek, in chemistry, physics, history, English and PPE (philosophy, politics and economics).

Not one of them had been specifically trained as a teacher, and it is quite clear that those who were "natural" teachers had the most success with their pupils. Many First Class Degrees were obtained by those who sat under the French and English tutors, few by those who studied theology. John Kelly was a very shy man with a pronounced stutter, a brilliant scholar himself, but like many outstanding academics, he was not able to communicate his knowledge to people like myself from small Grammar Schools who had not been taught, as our contemporaries from the "Public" Schools had, how to work on our own, how to research in libraries, how to write intelligent essays.

There were only two methods of teaching at Oxford. The first was the lecture. At the beginning of term a list of lectures was given to us which we had to attend, some in our own college, others in different colleges of the University. In the thirties lecturers and tutors were usually men who had been appointed to their colleges when quite young because they had first class degrees or had written a book, and the almost universal practice was for them to expound their subject from their own books. A prime example of this was a Professor D.C. Simpson who many years before had written a book on the Old Testament. His lectures were culled almost word for word from the chapters of this book. He constantly, used the Hebrew form of the word Jehovah, "Yahweh", and he was known as "Yahweh" Simpson. There was no discussion after the lecture and we might just as well have sat in our own rooms and studied his book.

Another lecturer, on Canon Law, was R.C. Mortimer of Christ Church. At the first lecture in the Autumn term of 1937 there were about thirty theological students present. At the next, about ten had given up. After about six lectures there remained only a girl theological student and myself. I often wonder, even now, if the girl turned up at the last lecture, for I did not!

Such are the ways of appointment in the Church of England that R.C. Mortimer became Bishop of Exeter. He was an opinionated High Churchman and by all accounts a not very successful Bishop. I met him many years later in a meeting of the General Synod in York when the Report "Christian Initiation, Birth and Growth in the Christian Society", the result of a Commission of which I had been a member, was presented. It made certain recommendations about Baptism and Confirmation to which I shall refer later. They were very much reflections of what the clergy in the parishes were thinking in 1971, and were perhaps too revolutionary (e.g. that children should be admitted to Communion without Confirmation but with due preparation, and that people baptised in adult life should not have to submit to Confirmation). We sat next to each other at dinner in York University one evening, and not knowing who I was, he declared loudly to all and sundry: "I shall not allow that Report within my Diocese!" Such ancient prelatical behaviour on the part of Bishops has, I hope, come to an appropriate and unlamented end.

I took lectures on the Epistle to the Romans from Canon H.L. Goudge, also of Christ Church, and father of the novelist Elizabeth Goudge. He was a lovely man, small, with a hunched back, always dressed in deep black, the only lecturer who attempted to relate the Bible he was expounding to life. He taught the New Testament and to him I owe the beginning of such understanding as I have of the life and writings of St. Paul. He was also the only "don" who attempted to make any contact with students from outside his own college. He would invite us to tea in his rooms off Tom Quad at Christ Church, and being a widower at that time, would pour the tea and offer the cream cakes himself. His books on Church Unity and on Bible subjects, his great one volume commentary (the three "G"s - Gore, Goudge and Guillaume had collaborated in writing it) and his excellent sermons influenced greatly my generation of ordination candidates and clergy.

H.J. Carpenter, tutor, and later Warden of Keble College was another rather dull lecturer. Later, he became Bishop of Oxford. It is said today that the Bishops' bench has no great scholars sitting on it. That may be true. In the thirties and forties there were scholars in abundance. Carpenter had a string of first class degrees from London and Oxford, and an honorary Doctorate from Oxford. He was co-chairman of the long drawn out Anglican-Methodist conversations which came to nothing, and of the Anglican-Orthodox Commission for joint Doctrinal Discussions. Ordained in 1927, he spent 2 years as Curate of Leatherhead and then twenty eight years as an academic. As a Bishop what did he know of the needs and problems of the parish laity and clergy? Yet another academic from whom I took lectures was R.M.P. Milburn, a Hebrew and Greek scholar who was Fellow and Chaplain of Worcester College for twenty three years, who then became Dean of Worcester Cathedral and later Master of the Temple, in London.

It was no wonder that many students gave up attending lectures after experiencing their almost universal dullness. If only the lecturers had been taught how to hold their audience's attention in the first two minutes! If only their lectures had been lightened with a little humour! If only we had been allowed to question what they asserted, and they had discussed their work with us! If only they had given us copies of what they had said! In my years at Rochester I lectured on a great variety of subjects, to parishes, students, clergy, teachers, and I always made time for discussion and always had copies of the lecture available afterwards for those who wanted them. The lecture as delivered at Oxford, at least in the Theological Faculty in the thirties, was a failure, a totally inadequate educational instrument.

The second method of teaching was the tutorial. Because this was a dialogue it was a more effective tool or medium of learning and instruction. In the tutorial session which took place once weekly one could also get to know the tutor, an absolute pre-requisite of the learning process. A list of books was given - related to the subject of the essay to be written, and some guidance as to the lines of thought to be pursued. There were usually two of us theological students sharing a tutorial, but this was not a satisfactory arrangement. I assume it was because the number of students then reading theology was too great for face to face, one to one, encounters, which would have been the ideal. My essays were on the whole well-received by my tutor, John Kelly, but they had been written with books at hand enabling copious references to be incorporated. This had no relation whatsoever to the form of the examination which was later to be taken, which was an exercise in pure memory. Therefore if you had a poor sense of recall and a faulty memory you were at a great disadvantage. We were not even allowed to take a Bible in to the Examination Schools.

The first University examination to be taken at the end of the second term of the first year was Pass Moderations or, if you were a scholarly type and capable of better than merely good work, Honour Moderations. My subjects were French, Latin, History, English and Logic. I failed the Latin paper and had to retake the exam at the end of my third term. The failure was due (and I was not the only one) to the fact that University life had given me my first taste of real freedom. I had spent my time not in studying as I should have, but in exploring the Oxfordshire countryside, in walking the towpath to Abingdon, in cycling thirty or forty miles; or at the theatre, where operas and pre-London releases could be enjoyed, and in the cinema watching Deanna Durbin, Nelson Eddy and Jeanette Macdonald, the Marx Brothers, Simone Simon, Jean Gabin, James Cagney and all the rest of the stars from Hollywood, France, Russia and Britain, on the silver screen (though the screen at the "flea pit" in the Cowley Road, where one could get a good seat for sixpence, had several large patches on it!)

I am not a natural scholar and I would probably be right to claim that I was a "late developer", for in subsequent years I have written a great deal for the use of students and clergy and their parishes. None of it has been published commercially though many have tried to persuade me to do that, because most of what I have written has been "immediate" and contemporary, and thus quickly out of date as far as current references go. In any case a best seller in theology will only sell a thousand or two thousand copies. It is interesting that some of the novels entered for the prestigious "Booker Prize" sell only a few thousand copies. Some of the material I have written has run into as many as three thousand cyclostyled copies, and I only mention this here to reinforce my argument that material produced only from memory in an examination room is not a proper indication of intellectual ability!

So at the end of my third year I obtained only a Third Class Degree. In the years before the war of 1939-1945 this was the commonest degree awarded, so I was not alone, but like a conviction for felony, it remained on my "Curriculum Vitae". On one occasion when I was being considered for what the Church insists on calling "an important post" (as if the position held by the most junior curate is not just as important in the eyes of God as that of the Archbishop of Canterbury!) the Bishop said to me: "I see you have not put down the class that you obtained in your degree in Crockford" (the clerical Directory which at that time used to include many details of one's career.) Though I was called for interview I was not given the post, presumably partly because I had only a third class degree! A very large proportion of clergy today do not have a University degree at all. Are they any worse as pastors and teachers for that?

I enjoyed my three years at Oxford intensely. They had cost, in total, £450, which my mother had paid from my late father's estate. I loved the Hall and its imaginative, diminutive quadrangle. I loved my little rooms in the 1934 Canterbury building. I loved the city and its architecture. I loved the Botanical Gardens where I would wander on a hot summers afternoon. I loved the Isis and the Cherwell, where friends and I would punt and laze. Edward Hinson and I struck up a warm friendship with an English scholar of our year, Douglas Holmes, who did gain a first class degree, having come from an ordinary Grammar School in Stafford. When war broke out he joined the Marines, was trained as an officer in Eastney barracks, Portsmouth, took part in the ill-fated expedition to Crete, and was killed, as were many Hall men of my generation. We had good times together, walking, cycling, punting, talking, widening our horizons. In the summer of 1937 we three went to Paris under Edward Hinson's guidance, the expert student of French. It was hot and steamy that August and most Parisians had wisely gone to the coast, but we saw and explored every famous building, travelling all over the city by Metro, eating cheap but delicious meals with wine and fresh fruit.

Unbelievably, the Guide Book which we used was called "Paris on £10"!

We explored Versailles with special interest that year, for a book had just been written by two Englishwomen who claimed to have seen a vision of Marie Antoinette and her court sporting themselves in their farm at Le Petit Trianon, with all kinds of circumstantial evidence. We went daringly to the Moulin Rouge and saw the notorious Mistinguette; we improved our French by going to the cinema and seeing two American films, one with Henry Fonda, and the other with Maurice Chevalier and I think Jeanette Macdonald, dubbed into French dialogue with some startling results. It was on the Paris Metro that I received what today would be called a "culture shock". My puritan senses were outraged by the sight of two young French people kissing in public. That certainly never happened in England, I told myself. The French reputation for depravity and shameless dissoluteness was plainly true! How innocent the young ordinand was at twenty years old.

In August 1938 we borrowed my mother's Hillman 10 car and toured the South West and Wales. We had intended to "do" the Lake District and Scotland as well, but after a fortnight of over-close proximity we decided that our friendship would not survive another fortnight so after fifteen days we went our separate ways and returned to our homes. It was the time of the Munich crisis in any case and it was felt that we should be at home. The crisis rumbled on until September 29th when Chamberlain and Daladier signed the agreement with Hitler which gave the French and ourselves a year's grace to prepare for what even then seemed to the wiser ones among us to be inevitable - War.

St. Edmund Hall was developing a reputation as a formidable adversary to much larger colleges in most sports, rowing, football rugger, hockey and athletics. Twenty years on, in 1959, the Hall was not only Head of the River in the summer "Eights Week", but walked away with the rugby, soccer and athletics cups. But games were not my strengths. I became President of the Chess Club though it did not have more than a handful of members, and of the Debating Society and the Liddon Society, a group of theological students who met regularly to discuss matters of faith and morals and to hear visiting speakers from home and overseas. The society was named after Henry Parry Liddon, one-time Vice-principal of the Hall, and later to be Dean of St. Paul's, the most dazzling preacher of the Victorian age.

One of the most difficult of all exercises is to relate the theory of religion to life. I have mentioned that H.L. Goudge tried to do this in his lectures, but little spiritual food was to be found in the life of the Hall Chapel. It was fairly well attended on Sunday mornings at 8 a.m. but for spiritual sustenance students had to link up with one of the many churches in the city. If you were of the High Church persuasion you attended the Anglo-Catholic Pusey House Chapel. If you were at the other end of the ecclesiastical spectrum you attended, as I did, St. Aldates. This had, and still has, a large and lively undergraduate body. Famous preachers could always be heard and meetings attended. One of the great occasions of the year was the "missionary breakfast" held in a large room on the first floor of the big store, Elliston and Cavell's, now Debenhams, where as many as three hundred students would assemble to eat breakfast and to hear inspiring speakers from overseas. John Kelly did gather the ordinands together regularly for worship and usually a drubbing down for not living up to our profession, when one of our number had in some way disgraced himself (too much beer perhaps), and "let the side down".

In 1937 I was "captured" by the Oxford Group. This was a strange quasi-Christian organism which later became known as Moral Re-Armament, founded by an American, Frank Buchman, who had gone through some kind of conversion experience and had sent letters of apology to all those whom he felt he had wronged. The tenets of the Group were simple. They were based on the four absolutes, absolute honesty, absolute purity, absolute unselfishness and absolute love. The first demand made upon members was that they should listen to God's guidance daily, preferably in the early morning, and share that guidance with others. Every member was expected to be an evangelist, and the form that evangelism must take was to "challenge" one's family and friends on the basis of the absolutes, and get them to share with you in listening to God's guidance, and recording it, and then carrying out any directions which that guidance appeared to have given you.

The Bible was studied in the light of the four absolutes, and though one was not prevented from keeping up one's membership and commitment to a Church, this was not felt to be necessary. Most members of the Group in my time were rather critical of the Churches and did not take part in their worship. When one had been a member of the group for long enough and had a proved commitment one was allowed, and expected, to make a public profession of conversion. The watchword of the Group was "Life-changing" and its slogan was "Change men, change nations, change the world". It came to make the most extravagant claims that it had actually changed nations by changing some of their leaders. It set its cap at the important people in the theatre, in commerce, in music, in local government. We held rallies in town halls and large Hotels. I recall one rally in the prestigious Dorchester Hotel in London when a famous actress, Margaret Rawlings, whom I suspect a member of the Group had thought to have life-changed, for she was a guest speaker, rounded upon us all, and made a plea for reticence and modesty in religion, and non-invasion of a person's privacy. This was fully reported in next day's papers alongside a photograph of the actress in a rather less than modest and reticent pose.

Looking back on it now, I am amazed at our naïveté on so many elements of the Group's philosophy. There is of course nothing wrong with putting before mankind the high ideal of the four absolutes. If all mankind were completely honest and loving, pure and unselfish, there would be no wars, no Aids, no need for policemen, judges and juries. We should all drive our cars unselfishly and the pornographic shops and magazines would close down. I believe in absolutes, but when it comes down to particular cases, for example in the matter of honesty - truth - there are occasions when it is difficult to decide what *is* absolutely honest. Doctors face this dilemma daily. Again what is it to be absolutely loving? In family relationships does one not sometimes have to be "cruel to be kind" - with children for example?

Another weakness of the Group was its infantile dependence on Frank Buchman. He was a spiritual dictator who could sometimes be very cruel to his colleagues. He had become self-opinionated because of the adulation and hero-worship he received, and he exploited the fact that he was the founder of the organisation. I often heard it said, when the "guidance" among us seemed to be contradictory, "We will get Frank to ask guidance on this one," the presumption being that if our guidance was wrong, Frank's would certainly be right. Indeed the whole concept of divine guidance was flawed. We would sit in a circle for half all hour, writing our thoughts down in notebooks and then the leader of the group would say: "What comes?" then we would each recount what had come. If nothing seemed to "come" we would make up something and put it down so that we might not incur the incredulity of our fellows that we had received no guidance! And what we did "receive" was often so banal as to be laughable. Then the guidance had to be "checked" to see if it fitted in with the absolutes, and one member could question another's guidance. This makes nonsense of the whole process, and is at odds with the traditional Catholic view of the way in which God does guide us; and of the way in which for centuries the Church has helped its members in the preparation of their confessions.

The philosophy of actually setting out specifically to change someone's else's life is to me a total contradiction of the necessary Christian virtue of humility, and of the doctrine that all men are sinners. Why should I assume that someone else's life needs changing? Am I so sure that my own life doesn't need a drastic overhaul? I found no humility in the Oxford Group. There is indeed a sense in which a Christian is absolutely sure of the Faith, but it must be a humble sureness. I have mentioned my friend, Hugh Durham who was so constantly "got at" by Groupers that his mind was in a turmoil. I have remarked how he had come to Oxford as a convinced Christian, a dedicated ordination candidate. When they had finished with him he had lost all self-confidence, and lost his faith, and one day he walked all the way home to Liverpool and did not come back that term. He ceased to be an ordinand. One must be sure of the Faith. It is pure pride to be too sure of oneself.

Nor could the Group face even the mildest criticism. If someone was reported to be critical, and many were, including Hensley Henson, Bishop of Durham, who wrote an unanswerable and devastating critique of the Group and its tenets, then we would aver: "That man must be defeated in his own personal life" to hold such a view. What arrogance! I left the Group and resisted all blandishments to return, but I owe them a great debt, in teaching me in a negative way the truth about guidance as well as the importance of a high ideal in life and in religion. When it finally relinquished its tenuous hold on the last vestiges of Christianity with the idea of a universalist and syncretistic morality to which all men must come whatever their former religious faith, then it was the parting of the ways for many of us. Nor would it be forgotten that Frank Buchman had said "Thank God for Adolf Hitler." Like many Americans of the time, far away from what was happening in Europe, though Buchman should have known, he saw Hitler as the last bulwark against Communism, the great Satan, the great bogeyman. This festering sore in the American mind came to a head in the McCarthyism of 1950-1954 when Senator McCarthy held his witch hunts among two hundred members of the State Department whom he alleged to be Communists, along with others in the realms of literature, music, business, the film world and many areas of American life.

That rather long digression on the Oxford Group is not irrelevant. It was part of my total Oxford education, part of my spiritual pilgrimage, and had a part to play in my low academic attainment, since for two years I spent a large part of my time in Group activities when I should have been at my books. It also caused me to think more deeply about religion, what it truly is, and who and what it is for. For example, it seemed to me even then, to be wrong, that the headquarters of the Group should be based in Brown's Hotel, one of the most prestigious and expensive hotels in London. It seemed to me to be wrong then and wrong now, that we set our targets among the middle and upper classes, believing that somehow, if we won over a famous person, or a rich person, that would be more pleasing to the God from whom we sought guidance, than to change the life of a shop girl. So too the Group had an inordinate interest in money and material things. Members of MRA would of course deny those attitudes, but in the thirties they were the prevailing modes of belief and action.

It worries me still that my first Vicarage was one of the largest houses in the parish, with 17 rooms; and today, that the Diocese of Guildford is reportedly about to spend up to £400,000 on building the new Godalming Vicarage: £325,000 on the building, the rest on fees, when thousands are homeless. It worried me when I was a Vicar in his Diocese that George Reindorp, the Bishop of Guildford, (more of him later) tried to institute "important" and "less important" parishes with appropriate differentials in stipends, on the basis of the number of primary and secondary and preparatory and Public Schools, and hospitals and nursing homes, within the parish boundaries. If a man takes seriously the Ministry entrusted to him, he is fully occupied, however many school governing bodies he sits on. Indeed, he may be a more effective parish priest if he sits on fewer committees and attends fewer "important meetings". But I must not digress any more from my Oxford theme.

In the years following the Hitler War I returned to Oxford for conferences and observed some of the changes that had taken place. Most of the students were more mature than we were, sanctions and regulations had been loosened, more women undergraduates were to be seen. In Blackwell's, the bookshop where I had spent many hours just browsing, students were still having free reads. Cricket was still being played in the Parks, and punts were still being poled along the Cherwell. The deer were still in Magdalen park, but many new architecturally innovative buildings were rising all over the city. The number of bicycles, always large, had increased, as had the traffic in Broad Street, now largely a car park, St. Giles and Cornmarket Street.

This year I again spent a few summer days in the city. Prices in the pubs and hotels and eating places were enormous. I paid £15 for the kind of supper for which I had paid one shilling and sixpence in the Cadena in 1936. At eleven o'clock at night the streets were full of undergraduates, sitting on walls and even on pavements, many of them behaving in the way that had so shocked my puritan soul on the Paris Metro in 1937. Like us they were deep in philosophical debate, still asserting opinions as truths, just as we did; intellectually putting the world to rights and passing critical judgements on the University, their tutors, on Government, on Church and State. "Plus ça change, plus c'est la même chose." Nothing much changes. Alphonse Karr wrote that in 1849. He was wrong and he was right. Things change, habits change, buildings are changed, but basic human problems and concerns, hopes and fears, do not change. (Certainly the clothes that undergraduates wear have changed - not a sports jacket or tie was to be seen!)

Oxford has housed a University for more than 800 years. In all that time it has been a centre of religion, learning and some good manners, and all who have had the good fortune to live and study within its mediaeval or modern walls must be grateful for what it has given them. It is difficult to assess what that gift means, for it deepens and develops through the years. I owe more to Oxford for what I am and believe today than I owed it when I was a young man. I have been critical of the teaching I personally received but Oxford gives more than formal teaching. It is what happens when students gather for talk and debate late at night as students have done for 800 years, and on into the early hours, that remains. It is a spirit, an essence, a character, a meaning, that soaks into a man's whole being, that remains when the logic lectures and the dull repetitions of the discourses of long-dead dons have been forgotten. Yet this is astonishing, for how long does a student taking a degree at the end of his third year spend in Oxford? Nine terms of eight weeks, that is all; less than a year and a half. That is a short enough period in all conscience for a radical development of body, mind and soul, brain and personality. In that so short time we add to the sum total of our knowledge and experience; we learn to tolerate the opinions of others and to present our own ideas with confidence, and we are prepared for the even greater task of continuing to learn for the rest of our lives.

Like all other Universities today, Oxford is expanding its teaching and research and is receiving less Government funding to do so, but it will survive. St. Edmund Hall has been threatened with extinction, absorption, change of character, many times in its seven centuries of life, but it too will survive.

Oxford houses several theological colleges and when the time came to decide which one of many throughout the country I would proceed to after taking my degree, it was mainly a question of whether to stay within the University orbit, with all that it offered of continuity and continuing theological study, or pass on to a different world of a more tightly knit institution, independent of and not in any way conditioned by, proximity to a rather over-powering academy. In Oxford, St. Stephen's House and Cuddesdon were more Anglo-Catholic in tone than I wished to become, Wycliffe Hall was more Evangelical, Ripon Hall had the reputation of being "Modernist". Beyond Oxford, Salisbury, Wells (now, sadly, closed) and Lincoln, were all of high reputation and of no pronounced exclusive churchmanship. Those whom I consulted gave high praise to Lincoln so it was to Lincoln that I went in January 1940. (Sadly, too Lincoln is to close in 1995.)

I left Oxford in the summer of 1939. Hitler invaded Poland on September 1st, and Britain declared war on Germany on Sunday September 3rd. I heard Neville Chamberlain's sad broadcast in the house of friends in Sussex near the farm in Steyning to which my mother had moved when she married, five years after my father's death, a jolly farmer of the strict Baptist persuasion, John Cross by name. The two things did not seem to go together. The strict Baptists had a very narrow and restrictive attitude to life and faith - no cinema, no theatre, no dancing, no alcohol, but it was not for his faith but for his jolliness that my mother was attracted. She was still, at fifty one, a good looking and eligible widow, an excellent housewife and cook, with an income of her own. John Cross was of similar age, with four grown-up children whose wife had deserted him some years before, and he had been divorced. He was a heavy smoker of Player's cigarettes and died a few years later of a hideous lung cancer. He was at that time a nondrinker and belonged to a strange organisation called the Rechabites. They are referred to in Jeremiah 35 as a group of people who would not take strong drink because their forefather Jonadab had forbidden it.

The Rechabites took one sentence in this passage literally, as many fundamentalist Christians do with other passages of the Bible, but the folly of treating every word of the Bible as of the same value, of taking the Old Testament as having an equal authority with the New, and of taking admonitions out of context, is illustrated when one goes on to read further. Certainly the passage says:

"We will not drink wine, for our forefather Jonadab, son of Rechab, laid this command on us; You shall never drink wine..."

But it goes on to say:

"neither you nor your children. You shall not build houses or sow seed or plant vineyards; you shall have none of these things. You shall remain tent-dwellers all your lives."

John Cross's children certainly did not obey this command, nor, as a farmer, did he! He lived in a house, he sowed seed, lots of it, and he did not dwell in tents! It was not difficult to persuade him during our many theological discussions (he was very worried about the religious implications of his divorce) that to take Jeremiah 35 literally into his way of living was contradictory if not impossible, and he soon became happy to drink the occasional glass of beer, whisky or sherry, which he enjoyed. What his strict Baptist friends thought of him I can only guess. I don't know if the Rechabites still exist in this free society. There are other, much more cogent and intelligent reasons for not partaking of strong drink. A pity that smoking too is not forbidden in any Bible passage. John Cross was a strong supporter of the Lord's Day Observance Society which frowned upon the opening of theatres, shops and cinemas on Sundays. John would not go into a shop to buy his cigarettes on what he called "The Sabbath" (though the Sabbath is Saturday) and so he had installed a cigarette machine in his office. On Sunday mornings before Chapel where he was a Deacon, he would solemnly insert his shilling in the slot and take out his cigarettes. It's amazing how much we fool ourselves.

But John Cross was a hospitable and generous man. He welcomed me and my family into his ramshackle 18th century farmhouse and in the midst of his 325 acres I found the peace and quiet I needed to continue my reading and thinking in preparation for the intense and rather "out of the world" period which I must now undertake as I proceeded towards Ordination.

CHAPTER 7

LINCOLN

"Discreet and learned Minister of God's Word."
First Exhortation, Communion Service.
Book of Common Prayer.

"As I take my shoes from the shoemaker and my coat from
the tailor, so I take my religion from the priest."
Samuel Johnson (1709-1784)

"A man who is good enough to go to heaven, is good
enough to be a clergyman."
Samuel Johnson (said on April 5th, 1772)

"Terms like grace, new birth, justification, which with St. Paul are
literary terms, theologians have employed as if they were
scientific terms."
Matthew Arnold, poet (1822-1888)

In January 1940 I left Sussex for Lincoln. I had spent the last six
months reading and studying and working on farms for John Cross
and his brother-in-law, Walter Wills, with whose daughter Frances I
believed myself to be madly in love. She was tolerant and friendly
but did not share my feelings. Wills was a sheep farmer and I helped
him too, building a garage for his farm machinery, painting a lorry
battleship grey - not for camouflage reasons, although we were in the
flightpath of the RAF and German bombers, but because that was the
only colour of paint available at the time. And, using my mother's
car, I acted as chauffeur for all and sundry, before petrol rationing
became very restricting. I taught Frances to drive and she passed her
driving test in Brighton, not an easy town to drive in, at the first
attempt. I was also at the same time in love with Wills' other
daughter, Doris, but she married another local farmer; and later with
a lovely girl called Daphne - whose surname I cannot recall, a friend

of Frances, who was one of the first victims of the polio epidemic which struck Britain in the late thirties and early forties. It is a horrible disease, due to a virus which attacks the spinal cord and causes paralysis. It has been practically eliminated by the Salk vaccine, but this was not available until 1954. I was deeply moved by her death at the early age of seventeen.

For John Cross I built two concrete silos, cylindrical towers in which silage (green fodder kept succulent by the addition of molasses, and fermented inside the tower) is made. Like my father, I enjoyed using my hands, but I was not really used to the work, which strained all the muscles and tendons of my right arm. I went to the local doctor who told me I had "teno-syno-vitis".

"What on earth is that? It sounds disabling, if not fatal?"

"Oh, you will not die. It's only an inflammation caused by unaccustomed manual labour."

Today the condition is called "RSI", repetitive strain injury, and seems to be common among secretaries. One of them has just been awarded £35,000 in damages against her employer. "No comment," as they say. He strapped my arm from wrist to shoulder, and for good measure my ribs as well, in the old kind of Elastoplast which when removed tears away all the hairs and some of the skin (or so it seemed) as well. Thus partially cocooned in plaster, I left Sussex by train in brilliant sunshine, and arrived at Lincoln in four inches of snow.

It was 1940. Before making their final decision to attend theological college all prospective ordinands had been sent various letters setting out the pros and cons of continuing to prepare for a "reserved occupation" or joining the Forces. It was pointed out that if the Government had not assessed the Ministry of the Church as an "important" occupation (like farming or work in munitions factories) they would not have designated it as "reserved". The classical arguments for the "Just War" were rehearsed and we were reminded that we would face a great deal of suspicion and reproach, if not downright hostility and abuse, for being able-bodied young men not in uniform. It was a very hard decision to make. I would have been an Officer straight away in view of my OTC background, and the fact that I had passed Certificate "A", the OTC exam. My practical knowledge of tactics and strategy would have been elementary since we had been trained on the *Infantry Training Manual 1920* which had five lines on air attack, and four lines on gas attack! Yet, for some years I had been convinced that I had an over-riding call from God to be a priest. Many other professions and vocations would have been open to me before war came - I could have trained for the Law which had always appealed to me as a place where logical argument reigned supreme, or as a teacher or as a pilot, though my inadequate right eye would have probably prevented that.

I had greatly enjoyed my elementary "training" as an "officer" in the "Corps" and I had been fascinated by the development of air flight. The Schneider trophy had been competed for between seaplanes of any nation since 1913, and Squadron Leader Orlebar was a hero to many of my generation. Britain had won the trophy outright by victories in 1927, 1929 and 1931, years when I was at school. The planes which won in those years were the forerunners of the amazing Spitfires which largely won the Battle of Britain in 1940. I admit that I was in many ways physically a fearful coward, but I am encouraged by the fact that most war heroes have admitted to fear of physical pain.

Though I was by instinct and conviction a pacifist, it was not merely physical fear which made me accept the status of "reserved occupation", though who will not admit to such a thing before joining the Forces? The idea that war is an exciting, glorious adventure had died with the 1914-1918 war, with the Spanish Civil War, and with Italy's barbarous invasion and treatment of Abyssinia in 1935. It was rather the idea that I could be of more use to humanity preaching and living the Christian idea of love for God and neighbour.

I *did* suffer abuse and scorn as the war proceeded and I did find it difficult sometimes to justify my decision. In the Windsor Youth Club in 1941 swastikas (originally these were primitive religious symbols of Greek origin - Hitler did pervert everything he touched!) were daubed on the walls. A large one was even painted many years later in the road outside my Vicarage in Surrey in 1951. Matters were not improved by the fact that my surname is plainly German. Some of my contemporaries opted for service, but most felt the same as I and proceeded towards ordination. A number later became Chaplains to the Forces. Many Chaplains performed heroic deeds on the battlefield and many died in action. The Bishop of Oxford, after I was ordained, would not authorise men under thirty to become Chaplains, and would not send married men into the Forces. So on both counts, as I married at twenty-six and had my first child at twenty-seven, I was ineligible for active Service as a Chaplain. This too was a cause of criticism on the part of some lay people in the parishes which I served during the War, but it had to be endured, not defended and justified.

I have been critical of both my schooling and my University education. I am critical too of my theological training, mostly on the grounds that the men who were in charge of the theological colleges were themselves ill-equipped to prepare us for the *parish* ministry. Eric Abbott, the Warden of Lincoln, was thirty-five when I came under his authority and spell. He had spent the statutory two years as a Curate in Westminster and from then on his career was entirely academic, mostly at King's College London. After a spell at Lincoln he returned to King's as Dean and later became Warden of Keble College and then Dean of Westminster Abbey. He was an intensely spiritual man who had an abiding influence on ordinands over many years but his knowledge of the parish and of the men and women in the pew was minimal.

Eric Mascall, like Eric Abbott, was a Cambridge scholar, and he too had been a curate in Westminster, and earlier in Southwark, but his experience of parish life covered only five years. There is no doubt about his intellectual brilliance and he was the author of many influential works of theology. He held degrees and honorary degrees from London, Oxford, and St. Andrews as well as Cambridge. He was my tutor at Lincoln but his sharp theological mind was not attuned to the needs of those who would spend their whole lives preaching to mixed congregations of no more than averagely intelligent parishioners, preparing the products of Secondary Modern schools for Confirmation, visiting the sick at home and in hospital, trying to help the bereaved in the back streets. Neither Abbott nor Mascall was married. Christopher Evans was another unmarried prizeman from Cambridge who had been a Curate in Southampton for four years before becoming Tutor at Lincoln, and he was somewhat less academically oriented. Eric Mascall has since died (1993).

Geoffrey Bentley was yet another Cambridge scholar who had spent two years only as a curate in the Portsmouth Diocese before becoming a tutor and lecturer in ethics at Lincoln. For fourteen years from 1938 he was also Chaplain of Lincoln County Hospital and he gave us our first introduction to what is a large part of a priest's ministry, visitation and service-taking in Hospitals. He would vet the sermons we proposed to preach in Hospital (in theory that is; we did not in fact ever preach them) and I recall preparing an absolutely stunning sermon which took twenty minutes to read to him. It was then that I learned a lesson I have never forgotten, two lessons in fact, (a) that the attention span of patients in Hospital is no more than a few minutes, (b) that you never talk about illness to folk in Hospital. I learned much later, after being invited to preach at a bell-ringer's service, that one should never preach about bells to bell-ringers either.

In an interesting book of self-disclosures by a varied selection of members of the Church of England (*Revelations* by Mary Loudon) Dr. John Habgood, Archbishop of York, a scholar with a first class degree in Science ("I have no theological degree, all my DDs are spurious.") questions the custom by which he came to be a Vice-Principal of a theological college, Westcott House in Cambridge, with such limited parochial experience and having "only done eighteen months theology". He does not however question the principles or policy by which so many members of the staffs of Theological Colleges with minimal parish training became diocesan Bishops.

We had lectures on Liturgy from a Canon Chancellor of Lincoln called Srawley who had once written a book, and a Brother Edwin from Kelham tried to teach us how to sing the Office. From time to time we had "teaching weeks" when high-powered women from the Church of England Board of Education would come and induct us into the mysteries of teaching in school and Sunday school. They were the most practical and down to earth people who ever tried to help us. From them I learned to enjoy teaching in school and Sunday school; from them I learned the importance of gaining and holding the attention of children; and the art of story telling and illustration, which has been with me ever since, and which I have tried to impart to others.

Some of us were also inducted into the practice of prison visiting and twice in our course we were taken to a country village near the city and allowed to preach to an ageing Evensong congregation while one of the staff of the college sat at the back and took notes. Their comments at a discussion later were no doubt of some value, but they themselves were not interesting or eloquent preachers, and most of their sermons were theological expositions, totally unsuited to parish congregations, so little that would be helpful for the future was learned. This was not their fault. They were expected to achieve the unachievable, given their own background and training. Preaching must come out of experience not only of God's love for mankind, but of mankind's suffering and needs. The four staff only had twelve years parochial experience between them. At that time they had no children of their own, though Christopher and Geoffrey were married later, and their contacts with the so-called "working classes" with whom most of us would later have contact, were minimal.

The Vicar of St. Peter at Gowts (lovely dedication) in down-town Lincoln was a greater help. We met with his young people and learned about the problems of adolescence by assisting with his Youth Club. I remember how baggy the knees of his trousers were and I have a photograph of him to prove that my memory in this matter at least is trustworthy. He was obviously a man of much prayer.

We were not a large company, about forty men of diverse ages and varied backgrounds. John Ford, father of the TV newsreader Anna, had been an actor. One man had been an insurance agent, another had worked for a tobacco firm. One was blind. Some came from clerical families, others from non-Church backgrounds. Most had University degrees. There were no women and none from other denominations as there are at Lincoln today. We lived in a very close community with our lives dominated by community activities, prayers, meditation, lectures, meals, discussion sessions, sermon sessions, and the Chapel was the centre of our life. When I took a "teaching week" for the students at Westcott House, Cambridge, in the late sixties I remember being surprised at how little of the daily routine was spent in chapel, and how not every student attended, or was expected to attend every service. This was the sixties, the age of rebellion against authority and the establishment, and the virus, if that is what it was, had entered the Church as well as the rest of society.

In wartime little heating was available and coal for our rooms which had no central heating was in short supply. The attractive little chapel had no heating at all, so it was no wonder that we all suffered from colds from time to time. We were expected to be in chapel at 7:30 a.m. for Mattins, followed by daily Communion. At 9:30 a.m. we returned again for half an hour's meditation on a book or subject of our own choosing. Back again at 12.15 p.m. for the office of Sext (the sixth hour, the fourth of the seven monastic hours, lauds, prime, terce, sext, nones, vespers or evensong, compline). Evensong in the afternoon and compline at 9:30 p.m. Attendance was obligatory except at Evensong. The music was plainsong for the chanting of the psalms, Merbecke for the Holy Communion when sung, and hymns from the English Hymnal. At the beginning and ending of each term the Warden would preach a sermon, sitting in a chair before the altar, and other staff would address us from time to time during each term. The Angelus was rung at 12 noon to remind us that "the angel of the Lord brought tidings to Mary" and we said our own prayers internally when we heard it, wherever we were, and whatever we were occupied in doing. The routine was tedious and hard to make real. I have never found the recitation of psalms for the day helpful. There is so much that is unchristian among the glorious Hebrew sacred songs. Yet it was a most valuable discipline which is apparently missing from much theological training today.

This routine was often interrupted by the war. North of Lincoln was the RAF base at Scampton from which bomber planes flew regularly. From there flew many of the planes that attacked the Mohne and Eder dams with Barnes Wallis' "bouncing bombs" in 1943. Wallis was a much underrated aeronautical engineer who had designed the airship R-100 and played a leading part in the development of Concorde and swing-wing aircraft. At night when the air raid sirens sounded we would descend the steps into the basement of the College which had been a hospital in a previous existence, the basement being the old mortuary, carrying our blankets and spending an uncomfortable time until the "all clear" was sounded. A gruesome place to be.

If you look up the word "Lincoln" in a concise Encyclopaedia today you will find it described as "an industrial city (excavators, cranes, gas turbines, power units for oil platforms, cosmetics) pop. 1981, 76,200. A flourishing Roman colony, Lindum, with a big mediaeval wool trade. Paulinus built a church here in the 7th century and the 11th-15th century Cathedral has the earliest Gothic work in Britain. The 12th century High Bridge is the oldest in Britain still to have buildings on it."

The theological college stands not far from the Cathedral on a high hill and the winds from the Ural mountains blow straight across the cold sea upon them both. How cold it was for three quarters of the year! Cold, but mostly dry. Which is an apt description of the worship of the Cathedral in wartime. We attended Sunday Mattins as a body, in the magnificent setting of the choir, but Cathedrals are much too cavernous and empty for small groups of worshippers. They come into their own on the great Festival occasions. Nevertheless one could not help but be moved and influenced; as at Oxford, one was part of something, study, worship, a groping after truth, that had been going on upon the same spot for many centuries. The spirit of Hugh of Lincoln, Bishop in 1186 was still there. The spirit was there of the saintly Victorian Bishop Edward King, bishop from 1885 to 1910, who had been arraigned before the courts for wearing a coloured stole, and whose pastoral lectures were still in print and of continuing validity. There were in Lincoln aged worshippers who remembered being confirmed by Bishop King.

There was little evidence that the life of the Cathedral impinged upon or entered into the life of the "industrial city". Because of its industry Lincoln was the target of German bombers, and some damage was done, but on the whole the city and its factories were largely unscathed. The two worlds of industry and religion were then, and still are, poles apart. The Industrial Christian Fellowship was founded to bring the two worlds together. Does it still exist? Industrial Sunday was instituted to remind industry of its dependence upon the God who put the coal and iron into the earth, and to remind the Christian Church that part of its message is the redemption of the *whole* of life. So the Sunday was linked to Rogation Sunday when prayers are offered for the crops and the whole work of agriculture. In many churches and Cathedrals the products of industry were brought into Church in the same way that I used later on at Chertsey to bring the plough into Church on Plough Sunday in January.

The sermon was an important element in the worship of Mattins and as a prospective preacher I was keen to learn from the Dean, the sub-Dean and the Canons of Lincoln, so in my own kind of shorthand I wrote down every word that they preached. This was thought by my colleagues to be a kind of masochistic eccentricity, but I did learn how to expound a text (and how not to); I learned how important illustrations from "real life" are because there were very few in the sermons heard at Lincoln; how to hold your congregation's attention; and how to lose it. I was much influenced at the time by the published sermons of the Methodist, Leslie Weatherhead, who preached at the City Temple in London to a thousand people morning and evening. He was a master of the art of (a) creating an immediate rapport with his hearers; (b) illustrating from immediate and current experiences rather than from the lives of the saints of former centuries; (c) making the life and personality of the man Jesus come alive for ordinary people; (d) not being afraid to use humour - Weatherhead pointed out how much humour there is in Christ's teaching; (e) interpreting difficult Biblical passages and doctrines in language they could understand; (f) answering the questions that are being asked by ordinary folk about the Faith and not the questions which the Clergy think they are asking. Nor did Weatherhead break either of two other cardinal rules of preaching - do not indulge your own ego by quoting in Greek or Latin, and do not use technical theological terms, even basic ones like incarnation and atonement, without some explanation, however simple. Later, when I write about the training of Readers in preaching I shall have more to say about this vital subject.

The purpose of a theological college is to train ministers and priests of the Church not only in the Word of God, the Bible (for theology is no less a science than biology or zoology or cosmology), and the "word" about living things: animals, the order of the universe; but also in pastoralia, the 7 Sacraments, preaching and teaching, liturgy (worship) and the conduct of it, prayer and the teaching of it in so far as it can be taught, ethics (the moral values of human conduct and the rules and principles that ought to govern the exercise of those values) and Church history, including the history of other denominations. There ought also to be some instruction in the other world religions and certainly a simple course of psychology and an introduction to sociology, the origin and development, organisation and function of human society. Which plainly is a five year course at least. Those of us who had read theology at University were expected to stay two years at theological college, making five years in all. Those who had not a degree in theology were expected to spend three years. Clearly, too, only the fringes of a large part of such a course could be touched. It was frequently said by our tutors that they were not there to teach us all we would need to know about the practice of our ministry and priesthood. That would come with our ordination to the Diaconate. As Deacons we would be subject to our Vicars or Rectors and to them we must look for the practical side of our education in parish life. The Diaconate lasts a year, and in wartime we were expected to continue our study alongside our ministry and we would take a Deacon's examination before ordination. Today much more time is spent away from college working in parishes *before* being made Deacon, and this is clearly an advance on the method to which we were subject where, on the actual day of ordination we would be plunged straight into parish life with a Vicar whom we had seen but once at an interview, and with parishioners, Churchwardens, Church Council members, fellow clergy in the Deanery, whom we had never met.

At Lincoln we were well taught in some of the disciplines I have listed above, particularly in prayer and worship and ethical problems, but of other Christian Churches we learned little. A prominent layman from the Russian Orthodox Church in Paris did come to lecture us but all I remember from his discourse was that Orthodox Christians make the sign of the Cross from right to left rather than from left to right. That is not to say that what he gave us did not penetrate our subconscious minds, and I believe that to be true of much that we were given. It's like the breakfasts we have eaten - we may not remember them, but they have fed and sustained us.

What is the priesthood to which we had been called? Eric Abbott especially was concerned to interpret to us the Catholic and Biblical doctrines of it.

The word priest is a form of the word "presbyter" in more than one passage, but the phrase most used in the Acts of the Apostles is "apostles and elders" and mention is made of elders being ordained. The debate continues as to whether the elders and presbyters were one and the same, or whether the apostles acted in any way like a modern Bishop. What is clear is that some men were set aside to serve tables (the Deacons) and some had priestly functions. Much more important in deciding what the function of the Ministry was in New Testament times is a series of phrases or descriptions of a minister.

The most striking phrase is *"Man of God"*, which occurs twice in Paul's letters to Timothy, but is found no less than forty nine times in the Old Testament, referring to men such as Moses, Elijah, David, those who exercised either prophetic or priestly functions in the Hebrew hierarchy. Time and again Eric Abbott would refer to our future ministry as "Men of God", as Paul wrote to Timothy, that we might be "perfect, thoroughly furnished unto all good works." We were to be men separated out by God for a particular purpose, the ministry. To be a man of God, we were told, is to be concerned with the things of God, not just Church, Bible, Prayer Book, Sacraments, but life in all its complicated fullness as given us by God. We could only truly be men of God if we were men of prayer. The ministry of the man of God we were told, is to the *"people of God"*, not just those who came to Church, but to all people, old and young, rich and poor, intelligent and foolish, saint and sinner, male and female. We were to teach and preach that the Gospel of redemption is for the whole man, not for his soul only.

The word *pastor* was not much used at Lincoln, since it had largely been appropriated by the Free Churches as a description of their ministers but it is a good New Testament word, used of himself by Jesus, for it means shepherd. This indeed is the theme of the Bishop's address to candidates for ordination in the "old" service, for they, says the Ordinal (the people to whom we shall minister), "are the sheep of Christ which he bought with his death and for whom he shed his blood." There is no joy in ministry greater than the joy of caring for the flock of Christ. Sheep, incidentally, are not the cuddly lambs of holy pictures. They are rather greasy animals, difficult to hold, difficult to control, much given to straying into inaccessible places, tending to follow each other without much sense! I have always been grateful as I have remarked earlier, to H.L. Goudge, one of my Oxford mentors, for pointing this out in one of his sermons. But "shepherd of the sheep" is still a good description of the priest.

Then we were taught what it means to be a *priest,* one who in Old Testament terms makes sacrifice for the people, holds them up to God, and interprets the ways of God to men, and conveys to them His gifts of grace. We were well schooled into performing the functions of the priesthood, the administration of the Sacraments. The Deacon is allowed to baptise but he does not celebrate the Holy Communion until he has been priested. There are seven sacraments, so in addition to preparation for our function at the font and the altar, we were advised to learn the Communion service off by heart. I have always been grateful for this advice - not only because I can say the service from memory but also because it enables the priest to *look* at the congregation and give real meaning to the words as he says them. It seems that this advice is not given to modern ordinands. I find that very few priests of recent generations can take their eyes from the service book for more than a second or two. This breaks the contact that the priest must have with those who are with him in offering the holy sacrifice. We were also instructed in the meaning and administration of Confirmation, Confession (penance) Holy Order, Matrimony, and Unction (anointing with oil of the sick), and in the practical care of a vestry - "a Lincoln man is known by his vestry" we were told often.

It is undeniably difficult to train one who will not be taking marriage services for some time, or hearing confessions, or administering unction, in all those activities, but we were expected to prepare a course of study for Confirmation candidates. It was realised that this is an academic exercise, a matter of theory, and it would be a triumph of hope over experience if what we prepared was to be of any value when the time came for it to be put to the test. In those days very few books of such courses were available so we were working without much help. Nor can you prepare something for people whom you do not know but no doubt it was useful for us to put down on paper what we thought were the essentials of our belief. Today books and visual aids are available in abundance for the priest who takes the trouble to read and use them. Many parishes do not now treat preparation for Confirmation as we were taught to, as a sort of intellectual steeplechase to be run before the great day. Many believe, as we tried to persuade the Church in our Report "Christian Initiation" (more of that later) that children should begin their preparation for birth and growth in the Christian society at the earliest age possible and that Confirmation should not be the occasion of crossing a hurdle, but the time when an *adult*, already trained as a communicant should make an *adult* commitment and should be commissioned for his role as an *adult* Christian. This would normally be at a much later age than the usual fourteen, a time notorious for its instability and uncertainty.

Another phrase used of the minister in the New Testament is *"steward of the mysteries of God"*, which I suppose is another phrase for priest. This is how Paul refers to himself and his ministerial companions in 1.Cor.4. A steward in Greek is a dispenser, which is important, since the modern understanding of steward would be a man holding the Master's purse strings, Clerk of the works, in complete charge of all his master's property. That is not what the priest is. He is servant of God, but he does "dispense" God's grace through the sacraments, through preaching and teaching, through prayer and worship. In the Church of England as in the Roman Church, he also dispenses absolution, God's forgiveness, and benediction, blessing, not his own, for no priest is able to forgive or bless in his own right, but only as a chosen and ordained instrument. "It is required in stewards," writes Paul, "that a man be found faithful." This was a large part of our training and teaching - the total dedication, consecration, devotion, whatever you care to call it, to God and our people. We were committed to Christ within the Church which is called his "Bride" till death should us part. All these things Lincoln and its staff taught me.

We were such a close community at what was originally called "The Chancellor's School" of Lincoln, the Chancellor being an important functionary of the Cathedral, who in earlier days presumably had the training of priests in his hands, that we were all friends, but I had a close intellectual friendship with an interesting character called Henry Brandreth, some three years older than I, who had a special interest in "Episcopi Vagantes", wandering Bishops, who seem to have exercised their vocation as Bishops in some very strange places and circumstances. He allowed me to read the proofs of a book he had written on them and gave me the chance to review other books for periodicals with which he had somehow gained a connection. Later he became Chaplain of St. George's Anglican Church in Paris and Associate Secretary of the Church of England Council for Foreign Relations. Harold Last was another close companion, a brilliant musician and organist in the college Chapel, later FRCO, and lecturer in New Testament and Music at King's College, London, who in later years gave his knowledge and expertise to a number of public schools. Not all of us were cut out to be parish priests and it is one of the glories of the Church of England that we can use our talents and vocations as priests in schools and colleges, hospitals and factories, monasteries and other religious foundations, even in airports, as well as in parishes.

I was very anxious to be ordained as soon as possible. Church law says that a man must be at least twenty-three before he can be made Deacon. I had reached this age in August 1940, so I persuaded Eric Abbott to let me take the General Ordination examination early. This exam was normally taken at the end of one's second year in College. It covered Old and New Testament Studies, Church History, Worship, Ethics, Prayer Book Studies. I took it in May 1941, passed and was ready for ordination at St. Peter's tide (June 29th) 1941. Early in that year we had been urged to make contact with possible parishes to give us a "title", in other words, accept us as Curates when ordained. Normal practice then was for incumbents looking for a Curate to write to the theological colleges of the Churchmanship of their parish to be put in touch with likely men.

I was given three names by Eric Abbott, the Vicars of the parishes of Eastleigh and New Milton in the diocese of Winchester, and Windsor in the diocese of Oxford. Gerrards Cross was in the diocese of Oxford, so my contacts there were strong. I had been confirmed by the suffragan Bishop of Buckingham and had preached in my own Church by permission of the then Bishop of Oxford, Thomas Banks Strong, soon to be succeeded by Kenneth Escott Kirk, so although I went to see the incumbents in the Winchester diocese, I looked forward to the possibility of being accepted at Windsor. It is strange that even in those days we were told that really the proper place to start one's ministry was in the North, and preferably in a "slum" parish, so when I had seen the Vicar of Windsor, the Reverend Ralph Creed Meredith, and been accepted by him for a title after my June 29th ordination, I was considered to have chosen an easy option! I discovered that Windsor had slums too, many of them in the back streets behind the barracks, in the smoky hovels behind the gas works and a group of cottages called "Prince Consort Cottages", designed by Queen Victoria's husband, but with no back doors so that there were no through draughts and the rooms stank.

The two incumbents in the Winchester diocese would have been willing to accept me. Eastleigh liked "Lincoln men" and had two working there already, and New Milton (now called Milton) attracted me as being by the sea, but as it turned out Windsor was, I am sure, the correct choice. It is easy to see the hand of God in choices that have been made and I believe this to be so in my own case, but I have always been chary of claiming too much for divine guidance (shades of the Oxford Group) since I heard the story of the Free Church minister who had been offered a rather desirable pastorate. His daughter was asked by a friend whether the family was going to move. "Well, father's still praying about it, but mother's packing!"

It is more than fifty three years ago that I left Lincoln for Windsor and I am aware that memory is a fickle jade and a poor instrument of recollection, but all my memories of Lincoln apart from the cold, are good and happy. I have criticised the system then prevailing for the training of the priest, but I have no criticism of any of those who helped to train me. They were a scholarly and dedicated group of men, of a higher calibre as a group than those serving any other theological college of the day. They all became well known in the Church and held important posts, wrote valuable books and to them I owe very much of what I am as a priest.

To Eric Abbott I owe most of all, as did all the men who were trained while he was Warden of Lincoln. Until the year that he had a massive stroke he still sent birthday cards to every priest who had been at Lincoln in his wardenship. I suspect that he sent such greetings to all the students he had had in his two periods at King's College London, first as Chaplain and after Lincoln, as Dean. There must have been hundreds of them! I had been married on my birthday and he always noted that fact as well. He was a man of prayer and rare sensitivity to his students' background. He knew that I had been reared in a rather hot-house evangelical atmosphere, and this came out in the debates that we had about the Church. He respected that fact, and he knew that I would be influenced by the "Catholic" atmosphere of Lincoln. I was indeed so influenced, and made my first formal confession to God under his guidance. That was a humbling and difficult thing for an evangelical to do, but it was a turning point in my life. I have heard many confessions of other people since then, and I always gave the penance that he gave me. As well as the formal acts he said, "Go away and write down ten things to be thankful for." Not two things, not five things, but ten things to be thankful for. That was a reminder that however low we are, however much we feel oppressed, weighed down, kicked in the teeth by life, we must always be thankful to God. And there are so many things in my life that I am thankful for, having gone to Lincoln is one of them, for it gave me a balanced view of the Church. "Be an *evangelical* Catholic, Stanley," Eric Abbott would say. I have tried to be such.

A quietly spoken, gentle man, he never lost his touch, even in the exalted position as Dean of Westminster, meeting all the time with Royalty and the famous. It was probably not the position he should have been given. It wore him out and he suffered a crippling stroke. He carried on but had to retire and his death came earlier than it should have done.

In his pastoral sermons he quoted more than once a poem written in earlier days, by the Reverend C. Hutchinson, and given to us as the ideal at which we should aim. It was called *A Priest's Prayer To*

Jesus. It is out of date, sentimental, but it speaks of the loving depths
of the ministry to which Eric Abbott pointed us:

> When mothers with adoring eyes
> Bring babies to the baptistry
> And place them in these arms of mine
> Christ of Bethlehem, look on me.
>
> When boys come running down the street
> and take my arm in intimacy,
> and humble me with trustful love,
> Christ of Nazareth, look on me.
>
> When boy and maid stand side by side
> with glad and shy solemnity
> and my words make them man and wife,
> Christ of Cana, look on me.
>
> When I stand up to preach to those
> whose goodness and humility
> rebuke me till I flinch with fear
> Christ of the Mountain look on me.
>
> When this too human heart of mine
> Lies held in friendship's mastery
> and I am torn by too much love,
> Christ of Bethany, look on me.
>
> When in the room of death I stand
> to solace pain and to set free
> the labouring hearts of dying men,
> Christ of Calvary look on me.
>
> When I am happy as a child
> for simple joys, unconsciously,
> when I forget who giveth joy,
> Christ in glory, look on me.

When I go tramping over hills
that look towards the sunlit sea
under a sky of windy clouds
Christ of Emmaus, walk with me.

When, without maid or wife, I see
the years creep on me, solitary,
and round me a great loneliness,
Christ of the Garden, look on me.

When I am sorry for my sins
and run back haltingly to Thee,
With broken vows and empty hands,
Christ of Compassion, succour me.

When at the altar day by day
I handle the good mystery
with these unworthy hands of mine
Christ of the altar look on me.

When at the last I come to pay
the price of my mortality,
when sister Death shall close my eyes
O Master Christ, acknowledge me.

I have used the poem many times when I have been the invited preacher at Ordination services, and during interregna when I have been trying to help ordinary congregations understand what to expect from their new incumbent; and although it is plainly a personal prayer or meditation for the individual priest, I know it has spoken also to the laity who through it have come to a different understanding of their relationship with their parish priest and of his ministry. When I hear of clergy who "do not visit" or who have a less than loving relationship with their church officials and devoted workers, I am sad that they seem to have lost the vision of the priesthood which Father Hutchinson put before us. If I am asked, "What made *you* want to become a priest?" I have to reply, "Many things and many influences." It was undoubtedly a divine vocation, an actual "calling" from God, mediated through many voices. There was the atmosphere of worship participated in from an early age - the music, the words of the liturgy, of the Prayer Book and the Authorised Version, but also the influence of dedicated clergy, even the unfortunate Fred Crosby. Perhaps it was the challenge of sermons heard, of Confirmation class teachings. Indeed as William Cowper wrote: "God moves in a mysterious way." No stranger mystery than the making of this priest, one of St. Paul's "weak things". But priest I am, and priest I remain.

(At the end of 1994 I have been sent news that the college in Lincoln is to close, and is to transfer its work to Sheffield. Numbers in theological colleges have dropped from 900 to 627 in six years and there is an over-capacity of 120 places. Colleges such as Lincoln are being urged to move closer to universities, where new links can be forged with the community and with the Theology faculties existing there. For many of my generation the ending of the kind of residential community which gave us so much will be a sad occasion, but new conditions demand new approaches. Perhaps we were too enclosed, too sheltered, too inward-looking. Students for the priesthood will gain much from living and working in the world in which they will have to serve and minister. It must be hoped that the life of prayer and worship will not suffer. Stop Press! The Bishops have ruled that the move to Sheffield cannot now take place. From July 1995, Lincoln Theological College will no longer exist. How sad that is!)

CHAPTER 8

CURATE

"I was a pale young curate then."
W.S. Gilbert. "The Sorcerer"

"A Curate - there is something which excites compassion
in the very name of a Curate!"
The Rev. Sidney Smith "Persecuting Bishops"

"Almighty and everlasting God, who alone workest
great marvels... send down upon our Bishops and
Curates the healthful Spirit of thy grace."
A very necessary prayer in the Prayer Book.

(A) WINDSOR

It is typical of English perversity that an Anglican *Curate* is in reality a subordinate, when the word means that he is in charge - has a a cure; and yet is subject to a *Vicar* who is his superior and in a sense his employer. Yet the word "Vicar" comes from a root meaning subordinate, someone who acts in place of the overseer, the "boss". The French approach the matter more logically. M. le Curé is the Vicar and M. le Vicaire is the Curate! Leaving Lincoln I was to be a "Curate".

I was made Deacon on June 29th, 1941, St. Peter's Day, by Kenneth Kirk, Bishop of Oxford, a theologian, author of several books of philosophical theology such as *The Vision of God* and *Conscience and Its Problems*; a tall, remote, academic figure with a thick body, thinning hair and heavy jowls. He was another example of the Bishop elevated from Milton's "olive grove of Academe" to be overseer and pastor of clergy and parishioners of whom he had minimal experience.

I remember little of the pre-Ordination Retreat in which we were required to spend several days in prayer and meditation in preparation for our ministry, but I do recall the text of Bishop Kirk's address to us at the end of the Retreat. It was taken from Peter's first letter, chapter 5 and verse ten: "The God of all grace who called you into his eternal glory in Christ will himself, after your brief suffering, stablish, strengthen, settle you on a firm foundation."

What the "brief suffering" was to consist of was not explained - there was to be plenty of suffering in the next fifty years, but the firm foundation has never shifted. On that day I was stablished, strengthened and settled into a way of life and ministry which has continued until now. I was to be a recognised and set-apart "man of God" and a "shepherd of the sheep". I have failed in that ministry many times, but I have never not been conscious of the guidance, the help and the forgiveness of God. Something does happen when a Bishop, (himself a sinner, but a successor by direct line to the Apostles and thence to our Lord Himself,) lays his hands upon the head of one who is to be made Deacon, or the Deacon who is to be ordained Priest. The congregation present at the Ordination, and the clergy present, pray earnestly for the gift of the Holy Spirit to descend upon the unworthy.

The words of the Ordinal are moving and full of deep meaning. The rite used in 1941 was that in the 1662 Prayer Book. The Archdeacon (whom I had met only once) presented the three of us who were to be made Deacon, to the Bishop, affirming that we were "apt and meet for our learning and godly conversation, to exercise our ministry duly to the Honour of God and the edifying of the Church." After prayer the Bishop posed a series of questions which we had to answer in the affirmative...

... that we trusted we were inwardly moved by the Holy Spirit to take this office and administration upon us.

... that we believed ourselves to be truly called by Jesus Christ to this Ministry.

... that we believed the canonical Scriptures of the Old and New Testaments to be a revelation of God Himself, fulfilled in Jesus Christ.

... that we would "diligently read the same to the people assembled in the Church" where we would be appointed to serve.

Then the *duties* of the Deacon were rehearsed...

... to assist the Priest, especially at the Holy Communion.
... to read the Scriptures and the Homilies. (The Homilies were sermons or instructions prepared in Elizabethan times for the use of clergy who were illiterate, as many were, and unable to prepare their own sermons and instructions. They would have been of little use to a wartime congregation in the Royal Borough of Windsor, and probably hadn't been heard for several hundred years!)
... to instruct the youth in the Catechism.
... to baptise infants in the absence of the priest.
... to preach if authorised to do so by the Bishop.
... to "search for the sick, poor and impotent people of the parish, to intimate their names to the Curate (i.e. the Vicar) so that he could exhort (!) and relieve them with the alms of the parishioners and others."

Following our assent to these propositions we were exhorted to fashion our lives and those of our families according to Christian doctrine, to make us all "wholesome examples of the flock of Christ". Then, finally, we promised to obey the Ordinary (a mediaeval name for the Bishop in his juridical office) and other Chief Ministers, "following with a glad mind and will their godly admonitions."

The Alternative Services Book of 1980 has taken most of these promises into its Ordinal, in more modern language, and has added a few more about accepting the Christian faith as the Church of England has received it, about promoting Christian peace, unity and love, among all Christian people, and about continually stirring up the gift of God that is in us to make Christ known to all men.

After prayer for the gift of the Holy Spirit and his sevenfold gifts of grace the Bishop lays his hands upon the candidate's head saying "Take thou authority to exercise the Office of a Deacon in the Church of God..." and, handing him a New Testament (in Greek in our case), he says, "take thou authority to read the Gospel in the Church of God and to preach the same..."

There are some excellent changes wrought in the 1980 Ordinal, especially the Bishop's prayer before the laying on of hands, the moving Litany, the Proper Preface and the post-Communion sentence and Collect, but I regret the passing of the phrase "Church of God" and the substitution of "your Church". I have always believed that I was ordained as a minister in the Church of God and not just in the Church of England. No doubt this is the intention of the new service, but it is not made clear. In the new Ordinal, at the ordination of Priests, other priests share the laying on of hands with the Bishop.

I had bought a pair of new shoes for this great occasion. It was a very foolish thing to do; at the end of the service my feet were swollen and uncomfortable. But after the lunch and Bishop's reception which followed the service, and which was attended by our relations and friends, the clergy who had examined us and rehearsed us for the occasion, together with the priest who had taken the Ordination Retreat, and my mother and step-father (a Baptist duly impressed), I made my way to Windsor, and to my new lodgings down by the River Thames in the small semi of a non-churchgoer, the only parishioner found by the Vicar who was willing to take me.

The Parish Church of New Windsor was built at the beginning of the 19th century with a large gallery on three sides and slim iron pillars. It was a time when architects were beginning to experiment with iron as a building material. The first iron bridge had been erected in 1779 but the iron and glass Crystal Palace was not built until 1851, so the 1803 Church of St. John the Baptist was something of a pioneer. It held more than a thousand worshippers when full to the galleries. Not far away there was a "daughter Church" of All Saints, built at the turn of the century at a time when it was thought that provision must be made for the "working classes" who would not be comfortable worshipping with the landed and other gentry at the parish Church, dedicated to St. John the Baptist.

St. Peter's Day, June 29th, was superseded in the ecclesiastical calendar by the Sunday within the Octave of the patron saint, John the Baptist, whose day was June 24th, so my first appearance as the new Curate and Deacon was at the 6:30 p.m. Festival Evensong for a Patronal Festival. It is the church service which of all the thousands of services I have attended or conducted, stands out most clearly in my memory and affection. The church was crowded and I was to be Chaplain to the special preacher, the Bishop of Buckingham, Philip Eliot. This was a particular joy and privilege to me because he had confirmed me at Gerrards Cross St. James, in 1931, ten years before.

It was an extraordinarily hot June evening and poor Bishop Eliot, who had a lame leg, was perspiring freely in his heavy cope and mitre as he processed gamely round the church for the first hymn, followed by me, his temporary Chaplain. I must not pretend that I was not conscious of the eyes of the great congregation straying from their hymn books to catch a glimpse of the new young Curate in his clean new cassock, surplice and scarf, with his rabbit-furred BA hood hanging down his back. I hope that the agony I was enduring in my new shoes was not evident! The singing of the choir and the playing of the well-qualified and expert organist were magnificent, and I have never heard that great hymn "Thy hand O God has guided" so well sung as it was in procession that day. I still have the scarf. After thirty years the cassock was too small. The white BA hood became a red MA hood in 1943.

On Monday June 30th, the next day, I came down to earth. I was expected in the Vicar's study at 9 a.m. together with my fellow Curate, an experienced priest who had spent several years in Canada, and who was in charge of All Saints, Arthur LeDieu, a married man with children.

My Vicar, Ralph Creed Meredith, was an Irishman (typically Irish to have a Welsh name!) born in 1887, a graduate and Philosophy prize-winner of Trinity College, Dublin, who had served his first curacy in Dublin. He then moved to England to a series of curacies in Leeds and in the Midlands where he had married a daughter of the Aynsley China family and had become first priest in charge of the conventional district of Bournville - home of the Cadbury's and their factories - and then its first Vicar. In 1924, having signed the document (which I also had signed in 1941) which accepted the right of the Church to invite us to serve overseas in the colonies and Dominions, Creed Meredith was sent to New Zealand as Vicar of Wanganui in the North Island. There he was a dynamic and "successful" incumbent of Christ Church, opening up remote areas of his parish and establishing two mission churches, until illness forced him to return to England in 1931 for surgery which at that time in New Zealand was not obtainable. After a long illness and a lengthy convalescence he had become Vicar of Cheshunt in Hertfordshire, which he left after eight years to become Vicar of New Windsor, a parish in the gift of the Lord Chancellor.

My first Vicar was a remarkable man. He had been ill for most of his childhood and he had a short and twisted lower leg, yet he was an athlete of no mean ability, a champion player of badminton and tennis, and a pioneer of croquet in New Zealand. He had not been to school, having been educated privately. His father was a well-to-do lawyer in Dublin, Sir James Creed Meredith, and he was one of a large family, for Sir James' first wife had died and he had married again. One son by the first wife became a judge, another a high ranking Indian Civil Servant. One daughter spent fifty years in India as a CMS missionary, another married a Curate in Northern Ireland; there were two more sons and Ralph was the younger of the two. A remarkable family altogether, and its influence continued throughout Ralph's life. At no time had he ever lifted a hand even to boil a kettle or clean his own shoes, and he regarded it as a solemn duty of his class to provide servants for his wife and family, however poor he might be. In this he was of course a product of his own Victorian generation and his own Irish upbringing in an affluent household with many servants. No blame attaches to him for any of this, though it did cause some tension, even unhappiness, in his relations with his daughter Myfanwy who had other ideas and saw no reason why she should not be friends with the daughter of the Church room cleaner at Cheshunt, or go out to dances with "the boy from the gas office." When I married Myfanwy, Ralph expressed some relief that I had rescued his daughter from - I am not clear what, but rescue her I had, and I was accepted as a worthy son-in-law in spite of the fact that my own father had left school at the age of ten and there had certainly been no servants employed in our family apart from the occasional "daily woman" and pram-pusher.

My Vicar was a hard worker. Though he found early rising difficult and he was always five minutes late for the weekday celebrations of the Holy Communion, he was rarely in bed before midnight, writing letters and composing his sermons in long-hand.

He was an assiduous visitor and trained his curates to be the same. Each Monday morning we had to produce a list of homes and people we had visited the previous week, with some note about them, with names of possible confirmation candidates, people needing sick or other kinds of visits, and services we had attended. We were expected to attend Evensong which was said daily in the parish Church if we were not otherwise gainfully engaged. All this was to be recorded on a sheet specially printed for the purpose. The Vicar took literally and seriously the admonition to the Deacon in the 1662 Ordinal that he should "search for the sick, the poor and impotent people of the Parish, to intimate their estates, names and places where they dwell unto the Curate (Vicar!) etc..." If there were fewer than twenty names on my list of visits I had plainly been slacking! Once a month I would visit each one of the forty-eight old women in the Victoria Street almshouses and then I could happily fill the printed sheet with names.

It was the Church that performed most of the social work in those wartime days. The almshouses had been built by the Church. The all-range schools, infant, junior, and senior schools in the parish were all Church schools and each Friday I would spend the morning teaching the children in one or other of them.

It was the Curate who helped to staff the large Windsor Youth Club of three hundred boys and girls in premises opposite the Parish Church. We also had our own youth club of Church boys and girls in our own premises in Church Street with some forty or fifty members. With them I played the usual club games, table tennis, snooker and the rest. With them I produced a yearly missionary play, and a Nativity Play held in All Saint's Church. I am amazed at the self-confidence of this young man who organised the productions, found all the costumes, constructed the angels' wings for the Nativity plays out of wire and sheets and silver paint. The wire had come from a fence in the allotment of the Churchwarden, Mr. Foreman. The material for the wings was an old sheet from my second landlady, Elsie Hawes, a true saint of the Church. I have the photos of those plays still, and I am ashamed that I never thought to iron the costumes which I had discovered in an old trunk in the Church Room. They look so creased! But I am sure that in wartime few noticed and none minded.

In the town Youth Club where I spent several evenings a week I organised a choir and conducted concerts with the minimum of musical knowledge or skill. I instituted a discussion group, played games, and generally made myself useful, as required to by my Vicar who, with his eye to the main chance, had persuaded the Youth Club Committee to pay £100 a year towards my stipend. This put me at some disadvantage because he had not told *me* the position and I only discovered it when the annual balance sheet was posted on the Youth Club notice board and my Vicar had been complained to that I was not earning my money. Nor was I, for my whole stipend was only £200 a year and I was certainly not spending half of my fifty or sixty hour week (I was a bachelor so had nothing much else to do except work) in the Youth Club. I fear that for this regrettable lapse on my future father-in-law's part I did not always feel ready to "Obey the one to whom the charge and government over me was committed, with a glad mind." I felt he had acted with something less than a proper candour towards me.

But I was only the Curate and that put me in my place. There were other irritations. Each month I was expected to go and *collect* my cheque for £16.3s.4d *in person* from the Treasurer. There was no reason why the cheque could not have been sent to me, or handed to me on a Sunday or even pushed through the letterbox of my lodgings. No, I must go cap in hand and ask for it.

Then there were the sermons. I had been "licensed" by the Bishop to preach, and the usual rule for Deacons was "not more than once a month", because in the year as Deacons we had to study and prepare for examinations for the Priesthood. So I prepared a monthly sermon with great effort and research and much re-writing, and presented it to my Vicar. He was very critical when I happened to use the word "I". "Who are you?" he would write alongside. Though he had an immense amount of experience and could have told many good stories about his life as a Curate in the slums of Dublin, Birmingham and Leeds, or about New Zealand, he would never say "I", always "One". I felt that to be pedantic and it reduced the personal value of what he was preaching. Certainly we preach Christ crucified, but we also must preach "that which we know, have seen and handled of the Word of Life." "One" cannot do that without saying "I".

On the first Sunday of the month the Mayor and Corporation of Windsor attended morning service and one Monday morning in Staff Meeting, the Vicar said, "I think you could be allowed to preach one Sunday when the Mayor is present. You realise what a great honour that will be, don't you?" The Mayor was the local grocer. He was also the Churchwarden, so he had heard me preach anyway, but before the great day there had been a local election and there was a new Mayor, a woman who only came to Church when this great event took place. So it was thought to be an even greater honour for me to preach to the Lady Mayor! I think it was a good thing that I should have my pride humbled, though at the time I resented the suggestion that to preach to a Mayor was an "honour". I believed it to be an honour to preach to anyone in the name of Jesus Christ, and I did not think, and do not think, that God takes note of the worldly status of those who listen to the Gospel, however well or however badly it is preached.

Dear Walter Foreman, the Churchwarden who pulled his allotment fence to pieces to give me wire for the angels wings, I shall for ever be grateful to him! After one sermon he said to me with a loving but painful frankness, "Why do you look so *miserable* when you preach?"

"Do I? I wasn't aware of it. Thank you very much!"

For several sermons after that I would put at the top of the first page in large capitals "SMILE!" Would that more Churchwardens and sidesmen would be honest with us clergy and tell us truly what they felt about our conduct of services, our sermons, our attitudes at meetings. I was more than a little pleased when, as Myfanwy and I were preparing to leave Windsor for Bath, her father said, "Thank you for your preaching ministry. Your sermons have been greatly valued here."

Like most young unmarried Curates (I suppose) I had lots of invitations to take tea with widowed and spinster members of the two congregations. There was Miss Goddard of Frances Road, a tall, spindly lady of advancing years, with a black velvet band round her throat, much lace and what used to be called a "modesty vest" held in place by a cameo brooch of blue enamel. The tea was dispensed from a large silver teapot sitting on a silver cradle. Each cup was heated from another silver pot holding boiling water, over a spirit lamp before the tea was poured into the delicate porcelain cup. Tea first of course, then the milk! China tea was the norm but Indian was available on request! The sandwiches were of white bread and thinly sliced cucumber, approximately one and a quarter inches square, no crusts. Only one cake was available, a deliciously light Victoria sponge. Our conversation was equally delicate, concerned with the progress of the war and various doctrinal problems. From time to time, at Christmas usually, Miss Goddard would present me with a 5/- Book Token to buy myself a work of theology (she assumed), but I must confess that I rarely spent it on such. On my next visit she would ask me what I had bought with the token and blushing inwardly at the manner in which I was being "economical with the truth" I said, "A book about the American Civil War". It was in fact Margaret

Mitchell's *Gone With The Wind*, at 3/6d and considered at that time to be a rather risqué novel, not to be read by nice people. Miss Goddard would not have approved.

On Sunday afternoons I conducted a service, with talk, for a large group of adolescent boys and girls called the "Senior College". They had their own service book, a simplified form of Evensong, and up to about thirty youngsters attended regularly at 3 p.m. Is there a single parish in Britain today where thirty boys and girls aged from thirteen to eighteen will gather on a Sunday *afternoon*, in a Church, to worship God and learn about their Faith? After the service we would walk, if it was fine, in Windsor Park, strolling up to the "Copper Horse" at the end of the elm-lined Long Walk and back, discussing life and love, human relationships, friendship, death, war and sacrifice. I valued these walks and talks more than I can say. On them I got to know the hopes and fears and loves of many young people in a way not to be found in the ordinary Youth Club, certainly not in the big Town Club with its three hundred members and where I was resented by the paid woman leader who was a Baptist, and by the voluntary man helper who was also uncooperative, and where almost none of the young people came to the precious "Chapel" set aside for their use and a late evening "Epilogue". That chapel was a lesson in how not to "do" religion. It had small Church pews donated from the Castle and a set of beautifully tooled leather unopened and unused Prayer Books (1662) with the Royal Victorian monogram on them. The only thing that could be said for it was that it was a "quiet place" to which a boy or a girl could come on their own for a while, or where they could have a chat with me on some problem or difficulty in their family life or school life.

I prepared many of the "Senior College" for Confirmation and in subsequent years I discovered how high a proportion of them had remained loyal and active in their Christian life. This was especially true of the older boys who were called up and had to maintain their faith in the Forces and of some of the girls who voluntarily joined the women's services, the ATS, the WRAF and the WRNS. Windsor was a "garrison town" and soldiers were much in evidence, and this was a continual reproach to a non-combatant in a "reserved occupation". Swastikas continued to be daubed on the walls of the town Youth Club, and the occasional "Heil Hitler" was muttered behind hands when I came into the Club. These were the reactions of a minority of prejudiced, bigoted and ignorant young people for whom, as their parents had probably taught them, all Germans and all with German names were the enemy.

They were not the reactions of the older parishioners who were universally kind to me, nor of the teachers in the schools where I taught "Scripture" on Fridays, nor of the staff of the famous King Edward the Seventh Hospital where I visited the wards, took services and early on a Sunday morning after I had been priested in 1942 - at 6 a.m. I recall - celebrated Holy Communion for the Sisters and Nurses. Hospitals seem to have been a large part of my ministerial life and I regard the exercise of a Christian ministry in them as an essential part of a Priest's fulfilment of his divine office and vocation. It was at Windsor that I learned about what pain and suffering and war can do to human beings at all ages, to their minds and souls as well as their bodies. G.K. Chesterton writes of the "easy speeches which comfort cruel men." I discovered that no easy speeches can comfort the dying or those in deep pain. It is natural for the clergyman to fall into the same easy assurances which relatives give to their sick kinsfolk about illness, when more often than not from the man with the clerical collar, the patient expects *spiritual* help and strengthening.

The wards of the Edward the Seventh Hospital in 1941-1943 were full of soldiers from several nations, rescued from the countries overrun by German forces - French, Belgian, and Polish, as well as English. For the English soldiers I would write letters; for the Poles I could do little but hold their hands and look into their eyes with compassion and sympathy. My knowledge of French was fairly competent and the French and Belgian soldiers appreciated a somewhat halting conversation in their own language. My abiding memory of these Hospital days is the stink of gangrene and the sad eyes of those who had lost limbs and were far from their own homelands.

On more than one occasion I visited parents who had just received news that their son had been killed or was posted missing from the battlefield. This was a sad experience, for what could one say? "No greater love than this, that a man lay down his life for his friends"? No easy speech could overlay the basic wickedness of war, or assuage the pain and misery of loss. In any case, what did I know of suffering or of the distress of bereavement when wives had lost husbands or mothers had lost sons and sisters had lost brothers? My lot had been cast in pleasant, tranquil places. Could one speak of the sacrifice of Christ on the Cross at such a time? On Remembrance Sunday we sang Sir John Arkwright's *Hymn For the Fallen* with deep feeling, and we saw at that time no contradiction or blasphemy in the verses that equated the sacrifice of our soldiers with the sacrifice of Christ...

> "These were his servants, in his steps they trod
> Following through death the martyred Son of God;
> Victor he rose; victorious too shall rise
> They who have drunk his cup of sacrifice."

Today many parish clergy refuse to allow that hymn to be sung, much to the disgust and resentment of old soldiers and sailors and airmen, especially those who remember from personal experience the sacrifices of the Great War, or the Hitler War.

In 1942, after a year during which I had to study set books and write a 10,000 word thesis on a subject of my own choosing I had to take my priest's exam and have an interview with the Archdeacon. On a lovely hot June day I cycled the twelve or so miles over to Wargrave where he had a charming house by the Thames. We talked about the books I had been required to read, about my work and my relations with my Vicar. Had I any difficulties which I wanted to discuss with him? No, I was very happy in my work. We sat in deck-chairs on his wide lawns and drank tea and ate more cucumber sandwiches. I left to cycle back to Windsor. I never spoke to the Archdeacon again.

I chose for the subject of my thesis: *A Study in Repentance*. It is a fascinating theological subject much neglected by the modern theologian who would rather discuss the guilt feelings implanted in us by our religious upbringing and the teachings of the Church. In the accounts of Jewish religion in the Old Testament, the "people" are always being urged to repent of their sins, though the noun "repentance" itself occurs only once, in Hosea. More often than not it is *God* who repents - even right back at the beginning where He actually is sorry that he made man at all (Gen 6.6). This of course is not a sorrow for sin, but a figure of speech, attributing to Him the feelings that He would have had if he were a man. Perhaps, looking upon the world, He has those same feelings today!

The first element in the preaching of both John the Baptist and Jesus was "Repent!" In the preaching of Jesus, pre-eminently in the parable of the Prodigal Son, or the Forgiving Father as it should be called, repentance is allied with, and inseparable from, forgiveness. I had to work all this out, using what I could glean from the early Fathers and the Mediaeval "Schoolmen" on the subject, with appropriate references. Psalm 51, David's great prayer of penitence after he had confessed to the sin of putting Uriah to die in the forefront of the battle so that he might steal Uriah's wife Bathsheba, is a classic expression of penitence. A study of the Lord's prayer and the relationship between our own sin as forgiven by God, and the forgiveness we must offer to others, was a key theme of the thesis, as was the cost of penitence and the cost of forgiveness. Then came Baptism - "repent and be baptised" was the constant challenge, from John the Baptist and Jesus, right through to the first conversions and on beyond. My impression is that the preaching of the modern Church largely lacks this element. Perhaps because we are afraid to talk about sin and would rather use words like "disposition" and "aberration", "deviation" and "abnormality". Since we do not preach repentance we do not preach the greater message either - forgiveness. Enough sermon.

My efforts were well received and as the one who gained most marks in the exam I was appointed "Gospeller", the Deacon who would read the Gospel in the service of the Ordination of Priests. This was no great achievement since there were only three Deacons to be ordained at Petertide in 1942, once more in Christ Church Cathedral Oxford, under the hand of Kenneth Kirk. I had my final interview with him, and all I remember of it was that he advised me to read the whole of Jane Austen's works each year, and that I was not to marry or hear confessions without his permission. Not until I had been in Priest's orders at least five years in the case of confessions.

Ordination day was as hot as it had been at a similar date in 1941. My shoes did not hurt on this occasion. We had a valuable three day Retreat beforehand, and relations and friends turned up in force, or as much force as the exigencies of travel in wartime allowed. I suspect that John Cross, my step-father, used some of his farming petrol allowance to bring my mother and sisters to Oxford.

The day of a man's Priesting is the greatest day of his life, paralleled only by the day of his marrying. There is a similarity which has been noted for centuries in the Church. The Church is called the "Bride of Christ" and in the Roman Catholic Church in particular the celibate who is to become a priest is reminded that he is giving himself to Christ as a man gives himself to a woman in marriage. The metaphor or simile falls down of course at many points, but just as the marriage service requires the partners to promise love and loyalty "till death us do part", so the Church has always taught that the priesthood is a lifelong commitment. Once a priest, always a priest. This I was taught at theological college. This I firmly believe, and in the 1662 service which was used on that day the following phrases occur:

"The Church and Congregation whom you must serve is His *spouse* and His body."

"Consider with yourselves the end of your ministry towards the children of God, towards the *spouse* and body of Christ."

The framework is similar to that of the service for making Deacons, with corresponding questions and answers, but in the 1662 service the Bishop gives a long and moving, almost frightening, exhortation about the weighty duties and responsibilities of the Priesthood:

"You have heard... of what dignity and of what great importance this Office is... how weighty the charge to which you are called...to be messengers, watchmen and stewards of the Lord; to teach and to premonish, to feed and provide for the Lord's family: to seek for Christ's sheep that are dispersed abroad and for his children who are in the midst of this naughty world... that they may be saved through Christ for ever." "And if it should happen that any member... take any hurt or hindrance by reason of your negligence, ye know the greatness of the fault and also the horrible punishment that will ensue." "See that you never cease your labour, your care and your diligence... that there be no place among you either for error in religion or for viciousness of life." And there is much more in the same vein!

At the laying on of the Bishop's hands, and those of other priests today, the Deacon is told: "Receive the Holy Ghost for the Office and work of a Priest in the Church of God... whose sins thou dost forgive, they are forgiven and whose sins thou dost retain they are retained.

Be thou a faithful dispenser of the Word of God and of his Holy Sacraments." The newly ordained priest is then handed a Bible with the words: "Take thou authority to preach the word of God and to minister the Holy Sacraments in the congregation where thou shalt be lawfully appointed thereunto."

So now I was authorised and able to pronounce the Absolution, to celebrate the Holy Communion, to perform marriages, and administer the Sacraments of baptism and Holy Unction. I was not authorised to perform the other two, Ordination and Confirmation, though in some communions priests are allowed to confirm. There are Anglican clergy who would like to do this, but the Bishops would object strongly.

My training continued. I learned what to do with my hands when I celebrated the Holy Communion - how to say the service by heart, without always looking at the book. I visited, took baptisms and funerals, prepared young people and older people for confirmation, took charge of the choir when the organist left to serve in the Army, showed film slides for missionary societies, conducted study sessions and Bible study groups, took tea with old ladies and rode my bicycle furiously round the parish. I had a cyclometer on it and was able to record a total of 4000 miles in my two and a half years in Windsor. In 1943 I acted as "Correspondent" (Secretary) to one of our Church Schools which Creed Meredith was determined to enlarge as a good Church Secondary School. He made a great appeal to employers in the area, especially in Slough, an industrial town near Windsor, and raised many thousands of pounds to improve and enlarge the School, telling the employers how excellent were the girls who came from this School. He wrote to the Queen and asked permission to invite Princess Margaret to open the new school and to call it "Princess Margaret Rose School". The Queen agreed and Princess Margaret who was born in August 1930 came to perform the opening ceremony. It was a great ordeal for a young girl not yet thirteen, and when at a meeting many years later I reminded her of the occasion she remarked, "Yes, it was one of the most awful things my mother made me do!"

My life at Windsor was made pleasant by the kindness and affection shown to me by the Hawes family. I was not very happy in my first "digs" by the River Thames and this had become known in the parish in some way, and one Sunday morning after service one of the Choirmen came up to me and said: "My wife and I would be willing to give you a couple of rooms in College Crescent if you can afford thirty shillings a week." I went to see Elsie Hawes and moved in the following week. Not only did she give me two rooms and full board for that paltry sum, but I was allowed the use of another room which had a large dining room table to do my writing and typing on. How she managed I can only guess. I remember that spam pie was a staple food. I was not surprised when she said rather diffidently one morning after breakfast, "I wonder if you could afford another 5/- a week?" which of course I could and did. I spent little on myself apart from books, although with my first month's cheque of £16 I went to Dyson's the music shop on Castle Hill and bought a wind-up gramophone, and three records, for the total sum of £5. I had no radio of my own and there was no TV in the house, but music was a boon and a balm to a jaded soul after a day's visiting and meetings. The family at No. 11 College Crescent will always have a large place in my fond memories.

Unlike some of my contemporaries I was very happy in my first curacy. I had a strict disciplinarian as a Vicar. From him I learned the discipline of the desk and the study. However hard he had worked at night, in the morning Ralph Creed Meredith's desk was clear, with a pen and a pad of notepaper the only articles on it. From him I learned to answer letters the same day if possible. This stood me in good stead years later in Rochester where my Secretary and I would begin work at 8.30 a.m. clearing the desk of the large morning post, and making notes for the future replies to letters which had expected no immediate answers.

Each morning had to be set aside for reading and study, for sermon writing and preparation of talks to various groups, and for Hospital talks and confirmation classes. At 2.15 p.m. I was expected to set out on a round of visits, and apart from occasional appearances to take said Evensong in the parish Church at 4 p.m., I was expected to stay out visiting until 5 p.m. Two evenings had to be spent at the town Youth Club, and two at the Church Club. There were often other evening meetings and study groups. The rest of the time, as they say, was my own! I do not begrudge this strict time table, nor do I apologise for being a willing supporter of the "work ethic" attributed to Protestants. I think it was right to expect hard work from a bachelor. When I became a married man I had to look at life with different eyes, and had perforce to balance the needs and obligations of a family against those of the "job".

Times have changed drastically since the 1940's. The Church now has to battle against forces of moral slackness, cynicism and unbelief which we did not know. The family has disintegrated. The number of divorces has risen from 25,000 a year to 150,000 a year, and children from separated parents and broken families do not join Sunday Schools or Church Youth Clubs. Instead they roam the streets and the discos. When the priest makes most of his visits, it has to be in the evenings when the TV will *not* be turned off for him, or on Saturdays and Sundays. The State now provides those things once provided by the Church, and no one feels they have to go to Church or be friendly to the Vicar, to obtain shoes for their children, money, food and coal for their fires, as many did in wartime Britain. There is no *real* material poverty in the welfare state. That will be denied by some, but the apparatus is in place to ensure that no one *need* go naked, hungry, cold or shelterless. That was not so in 1941. On one of my school teaching days I was in the school at lunch time and saw the children eating their sandwiches. One child had two thick pieces of bread spread with stale lard. That was her lunch. There *was* some abject poverty in the Royal Borough of Windsor and I had to minister to it.

In March 1943 my life was changed. Mary Myfanwy Patricia Creed Meredith, the Vicar's daughter and first born, aged twenty-six, came home from New Zealand. She had so loved her childhood in Wanganui from the age of eight to fourteen that she had determined to go back when she had the chance. Trained as a teacher of Physical Education at Dartford PE college, she had done her initial two years stint at a school in Clacton, and then had emigrated in December 1939 to a Presbyterian boarding school called "Iona" at Havelock North in New Zealand's North Island, on a three year contract. The war was not going well in 1942 and she thought she might never see her parents again, as bombs had been dropped near Windsor on several occasions. After a frightening voyage in convoy she had arrived back at Liverpool in March 1943. My first sight of her was of a beautiful, dark-haired, brown-eyed, smiling face in the Vicarage pew, a few feet away from the lectern where I was reading the lesson. She was dressed in a tan-coloured suit, with a broad-brimmed matching tan hat. Do I believe in love at first sight? Of course I do. Do I believe in mutual attraction at first sight? Indeed I do.

We met that night after Evensong in the Vicarage drawing room - a snack supper with bridge rolls and fish paste. My experience of the opposite sex was minimal. I had escaped the attentions of the many young girls in the Senior College, and more especially of one of their mothers who had thrust her daughter at me on every possible occasion, who had offered me a daily glass of milk after Friday mid-morning Communion and had insisted on a monthly tea party before Evensong on Sundays. When I met Myfanwy all thought of Frances and her sister Doris fled. She was so vital, always smiling and with a most attractive New Zealand lilt to her voice. In those days almost everyone smoked and Myfanwy had a stock of American cigarettes called "Lucky Strike" and after supper she threw a packet to me. A strange beginning to a life together which lasted forty-eight years.

She bought a bicycle and together we cycled everywhere. We walked in the Great Park. We went to the cinema. She obtained evening work at the Slough Social Centre taking evening classes in PE and indoor games. I would cycle to meet her at the end of her evening. I went to tea at the Vicarage. She came to tea in my room at No. 11. We wrote to each other every day, sometimes twice a day. We went out to dinner with friends. We fell deliriously in love. We had met for the first time in March. On May 6th, 1943 we got engaged on the leather davenport in the Vicar's study - not the desk - the sofa. It was 12.30 a.m. and everyone in the Vicarage was in bed. I should have gone home hours ago. We heard footsteps descending the stairs outside the study door and it opened. "Stanley! What are you doing here at this time of night?"

It was Myfanwy's mother, Sylvia.

"We have just got engaged!"

"I can't help that Stanley! Go home!"

Abashed but walking on air (what a cliché!) we parted at the front door and I went home.

The official announcement went into the papers on May 10th and we were married thirteen weeks later to the delight of the whole parish who turned up in force to see Myfanwy walk to Church when they had expected at least a local taxi.

It was a very hot day, my birthday, August 17th, and the Church was crowded with eight hundred people. The reception in the

Vicarage garden for several hundreds was organised by the Mothers' Union with tea and sandwiches. The Merediths were teetotallers, so the toasts were drunk in lemon squash or tea. I gave the worst speech of my life, so Myfanwy said! That night we stayed at the Great Western Hotel in Paddington station and in the morning took the train to Penzance in Cornwall. The train was packed with soldiers as well as civilians and I had to stand most of the way. We had written about fifty letters trying to find a hotel or boarding house near the sea for a honeymoon, without success. We landed up in a primitive farmhouse at a village called Morvah, near the Pendeen lighthouse on the north Cornish coast. The taxi from Penzance station to Morvah at about 9 p.m. at night cost £10, more than two weeks stipend. We were too much in love and too tired after an eleven hour train journey, to protest at such a charge for a mere 7 miles, but there were no buses. If we had protested we would have been met with the usual wartime reply "Don't you know there's a war on?" Nevertheless, from that moment on we were "in love" with Cornwall.

The honeymoon was an almost total disaster. It rained for thirteen out of the fourteen days. The coast was shrouded in fog and the fog horn sounded relentlessly. We could not sleep on the hard flock mattress and neither of us had ever shared a room with another person. We were over-tired by the excitement and exhausting wedding ceremonies. No doubt we made love too often as well.

I know that clergymen should not project their own unhappy marital experiences on those to whom they may be giving advice in wedding preparation talks, but since that occasion I always warned prospective brides and bridegrooms not to expect too much in the first days of marriage, and to postpone the honeymoon for at least a year. Today, of course, many of those who get married in Church have been living together for some time anyway, so the advice would be superfluous.

We returned to our little flat in Bolton Crescent. It had been added to the house of the Headmaster of the Royal Free School, a Colonel Froome, as a "granny flat", but granny had died. It was one room down and one room up, with a ladder between the two, with a tiny kitchen of sorts with a small gas oven, below the ladder. After Church one Sunday morning very soon after our return from Cornwall, I got back to the flat to find a small joint of roast beef lying on the carpet under the ladder, with the baking tin and a pool of cooking fat alongside, plus some roast potatoes. From the room above came the sound of heart-rending sobs. Myfanwy had been well fed in New Zealand which could not, during the war, find export markets, so everyone there had lived on butter and cheese, milk and lamb. She was therefore, to say the least, at that time, a well-built woman. She was too big for the tiny kitchen, and in attempting to baste the beef had dropped the tin. A veil must be drawn over subsequent events.

We enjoyed our little home when things had settled down and we entertained my fellow clergy of the district and their wives, Myfanwy's fellow teachers, and some parishioners, particularly the young; though the "College" girls were not so keen to come to my home as they had been before I married!

(B) BATH

When Myfanwy became pregnant it was plainly time for me to find a new cure. My salary was at that time £220 a year, out of which I paid £104 a year for the flat, and plainly Vicar Meredith did not want a young married curate with a baby on his staff. He knew that he would not get as many hours work out of me as he had done when I was a fancy free bachelor. I needed more money to keep a wife and child, so we parted amicably. We left for Bath on January 1st 1944.

After various applications to Vicars and Rectors through the columns of the Church Times which came to nothing by mutual consent, I became Curate of the parish of All Saints, Weston, Bath, at the princely stipend of £250 a year plus a house. My new Vicar was Prebendary Francis Bromley, pronounced, as I was firmly told, "Brumley", a seventy year old widower who had been at Weston for a very long time and was regarded as something of an ogre by the parish. His previous curate, Laurence Fussell, had been with him all through the war and had left to be Vicar of Wellow a parish in the same diocese of Bath and Wells. Laurence's wife had been a great help in the parish and Prebendary Bromley expected Pat (Myfanwy) to be the same, in spite of the fact that she was pregnant. This was plainly impossible, and Vicar Bromley never forgave her for the fact that she would not take on the job of Enrolling Member of the Mothers' Union.

Myfanwy had become "Pat" very soon after we met because, she said, no one could pronounce or spell her Welsh name. That is, she became "Pat " to all except her own family who refused to use the name. I thought this to be quite illogical, as they did not use her first name, Mary, and they had given her Patricia as her third name anyway. All her school and college friends had called her "Miff", a name frowned upon also by her family. It was even further a strange attitude since her brother, James Noel Michael Creed Meredith was always known as Michael.

I worked hard as curate of Weston, but my Vicar was a sad, unhappy, cynical old man. He should have retired when Laurence Fussell left for Wellow. Once again I had a big Youth Club, and an enormous "Bible Class". I spent many hours as Chaplain to the large Hospital in the parish, the Royal United Hospital, Bath. I visited assiduously and refereed, without much technical knowledge, the village youth Football Club, the All Saints. There was a senior club as well but luckily I was not asked to referee them. I had hated football at school. We had very good congregations and several senior naval Officers, Captains, and Rear Admirals, were regular attenders at Church, as the Pay and Pensions department of the Navy was based in the Bath area.

My Vicar called himself "an old-fashioned High Churchman", a phrase without much meaning since all it meant was that he used the 1662 Prayer book and did not like the 1928 alternatives. He did not hear confessions and we did not wear vestments, or observe any of the so-called "high Church" services in Lent or Advent, or at other times. But he did stick to the old Prayer Book, and once told me, when on "Industrial Sunday" I had used some special prayers for industry prepared by the Industrial Christian Fellowship, "we do not use in this Church prayers which cannot be found in the Prayer Book." This was quite inconceivable to me and I said so. The 1662 Prayer Book was based upon words written originally in 1549, two hundred years before the industrial revolution which had transformed the face of Britain. Bath was in many ways an industrial city, and firms such as Stothert and Pitt had large factories in the city. Indeed they had been targeted in air raids on Bath. Where would one find appropriate prayers in a mediaeval base for a 17th century book? I assume that he was not able to retire for financial reasons, because he hung on way beyond the time that he was able to do his work or minister effectively. He was too worn out to write sermons, so he would take a volume of Charles Kingsley's addresses or some later volume, and he would preach from it without acknowledgement. He did it very well, and very few would have known.

He was always criticising the junior clergy in the area and once said to me - "that young man over at... sits on his backside in his study and expects people to come to him..." Dressed always entirely in black he was a brooding figure in Weston. His recreation was to play bridge with several elderly people in the parish, and in the summer to play bowls most afternoons and evenings with the men. During our time in Weston Peter was born in June 1944 during an air raid on Windsor where Pat had gone for the birth, and Jill was born at home in 28 Eastlea Road, Weston, in October 1945. The war ended while we were there and there were great celebrations, street parties and services of thanksgiving for the ending of the war in Europe in May 1945, and in the Far East after the dropping of the atom bombs on Japan in August of that same year. The bells were rung again and the blackout came down, but austerity continued for some years after. American troops had been stationed near Bath for some months before the allied landings in Europe in June 1944, and many of the village girls had taken themselves down into the city of Bath in the evenings, and at weekends, to go out with them. The number of children born out of wedlock rose and the number of babies in the Children's Society home in the parish increased. I had to baptise many of them. Eleven at one service was my record. Some of the girls had a great shock when they gave birth to black babies. They had gone out and slept with what they thought were white soldiers, but many of those "white" men had had black antecedents on one side or the other, and the black babies were "throwbacks".

Pat was anxious to get back to work, for even £250 a year and a house was not enough for a family of four to live on. We sold many of our wedding presents and I sold a large number of books back to Blackwells of Oxford. We sent our old clothes to a firm in Victoria Street, London, who paid us a few shillings for them. When Pat obtained a post which gave her a few hours teaching at the local Technical High School, and I ran a Course on RE for "O" level candidates at the Evening Institute, we had a few shillings extra and employed a lovely old Somerset lady whom we called "Nanny Hayward", to push the pram out for the afternoon two or three times a week, which gave us some respite. The next nanny was not so successful. She was a Mrs. Smith who assured us that Peter was well looked after until one day we saw her shopping in Woolworth's in Bath. Peter was at Mrs. Smith's basement flat being looked after by the lodger, and we can trace some of his nervousness in later years to this incident. To be left in a dark room with a total stranger at an early age must have been a frightening experience for him.

When Prebendary Bromley decided to retire and a new Vicar came it was time for us to leave too. We were not sorry. Weston had not been a happy cure, for I was frustrated at not being allowed to do any of the things in the parish that I had wanted to do. I was young and had new ideas about parish life and work with various groups. I had ideas about worship, about the use of the Church schools, about conferences and teaching weeks, that had been put down by the tired old priest. We had plenty of manpower and woman power in the parish, plenty of willingness to learn and participate in parish development, but none of it was being used. It was time, I felt, for me to have my own sphere of responsibility. I did not expect a "living" after six years as a Curate, but a "sole charge" in a larger parish was possible, where there were two churches. There were not many things about Bath that we would miss except perhaps ground coffee from the shop in Milsom Street at 3/6d a pound, Bath Oliver Biscuits, and occasional visits to the Theatre Royal where a New Zealand friend of Pat's was working. We had seen and heard Richard Tauber in person at the Pavilion, and I had preached to a thousand people in Bath Abbey. We enjoyed taking our friends, some of them from overseas, round the old City of Bath with its Pump Room and Royal Crescent. The famous Assembly Rooms had been destroyed in the "Baedeker" air raid in 1942. We had no car, so all our trips into the countryside were by bicycle, with a child each on the back, or by train to Bathford or Limpley Stoke.

I had *not* enjoyed the endless wartime queuing for fish and meat, for baby food at Boots, for the occasional Fuller cake or Foort's huge dry, sugarless, tasteless biscuits. We had *not* enjoyed the weather which seemed to be endlessly cold and wet. In the winter of 1946/47 the snow drifts lay six feet deep in Weston. I had not even enjoyed my first garden, since the soil at No. 28 Eastlea Road was solid clay. But we *had* enjoyed making new friends, the Bones, who remained faithful correspondents until they died. Neville was Peter's godfather;

and the Stares across the road who had a boy, David, of the same age as Peter. They had a car too, a small Standard 9, and were very generous to us in the use of it. During a visit from Pat's brother Richard, eighteen years younger than she, who was plainly sickening for whooping cough, both children and I caught the dread disease and it took us months to recover. We gave it to our neighbours and their children who were not best pleased. We would walk daily around the houses going one way, and they would do the same walk going the other way and we could hardly bring ourselves to greet each other. We did not enjoy good health in Bath!

I had requested an interview with the Bishop of Bath and Wells in his incredible moat-surrounded Palace in Wells but Bishop Bradfield had nothing to offer me, so once more I turned to the pages of the Church Times and saw there an advertisement for a priest in charge of All Saints in the parish of Chertsey in Surrey. Eric Abbott from my days at Lincoln had recommended me to an old college friend of his who was patron of the living of Steeple Claydon, the home of the Verney's, but though the then owner of the estate and I had got on well together, it did not seem a right move. We had lunched on cold roast lamb and potatoes in the huge first floor ballroom of Claydon House, attended by one aged and rather decrepit maid in lace apron and Lyons type "Nippy" head-dress.

The Claydons were not for me, in spite of the continuing presence of the spirit of Florence Nightingale who had lived in the Hall for many years. So to an interview with the Vicar of Chertsey, in the Diocese of Guildford, Cuthbert Lempriere Holthouse I went. He was a gentle, unassuming, diffident man with a delightful second wife called Theodora. She was indeed a gift from God, a lovely woman of ample proportions, always welcoming and always smiling. In spite of the fact that I lunched with them (again!) on cold lamb and potatoes garnished with a pickle that had grown a mould, for which an apology was made in the letter which accompanied the offer of the curacy, we had seen eye to eye on many matters and I was happy to accept. The stipend was a small improvement - £275 a year and a house, plus the Whitsun offering.

I was not sorry to leave Weston, All Saints, though we were sorry to lose our friends. The sad old Vicar had even said to me while I was preparing for our last Sunday there, "Mind now, we don't want any farewell sermons!" He wouldn't even let me say "good-bye" to the parish in my own way! Very inhibiting it was!

(C) CHERTSEY

We arrived with furniture in our new curatage in Eastworth Road, Chertsey on August 17th 1947. Pat had obtained a full-time post as PE mistress at Twickenham Girls Grammar School, so financial considerations played less of a part in the decision to leave Bath. We had also obtained the services of a former maid at Windsor Vicarage, a charming, attractive blond-haired girl, Peggy Gidden, who came to us as "nanny-housekeeper" at some very low salary plus keep, and her own room in the 3-bedroomed detached house in Eastworth Road which went with the "job". She was a great success and stayed with us many years, looking after the children, running the Guides at Chertsey and at Shottermill, and being a friend to Pat, until, with the children happily at School, she left to become a nurse at Hackney Hospital. Having left school at fourteen, as so many young people did in those days, she had no "piece of paper", but the potential was there and only needed to be discovered and brought out. She ended up as an Assistant Matron of a large London Hospital, having made her mark as a sister Tutor because she already knew all the illnesses to which children can be heir and how to deal with them, as well as how to make egg custard and all the other delicacies with which sick patients are to be won. All this from *practice* on our two children, Peter and Jill.

St. Peter's, the parish Church of Chertsey had a long and distinguished history. Cranmer had written a large part of the 1549 Prayer Book in a former monastery alongside the Thames. But the ancient Church had been ruined inside by the Victorian decorators. The town was frequently referred to us a "dump" for it consisted largely of housing estates built between the wars, and long roads of semi-detached and small detached houses running in all directions to Staines, Addlestone, New Haw, Weybridge and Woking. It had a good railway service to London and was in the "commuter belt", not far from London Airport as it was called then, now Heathrow. The population in 1947 was about 10,000, it is now more than 15,000, Pat was able to get to her work in Twickenham by train.

The daughter Church of All Saints of which I was now "Priest-in-Charge" had been built of red brick in 1901. Correspondence in the archives shows that the then Vicar had *instructed* a portion of his congregation, presumably those who lived in the Eastworth Road area, henceforth to take themselves on Sundays to All Saints and not the parish Church. I was thrilled to have my own cure and I must record that Cuthbert Holthouse was very good to let this rather active young Curate have his head. We met regularly for "staff meetings". He allowed me to write about All Saints in the parish magazine, and the only point of contention we ever had was in the matter of the Electoral Roll. The Roll, as its name implies, is a list of all those who are willing to identify themselves as members of the Church of England. They become entitled, by signing the roll, to elect the Parochial Church Council at the annual parochial Church Meeting, held just before or just after Easter. The Rules governing the Roll have been slightly changed since 1947 but at that time it consisted of those of either sex who were eighteen years old or upwards, baptised, resident in the parish, not members of any other religious body, or if not resident in the parish, had attended public worship in the parish during a period of six months prior to enrolment.

I did not believe then, and I do not believe now, that the electoral roll is a true record of committed Church people. Certainly every regular worshipper should put his name on the roll, but my quarrel with Vicar Holthouse was that he tried to get people to sign the roll, even knocking at doors to do so, who were not regular worshippers, in order to boost the numbers on the roll. A glance through any Diocesan Directory which records Easter communicants and the number of those on the Roll, demonstrates the strange divergence between the two figures. Taken at random and without identifying them, in the Guildford Diocese there were parishes with 300 on the roll and 70 Easter communicants; 220 on roll, 280 communicants; 266 on roll, 373 communicants; 170 on roll, 95 communicants. At Chertsey the number on roll vastly exceeded the number going regularly to Church. It may seem a small matter but to me it was a matter of basic honesty. The other problem of the Roll is that few regard it as a sign of their obligation to do what the Roll was intended to do - to provide a voting body at the Easter "Vestry" meeting. In many parishes with hundreds on the Roll, only a few dozen attended the annual meeting to appoint the Churchwardens and elect the Church Council.

Congregations at the parish Church were small but very loyal to Cuthbert Holthouse. I have remarked earlier that I was grateful to a Windsor Churchwarden for being honest with me. If only the worshippers at St. Peter's had been honest with their Vicar. He could not be heard beyond the front pew but no one had told him so. St. Peter's is a large and echoing building, and though the Vicar had good things to say, and though his conduct of services was reverent and thoughtful, why should people go to a cold and rather ugly building to hear only murmurings? One consequence of this was that the congregations at All Saints began to grow. The choir expanded, in spite of the fact that the organist I inherited was over eighty, deaf, and suffered from arthritis in her fingers.

It was sometimes disconcerting to hear the organ begin to play in the middle of a lesson or just as I was starting to pray! When I discovered on my first Sunday that the organ was still being pumped by hand, by a devoted and most loyal old pensioner who was blind, but who found great difficulty in keeping the bellows full, it seemed to be obvious that my first money raising task would be to fit an electric motor. We did this, and at the same time added two much-needed stops. The organ-blower was quite relieved to give up his chore. The total cost of this work was in the region of £110 and the money was raised by a letter of appeal which I personally sent to more than a hundred local worthies, including the shopkeepers, doctors, dentists and other professional and commercial notables. Looking back, I am amazed at my cheek in asking strangers for money for a Church organ, and some of my correspondents must have approved the new Curate's audacity because they sent me cheques and ten shilling notes. Our dentist was a Mr. Murray Bruce and I remember still the letter he wrote with his contribution of 10/-. It was rather sharp and sarcastic since he was not a churchman and said so, but he admired my effrontery and hoped that many others would do the same.

When the work on the organ was complete I invited six organists to give public recitals lasting an hour or so after Evensong on successive Sunday evenings. This was something new in Chertsey's church life and the recitals were well attended and the "silver collections" as folk left completed the fund raising effort. I had spread my invitations as high as I could, and though Dr. Harris, the organist of St. George's Chapel in Windsor Castle, could not take part, Anthony Caesar, a Music Scholar of Magdalene College, Cambridge, a master at Eton and already a FRCO, did. We met many years later when, now an ordained priest, he had become a Queen's Chaplain and Sub-Dean of the Chapels Royal, at St. James' Palace. He could not clearly remember, more than thirty years later, his visit to an insignificant daughter church to play on a rather undistinguished organ. Another achievement was to obtain the services of a then famous cinema organist, Harold Ramsay, who was a brilliant executant and later became organist at the great Mormon Tabernacle in Salt Lake City in the United States. He came to give his recital in riding boots.

Poor Miss Mallam of the arthritic fingers was not invited to give a recital and very soon afterwards I had to ask her to retire. This she did with the greatest reluctance, not being willing to admit that the task of organist was now beyond her. A year or so later she died and her sisters accused me of hastening her death by taking away from her the only thing that made her life worth living. This I thought to be unfair, but it introduced me to the problems of personal relationships within church life which anyone with a "sole charge" had to deal. In other circumstances the burden could have been placed on the Vicar!

At All Saints I was inducted into the perennial problem of the Church - money raising. In 1947 there was already in existence an embryonic stewardship scheme called the "All Saints Circle" but it had few members. It was an envelope system. This we expanded until we had more than a hundred members each making a contribution each week at a figure known only to the recorder. I thought it would be important to let it be known that a worshipper was a regular subscriber to church funds and names were inscribed on a colourful board in the porch, in the form of a circle. We had no church hall, so the All Saints' Committee agreed that we should build one. The Vicar and his PCC were of course kept informed of what this active daughter Church was planning! They had no objections but I suspect that they had some reservations in case the upstart child should upstage the parent.

A kindly local architect prepared the plans at little cost to us, and another good friend made a magnificent model of the proposed building which sat in the porch. The Diocese had no objections and we began to raise the necessary funds. The total cost of the hall which was to be built on to the East end of the Church on a piece of grassland adjoining was to be £7,000, and it would have provided a much needed meeting place for clubs and societies not only of the Church but of the local community, and for all ages. By the time I left Chertsey for Shottermill we had raised more than half of the money. What happened to it I do not know. There was at one stage a suggestion that the money should be used for repairs to the parish Church which would have been a disgraceful betrayal of all those who had worked so hard for the project. I assume that the money has been swallowed up in the parish finances anyway, since during the long incumbency of George Archibald the parish found it impossible to appoint a priest in charge of All Saints, or raise enough money to keep the church going, so it was pulled down. I am prejudiced of course, but having left it in a flourishing state, with a large Sunday School, keen workers, a steady income, a zealous body of young people, I can only regard its demise as a tragedy for a parish which so badly needed it as a spiritual powerhouse, a place of care and concern, a household of faith and worship and teaching, for half the fifteen thousand people who now live in Chertsey.

Opposite the Church in Eastworth Road was an unusual foundation called the "School of Handicrafts". Such foundations do not exist now, for under a mass of legislation in recent years the work that they used to perform is now the responsibility of the local authority and the various social services departments. The School of Handicrafts was a private, independent foundation for deprived boys who had been sent to it by local councils as in need of care and protection. They were a sad collection. One boy had seen his father kill his mother; another had been found in a bus shelter in Esher and, unbelievably, had been named John Esher; another was the illegitimate son of a peer of the realm, cast off by his father. There were thirty or forty of these boys being looked after by a remarkable little man and his buxom wife, Mr. and Mrs. Henry Portwood. They had two assistants, a husband and wife, and a fifth member of staff who ran the small farm attached to the school. The boys attended the local school, Stepgates, in Chertsey, but also had handicraft training in farming, boot and shoe repairing, carpentry and elementary engineering. The boys came to morning service at All Saints and I prepared them for Confirmation during their time at the School. Some of them did extremely well and took up good positions in later life after they had received further or higher education. One became a priest. Once a year in the grounds of the school we held a grand fête which raised for those days a magnificent sum of £200. It was also the scene of the "All Saints' Flower Show", an event attended by all the local flower societies at which the grower known locally as the "Dahlia King" would mount a splendid and imposing display of that rather gross and harshly coloured flower, some of the blooms being a foot across. Home made cakes and jams would be judged, my own rather cloudy marmalade and rather pippy raspberry jam not being among the winners. What would the Church achieve if it were not for the dedicated and devoutly committed folk like the Portwoods? Eventually the School had to close, the boys were dispersed, the buildings sold to the Roman Catholic Church, and the Portwoods went to Bristol to take over the imposing premises of the YMCA there.

Chertsey had once had a large Church School and the Church retained the buildings when the local authority built a new school at Stepgates. On several week nights in the old Church school premises, Elizabeth Derry, a teacher at the local Girl's Grammar School, her sister Constance, and I, ran a flourishing Youth Club. It is almost laughable now to recall the kind of things we did with those youngsters. Miss Derry taught the girls how to make gloves, I taught the boys how to make balsa wood aeroplanes and models. We played table tennis with them and always ended with a "religious" talk and an epilogue. We had discussions and debates, and as at Weston Bath we ran a small library and play reading circle. For those days we were in a small way pioneers, for it was an "open" club, with no strings attached, no regular church-going required as a payment for entry.

The Derry sisters were a great and dependable strength to the parish and especially to All Saints. They supported every effort we made to make All Saints a place of influence within the community. They ran the two branches of the Sunday school, which was held in the church because we had no hall, the infants in the vestry, the juniors and seniors in the Church. They gave full support to meetings of the Sunday School PTA. This was an idea of mine which I have not met elsewhere whereby as in a day school, parents and those who taught their children would meet socially, and discuss what we were trying to do in the Church on Sunday afternoons. We did not get a large number of parents (very few fathers!) but that is the experience of the day school as well. Those who came found it valuable and interesting. It was all part of my training to become eventually an incumbent, with the powers and responsibilities, the awesome freedoms and daunting authority of "the Vicar". The Derry sisters retired to Padstow and some years later we met again when we bought "Zansizzey", and we enjoyed sharing memories of All Saints' Chertsey.

When Cuthbert Holthouse moved to another parish and I had spent three happy and profitable years at All Saints, I felt it was time to move again. In those days it was expected that a curate would spend time in at least three parishes before he aspired to become an incumbent. Ten years was thought to be a necessary period of probation for what the dictionary calls "being able to take rational decisions without supervision", a good definition. I wrote to the Bishop of Guildford, who replied that "if you are patient for a while I may be able to offer you something in the near future". Meanwhile my new Vicar was George Archibald, aged thirty-eight, who had been trained at the High Anglican Theological College at Kelham, had served as a Chaplain in Eastern Command from 1944-1947, and as a Curate in three parishes in the Diocese. He came from being in charge of the conventional district in which the new Guildford Cathedral was to be built and he came with a high reputation as a fine parish priest. We were very much of an age. I was thirty-three and he was only five years older than I, so he left me very much on my own in the final months that I spent at All Saints. He was a shy man who found it difficult to communicate and this vast parish was more than he could cope with. Chertsey should have had two or three curates to do the necessary chores even in those days when clergy were more available than they are now.

In October 1950 the Bishop of Guildford, one Henry Colville Montgomery-Campbell, a true Anglican eccentric, wrote to tell me to arrange a meeting with the Archdeacon of Surrey, at that time the Rector of Haslemere, who had in his gift the living of St. Stephen, Shottermill, near Haslemere. The system of patronage in the Church of England is a cause of some debate, and to many, of real worry and concern. Patrons come in many shapes and sizes. They can be Bishops or Diocesan Patronage boards, private individuals, University Colleges, the Crown, the Lord Chancellor, trusts of particular churchmanships, Cathedral Chapters, schools, almost anyone or any body in fact. For example, the parish of Chertsey was in the gift of the Haberdasher's Company and Christ's Hospital (school) alternately. George Archibald had been at school at Christ's Hospital, so in the eyes of the Patrons, he was plainly a strong favourite for the parish against all other comers. It is not a good way to choose a Vicar, just because he has been to a particular school.

Archdeacon Ritchie took me round the parish of Shottermill which lies at the West end of Haslemere geographically and the East end socially, and I called to see the Vicar who was leaving, Leslie Towner, his wife and three grown up children. He had been Vicar from 1939 until 1950 and had seen the parish grow in population. After eleven years he felt, as we all do after so long a period, that he had no more new ideas to offer. "It is a good thing to move," someone once said of the clergy, "because all your sermons and all your wife's dresses are new." I was offered the "living" and accepted it.

Being a priest in charge of a "sole cure" is an essential preparation for the work of an incumbent, and not all clergy are fortunate enough to have that advantage. I learned much at All Saints, including how to take the chair at committee meetings. I learned some of the vagaries of human beings, especially the religious kind. I learned why people come to Church and why they don't. "I don't ever come to Communion", said one lady to me in the street, "because I can't bear the thought of drinking blood." How does one answer that statement? It is a more common feeling than some will admit. The street is not the place to have a discussion on such a weighty matter.

I learned to cope with the frustrations and disappointments which follow the collapse of some pet scheme. I learned that many people resent the role of the Church in society, in the education system, in social care and even in matters like a "Flower Show" being called after the local Church. I remembered the local resentment that the two football clubs in Weston, Bath, should also be called by the name of All Saints. I learned in my regular visiting that there are folk in the back streets and in the big houses who don't particularly want to talk about the weather or what is on the radio (TV now); but *do want* to talk about God, about how difficult they find it to believe in Him in a world of so much pain and suffering, about their disappointments in prayer. At Chertsey I saw much more of my fellow clergy in the meetings of the Deanery Chapter and in various conferences. We discussed all the same things that clergy still discuss - problems with baptism and Confirmation, cemetery fees, Bishop's rules and regulations, forms of worship, family services and so on. The first talk I ever gave at a Chapter meeting in 1949 was on Baptism, *Infant or adult, exclusive or open?* I recalled that it was that same subject on which I had become heated at theological college discussions in 1940, and when I sat on an Archbishop's Commission on Baptism and Confirmation in 1970, we had exactly the same debates. Today, more than twenty years after that Commission the problems are not resolved.

We enjoyed our little detached house in Chertsey. On Saturday afternoons we would take the children on to St. Anne's Hill, or to the lock on the River Thames on the back of our bicycles. When I inherited a little money from my father's estate, held up by the legal gentlemen for fourteen years since his death in 1934, we had our first car, a blue Vauxhall 10 for which I paid the exorbitant sum of £420, second hand.

It was while we were in Chertsey that I began to take an interest in Divine Healing, and also in the work of the Diocese. This was initially related to the fact that the Diocesan priest who was concerned with the pastoral care of the deaf asked if he could use All Saints each month as a centre to which the deaf folk in the area could come for a Communion service. As he celebrated the Eucharist his lay assistant translated the words of the service into fluent sign language for the worshippers. "The deaf hear" was one of the evidences that Jesus sent to John the Baptist when he asked if Jesus was the promised one. The healing of the deaf and dumb man (the two impediments go frequently together for obvious reasons) which is recounted in Mark chapter 7 is an example of a miracle where Jesus used natural means, saliva, as well as prayer and touching with his hands. It is interesting also for the fact that "Jesus took him away by himself" for the healing ministry. The ministry to the deaf is a little publicised ministry. There are at the moment fifteen full time and thirty part time and non-stipendary Chaplains who have learned the sign language that they must use to communicate with their "parishioners" who are scattered throughout a diocese. The Church's Board for Ministry has a staff member, Canon James Clarke, a man himself involved in the ministry from his time in the Leicester and County Mission to the Deaf since 1968, to represent the interests of the hundreds of thousands of deaf people, to support the Chaplains and provide training opportunities for them.

At All Saints, as I visited the sick at home, and patients in Hospital in Chertsey and Guildford, it was borne in upon me more and more forcibly that the ministry of healing was being sadly neglected by "the Church". A large part of Christ's own ministry had been to heal, and his command to the twelve and the seventy when he sent them out on their mission was a twofold command: "preach the Gospel", "heal the sick." We said prayers for the sick in our Church services, though in those days we dare not mention them by name but they were very formal and very generalised prayers. I believed as we all did, that all healing comes from God, and it can be mediated in a hundred ways, through doctors and nurses, psychiatrists and practitioners in alternative medicines, as well as by relations and friends; but was there a particular contribution that the Church could make? I knew that certain individuals had gained great notoriety for their individual healing ministry and some of them held crowded meetings and services of healing at which it was reported that some had thrown away their crutches, others had got up out of their wheelchairs. One famous healer claimed that he was indwelt by the spirit of Louis Pasteur, and the claims of Christian Science and Mrs. Mary Baker Eddy were well known. But the Church of England? Yes, there were two societies, the Guild of Health and the Guild of St. Raphael, which published little books of prayers and healing services, and to which parishes and individuals could be affiliated. We linked up with the Guild of St. Raphael and began to use the threefold ministry of the ancient Church - prayer, the laying on of hands and holy unction, anointing with oil. Theory was put into practice and our healing services became a feature of parish worship. It would be wrong to claim that many miracles of healing took place, but certainly many people's health did improve. One lady who was bedridden was able to get up and live a normal life.

Often, where actual healing did not take place a new attitude to sickness was discovered. We began to see that we are responsible by the way we live for a large part of our own and society's sickness. "Prayer does not change things, it changes people" is an old Wayside Pulpit statement. It is very true in the realm of divine or spiritual healing. I always used the laying on of hands when I visited the sick, and in certain situations, particularly poor eyesight or deafness, I used holy Unction. This is anointing with oil which has been blessed (often by the Bishop on Maundy Thursday) and is kept with the Reserved Sacrament for the purpose of healing, not just for the anointing of the dying, as in the use of what is called Extreme Unction.

It was in Chertsey that I learned the value of this threefold Ministry and I developed it as Vicar of Shottermill and wrote a great deal about it for parishes when I came to Rochester.

From time to time I would be asked to bury suicides whose bodies had been dragged up out of the river Thames. Those were sad occasions, for often the bodies had been unrecognisable and were of people quite unknown. A funeral where there is not one mourner is a most melancholy event. In the geriatric wards of the local hospitals I saw human beings without dignity or hope and I became convinced that both the Church and the medical profession should take the question of voluntary euthanasia more seriously. To these two problems, suicide and euthanasia I shall return later, when I had to face them in personal context.

In Chertsey I became aware of the importance of the Diocese. In the Oxford Diocese I had no dealings with Diocesan House, and had never, as a very new young Curate, been invited to take part in any diocesan project or committee. Then too it was wartime and travel was difficult and the Oxford diocese was a very large one, consisting of the three counties of Buckinghamshire, Berkshire, and Oxfordshire. In the diocese of Bath and Wells the same was true. We had few diocesan events. The only one I was ever asked to attend was a meeting that Bishop Wand held to inform us what was being proposed in the 1944 Education Act for Church schools. I remember his defence of Church schools, especially the village school, and saying, "I care passionately about them because I am a product of one of them". Vicar Creed Meredith was a great advocate of Church schools and indeed had been a local Secretary of the National Society which had been responsible for building many of them, but it was a sign of his own double standard that he would not send any of his three children to one of them!

In the Guildford Diocese I was appointed to various Diocesan Committees, and began to be interested in raising money for the new Guildford Cathedral on Stag Hill. I was particularly interested in the Children's Committee and the Missionary Committee. Pat's aunt was a famous CMS missionary in India and Pakistan so we linked up with her and she visited us to talk to the keen missionary supporters in the parish. The training of Sunday School teachers was in those days a matter of growing concern and I took part in leading training days and residential conferences for such teachers. This was not something new. I had attended similar gatherings when I was a young fifteen year old teacher at Gerrards Cross in the 1930's. But there had been advances in teaching techniques since then!

While we lived in Chertsey Pat continued to teach. She loved her job at Twickenham. She was a brilliant teacher of netball and hockey, and her teams won all the local schools competitions, as they did later in West Sussex when she taught at Midhurst Secondary Modern and Grammar Schools. As I shall write in a later chapter, being the wife of a parish priest is no sinecure. Indeed it carries with it considerable burdens. There is first of all the resentment of Church people that the working wife will not have time, especially if she also has children, to be the "unpaid curate". That is even more true if her husband follows, as I did at Weston, and was later to do at Shottermill, men whose wives had taken a leading part in parish life. Dr. Jenner's wife stopped me in the street in my first month at St. Stephen's saying, "I am just off to take such and such a meeting, and if your wife was doing her job, it would be she who would be taking it."

I was astounded and dismayed by such an attack. I forced myself to reply very firmly, "Yes, and if the Church and parish paid me a proper stipend instead of £400 a year and a house with seventeen rooms and two acres of garden, she might well be doing so."

This was not in fact wholly true. Pat had been born into a clergy family and she had seen the life of a Vicar's wife at first hand. It was not the kind of life that appealed to her. She did not want to spend the rest of her life delivering parish magazines and going to women's meetings. Her mother had not been trained to a profession. She had, and she felt it to be her vocation to use her training in the field of physical education, and not waste it by not using it. The problem is still with us, though more parishes and congregations are coming to terms with the actuality that clergy wives often go daily to work, not only because they have been trained as doctors, nurses, teachers, secretaries, but also because financially they must.

Then there is an even more traumatic decision to be made. When her husband was ordained, the clergy wife had not been "admonished" and made to take certain promises. She was not therefore bound by any ecclesiastical or religious oath to her husband's job. But she was bound to him by equally solemn vows taken in marriage. Pat had not said the outmoded, archaic and often misunderstood word "obey" in her marriage vow, but she knew that loyalty to me might require her to give up a much loved teaching situation when I moved. This was no great problem when we left Bath because her post was only part-time and temporary. I knew therefore what a sacrifice I would be asking of her when I accepted the living of St. Stephen's. She was very sad to leave Twickenham, and indeed for a term she struggled to get there by train, but as will appear later, "all things do work together for good..."

CHAPTER 9

VICAR

"If he departed as he came with no new light on love or liquor, good
sooth the traveller was to blame and not the Vicarage, nor the Vicar."
(A comment on those itinerants who call on the Vicar!)

"His talk was like a stream which runs with rapid change
from rocks to roses. It slipped from politics to puns, from
Mahomet to Moses. Beginning with the laws which keep the
planets in their radiant courses and ending with some
precept deep for dressing eels or shoeing horses."
(The Vicar's conversation.)
W.M. Praed. (d. 1839) "The Vicar"

Our introduction to Shottermill was not auspicious. We moved
from Chertsey on January 1st 1951 in deep snow. Neither my
predecessor nor the members of the parish had thought to heat the
Vicarage, which was a huge, seventeen roomed house, with no central
heating, and it had been empty for three months. It was cold and
damp and dirty. Peter had mumps and on the car journey from
Chertsey to Haslemere he had said plaintively, unaware that with six
inches of snow outside we would not be able to do what we usually
did, "Are we going to stop soon for a picnic?" He was six and a half,
Jill was five years and three months. In Chertsey both had been to
Stepgates, a terrible Infant School run by a cruel martinet of a
teacher, and were to be very happy at the School at the end of
Vicarage Lane.

It is best to draw a veil over most of those early days in the
Vicarage. It had many drawbacks. Lack of central heating was one.
Another was that it had a 110 volt electricity supply and none of our
appliances would work. No money had been provided by the parish
or diocese for repairs. The Bishop gave me £50 for expenses from his
private fund. The rest we paid for ourselves. I could get no grants,
so I had the Vicarage completely rewired to 220 volts at my own

expense. I paid for several of the rooms to be redecorated. The house was a pseudo-Georgian building put up in 1910 at the cost of £1,780. It had dozens of large sash windows and while still in our house at Chertsey, Pat and I had made all its curtains with 170 yards of material. The lounge was 26 feet long, and I had expended the rest of my inheritance on furniture and carpets for all the rooms of this monstrous building. There were many tears and recriminations in those early Vicarage days.

Yet a large house is in many ways an advantage - apart from the cost of running it. We had room to house Peggy Gidden, now our "housekeeper" and still our friend, in her own quarters. With Pat at school and myself out in the afternoons at meetings or visiting houses or the Hospitals, she was always there when the children came home from school. We let the top floor of three rooms to a dear woman, Mrs. Edwards, in exchange for housework, no money passing. She also cleaned the Church. Her husband was supposed to help me with the garden as part of the bargain, but he never did. He was a strange, lazy, perverted man, who on his return from his day's work, put on his pyjamas and sat himself down to read comics and the Daily Mirror. There were also two rooms available for the use of the woman parish worker, one of them a kitchen with fridge, sink and cooker, the other a large bed-sitting room. For this I charged a small rent.

Then it gave us immense pleasure to be able to house those, teachers mostly, who could not find digs locally to their school. Some stayed with us for years, others a shorter time. One teacher at Pat's new school in Midhurst brought his wife and small son to stay with us for many months. It seemed right to share "what we so richly enjoyed". The huge garden was also a blessing. The children entertained their growing number of friends in it. It was large enough to house a small cricket pitch, a long jump and high jump pit, a clock-golf course and much else. On the first Saturday in July which, for twelve of the fourteen years we held it, was a fine day, we put on a grand Garden Fête, raising initially £80 and then about £250, which was a great deal of money in the 1950's, attended by up to a thousand people. We used the choir, the Brownies and Guides, and members of the junior organisations, to sell tickets and programmes at sixpence (2½p) a time among the 800 houses of the parish.

Getting ready for the Fête was a real burden. The huge lawns had to be mowed, the flower beds cleared of weeds and several hundred annuals planted and watered. We never knew what the weather might be and I had sleepless nights wondering what we would do with all the stalls if it rained, and whether the 750 Walls Ice Creams which I had ordered at a discount would be enough. The men and women of the Church were magnificent in planning and running this great social occasion. The Haslemere Town Band would play. The local butcher, who was also the Churchwarden, gave us a live pig to bowl for. The children from the village school up the lane, an all range school at that stage, put on dancing displays under their admirable Headmaster, Bob Oldham. It was a pity that we could not use the bottom half of the two acre garden which had been converted into allotments during the war and let to villagers at 2/- a year, but only three sections were still being worked and the rest was weed-infested. I have moved too far ahead of myself. This was all to be in the future.

My "Institution and Induction" took place in deep snow on January 4th 1951. Some faithful ones had undergone a difficult journey from Chertsey and the Bishop had struggled through from his mansion in Farnham Castle, driven by his daughter. The attractive small Church which held about two hundred and twenty people was full as the tall, gaunt, whimsical Bishop, Henry Montgomery-Campbell, a chain smoker who kept his fingers free from nicotine stains by the use of a wire contraption attached to his first finger, declared at the Institution: "Receive the cure of souls which is both thine and mine." The legal forms had all been signed beforehand and I had taken all the oaths to the Queen, the Bishop and others. The Archdeacon then "inducted" me, acting on a mandate from the Bishop, into the "rights and appurtenances" of the benefice, i.e. the Vicarage and a stipend. We processed round the Church to the main door, and then into the choir vestry where I tolled the Church bell to inform the people of Shottermill that I had "taken possession" of the benefice. There is in the Church a superstition that as one unconsciously tolls the bell a particular number of times, that number will mark the years which will be passed in the parish. I tolled the bell seven times, and stayed fourteen years. So much for superstitions.

Then we made visits to the Baptistry, the chancel, the pulpit, the altar rails and the priest's stall where I made promises to baptise, prepare people for confirmation, celebrate the holy Communion, preach and say the Offices of the Church. In those days the congregation was not invited to take part or help the parish priest in all these activities, but today the principle is of priest and people co-operating in the ministry, the *whole* ministry of the Church. Today also, representatives of other Churches and of the local community are invited to participate in this ceremony. The Roman Catholic priest in Haslemere had been invited to attend but had not accepted the invitation. This reflected the attitude of the Roman Catholic Church to the Church of England in 1951. The relationship is a little happier now, though Rome will still not accept Anglican Orders as valid. This sheds some light also upon the fears that the ordination of women will adversely affect our relationship with Rome. Why should we worry about their accepting our *women* priests when they won't even accept our *men* priests?

From my time at Stephen's Shottermill I date my support of women's ministry, and of the ordination of women to the priesthood. It has always seemed obvious to me that the life of the Church depends largely upon its women members. They form the majority of worshippers on Sundays and in most parishes the totality of worshippers on weekdays. They perform all the "chores", keep the church building clean and flower decorated, teach in Sunday School, run many of the clubs and societies. Take away the women and who would be left? I know that the men are at work on weekdays, but then today so are the women! Shottermill parish magazine for January 1951 shows that women ran the:

Electoral Roll
Bishop's Challenge (a diocesan fund-raising scheme)
Mother's Union
Bible Reading Fellowship
Parish Secretaries for CMS, SPG, UMCA, Missionary Societies
Mission to Seamen
C. of E. Children's Society
St. Stephen's Fellowship

On the Parochial Church Council in January 1951 were nineteen women and three men together with two men Churchwardens, and the Treasurer. My predecessor, Leslie Towner, was a man of prayer and was known as such in the parish, but he was not one who could communicate easily with children or men. He was much influenced by Alfred Field, a layman in the "Catholic" tradition who had been an assistant in the Army and Navy Stores when a middle-aged lady had fallen in love with him. She was very rich and they married. After her death Alfred freely used the money she left him for charitable purposes and for the Church in its many aspects. He helped young men in their preparation for ordination, he provided money to St. Stephen's for the enhancement of the Catholic atmosphere by pictures, altar frontals, Lenten array, vestments. He was a most generous man. He would say to me: "When next you are in London, don't forget to go to Mowbray's and buy yourself some theological books and put them down to my account." He was the first to respond to any appeal for financial contributions to missions or the Church fabric, and was a devout and regular communicant.

I "inherited" an excellent woman worker, Kathleen Chase, who was being paid a quite disgracefully small salary. She was an assiduous visitor and in her quiet way in the parish, and in Shottermill's Holy Cross Hospital - a Roman Catholic foundation for TB patients who were mostly Anglican - as well as in her work with children and young people, she was an indispensable asset to the Ministry. My shock and anger can be imagined when it was suggested in a Church Council meeting early in my incumbency that in order to meet a possible bill of £800 (at least £12,000 today) to repair the ravages of the mason bee in the soft stonework of the Church, built in 1841, we could pay the bill by sacking the woman parish worker and saving her salary over a few years. It was an infamous suggestion, indicating a complete misunderstanding of ministry, stewardship, the Gospel and every other aspect of our Faith; and though it was briefly discussed and supported by some, albeit with little enthusiasm, my response was, "if Kathleen goes, I go too, the same day." This ensured that the proposal was quickly rejected. She stayed. I stayed. The money was easily raised. The incident shows how hard we would have to work to teach the true meaning of the Gospel and the true place of women in the Church.

In 1952 I was able to propose to the PCC that her salary was raised by £120 a year and this was accepted; no one suggested that *my* stipend of £400 a year should be raised. Out of it I paid local rates of £69 a year and a Diocesan dilapidations charge of £49, plus stamps, stationery, car, telephone, garden, heating, and all office expenses. When we had a directive from the diocese that PCC's should *consider* paying the incumbent's rate bill, a school teacher member of the PCC said, "I should like someone to pay *my* rates please." Though I think some members were shocked at such a veiled attack, the statement prevented for some years the adoption of the diocesan suggestion. Was it any wonder that Pat had to continue working as a games mistress in Midhurst? Rather than ask for financial help we sold more wedding presents and books, and having given up smoking, I sold my solid silver cigarette case, a twenty-first birthday present, for £5. My car was in need of expensive repairs, and a keen member of the congregation, John Griffin, who was general secretary of the British Legion, offered to let me have one of their second hand staff cars, an Austin A40, for whatever I could get for mine. That was a generous gesture indeed, for the Austin had only done 12,000 miles. John Griffin was a powerful figure in the Church. He and his wife came to St. Stephen's although they lived in Haslemere, because of our Catholic tradition, and continued to be my friends and supporters all through my time at Shottermill.

At thirty-three I was full of energy and full of ideas. I had a vision of what a parish should be, and of its place in the community. Some ideas I had tried out at All Saints, Chertsey, but now I had the opportunity and the authorisation, to put theory to the test, to put hypothesis to verification, assumptions to the proof. Before each of my moves I had gone into Retreat to look back on my mistakes and to ask guidance for the future. Retreat is a bad name for an experience which is mainly concerned with advance into a greater spirituality, a deeper understanding of a vocation accepted. Retreats should end in resolutions, and the resolutions I made before going to Shottermill were related to the dangers and opportunities of being a Vicar, burdened with all those admonitions in the service of Induction and Institution as we had processed round the Church.

At the Church door - how to make the people of the parish feel that it was always open for them? In my fourteen years it always was open, though we did have thefts from the boxes and some vandalism.

At the Baptistry - what should St. Stephen's be doing for the children? I had always believed in an open baptism policy and in the whole of my ministry I have never refused to baptise a child. I have imposed conditions on myself and on the parents:- visitation and discussion beforehand, full explanation of what baptism involves, letters to godparents not able to be present, follow-up by myself and willing volunteers from the congregation, and the provision of godparents from the congregation where parents could not provide their own.

These are all pastoral opportunities which the priest denies to himself and the Church at his and their peril if he adopts a rigid baptism policy. In a long experience I have found that God's Spirit is at work in the most unlikely and stony soil.

At the Chancel steps where the confirmation candidates kneel before the Bishop - what is the Church's ministry of teaching and evangelism to those who present themselves, often from pagan backgrounds, for admission to Holy Communion? I remembered how one mother in Windsor in 1942 had approached me to prepare her fourteen year old son for Confirmation. Neither she nor her son had been inside a church for years. She said: "I want him confirmed. Look at what Mr. Churchill is doing for the country, and he is confirmed." I had no evidence that Churchill was confirmed though I assumed that he was, and I hoped at the least that it was having some effect upon his leadership of the nation, but it seemed a strange argument. However, the lad began to come to Church with his mother (as required!); he was confirmed and later offered himself for the priesthood. Never underrate the power and penetration of the Holy Spirit in human life!

We had stopped "at *the place where the prayers are said*" - what was required of me, of the parish worker, of the congregation, in the realm of prayer and worship? The parish woman worker and I always said Mattins at 9:30 a.m. and Evensong at 4 p.m. on weekdays publicly in Church, together if possible, on our own if not. At the altar rails the place of communion with God and with each other. Sunday worship - what would be its form, its impact? Very soon I was to receive letters asking me to "restore Sunday Mattins to its proper position." Many, I was told, had gone off to Haslemere Parish Church because they had been deprived of their full choral Mattins. One of my resolutions was to make no changes until I had fully consulted all concerned, and for practical purposes that meant the two hundred names on the Electoral Roll. I knew that, as at Chertsey, this did not in fact represent the actual regular worshipping body, but it was the legal list and those on it had a right to be consulted. When I did this at the end of several months and after discussion with the Church Council (after two Annual Meetings, roughly half and half, men and women) eighty-eight people replied, and as a result we restored Sunday Mattins as a full choral service at 10.30 a.m. with a sermon at the end in the usual place, but followed, after a short break in which worshippers could come in if they had not come in during the short break *before* the sermon, by the sung Eucharist. A compromise indeed. Many of the Mattins people had already been to Communion at 8 a.m. and did not want to be present at another Communion. The Sung Eucharist worshippers had the whole service-with a sermon at the beginning rather than after the Creed (as it was in 1662). The only folk who had cause to complain were the members of the Choir who gallantly sang each service and were in Church from 10:15 to 12:15. None did complain. Nor did the excellent succession of organists.

Today, prospective incumbents are sent on the ecclesiastical equivalent of management courses. There they are no doubt warned about the dangers of change, the need for consultation; they will be told about management by creative tension and backward reaction. They will be told about structures and the necessity of job satisfaction, about motivation, about the books available, about parallels between the Church and a business. In 1951 we had no such help available. We were expected to have learned how to "run" a parish from our former Vicars, from the successes and mistakes which we had made. I did not make any conscious plan, and in my first letter to "My dear people", as we all began our parish magazine letters in those days, I asked them to pray for me, to join me in worship and to make themselves known to my family and myself whenever they saw us in the street or in shops. I asked them to be particularly understanding that Pat would be at work every day, including Saturdays when she had team games to supervise. We would both stay in on Friday evenings and would be delighted to have parishioners call on us. Week after week we stayed in and no one called. They had not been used to calling at the forbiddingly huge Vicarage except for baptism forms and sweet coupon signatures, wedding preparations and banns forms. Then one Friday evening there was a good film at the "Rex" cinema at the bottom of the road, so we went out. That was a fatal mistake; two ageing spinster sisters *did* call and found us out, in more senses than one. They never quite forgave us. That was one idea that didn't work.

How to get to know the people. That must be a priority for every new incumbent. In his interview with me, Bishop Henry (as they would call him today - we were not so familiar) had said to me in his direct, forceful way: "No riding about in a car, now. Get about your parish on your own two flat feet." It was wise advice, especially from one who had never driven a car. To pass the time of day with everyone, wearing my clerical collar to identify myself, to visit every house on foot, that was the only method of getting to be known, and getting to know at least a few of my people.

We tried other ways. There were a hundred pre-fabs in three roads in one part of the parish, roughly divided into thirty odd houses in each road. We visited them all and invited the residents, road by road, to an afternoon social occasion, hoping that in such a way they would not only get to know their parish priest and parish worker, but also get to know each other. This experiment had limited success, partly because the roads were at the top of a steep hill, and pushing a pram back up a steep hill is no fun, but also because it was something new and there was a suspicion that "the Church" was trying to take advantage in some way of the pre-fab residents. I never did understand why they should think that, as we later had quite a number of children in the Sunday school from there, though we had to provide car transport for them each Sunday. For young mothers with children we held regular "Pram Services" on the same day as they attended the clinic in Vicarage Lane.

Without consciously doing so, I identified over the first few months what I considered to be areas of need and areas of possible growth. First there was a need to weld together a divided congregation and parish. Those who came to the early service and Mattins were from the more well-to-do areas of Shottermill, from the large houses in extensive grounds on the Hindhead road. Hindhead had been part of Shottermill until the early years of the century, and correspondence in the Church chest showed that the richer folk there wanted their own church building, while the folk at the bottom of the hill were reluctant to let them go because it would mean a loss of contributions! Hindhead got its Church in 1901. The people from Lion Lane and the less well to do areas came to Evensong. The Sung Eucharist had a mixed group of participants.

Next there was a need to make contact with everyone in the parish. This should not be difficult since there were only eight hundred houses in all. The parish magazine produced monthly was a small printed affair running to about two hundred copies. This was an area where development was possible and would be a useful means of contact and teaching if it could be delivered to a larger number of homes. Other information, about plans and forthcoming events could be printed and pushed through every letterbox in the parish. We had done this in Chertsey with a far greater number of homes.

Then there was plainly a need to teach the faith to those who were more or less active members of the Church. Time and again I had heard the plea, in Windsor, Bath, Chertsey, "We need more *teaching* sermons. We don't really know what we believe, we Anglicans." This was usually accompanied by the wistful complaint, "The Roman Catholics know what they believe." This gave me the incentive to work out a scheme of teaching by series and courses of sermons on the Creed, the Lord's Prayer, the Ten Commandments, the seven Sacraments, Prayer, the books of the Bible, the messages of the prophets, and much more, in both morning and evening worship. Each Lent I prepared courses of teaching for the additional weeknight services which came to be very well attended over the years. (An example of a very full programme for 1962 is in an Appendix.)

The Parish Magazine also should be a teaching agent, not just a list of past trivial activities where Mrs. A. presided at the tea urn and Mrs. B. gave a talk on dried flower arrangements. The question of what should be taught to the growing number of children in the morning and afternoon Sunday Schools was discussed with those responsible, and the Sunday School adviser in the Diocesan office, as well as with the parish worker and her teachers. At Evensong, particularly in the winter months when the Church did not need to be blacked out, I would show films and filmstrips. At Evensong also we had occasional hymn practices and psalm practices during which we learned many new hymns and chants. Very early on the PCC agreed that we should hold open air services in the summer months. These were very helpful to members of the congregation who had to make a public appearance as committed Christians, and it strengthened the faith of many of them, though its missionary or evangelistic value was limited. It may be that someone sitting at an open window heard something which helped them in their life.

I was very concerned about the lack of *men* either in the worshipping congregation or in positions of responsibility in the

Church and began to consult with the keen and faithful few men that we had. But most of all there seemed to be great possibilities of advance in work among the *children*. There was no Church School in the parish as there had been at Windsor and in Bath, for the Shottermill schools had closed down in 1929, one of its buildings having become a wholesale sweet store, and the other continued to be used as a Church Hall. So in the February magazine 1951, a few weeks after my arrival in the parish I made the following suggestions:

"... that there should be a CHILDREN'S CHURCH to supplement the Junior Sunday School. The weakness of a Sunday School meeting in a church hall is that only on rare occasions do the children come into Church to learn what goes on there. The children would have their own Churchwardens, sidesmen, council, read their own lessons, run their own little Church." (As I found it, the children's work was divided between morning and afternoon Sunday Schools with some families having children in both.)
"... that all children over twelve should come to the Sung Eucharist anyway."

This did not solve the problem, although the afternoon service became popular and well attended for a few years, but declined when, with the improving financial climate, more families bought cars and took themselves off to Bognor or Southsea or the Witterings on Sunday afternoons. These seaside places were only about thirty miles away. In the end we had to abandon the afternoons and return to full morning Sunday Schools for Kindergarten and juniors at 10 a.m. with them coming into Church after their lessons. Later still we had classes held in the Lady Chapel before service. At its most popular we had one hundred and forty children on the books, for children's Sunday worship and teaching. An example of a house-to-house delivery, *You and your children*, is in an appendix.

The active life of the Church has to be lived from Monday to Saturday, and not just on Sundays. Generations of boys and girls and men and women had looked to the Church of England for entertainment, education, physical activity, even training in various skills as well as "religion". This activity had its finest flowering in times of poverty and unemployment, times when the State made no provision for such things. As a Curate I had produced plays, set up youth libraries, organised clubs and games, shown films and film strips, taught and conducted a youth choir and done all the things that Curates were expected to do in the nineteen forties. Just as the Curate of Gerrards Cross had taken us out for sardine sizzles and sausage suppers, I had done the same. Could the same activities be provided at Shottermill? We had the premises, we had few helpers, but on Lion Green we had a fine stretch of grass. So in April 1951 we started up the Young Pilgrims. They were children from 9 - 12 years and they met on Tuesdays from 6.30 to 7.30 p.m. in the Church Room (the old school) for games, talks, handwork and such like in the winter, and on Lion Green in the summer, for cricket and rounders. "The subscription is to be one penny," I wrote, "and *any* child can join. This is important, because although we shall expect the children to attend Children's Church as well (they will enjoy that as much as their games) no child in the parish will be excluded. We shall appreciate offers of adult help too." On Sundays at 3 p.m. (until we had to abandon Sunday afternoons) we sang the Pilgrim's Hymn (Bunyan's *Who Would True Valour See*) and I would give what I hoped was an interesting and bright talk with visual aids suited to the age group. The admirable Peggy Gidden was already planning to run a Guide Company attached to the Church and I hoped that in due course a Brownie leader would be found. She was. But I was unable to find a man to lead a Scout Troop. About forty 9 -12's joined the Young Pilgrims.

Over the years we experimented on Sundays with times and places according to the varying social conditions which were affecting the Church as well as the community. For example, in the 1950's Television began to have an impact on people's lives and on the way they spent their evenings, their Saturdays and Sundays. Later on in the 70's the whole Church was to change the time of Evensong so that people could be home from Church in time to watch *The Forsyte saga*. Later still, the long running *Upstairs Downstairs* had the same effect. The Cinema had its effect too. We had the only Cinema in the area, The Rex, and I was on good terms with the owner. Although the original agreement with the government had laid it down that cinemas could only open on Sundays if the owners paid a proportion of their takings to charity, this soon came to an end. The Rex now had afternoon shows. The type of film shown was also initially controlled, but soon this control too was removed.

Sunday afternoon services became rarer except for occasions such as the Christmas Toy Service, Mothering Sunday, Harvest and other "Family" occasions. Evensong continued to be well attended, with a full choir.

For the older children we had what we called Junior Fellowship in the Church Room for the 14 plus age group, on Tuesday and Thursday evenings, and for a while an In Betweens Club on a Saturday. For adults there was the St. Stephen's Fellowship, Mothers' Union, and we soon started a Young Wives' Fellowship and a Men's Society, affiliated to the Church of England Men's Society which had once boasted hundreds of thousands of members but which was struggling to survive. These organisations all made their contribution to the life of the parish and they all came together on Sundays at the Eucharist, or at least that was the intention! I kept the parish informed of what we were doing by regular circularisation of every house with leaflets and pamphlets, sometimes illustrated.

The year after the experiment with open air services on Sundays at 6.30 p.m. we began what we called "People's Services". Of course all worship is intended for all people, but it had been borne in upon me that most worshippers found the psalms difficult, although we provided pointed psalters in the pews, and that some of the set lessons were difficult to understand, so the "People's Services" had popular hymns, no psalms, simple readings and a short simple address. They brought in a number of new faces, but as is usual with such experiments, some regulars stayed away because they missed the psalms and the canticles! Once a month we held a Youth Service Evensong when all former confirmation candidates were invited and at which all responsibility was taken by the young people themselves. These were well attended but there were always one or two of the older ones from the normal congregation who absented themselves and one or two sidesmen were rather put out that their duties had been taken over by teenagers! But many more men were coming to Church and to meetings of the Men's Society, and we soon found no difficulty in having a full rota of sidesmen and welcomers on duty.

One of the joys of ministry was to have a Hospital within the borders of the parish. That may seem a strange source of joy, and I am aware that a Hospital is not the place where much pleasure can be found. A great deal of love and unselfish service, a great deal of caring ministry, yes. For me the joy consisted of ministering healing to the sick, as the Church had been empowered to do by its Master. Holy Cross was a Roman Catholic foundation with one hundred and thirty-five beds but the number of patients from that Church was very small, although the staff were all of that faith. This was occasionally a stumbling block, as when a devout Irish ward maid insisted on giving the Anglican communicants their breakfast before communion, I think with a mischievous intention. I protested to the Mother Superior who expressed regret but remarked "if your people had been properly taught, they would have refused breakfast." This was a very naughty response, as I pointed out: "My communicants certainly would not want to cause any such disruption to your catering and nursing staff." We sorted out the problem amicably and for fourteen years we had a happy relationship. This was partly due I am sure to the respect we engendered because of our industrious and diligent care of all the patients whatever their denomination, by our visiting every bed on Friday afternoons and by the regular sick communions which I celebrated, often for as many as twenty patients, on a Saturday morning from 6.30 a.m. onwards. Holy Cross at that time (1951) was a specialist Hospital for patients suffering from Tuberculosis, set as it was high among the pines, trees supposed to be beneficial for chest infections. The patients were all girls and young women and they were a most cheerful crowd. They were not normally allowed outside the Hospital grounds, so they looked for friendship and help from outsiders like myself. I found them very responsive to the services I held for them in the lounge rooms, as most of them were not bed-ridden. Many of them were prepared for confirmation, and for that I took the Bishop to them. Later they were allowed to leave their isolation and come down to the Church. From time to time I would show them films and filmstrips, not necessarily on religious topics. Their two favourites were amusing cartoon strips which I often used at the Youth Club: "How to behave at home" and "How to behave on holiday." The simple jokes on the strips would be received with gales of laughter. Each month I had to have an X-ray examination to see if I had contracted the disease.

My best friend among the staff was Sister Mary Beatrice who spent a large part of her time looking through a microscope and identifying the tubercle bacillus which was ravishing the lives of these young women. She had been an Anglican in her earlier years, and we achieved a great rapport on that basis. One day she stopped me in the corridor in some distress and said "You know my fish pond in the grounds? All the fish are dying. What shall I do?" Just outside the parish, at Shottermill Ponds, was a trout farm owned by a Mr. Leney, son-in-law of a former Vicar, Edwin Frend, so I said: "I will ask Mr. Leney to come up and advise you. I suspect the fish are not receiving enough food, or the water is not being aerated by the correct weeds."

"You do that, please," she replied, "and meanwhile, I will ask the Chaplain to bless a medal and I will throw it in the water after mass one day."

Mr. Leney came up to advise her, and Sister Mary B. as we called her, threw into the pond the blessed medal. The fish recovered and it was a matter of gentle dispute between us as to whether the visit of the fish expert or the medal had done the trick. Some thought there about the different approach to miracle on the part of the Roman and Anglican Churches!

As the dread disease of tuberculosis began to be conquered the number of TB patients dwindled and Holy Cross became more a general Hospital, with a number of private rooms and a geriatric ward. I valued my contacts with the patients in the single private rooms, as it gave more time and opportunity to speak of the things that really matter. Freddie Grisewood, at that time Chairman of the famous BBC "Brains Trust" was a patient for many weeks. He was a faithful communicant of the Church of England and we had many talks. A number of other well known people from the Haslemere area came into the Hospital for various ailments and I was pleased and surprised that so high a proportion of them wished to receive the Blessed Sacrament on Saturday mornings.

I spoke just now of the *joy* of the ministry of healing. This does not mean that every patient for whom we prayed, or who received the laying on of hands as most did, or whom I anointed with oil in Holy Unction, got better. On the contrary "it is appointed to all men to die" and if nature (or God) did not have its way through the ageing process which often includes disease, we should all live forever. What did happen, even in those who did not recover health, was that a sense of peace was engendered, and the strength to cope with the illness was given.

The geriatric ward housed between fifteen and twenty old ladies. Some of them were blind, some paralysed, some both, most were incontinent and senile. No doubt some were suffering from

Alzheimer's disease, which although discovered in 1906 has no known cure. It is a degenerative disease of the brain cells causing loss of memory and intellectual impairment. In 1989 a link with high levels of aluminium in drinking water was discovered, though this has recently been questioned by other researchers.

Sadly, one or two had no intellectual impairment but were still in the same ward as the decrepit and senile. The staff were on the whole kind and considerate, but to care for such folk causes great strain and the temptation to speak sharply or be unsympathetic to their cries for help must have been strong. My belief in the necessity for a re-think about the moral dilemmas of illness in old age led me to strengthen my concern that the case for voluntary euthanasia should be reopened. It was not possible to voice such a view in a Roman Catholic Hospital and I did not do so, but I saw no purpose in prolonging the life of many in that ward. There was no dignity in their state, no comfort, no peace, no human life that could be called such, as these sad creatures moaned and groaned, with lolling heads and drooling lips. There seemed to be no purpose even in struggling to get them out of bed into an arm chair.

When I first entered a men's geriatric ward in the old folk's hospital in Old Windsor in 1941, I could hardly bear the stench and the sad sounds of crying and distress. Here, ten or fifteen years on, it all came back to me. As a Christian I believe that human life is a sacred gift not to be taken from us lightly. I believe that God is at work through the dedicated doctors and nurses who care for such sad wretches; I am sure that the medical profession does its best through surgery and drugs to relieve extremes of pain, but I also believe that there comes a point at which the life cannot be called "human", and that if any pretension to dignity or quality has had to be abandoned, where relatives request it and the patient is not able to express himself or herself, life should be allowed to slip away with dignity. This was the judgement of the Law Lords in 1993 in the case of Tony Bland, a victim of the Hillsborough soccer disaster, who had been kept alive as a "vegetable" for three years. They insist in their judgement that their decision is not an open door to euthanasia, but it will re-open the debate. I shall have much more to say on this subject when I come to record the twelve years of pain and distress that led to my lovely wife's death in 1991.

My relationships with the Roman Catholic Church have been mentioned already in the case of the Irish ward maid who gave communicants their breakfast. On two occasions when I returned from my summer holidays I found that Anglican patients who had been receiving the Sacrament from me regularly on Saturday mornings had been "converted" to Roman Catholicism. One of them, an elderly woman of considerable intelligence, was crying when I called to see her on the Friday afternoon.

"They won't let you give me communion tomorrow morning," she sobbed.

"Why is that?"

"I have become a Roman Catholic. I don't know why. It was a silly thing to do."

I told her that as far as the Anglican Church was concerned the sacrament which the Roman priest would henceforth bring her was the same sacrament, and that we had no quarrel with Roman Catholic sacraments, only with some of the dogmas which had been added to the apostolic faith.

"But I have agreed to leave my money to them when I die."

"If you did that willingly and not under duress then that is a decision which is freely yours, and I am quite sure that the Hospital will make very worthy use of it."

I could say no more and it was not an issue which I could take up with the Hospital authorities. The other woman was a member of my own congregation and this was a sad "conversion". She died very soon after and her funeral service was in the Roman Catholic Church. I attended, but sadly none of her few friends felt able to.

This was all a very long time ago - nearly forty years and I would like to think that such things do not happen today, and that no proselytising takes place in similar circumstances. There were two other incidents which I feel I must record in this context, because I *hope* that they illustrate, as in the events in Holy Cross, that times have changed in the relations between our two Churches, and particularly in Roman attitudes to prayer and marriage.

It was the custom of the Rural Dean of Godalming, the Deanery to which Shottermill belongs, to invite to the regular meetings of the clergy Chapter of the Deanery, the local Roman Catholic priest in Godalming parish. I noted after one or two such meetings that although the priest took part from time to time in our debates and discussion, as any visitor might by invitation do, he would never say prayers with us, not even the Lord's Prayer. So I asked him outright after one such meeting:

"Why will you not even say the Lord's Prayer with us?"

He replied: "Because when I say 'Thy kingdom come, thy will be done' I don't mean the same as you do. I mean, 'may the time come when all men will offer obedience to the Pope as the head of the one true Church which on earth *is* the kingdom of God.' "

There was no answer to that travesty, that caricature of prayer. I do not know if modern Roman Catholics make inward reservations when they pray with us, as happily they do now. I hope not, but it is foolish to pretend that the things which divide us are not still very numerous and real.

The other incident concerned a Roman Catholic girl who was marrying a young Anglican policeman from Shottermill. When they came to see me for their wedding preparation, and the question of baptism arose, the girl revealed that she had been baptised as a Roman Catholic and that although she had been to a convent school, she was no longer a practising Roman Catholic. "Nevertheless," I said to her, "I think you should go and tell the priest that you are marrying an Anglican at St. Stephen's." This seemed to me to be the honest thing to do. The girl was reluctant but did as I suggested. The next week she and her fiancé came to the Vicarage for further instruction and discussion about marriage and the wedding service. The girl burst into tears. "I did as you wanted me to, but I wish I had never gone. He sat me down and gave me the most terrible lecture. He said that every act of intercourse would be an act of fornication. That if we had children they would be illegitimate in the eyes of the Church." I spent a long time that evening outlining the differences in attitude between our two churches to the priesthood (I was not a "true priest" in the eyes of Rome and therefore any sacrament I celebrated was not a true sacrament) and to marriage and the upbringing of children. The girl was reassured and comforted, but I suspect that the priest had made her an enemy of the Roman Catholic faith from then on. It was a foolish and cruel thing for him to have done. They were married and were happy together and came to Church until the young man was moved to another police post. I hope they still live happily and that their children, if they had any, are good Anglicans too.

I continued the healing ministry that I had begun in Chertsey, with services of prayer, the laying on of hands, and communion of the sick from the Reserved Sacrament. We compiled a list of the sick and sent it, with their permission, to a number of the faithful who had promised to pray at a certain time of the day for each one on the list. I was chary of mentioning people by name in the public services of the Church, though this is a common practice today, because one such person prayed for had not been told in advance and when they were told afterwards they objected very strongly. How difficult it is for the parson always to do the right thing!

We Anglicans have our irrational prejudices too, as well as our strongly held convictions about our own ministry and sacraments. How long has it taken some of us to acknowledge that a Free Church minister can exercise a true ministry even if he does not claim the name of priest? There are those among us who would still doubt the efficacy of the Holy Communion conducted by a non-conformist minister and who would protest against any move for unity which did not involve Free Church ministers renouncing their orders and being re-ordained by a Bishop. This was a matter of contention between the Methodists and ourselves when unity between us was being discussed, and came to nothing, twenty years ago and more.

In the 1950's we began to hold united services in Lent in the various denominational Churches in Haslemere, Methodist, Congregational, St. Bartholomew's, St. Christopher's the daughter church of Haslemere, and St. Stephen's. One of my most active and faithful members would not come to the service in the then Congregational church. I asked her why. "Because of that horrible wooden chandelier in front of the pulpit!" she replied. "And because the pulpit is in the middle of the church where the altar should be, and because the choir is sitting in what ought to be the sanctuary." I wonder where she got those prejudices? Of such trivialities are divisions made. The united services were the catalyst for other united efforts between the churches but it was a sadness that the Roman Catholic congregation did not join us.

It is always unwise to claim miracles of healing as the result of prayer, the laying on of hands and anointing with oil, but some remarkable things did happen. A woman stopped me in the street and said, "I understand that you have services for healing. When do they take place and may I bring my little boy?"

"On Fridays after the 10 a.m. communion service we have the laying on of hands, and on Wednesday evenings at 6:30 p.m. some of us meet for silent and spoken prayer for healing and intercessions for the sick. Bring your little boy on Friday."

The mother came, with a sick three year old whose illness had been diagnosed as diabetes, and about whom the Doctors were very worried. They had warned his family that the prognosis was not good and his chance of survival beyond five or six years was doubtful. The boy received the laying on of hands and was anointed over a long period. He continued to receive medical attention which I believe to be essential, and the GP was informed of what was happening in the Church. He did not object and indeed he encouraged the family. The boy recovered completely.

This incident raised the whole matter of the relationship between the clergy and the doctors. I discussed this with the local clergy and ministers and we set up a clergy-doctor meeting from time to time. But the doctors were much more reluctant to share their problems with us than we were to share ours with them. The medical profession was very suspicious of alternative medicine at that time, and even more suspicious of "spiritual healing". Those suspicions have largely disappeared today particularly among the younger doctors. Of course we understood their dilemma. The secrecy which exists between a doctor and his/her patient must not be breached. Confidentiality must not be compromised. We clergy understood this, but were convinced that there were areas where we *could* share experiences and find mutual solutions. The doctors were not so sure. So we explored realms where the interest was mutual - particularly in the realm of psychosomatic illness, the effect of the mind upon the body and the body on the mind. Some of the doctors were agnostics about religion. They found it hard to accept that religion had any place at all in healing, though they must have known that belief in divine healing was ancient, widespread and growing. These meetings were in my view very helpful, to us at any rate, and I was sorry that after a few years they ceased to take place.

Kathleen Chase had come to the parish in May 1947. She left us in August 1955 for the parish of Whitton near Ipswich, a large new housing area, much more populous than Shottermill. The parish had received much from her in those eight years, not only for her visiting and work among the children. The spotless beauty of the altar

The author as Vicar of Shottermill

Pat

Top: Denham Village, Bucks
Bottom: Denham Church, St. Mary's

R.G.S. High Wycombe, Sixth Form 1933

Top Left: S.H.H. Edward Hinson, Douglas Holmes at S.E.H.
Top Right: We three on the Eiffel Tower, Paris
Bottom: St. Edmund Hall, Oxford

S.H.H. and Theological College, Lincoln

Top: Lincoln Theological College 1940
Bottom: Rochester Theological College 1969

Lincoln Cathedral, 1940

Top: Windsor Parish Church, 1941
Bottom: All Saints, Weston, Bath, 1944

Wedding Day, 17th August 1943

Left: Honeymoon, August 1943
Right: Peggy Gidden, 'Nanny' and friend

Top: 'Nativity', Senior College Play at All Saints, Windsor, 1942
Bottom: St. Stephen's Church, Shottermill, Haslemere, 1951

Top: Shottermill Church. Ordination of a Deaconess, 1964
Bottom: The Vicarage Shottermill, Fête Day with Haslemere Town Band, 1952

Top: A Parish Breakfast, Shottermill
Bottom: Pat with Father, Mother and Aunt Winnie

Top: Pat the D.Sc Teacher
Bottom: Pat in party mood

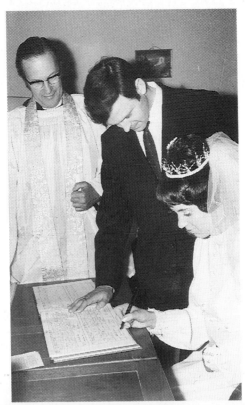

Top: I marry my Secretary
Bottom: I marry my Niece

Top: Our house 'White Friars', Rochester
Bottom: Jill and Peter at 'White Friars'

The Queen's Chaplains, Windsor Castle 1985

Top: St. Saviour, Trevone
Bottom: St. Saviour, Trevone, Interior

Top: 'Cedarwood', the house we designed
Bottom: Trevone Bay, the Cornwall I love

Like many who retire through ill health she lived on for another twenty eight years. I was privileged to take her funeral, for she had lived for a few years in the Clergy home at Hindhead and what I said can be read at the end of this book.

After five and a half years with us Jane had left and I appointed another Lay "woman worker" (not a very nice title or description we had decided over the years) one Mary Dee. She was very different from Kathleen, or Alma, or Jane. Large and friendly with an infectious laugh she soon found her own niche and stayed with me until I left for Rochester in 1965, and carried on with my successor. While she was with us she studied to become a Deaconess and it was a joy to me and the whole parish when the Bishop came to St. Stephen's to ordain her. The Bishop asked me to preach the sermon and I took the opportunity to say what I believed about women's ministry. This was long before the issue had become a matter of debate in the General Synod, and what I said is also to be found at the end of this book.

Whatever happens now in the Church when women have been ordained priests, and I do not personally believe that there will be a great split or many defections, I must record my conviction that, having worked with women colleagues for fourteen years in a parish and for a further sixteen years in a diocese, with those colleagues doing vital work among young people, children, and in social work, and having worked daily in those sixteen years with four admirable Secretaries, I *know* that women have no less a contribution to make than men at every level in the Church. That would include for me, the episcopate.

I was recently in the diocese of Dunedin in New Zealand and enquired there about their woman Bishop, Penny Jamieson. "She is doing a magnificent job," I was told. "She is a true Bishop, and a real 'pastor pastorum,' shepherd of the sheep." I would have had no hesitation in recommending some of those women colleagues (not all!) for training as priests. True ministry is of God. It is God who consecrates, ordains, presides at the altar, not man. His grace is not dependent on gender or on man-made rules and regulations. We do well to remember that He was born of a woman, that the faithful women ministered to Him before and after death, when all the men had forsaken Him and fled. His first Resurrection appearance was to a woman, and it was *she* who was commissioned to tell the good news to others.

In my youth in Gerrards Cross, I had become interested and involved in Missions. St. James's was a strong "Missionary parish" supporting the Church Missionary Society and other evangelical missions. I had painted the posters for the missionary fêtes and sales of work, attended courses, and helped at various missionary gatherings in the parish. I was anxious to revive this interest in a practical way at St. Stephen's so in addition to the usual fund raising efforts, when we ran our first Stewardship Campaign in 1960, which doubled our income immediately, I persuaded the Church Council to "give away" to home and overseas missions not less than one quarter of our total yearly income. This met with some opposition - "Charity beings at home," some said, but I was able to persuade the PCC that, "What we freely give away, that we keep. What we keep for ourselves, that we lose."

In the 50's and 60's this country had not had the huge influx of refugees and others from overseas that was to come in the 70's and 80's. Many of us had probably not spoken to a coloured person, and only seen them at work, probably washing up in cafés and restaurants in London, or more rarely, as nurses in a hospital. I thought it was important for Christians here to meet Christians from overseas, so each year we had an "Overseas weekend," not a missionary weekend as such, when students working in England would be invited to stay with families in the parish from Friday night to Sunday night. In this way we met young folk from Nigeria, Kenya, South Africa, Pakistan, India, Hong Kong and other lands. They enjoyed the experience and so did we. On Sunday we had only one morning service, the Sung Eucharist and all Churchgoers were encouraged to be present. This was followed by breakfast in the Church Hall for as many as were willing to stay, and was usually a luxurious meal produced by Mrs. Ede and the Mother's Union. After the breakfast the four students invited for that weekend would speak for a while about their homeland and the Church and its problems and opportunities there. About one hundred and twenty folk would sit down to these breakfasts, including many young people, and girls from the Grove School, an independent school in the parish who came to Church on Sunday mornings and whose students I prepared for Confirmation.

These breakfasts were so popular (and I hope the whole weekend in its more devotional and religious aspect) that we instituted them as regular occasions, usually on the fifth Sunday in the month, and concentrated on a theme - missions, harvest, Whitsun, the first communion Sunday of the newly Confirmed. The breakfasts had become so luxurious and self-indulgent that I had to curb the enthusiasm of Mrs. Ede and her helpers by pointing out that many in the world were starving, so the porridge course and the sausages and bacon were cut out and the breakfasts became simpler and more in keeping with our intention which was to ensure that people, especially those from different areas and different levels of the community, could get to know each other in Christ. Having received the Sacrament of His death it was not really appropriate to go out from Church to another secular feast!

I suppose that because I had made my views known on various subjects at Diocesan and other meetings I was being asked to join a number of Diocesan Councils and Committees, usually to represent the Deanery. The list grew longer as the years went by, but I like to think that my work in the parish did not suffer, rather that it was bettered by my broader contacts, giving me a wider vision and understanding of the Church and its mission. It is so easy to become inward looking and blinkered when one's life and activity, one's whole thinking and planning, is concentrated on a building in one place. This is a particular danger and temptation to the residentiary canons of a Cathedral Church, as I found at Rochester.

During my time at St. Stephen's I served on the Diocesan Committees for Children, Missions, Press and Publicity, Moral Welfare, the Board of Finance, the Council for Religious Education, and as an inspector of Church Day Schools. Many of these Committees are known by different names today, and there is no doubt that the Church has too many committees and too many clergy spending their time unprofitably attending their meetings, but every parish priest should be given the opportunity to serve on at least two Diocesan Committees to provide the essential "Input" from the grass roots and to learn about the wider Church. At Guildford I soon became conscious of the tension that exists between the parishes and the diocese, the resentment that decisions are made "at the centre" without, as parishes think, sometimes wrongly, full and sensitive consultation. The cause of the tension was often finance. It still is.

In the first place Parochial Church Councils resent both the manner of assessing the imposed "Quota" which they must pay (voluntarily in theory), and the amount of it. Diocesan bodies regard themselves as providing a service to the parishes, and clearly that service has to be paid for. Whether the parishes use the service or think it valuable or worthwhile is another matter. Over the years the amount paid by the parishes to the Dioceses has multiplied exceedingly. Where in the 1950's and 1960's parishes may have paid hundreds of pounds, today they pay thousands. The amount paid to the Diocese of Guildford in my last year at St. Stephen's, 1964, was £293. Today I would guess that the figure has multiplied by more than fifty times without the total income of the parish having risen by an equivalent amount. Today the parishes bear a much higher proportion of the cost of the ministry, and whereas in 1951 my stipend was £400 and a house, with no expenses paid, the average incumbent now receives £12,800 and a house, and all expenses of office paid, sometimes with additional grants for heating, garden etc.

In the second place the parishes question the need for such a large central bureaucracy as is found in most Diocesan Offices. In most dioceses the number of employees, architects, surveyors, accountants, secretaries, schools officers, youth and children's officers, social work organisers, has multiplied. They all have to be paid the current rate for the job as laid down by their professional associations. In the 50's much of their work was done on a voluntary basis, or on a minimum salary. Perhaps at that time the Church could have been accused of taking advantage of the principle of vocation, but those doing the work did not complain and there is no evidence that it is better done today than it was then. Certainly there was some unconscious exploitation of the clergy and parish workers and their willingness to work for God in poverty, but now that the principles on which the secular world rules its life have entered into the Church, it would be a brave man who claimed that the Kingdom of God has been extended one whit by the changes.

A simple illustration of the difficulties may help here. As a parish priest I received a stream of communications from the Bishop, the Secretary of the Board of Finance, the Children's Adviser, the Diocesan Secretary and others in the Diocesan Office. As many as four stamped envelopes from Guildford might arrive on the same day. "Why can't they get together in that Office and put all these communications in one envelope, and save postage on three letters?" I would complain, and at clergy meetings we would grumble at the incompetence of those "at the centre". It was when I had my own function in a Diocesan Office that I saw the problem from the other side. It would have been impossible to co-ordinate a mailing from the various branches of the diocese in one envelope without employing yet another body to do so. Letters are written at different times by different secretaries, some are single sheets, others contain wads of paper, copies of other letters, literature to be circularised about forthcoming events. Where each of us had a communication for the Bishop of Rochester, these were put into a pile in the front office. It was easy to do that for one person, but it would have been impossible to put out two hundred piles.

The other reason, I would surmise, for the multiplication of staff, is the multiplication of paperwork required, and like many, I question the necessity of much of it. How much of it is ever seen again, ever referred to again? How many of the multitudinous forms which are filled in during the course of a year are ever taken out of their files or pigeon holes? I am reminded of the hoary story of the time when every incumbent had to fill in a lengthy form about the parish, its buildings, its finances, its personnel. Not having a parish now I do not know if these forms are still used. What purpose did they serve? The simplistic answer given was, "They assist central planning. They help forward planning." One question in the form related to the seating capacity of the Church. An incumbent who detested filling forms replied the first year: "25"; the next time the form came and asked, "What is the seating capacity of your church?" he put down "10,000". The next time he put "0". No one questioned his figures, so his conclusion was that no one in fact read them. Which is almost a cue for the other chestnut about form-filling: "What is the greatest obstacle to your Ministry?" was a question on one form. An incumbent replied with stunning honesty: "My wife, but God knows, I love her still!"

In Guildford diocese I entered into the realm of ministry which was to be a principal concern of my life for the next thirty years. On arrival in Shottermill I was invited by Surrey County Council to be one of their representatives on the managing body of the local County School, once the Church School, and then an all range school from five to fifteen. I regarded this as a signal honour, for the County to appoint a priest as its representative. I was asked to be Chairman and had a wonderful fourteen years of co-operation with its first-rate Headmaster, Bob Oldham and his staff. It being a County school I had no responsibility for its religious education but I visited the school every week, helped to appoint staff and encouraged the school to use the Church building as much as they wished. So, at Christmas time in particular, the children got to know the inside of a Church with their Nativity plays and Carol Services. After a few years the infants were given their own premises in a large house in Vicarage Lane, with their own Head and staff, but the same managing body. The new Head of the infants had been on Oldham's staff, and with a cure of her own she made it quite clear that she was now independent and would organise things in her own way. This was not always Oldham's way, and a strange tension grew up between the two schools which I had to work hard to minimise. It is a common complaint of junior schools that the infants who come to them at seven have not been properly taught or adequately prepared!

Between 1958 and 1959 we built in the school grounds one of the early Learners' Swimming Pools in the County. It was more of a battle to persuade the County to maintain it when it was built than it was to raise the money to build it. Once more I began writing letters to prominent people in the area asking for money, and in a few months more than £700 came in from friends and parents and children. Grants totalling £275 came from the County of Surrey and Haslemere District Council towards the £1,037 which the completed bath cost.

Shottermill School had by this time become a Juniors only school. As an all-range school its pupils had taken the 11+ examination and the successful ones had gone off to Secondary Grammar or High Schools in Farnham, Godalming, Guildford. Many of us felt that the Haslemere district was populous enough to have its own school, so against considerable opposition from the County Education Authorities and others, we had mounted a "Campaign for a Secondary School in Haslemere". We held meetings and put out publicity for the School locally, and lobbied the authorities and Education Committee in Kingston, the County Town. Eventually our efforts were successful and Woolmer Hill School in Shottermill parish was opened in 1956, as a three form entry school, with a former public school headmistress as Chairman and myself as Vice-Chairman. Woolmer Hill was on a high point on the edge of the parish with magnificent grounds which came to be used by local athletic clubs and other sporting associations. Its first Headmaster was Mr. R. Anning who in effect put the school on the map and stayed twenty-one years. He was a forceful character and a great Headmaster of what was one of the new breed of School, the Secondary Modern.

It is interesting to read the brochure we put out for the Learners' pool. We quoted a letter I had written to the Divisional Executive of the Education authority in Guildford: Learners swimming baths were recommended by the English Schools Swimming Association. The nearest bath was twelve miles away, and thirty to forty Shottermill children were keen enough to go every week out of school hours to Guildford sixteen miles away, paying 2/- week (10p) to do so. We had the space, the water, the drainage, the necessary dressing room facilities for a bath and if it were to be used by other schools in the area as we were willing for it to be, the County should make a grant! A meeting of parents, teachers, managers and friends was held and £70 in cash subscribed there and then, £280 was pledged and one parent anonymously sent me £100. Automatic chlorination and aeration was demanded (rightly) by the County architect, and largely by voluntary labour on the part of fathers the bath was built.

My next project was the provision of a *public* swimming bath in the parish. In this I had the support of the whole district and in particular of the then Chairman of the Haslemere Council, Dr. Rolston. Again we held meetings and discovered that we were not the first. Many years ago a fund had been created for the building of a bath in Haslemere and some £700 or £800 was believed to be hidden away somewhere. No one knew where. This mystery created a stir when the local paper took it up and many letters were forthcoming about its possible whereabouts. The wheels of local bureaucracy turn slowly and after many years of agitation, and after I had left Shottermill, Haslemere got its public swimming bath. It cost £20,000 and was not well built and has had to have an immense amount of money spent on it since.

I sometimes wonder why I spent so much time and energy on projects which do not appear to have any religious significance, like the building of swimming pools, and I console myself with the thought that the Christian religion is concerned with all life, and not just with what goes on in Church buildings. In 1952 and 1953 I involved myself in the campaign against the American use of napalm in the Korean War of 1950-1953. In the armoury of terrible weapons of mass destruction which armies possess today, napalm probably does not rate very high, but in the early 1950s it was seen by most of us as much more obscene than high explosive. It was a fuel produced from jellied petrol, used in flame-throwers and incendiary bombs. It stuck to the skin when alight and caused horrendous burns. It was the picture of Korean children set alight by napalm which roused many of us. At meetings where I spoke against it, I was in fact surprised to find that many ordinary people supported its use and resented a clergyman, "Poking his nose in matters which did not concern him." Napalm is still used by many armies in the field and perhaps my campaign should have been more widely based - against the idea of war itself.

In the late 50s and early 60s I became an "Inspector" of Church schools on behalf of the diocese. This involved visiting Aided Schools, by right, to "inspect" the Church teaching being given under the 1944 Act to all the children in the school; and Controlled Schools under the same Act where there were withdrawal classes to give specifically Church teaching on two occasions a week. "Inspect" was not a word I would have used myself, "Advise" would have been more acceptable. What did this untrained priest know which the trained teacher did not know, and what right had he to make comments and give advice? When asked that question as I was on more than one occasion, with polite respect of course, I would reply that a large part of a priest's ministry was in teaching; that in fact I had been trained in my theological college to teach RE or RI (instruction) and that I did not come to criticise but to confer. In order to allay such suspicions I would take a class myself with the teacher present, and if they were willing I would sit and watch them take the class. At break or lunch time I would meet with all the teachers and open my box of RE books and visual aids and we would have a valuable discussion. When I came to organise the "inspections" in the Rochester diocese I concluded that the teachers had a valid point and we came to use only ex-teachers (sometimes heads) or clergy with a bona fide teaching diploma or several years of teaching experience. We called them "Advisers" or "Visitors" and they were on the whole well received.

It is unfortunately true that the Church, as in Shottermill parish, has had to give up many of its schools in recent years because of failing rolls and re-organisation, and also for a lack of teachers with real Christian conviction. This is not a problem for Anglicans only. The Roman Catholic Church is finding it difficult to staff its schools with practising Roman Catholics. All this has undermined the daily instruction in the Christian faith, even in Aided Schools. Whether new legislation enacted by a Conservative government making a "mainly Christian" assembly compulsory, and affirming the necessity for "mainly Christian" religious instruction, will halt the decline remains to be seen. Our schools and our teachers are a reflection of our society. This is a truism, even a cliché, but it is no less an accurate statement for that. In any case the schools should not be expected in a multifaith and secular society to teach what the homes and the Churches should be teaching. The sooner we face the fact that we are a small minority in a largely pagan country, the better, and the fact that the Church of England is the "Established Church" of the country will not save us. That is why I placed great emphasis on the teaching ministry of the parish Church of Shottermill, why we circularised every house with information and perhaps provocative "propaganda", challenging the people to do more than bring their children to baptism, more than present themselves for marriage, more than come to the jumble sales and summer fêtes.

In the enlarged magazine with its Diocesan inset and a "Home Words" inset, which cost 3d in 1951 and had to be put up to 4d in 1960 and later to 6d, there were 16 pages of closely printed material plus a pictorial cover and 4-6 pages of advertisements. In it I answered the questions that folk were asking, and not just the ones I thought they ought to be asking. In 1952 in a series of twelve, one a month, for example, the title was, "Is this your Problem?" and questions asked included "Cremation or Burial?"; "Divorce and Remarriage"; "Earthquakes and natural disasters"; "Why doesn't the Church expel the Dean of Canterbury" (the notorious Red Dean); "Why are so many parsons narrow-minded?"; "Why did God choose the Jews?"; "What has the Church ever done for me?" In 1953/54 I went through the alphabet with "A simple ABC for the Christian" - Adoration, Agnostic, Almsgiving, Angels, Apostle, Atheist etc. etc.

In 1955 there was a new series of "Is this your problem?" which dealt with subjects such as the Church and politics; do you have to be baptised to get married in Church? If God made everything who made evil?   Mummy, who is God exactly?   How can God be Almighty?   The words we use for our services - what is a Eucharist? etc.   Then there would be reviews of religious books within the price range that ordinary folk could afford.   We had early on installed a book table at the back of the Church, which was much frequented and used.   In later years, series on Prayer, on Stewardship, on Missions, the Ministry, and another "Your questions answered".   The Vicar's letter dealt with a wide range of parish interests and difficulties.   Then there were the usual "Notes, News and Comments" with references to past events kept to the absolute minimum.   One of the series that aroused most interest was: "Some Modern Substitutes for Christianity", in which I reviewed the beliefs of sects like Jehovah's Witnesses, Christian Science, the Mormons, the Spiritualists.   Then there were examinations of national problems such as strikes, a new Betting Bill, General Elections, Religious Broadcasting, Space exploration (the first satellite had been put into orbit in 1957 and the first spaceman, Yuri Gagarin in 1961) and its impact on our conception of God as a Creator and our infinitesimal place in the Universe.   The advent of Premium Bonds gave rise to a discussion on gambling.

It is tempting to allow a parish Magazine to become a one man voice, so I invited various people to write articles.   A girl with multiple sclerosis penned a most moving piece about being tied to a wheelchair.   She was one of my most faithful communicants.   An old resident who ended his days after singing in the choir for *eighty* years wrote a series on "Shottermill past".   One wrote of her overseas experiences as a teacher.   It was always difficult to find parishioners who were willing to put pen to paper however, so the voice of the Magazine remained largely the Vicar's and I continue to regard these publications as a major teaching agent.   What a pity so many of them today are badly typed and cyclostyled records of things past, with no insets and little to recommend them.   The usual price seems to be about 25 or 30 pence, five or six shillings in old money, and my impression is that they are bought largely "to help the Church" and not for their religious or literary merit and value.

I was instituted to Shottermill by Henry Montgomery-Campbell. When he was translated to London he was succeeded as Bishop by Ivor Watkins, a large friendly man who worked hard and was very popular in the diocese. But he overtaxed his strength and died suddenly of heart failure. He was succeeded in 1961 by George Edmund Reindorp, Provost of Southwark, who came to the diocese with a reputation as a "showman", a flamboyant personality and friend of TV celebrities, somewhat of a self-publicist. His first Christmas card bore a photograph of himself with Royalty. All this was a veneer, covering the true, attractive person underneath. He had been a naval Chaplain, a Curate and incumbent in Westminster and Provost of Southwark Cathedral. He was enthroned as Bishop on April 12th 1961 and presided over the consecration of the first part of the new Guildford Cathedral, for which I had spent much time and energy in defending and raising money, on May 17th that same year. George Reindorp soon set the diocese alight with his dynamic and often controversial personality and a host of new appointments were made, and many of the older men in the diocesan hierarchy were retired. In a remarkable enthronement sermon he emphasised that he was a parish priest at heart:

"Whether my parish has been a hospital ship, a cruiser, a dockyard in South Africa, thirty thousand in Westminster, or a Cathedral parish Church in Southwark, the work has been the same, caring for souls, loving, learning, caring, laughing, crying in that glorious freedom which is the Christian life. So whenever your Bishop suggests to you some project for helping forward the spread of the Kingdom, please remember he will see it set fair and square against the background of the ordinary parish, though as you know, no good parish priest admits that his parish is ordinary."

I got to know George Reindorp very well. He cared deeply for people, and in particular for his clergy. Some of his "projects" were hare-brained and not always well received, as when he proposed that parishes should be graded in importance and their incumbents paid accordingly. How on earth (or in heaven) is "importance" to be assessed? Just because a man has a thousand houses and two schools in his parish and a Hospital, is the work he does any more important to God than the work of a man with two hundred houses, no school, no Hospital, in the depths of the country, if he fulfils his ministry as best he can? I had six schools in Shottermill and a Hospital. I did not consider my work more important than that of the Vicar of Grayswood a few miles away who had only one school.

But the new Bishop kept most of his promises to the clergy. He welcomed letters which contained comments and criticisms of his words and actions which had offended some laity and some clergy from time to time, and when I had written to him in this vein he replied immediately in his own execrable handwriting, or typing full of erasures and mistakes, to apologise and ask forgiveness. He would ring up his clergy late at night to have a chat about some matter of concern, too late for some of us!

When I had set up a course of sermons and study based upon a book published for the 1962 Lambeth Conference called "God and the Human Family" he willingly came to preach the first of the eight sermons, kept a large congregation enthralled for forty-five minutes, and in the discussion which we held in the Church Room after Evensong straight away (no refreshments) he gained an immediate rapport with the sixty or seventy people who had come by declaring: "This meeting is unique in the history of the Church of England. No refreshments are being served!" In the parish we had all studied the relevant chapter in the book, and each of the preachers was supposed to have done the same and was asked to preach on the subject of the chapter: the Family at Home, the Family and the Nation, the Family and the Neighbourhood, the Family and the World at large, the Family and Work, the Family and the Church, the Family grows up, God and Family Life. George Reindorp was the *only* one who had obviously read his chapter in the midst of a busy life, and preached on it. One or two of the rest had plainly not read their piece, others turned out an old sermon and tried without success to make it fit. This was a measure of the man. When I was elected to the Church Assembly and took my place in the great debating Hall of Church House, it was George who left his seat to come over and welcome me, though I was no longer in his diocese and had left some years before. His little books on preaching are gems of common sense, and his published sermons are direct, challenging, sometimes humorous, sometimes moving, models for the budding preacher.

George Reindorp was a close friend of David Say, Bishop of Rochester (the "tallest Bishop in the Church of England") and when David Say was looking for a full-time Diocesan Director of Education I guess he discussed the appointment with George. The Bishop of Guildford had already offered me several "livings" which I had turned down, much to his surprise, but I was not willing to leave St.

Stephen's at a time which would prejudice my children's education. Bishops sometimes forget the need to consult. When I turned down one parish the Bishop rang me up and said, "My staff and I (that is, his assistant Bishop and the Archdeacons) have discussed the matter fully and we think you should go to Camberley." But the staff and he had not thought to discuss the move with *me*! I protested at the lack of consultation and the lack of appreciation of my family situation. Jill was fifteen at the time, soon to take her "O" levels and it was quite the wrong time for her to change schools or lose all her friends. Later she became Head Girl at Godalming, and went on to Leicester University, so I was glad we stayed. Peter was away at school at Ardingly College, so he would have been less affected. When we eventually moved to Rochester Peter was twenty-one and Jill was nineteen and a half.

George accepted my protest and I think it was a cautionary tale which he took to heart when he mas contemplating moving other clergy from their parishes. Negotiations over the move to Rochester were lengthy and complicated. The Bishop of Rochester first wrote to me on February 20th, 1964:

"Dear Mr. Hoffman,

Although I do not think we have met, we have mutual friends and I am presuming on this to write and ask you whether you would be interested in being considered for the appointment of full-time Director of Religious Education in this Diocese. I want someone who will be primarily concerned with education from the cradle to the grave in our parishes and with the relationship between parishes and every kind of school and college. We have only a comparatively small number of church schools and I do not want the Director to be too much involved in the detailed work of buildings and trusts. I want him to be the leader of a team which includes a Youth Chaplain, a Children's Advisor, several Industrial Chaplains all doing educational work, a Moral Welfare education secretary and one or two others.

It is likely that the post will be paid at the rate of a residentiary Canonry i.e. £1,500 per annum and that I shall be able to give whoever is appointed the status of a Canon in the diocese.

I do not know how you are placed or what your plans are but if this kind of thing appeals to you and you would like to meet me and to discuss it further I shall be very happy to hear from you.

Yours sincerely,

DAVID ROFFEN. "

As I shall relate in the next chapter, no decisions on either side were made for many months, but as I end this account of being a Vicar it may "round up the record" if I recall some of the things that I wrote in the parish Magazine of December 1964. (I was not able to tell the parish that I was leaving until the letter I wrote for November's issue on October 13th.) In December I wrote:

"For one who like myself enjoys playing with statistics it would be tempting in this, my last letter, to tell you that I have preached about 1600 sermons, addressed at least a thousand meetings in the Diocese and district, and paid 14,000 visits (at least) and so on. But strangely these are not the things I am most conscious of. What I am chiefly aware of is a sense of omission - the things that I have not been able to do, the people I have not been able to visit, the young people I have not been able to influence for God, the occasions when I have disobeyed the guidance of God. I am aware of my inadequacies in the face of some great personal need or distress in one of your families. As we say in confession - 'for these and all my other sins which I cannot now remember I humbly ask pardon of God...' and your pardon too, knowing that I receive it from the most forgiving God and the most forbearing and understanding of parishes.

In this magazine we have never spent much time and space on the past which is beyond recall. It is the present that matters, the eternal "Now" of God, and the future which so quickly becomes the "Now". I have no qualms about the future of the Church. Men have written it off before, centuries ago and in our own day. They are wrong, for the Church is of God, and in spite of all that *we* do to kill it, it will survive because this is God's will. Nor do I have any doubt that the future life of the parish will be strong and secure and outward looking if its present members remain faithful to God, regular in their Communion worship, in their personal religious practices and in their service of their neighbours."

I ended the letter with the famous prayer about those to whom much is given and from whom much would be required and said, "Shottermill, its Church and its people, will constantly be in my prayers of thanksgiving and intercession. May I ask that we shall be sometimes in yours too?"

I know that we were, and eighteen months later, in Rochester, I received on the 25th anniversary of my Ordination as a priest, a lovely card of congratulations bearing the signatures of nearly a hundred members of my former beloved congregation at St. Stephen's.

In that same issue of the magazine I was able to record a relaxation of the official Roman Catholic attitude to members of their Church taking part in non-Roman services and in prayers with other Christians. I was able to express the hope that Father Borelli would be allowed to be present at the institution and induction of my successor, Dennis Hyde, but I felt obliged to add:

"We should be failing in our duty to our Christian calling if we did not also record our regret that these relaxations go so little of the way to break down the real barriers. We long for the day when a non-Roman priest is allowed to join in Rome's worship, when in a mixed marriage the non-Roman party does not have to sign the forms that so offend other Christians, when Rome learns that the Spirit of God can and does guide others into the truth. That is why we are thankful for small mercies, but look one day for greater concessions."

I continued:

"Perhaps it is true with Roman Catholics (as I think it is with us) that the people are way ahead of their leaders in this matter. For I must finally record my lasting impression of the charity and good sense of the staff of our Roman Catholic Hospital where I have spent so much of my time ministering to the sick. Here I have always been received as a true priest; the Sacrament I have taken from ward to ward has always (except on very rare occasions, and then only through the ignorance of a rigorously taught ward maid) been reverenced as a true Sacrament. In the days when I used to take the Bishop into Holy Cross to confirm tubercular patients, he was always regarded and treated as a Bishop. I have often been called out to administer the last rites to patients, and, what pleases me most of all, I have been accorded the very precious title (to all Roman Catholics and to not a few Anglicans also!) of 'Father'.

If any of them read this - and I believe some of the staff do in Holy Cross, I trust without getting into trouble with 'authority', will they please accept my gratitude for all their help?"

So I wrote in December 1964.

Nearly thirty years have passed. Some of those pleas have been answered and the Pope of Rome and the Archbishop of Canterbury have knelt side by side at the altar in Canterbury Cathedral. Many barriers however still remain and not least among them, the Ordination of Women. I am encouraged by the fact that there is a strong, if little publicised, movement within the Roman Church towards the abolition of the requirement that priests must be celibate, and, not only among Roman Catholic lay-women but among their priests and nuns, towards the Ordination of women. The Pope's fierce attack on Women's Ordination in 1994 ("forbidden *forever*") has not helped the movement to unity.

Because the life of a Vicar and the life of a diocesan priest would be so different in so many ways, I tried in my final magazine to list some of the things I would miss in parish life. I wrote:-

"SOME THINGS I SHALL MISS (and some I shan't!)
(Least important things first!)

> Our lovely countryside and the peaceful walks on
> Marley, Blackdown and the Punchbowl.
>
> Our beautiful house and lawns, the spacious rooms
> and secluded quietness (but see later).

(Most important things next.)

> Our lovely Church with its perfect 'atmosphere'.
>
> The crowded festivals and especially the Parish
> Communions and Breakfasts.
>
> The quite delightful choir girls and choirboys - and
> trying to beat some love and understanding of
> Church music into their thick heads.
>
> Preparing folk for Confirmation and marriage and
> taking the sacrament to the sick at home and in
> hospital.
>
> My work with the Schools and the privilege of
> trying to help them. (I will still have this work
> but it will be of a different kind.)
>
> Being made a friend and confidant of so many of
> you and for the welcome I have received in all
> your homes.
>
> Teaching you the Christian Faith on Sundays and
> weekdays, particularly in Lent.
>
> The regular preaching to an appreciative and
> attentive congregation.
>
> Singing the services. In a Cathedral I shall have to
> keep quiet!
>
> The loyal co-operation of our Parish Workers,
> Church Officers and Councillors.
>
> Being 'The Vicar' - with the privilege and right to
> minister to every parishioner, being able to say
> 'good morning' and 'good afternoon' to
> everyone I meet without exception. In Diocesan
> work you have 'no one to call your own'.
>
> The list of 'things to be thankful for' (when hearing
> confessions I used always to give as part of the
> penance - 'make a list of ten things to be
> thankful for') is endless.

I shall not miss:
  Having to cope with a house of twenty-one rooms
    (there were seventeen main rooms and four
    lavatories).
  Tuesday evening's 'Pop' music in the Club.
  Those long Church Council meetings - necessary of
    course, but so wearing after a full day's work.
  Having to unravel twenty yards of messed up steel
    wire when Jack forgets to wind the Church
    clock and it stops.
I honestly can't think of anything else."

Perhaps all our visual retrospection is observed through "rose-coloured spectacles" and perhaps it is a feature to be thankful for in our human nature that we tend to forget the bad and remember the good. There *were* unhappy moments in my ministry. I referred obliquely to one in my last letter. This was the case of a suicide some few days after I had taken the funeral service for the husband of a non-churchgoing woman. I had visited her after the burial but perhaps I should have detected a depression and done more to help her; but one morning she was found dead on the railway line that ran alongside her road. Then there was a row with a Treasurer who regarded his work as stopping the Church from spending any money! We lost young people to aggressive "fringe" churches, and some left us when we ran a "stewardship" campaign, not being prepared to "pay the price". But in spite of all it was a very happy time in my life, being "The Vicar".

CHAPTER 10

ROCHESTER

"It is a reverend thing to see an ancient
castle or building not in decay."
Francis Bacon (d. 1626)

"Beautiful city! So venerable, so lovely, so unravaged by the
fierce intellectual life of our century! Whispering from
their towers the last enchantments of the Middle age.
Home of lost causes and forsaken beliefs..."
Matthew Arnold (d. 1888)
(Written of Oxford, but why not of Rochester?)

The Bishop of Guildford had not intimated to me that he was the
"mutual friend" of whom David Say had written, but I guessed that he
was. I had not at any time felt any ambition for advancement in the
Church, but I had been a parish priest for nearly a quarter of a
century, and had been at Shottermill for more than thirteen years.
Was this the time to seek new directions for my energies and talents?
Moreover, was it time for me to allow the good folk of Shottermill a
change of Vicar, a change of voice and personality and approach? I
had fairly recently been thinking that I had no more "shots in my
locker", that I needed a break from the routines of parish life. I was
aware that the parish needed to be pushed in new directions in worship
and pastoral care.

I had long talks with Pat, who loved her work at Midhurst
Grammar School, now a mixed school with a Girls' boarding house,
where she was largely responsible for the smooth change-over and the
entry of the girls without any of the traumatic difficulties which often
accompany such educational upheaval. When she became, as well as
PE mistress, the Domestic Science teacher, after her course at the
Battersea College (where my sister had also trained many years
before) she and I had designed the new D.Sc. room at the school. She
got on well with the Head and the rest of the staff. She worked well

with Ken Allport, the boys' PE master, not always an easy thing to do, as they shared playing fields at Cowdray Park. It would be a wrench and she was well aware that it might be difficult for her to obtain another post as part PE, part D.Sc. teacher, though the fact that my sister Enid was a headmistress in Gravesend might have been a help. Enid was a first class Head and was well regarded in the profession, not only by her own staff and other schools, but also by the County authorities at Maidstone. New schools were being built in considerable numbers in Kent in the 60's to accommodate the "post-war boom" in children of Secondary ages, so such posts might be available. It would matter little to Peter and Jill where they came home for their holidays from College or work.

It would be a false humility for me to say that I was not flattered by the implications in the Bishop of Rochester's letter. George Reindorp had plainly told him that I was capable of coping with what was clearly a "big job" (in the Reindorp sense mentioned earlier!) and of leadership. This letter was to have considerable significance in the coming years, for David Say would seem not to have told the various people mentioned in the letter that I was to be their "leader", and I did find myself deeply involved with buildings and trusts. More of that in due course.

Pat agreed to my sending a reply that I was indeed interested in the post, though the question of the Canonry seemed to be ambiguous. Fifteen hundred pounds a year would be about twice what I was being paid as a Vicar, and I would certainly be receiving "expenses of office" which were meagre at Shottermill. It would be dishonest therefore for me to pretend that the money element played no part in our decision. In the event it transpired that not only would all official expenses be paid but also that I would have the use of a Diocesan car, which would free our own car for Pat's exclusive use, which would be important if the teaching post she obtained was far from our new home.

No formal offer of the post for me was made for several weeks, and the notice of my appointment did not appear until September 30th. This was largely due to the problem of the Canonry. There are a set number of Honorary Canonries in the gift of a Bishop and it is only when a vacancy occurs by death or departure that he can make a new appointment. The Bishop and I had several meetings in London and Rochester, and it also appeared that the house was a problem. A new house was being built in the Cathedral precincts for a new *residentiary* Canon, and we were sent plans of it in order to link them with our furniture and to plan rooms. Correspondence with the Dean, the Archdeacon and the Bishop did not make it clear - I don't think anyone was clear at the time - whether I was to be the Residentiary Canon. I myself did not wish this as I could foresee a conflict of loyalties between Cathedral and diocese - which my later conversations with Diocesan Directors of Education told me was frequently the case where the Director was also on the Cathedral staff.

At this time the Rochester Diocesan officers and staff were housed in an 18th century mansion overlooking the river Medway called White Friars, but were about to be transferred to new offices being built inside a redundant church, next door to the Cathedral, on two floors, while retaining the ground floor section as a Church, and a "Board Room" on the other side of the first floor. When the transfer was complete, White Friars could be made habitable again for me and my family. Meanwhile, for six months we would have to find accommodation for ourselves (and pay for it ourselves - a fact which Archdeacon Harland insisted on and which I resented, as I had been promised a house free of rent and rates and dilapidations. I think my cross words with the Archdeacon over this action on his part were to be remembered by him for all the time I knew him. He was not used to people who spoke their minds forcefully to him!). We found a small and inconvenient and draughty little house in Sole Street, the village where my sister lived and Pat was given a temporary post for two terms at her school, Wombwell Hall, a Technical High School in Gravesend.

When White Friars was empty the Diocese spent £3,000 putting it into habitable order, with a new double garage and we moved our furniture out of store and took up our residence there for the next fifteen years. It was a lovely house, with tall elegant rooms, and large windows with pleasant views of the Medway traffic, in particular the barges carrying wood pulp from Scandinavia to the paper mills at Aylesford. White Friars was perhaps even larger than the Shottermill Vicarage, for it had an attic and a basement. Later on we decorated the basement and used it for the many staff parties which Pat gave, and young people's parties for Jill and her friends. There was a large drawing room which I also used for meetings of clergy and Readers, my study and five bedrooms upstairs plus the usual offices. In 1967 Peter and his friend Andrew Rowland built an Enterprise (13'9") boat in the basement and (of course!) the window had to be removed to get the boat out. The front garden was mostly lawn, so was easy to maintain, but a clay soil side garden always did defeat me. I just could not eradicate the buttercups. Today I should not try to improve it and it would be my "conservation area" for the cultivation of wild life! Once again we were able to use our large mansion to help homeless friends and staff.

Pat had interviews at various schools in the area and in September 1965 joined the staff of Walderslade Secondary Girl's School as Deputy Headmistress to a Head who was a Methodist Lay preacher who had been a Youth Leader overseas. We always suspected that the fact that Pat was married to a clergyman weighed with her in the appointment, but Pat was a great disappointment to Miss Barbara Schofield who treated her as her own private assistant and had no idea how to use a Deputy as a channel of communication with her staff. She belonged to the "no smoking, no drinking, no dancing" type of Methodist and never forgave Pat for telling the children to bring some beer or brandy to school when, in Domestic Science, (then about to be called Home Economics) lessons, the girls were making Christmas cakes and puddings. Such attitudes lead inevitably to deceit, and when the staff held their own parties, they would bring their own alcoholic drinks to school in lemonade bottles.

Because Pat was such an outgoing person and such a marvellous teacher, with a genius for making friends among staff, and pupils and their parents, she became very popular, and her brilliant flair for teaching games soon brought to the girls of the Walderslade teams the same success that she had achieved at Twickenham and in West Sussex at Midhurst, but with a different type of girl. Walderslade was a "new" suburb of Chatham and was composed almost entirely of recently built housing estates. Many of the girls were from broken homes, some were from County Council homes for disruptives. It was not an easy school to work in, and Pat gave her whole being to it. When she returned home at about 5.30 p.m. each day I always tried to be there so that she could unwind and tell me all that had happened at school during the day. I am sure that this cemented our relationship, as I would also unburden myself of many of the problems and people that I had had to deal with during the day.

I was also able to help her when she was expected to "fill in" by taking RE lessons, and the morning Assemblies. She and Miss Schofield were poles apart as teachers, and many of the Head's methods and principles were contradictory. It was important that Pat could unload some of her real frustrations upon me, and I was able to help her with the administrative side of her work, the records and personal files and reports. We set up a most effective "work experience" system for girls for a day a week, but though this was long before "work experience" had become common in secondary schools, it collapsed because of the objection of the Trades Unions and the inability of the County to find insurance cover for the girls.

"Rochester," says one guide, "owes its long history and cultural significance to its strategic site. It guards the approach to London and the heartlands of England from the south-east at the first crossing of the Medway between its estuary and the impenetrable Weald. Here the ancient Britons fought against the Romans, the Romano-British against the Angles, Saxons and Jutes, the Anglo-Saxons against the Danes, King John against the Barons, the Royal Navy against the Dutch Fleet, and as late as 1940 the Royal Air Force against the Luftwaffe in the Battle of Britain. But the story of Rochester is not only a story of wars and rumours of wars; it is also the story of faithfulness to the Good News of Jesus Christ and of service to the Prince of Peace, for it numbers among its great symbolic constructions not only a bridge and a castle but also a Cathedral Church."

White Friars sat on a high bank a few yards from the Castle. It overlooked the famous Medway bridge and from its front door could be seen, across the dry sunken Castle moat, the West door of the Cathedral. We were in the midst of a small world of history reaching back to Roman times and it could not fail to impress and influence those who are sensitive to its atmosphere. The bridge was somewhat of a nuisance as well as a vital crossing for those who lived to the east of it and worked in Strood, Gravesend, Dartford, and all points westward to London; vital too to those who lived to the west and worked in Chatham, Rainham, Gillingham, Sittingbourne, Canterbury and all points to Dover in the east! I often wondered whether some scheme could be devised by which people were enabled to work on their own side of the Medway! It would have saved those endless time-wasting queues of traffic on the bridge which necessitated adding minutes to every journey westwards. The castle was a tourist attraction, but was a dead building and I often used it as an illustration of the contrast between Church and State, between a living community and a dead and empty shell dedicated to war and political strife; for the original Castle and the original Cathedral had both been built by the same hand.

Rochester High Street was part of the original Watling Street, the great Roman road from Dover to London and thence to St. Albans and Dunstable and on through to the Severn, and there are still visible Roman remains in the foundations of the south wall of the cloisters of the Cathedral. But Rochester's real history began when Pope Gregory of Rome sent Augustine to Britain to convert the English in 595 and made him Archbishop of Canterbury in 597 AD Shortly before his death in 604 Augustine consecrated, as Bishops of Rochester and London, two of his companions in mission, Justus at Rochester and Mellitus at London. At Rochester a Cathedral Church in honour of St. Andrew was built. Nothing remains of this building and little of the Saxon cathedral which followed it, and the key figure in Rochester's early history was a little man from the Abbey of Bec called Gundulf who was Bishop from 1077-1108. He was a great builder, responsible for the early Norman parts of the Cathedral, the Castle, (the present great keep was built later) the Tower of London, St. Mary's Abbey and St. Leonard's tower at West Malling, and the still standing chapel of St. Bartholomew's Hospital, Rochester. Later builders of the present Cathedral kept to Gundulf's ground plan, and additions were made in all the following centuries up to the early 19th when the central tower was rebuilt. It was in 1540 that what had been a monastic priory was dissolved and the Cathedral was given a new name (the dedication to St. Andrew being abandoned) and the foundation was re-incorporated under the name of "the Dean and Chapter of the Cathedral Church of Christ and the Blessed Virgin Mary of Rochester". The last prior became the first Dean.

I loved the Cathedral, and though I was not, to my great relief, to be a residentiary Canon, I was invited by the Dean to take services of Evensong and celebrate the Holy Communion there each week. It was always a haven of peace and tranquillity and after a morning's work in the office in the new Diocesan headquarters in St. Nicholas Church next door (what a commentary on relationships within the Church that a parish Church should have been built in rivalry to the

Cathedral, ten yards away!) I would spend half an hour quietly in some part of the Cathedral, sitting, admiring the diligence and technical expertise of Norman and mediaeval builders, meditating and praying and planning.

The Medway towns of Rochester, Chatham, and Gillingham had a population of some two hundred thousand at that time, a vast sprawling conurbation, with the famous Chatham Royal dockyard where ships for the Royal Navy had been built since 1588, and a mass of small and large industrial factories. I have never been a "city" man and I suppose that my pastoral work had been set in pleasant places where the response to the Christian Gospel was positive and encouraging in the main, but I came to realise what an uphill task the clergy in the old cities and the new housing estates had in such a vast built-up area. In a downtown parish of ten thousand there might be fifty people in church on a Sunday, whereas in a Kentish village of a thousand souls there would be a hundred. I remember one hard-pressed and harassed parish priest saying to me, "Your job will be to encourage us, to get us out of our depression, and help us not to lose our faith." What a task for a new "Diocesan Official"!

It was that view of the clergy "at the centre" which I tried to dispel. I never came to regard myself as one of "them" at the centre, as opposed to one of "us" at parish level. I was never able to forget that I had my own origins in the parish as a small choirboy in St. Mary's Denham, that I had been an active layman in the parish at Gerrards Cross, and that for twenty and more years my daily care had been for the people in parishes, their hospitals, their schools, their meeting places, their clubs, their youth clubs. I had spent a large part of my ministry in baptising, preparing for confirmation, marrying, burying, ordinary folk from ordinary homes in ordinary streets and roads in ordinary undistinguished little communities.

In 1973 I felt the need to preach a sermon in several parishes where tensions between parish and diocese had arisen, called "Fellowship in the Diocese". The "Diocese" (the word means housekeeping, management, government) of Rochester comprised West Kent and the boroughs of Bromley and Bexley. It had over two hundred parishes and at that time about three hundred clergy, and in the sermon I explained about the "Staff", Bishops, Archdeacons, and the various responsibilities of those at the centre who were concerned with finance, education, social work, industry, women's work, stipends, pensions, parsonage houses, stewardship, music, drama, worship, mission and unity, Readers and their training, post-ordination training, pre-ordination selection, etc. etc. And I had to explain that though as a parish priest I had often grumbled at the sums we had to pay to the diocese, I had come to realise that parishes get back from the centre much more than they are expected to give. I said, "We who work for the diocese would like to see ourselves, and be seen, as servants of the people in the parishes, who are called today 'resource persons' willing and eager to offer help and any expertise we may have in our particular spheres. Please do not regard us as 'them' away in far off Rochester. All of us are members of congregations and all of us spend an immense amount of time in the parishes... I myself spent twenty-nine Sundays in 1972 in parishes and on weekdays went into sixty-five others... today from my Diocesan Office I sometimes feel that it is I who have cause to complain: that clergy and teachers don't answer letters, that what we are trying to do is being blocked by ignorance and sheer stubbornness, that our motives are being questioned or our intentions misinterpreted. How silly all that is! How wicked! If Christians cannot communicate with each other in charity and understanding, who can?..."

I don't know whether today I could preach that sermon with a clear conscience and I don't know what effect my words had on those who heard them or whether they were even addressed to those who needed to hear them, but over the years I think that relationships between the parish and the centre improved and the fact that I was invited to preach in 179 of the then 203 parishes was reward in itself for all the efforts made, as was the fact that the majority of the parishes and the majority of the ninety odd Church Schools contributed in some way to my farewell gifts in 1980. If I had been tied to the Cathedral as a member of the Chapter my work with the parishes would have been restricted. As it was, I valued more than I can say the opportunity to join with the ordinary parishioner in the worship of his parish Church, mostly as the "visiting preacher" it is true, but also as a ordinary worshipper.

Today I would guess, Rochester's fame rests not in its bridge, its Castle or its Cathedral, but in its association with Charles Dickens who was born in 1812 and died in 1870 at his house in Strood, across the river from Rochester, Gad's Hill, now a school. His last unfinished novel, *Edwin Drood*, was set in and around the Cathedral.

Miss Havisham's house from *Great Expectations* can be seen as "Restoration House" in Rochester, and much of *The Pickwick Papers* is related to places in and around the city. The Dickens Festival was evolving in our time at Rochester and has grown into a well attended international event, with characters in Dickensian costume crowding the High Street.

Rochester is still an important river port for woodpulp, and if the Isle of Grain is included it was once one of the most important centres in the world for importing and refining oil.

One of the historic survivors of the Augustinian influence on Kent in the early centuries was the King's School, Rochester, reputedly founded in 604 AD in the episcopate of Justus, first Bishop of Rochester. It is a comparatively small school. Because it is a Cathedral foundation the Governors were made up of the Cathedral Chapter of Dean and four Canons, together with representatives of other bodies in the County and diocese, including the Diocesan Board of Education. When the time came for the Board to nominate its Governor the members nominated me, for various reasons. I lived in Rochester; I knew some members of the staff and some of the boys; I (presumably) had some knowledge of the educational needs of independent schools; and my own son had been at an independent Church School, the Woodard School at Ardingly.

It came as a shock to the Board as well as to myself, when we received a letter from the then Headmaster, Canon Douglas Vicary, turning down the nomination on the grounds that there were already too many clergymen on the Governing Body! Apart from the fact that this was probably a technically illegal act, it was an insult to both the Board and myself, however much, as a clergyman myself, I might have sympathy with that viewpoint. Vicary had had a distinguished career as a scholar of Trinity College, Oxford, with a first class degree in Chemistry and a distinction in the Theological Diploma. He had been a school Chaplain, a College Chaplain and a tutor at Wycliffe Hall, the evangelical theological college in Oxford. He had been one of my predecessors as Director, as well as a Minor Canon and a Residentiary Canon, before becoming Headmaster of the King's School in 1957. He had also been for five years Director of Post-Ordination Training, so he had certainly spent a great deal of his time in the company of clergymen! He and I got on very well together, and I was often invited to preach when the boys from the School attended their Cathedral services. In due course he relented and I became a nominated Governor.

Vicary had been appointed to all these Cathedral posts in the time of Christopher Maude Chavasse who had become Bishop of Rochester in 1939. Chavasse was a convinced and rather bigoted evangelical whose father had been a famous Bishop of Liverpool, and he had been deeply involved in the foundation of St. Peter's Hall in Oxford in 1929, becoming Master of the Hall. The evangelical influence on the whole diocese was very strong in Chavasse's time, and lingered on for many years after Bishop David Say was appointed in 1961. It was rumoured that so strong was Chavasse's anti-Anglo-Catholic bias that he had refused to conduct Confirmations in "Catholic" parishes, though I cannot affirm the truth of the rumour. David Say was a much more balanced individual, and without failing under St. Paul's censure of being "All things to all men", he was a welcome visitor in all types of parish and a true "Pastor pastorum" to all his clergy, whatever their ecclesiastical colour and background. The Chavasse influence had been strong in the appointment of Deans and Canons of the Cathedral as well as in the appointment of Heads of the School.

I suppose that Heads were more autocratic in the 50's than they are allowed to be today, and resented interference, especially on the part of their Governors. When I became a Governor of the King's School I was amazed to discover that the only member of Staff that the Governors ever met officially was the Head, and that even he was excluded from certain parts of Governors' meetings. It was of course normal for Heads not to be present when they were being discussed personally by the Governors in relation to their salary, housing, etc., but for all other matters it was essential, in my view, that they should be present and take a full part in discussion and debate. To be present only to give their regular reports and then withdraw was a custom in many schools in the diocese and County, I discovered, and I proposed that where possible Heads should be present for the whole meeting. This was accepted, with some reservations, by the King's Governors. I also ascertained that no Governors took part in the appointment of Staff except the Dean, a residentiary Canon, and the Head. I proposed that this should be changed and in future at least one non-Cathedral governor should be present at appointments. This proposal was debated at length and after a long period was also accepted, as was my suggestion that we should all meet some, if not all, of the

Staff in a social context after Governors' meetings. This was something I tried to institute in all the Church Schools in the diocese. I had been appalled to find that except for the Head, many managers and governors had never met any of the staff of the schools they were supposed to be managing or governing. I still wonder whether statutory bodies like Deans and Chapters whose knowledge and experience mostly lie elsewhere should be ex-officio governors of Schools like King's.

Cathedrals are ruled by Chapters, consisting of a Dean or Provost and a certain number of Canons, usually four. The word Cathedral indicates that in it there is the "cathedra" or Bishop's chair and it surprises many that in spite of his exalted position in the Church and diocese the Bishop has no real powers over the activities of the inner Chapter, though he may from time to time make a "visitation", and the Chapter is bound to take note and if possible act upon the Bishop's recommendations. The word "Chapter" relates to a section of a monastic rule which was read daily and publicly in religious houses. Some Cathedrals, including Rochester, were of monastic foundation, others were "secular". The "Greater Chapter" of a Cathedral consists of the Residentiary Canons, plus the Honorary Canons, installed as such for their seniority or some special expertise or contribution which they have made to the life of the Church in the diocese. There were twenty of us at Rochester, together with the Suffragan Bishop and the three Archdeacons of Rochester, Tonbridge, and Bromley. We met from time to time to consider matters of wide interest concerning the Cathedral. We did not control policy but could make general comments and suggestions. Cathedral finances were often a topic and at one meeting it was revealed that the working conditions of the Cathedral staff, the vergers and cleaners, were disgraceful, and that money must be found to improve them, as well as the houses owned by the Chapter in which they lived. The Cathedral was in possession of certain items of silverware, non-religious in origin, called "Tazzas" originally wine cups with a shallow bowl and a circular foot, but in this case, I understand, though we were never shown them, more like Elizabethan beer mugs. It was proposed that they be sold and the money used for the benefit of those projects. I had always been much concerned that the Church should use its treasures for *people*, in advance of *buildings*, and also that we should exercise a proper stewardship of our income, including overseas aid, so I proposed, and it was accepted, that of whatever sum was obtained for the silver, a tenth should be invested and the income applied to charitable purposes at home and overseas.

But the first hurdle had not yet been overcome. The Bishop had to approve the sale, and if anyone objected the case would have to come before a consistory Court. At first the Bishop was unhappy about the sale, as were some members of the Chapter, but after a long period of debate and discussion lasting many months, it was agreed that the silver should not be sold at public auction but, offered to museums. One suggestion had been that it should be put on view in the Cathedral, but the insurance costs of such public display would have been prohibitive, and in any case would nullify the whole object of the exercise, which was to capitalise on possessions which were never seen and which had never had, as far as was known, a "religious" use. Eventually the British Museum purchased the Tazzas, the conditions of the vergers' working spaces were improved and various home and overseas charities benefited to the tune of several hundred pounds a year.

Now that the Church Commissioners have "lost" some £800,000,000 of the Church's capital, the question of replacing the income from that vast sum has arisen urgently. When we were discussing the disposal of the Tazzas I was reminded of the 17th century chalice in the possession of St. Stephen's, Shottermill, which no one had ever laid eyes on, as it was in Lloyds Bank, and how I had since come to the conviction that to possess such an item was wrong if it had a large cash value which could be used for the benefit of *people* and the work of the Gospel. I know that when Judas (who was treasurer to the apostolic band) saw the "waste" of the precious ointment in the alabaster box poured over Jesus feet, he remarked that it could have been sold and the proceeds given to the poor, and that Jesus had replied, "the poor you have always with you. Me you have not always with you." I have always thought that those who use this as an argument against selling the churches' material treasures were mistaken in their understanding of what Jesus was saying, and in their exegesis of the text. The whole point of the story is that it took place only two days (or according to John, six days) before the Passover, i.e. not long before the death of Jesus, and though giving alms to the poor was always praiseworthy, anointing before a burial was a greater act of kindness. In other words Jesus did not say it was wrong to use valuable assets for the benefit of the needy; he said that *in this particular case* the woman was doing something that no one else would be doing for him, preparing him for death and burial. It is, in my view, now time that every parish should review its treasures and in the true spirit of stewardship, should use them to make provision for the "stewards of the mysteries", the actual people who have given themselves wholly to the work of proclaiming the Gospel, as well as looking after the poor and needy.

Dioceses are divided into Rural Deaneries. The word "Rural" like many ecclesiastical terms which are usually a relic of the past, (in modern contexts - in towns and cities for example), is a misnomer, even a joke. The Rural Dean is appointed by the Bishop as "head" or "leader" of a group of parishes covering a certain area. Neither the word head nor the word leader is perhaps an accurate description of what a Rural Dean is supposed to be and do, because most of his ancient duties (and the office is of some antiquity) have been taken over by the Archdeacon, the Bishop's legal officer. The office was revived in 1836 and the Rural Dean is the President of the Ruridecanal Chapter, i.e. the incumbents and clergy licensed under seal in the Deanery, and co-chairman (now - not in 1965) of the Ruridecanal Conference of Clergy and Laity of the parishes in the Deanery, which are now called "Synods" under the Measure of 1969.

In my musings on how to get to know and be known in the Diocese as a full-time Director and "leader of a team", it occurred to me very early on that the key clergy *should* be the sixteen Rural Deans who would be meeting in Chapter with all the clergy in the diocese from time to time and also with the key laity. In my first few weeks in Rochester I wrote to all the Rural Deans and asked if I might attend one of their Clergy Chapter meetings to talk about education in its widest sense, and to give them my vision of the future, and to ask them for theirs, in the various parts of diocesan life represented by the team. For this purpose I prepared a paper, to be sent to the Rural Deans in advance and with copies available for the clergy in their Deanery. The response, as always in the Church of England, was mixed. Some Rural Deans were enthusiastic, particularly the younger ones, who replied immediately with an invitation. Some were accepting but hardly enthusiastic. Others, the older, more cynical and disillusioned, were frankly not enthusiastic. Two did not even trouble to reply. In preparation for the meeting in their Chapter I paid a personal call on each Rural Dean to listen and take note. My reception by one clergyman was hostile, by one or two rather cold, but it was something of an achievement to have made contact within my first few weeks in the diocese with those whom the Bishop, at least in appointing them, had regarded as influential leaders of their colleagues.

I was myself very enthusiastic about the possibilities stemming from such Chapter meetings, but I was soon to be somewhat disillusioned. Clergy are always suspicious, as I have already remarked, of those at "the centre", of Diocesan officials for whom they have to pay salaries and maintenance via the parish "quota". My first meeting was with the clergy of the Rochester Chapter, and I thought it had gone well, when, in the discussion which followed my talk, one local incumbent asked: "Who says we need a full time Director of Education? Who pays your salary? I don't think we need you at all."

I was grateful to John Bickersteth, the then Vicar of St. Stephen's Chatham and later Bishop of Bath and Wells, when he took me aside after this meeting and said: "Don't worry about so and so. He speaks only for himself. We are glad that you have come to Rochester and we will do all we can to help you and co-operate with you." I learned later that the clergyman in question was both unpopular and incompetent and that his days in the priesthood were numbered, though he was not of retiring age. There were always some clergy who continued to be doubtful about whether I was needed, but on the whole they welcomed all the moves we made to help them in their parish ministry and where they had schools they were always glad of advice and the financial help the Diocesan Board could give when their buildings needed repair or rebuilding. The many booklets I wrote for parish study were always appreciated and were much used, and I was increasingly invited to preach - not necessarily, indeed, rarely, about education. I especially welcomed the chance to preach a course of sermons, in Lent, or Advent, because it made me settle down to discover what I myself believed and work out ways to make the Christian faith relevant (blessed word!) to the daily life the congregations had to live at home, at work, and in community.

Welcome too was the opportunity to prepare the girls of Cobham Hall for Confirmation. This was a select private ("Public") school housed in the great mansion of the Cobham family a few miles from

Rochester, and most of the girls were highly intelligent and articulate, and did not hesitate to question the assumptions of the Faith. They were daughters of well known actors, politicians, financiers and military families. Meeting their parents socially after the Confirmation in the Cathedral I came to learn how very ordinary and unassuming are many of the famous, and how untrue their public image tends to be. I had prepared the girls of another independent school, the Grove School at Hindhead, over many years when I was a Vicar in Surrey and both there and at Cobham Hall I discerned that families at every level of society have to face the same difficulties and dilemmas, the same problems of relationships within the family. Divorce has the same devastating effect upon the children of a marriage whether the parents are on the dole or possessed of a mansion and a hundred thousand pounds a year. The disruptive girl at the Grove who spent a whole afternoon slashing all the coats in the school cloakroom and later, on another occasion, stealing all the toothbrushes, had the same problems and was subject to the same unbearable emotional pressures as the girl at the Secondary Modern who was constantly stealing money from her fellows, or the girl at Cobham Hall who was always uncooperative and obstructive in lessons.

I was glad, since my work was often with teachers, to be invited to join the governing body of one of the Church's leading Teacher Training Colleges which had been built a few years before at Christ Church Canterbury. Geoffrey Templeman, the Vice Chancellor of the University of Kent at Canterbury at the time, was Chairman of Christ Church and I became Vice-Chairman, often chairing the meetings of Governors when the Chairman was otherwise engaged on University business. It was, to begin with, a time of growth for the Training Colleges, but later a time of upheaval as succeeding governments interfered with the running of the Colleges and the curriculum. It was also a time of student revolt and restlessness. One student had consistently failed his exams and was told that the College could no longer keep him as a student, and he was asked to leave. He demanded his "rights" to appeal to the Governors against this action, and to appeal to the College Visitor who was the Archbishop of Canterbury. He appeared before the Governors with his "friend" (a technical name for usually a lawyer, or student lawyer in this case, who would speak on behalf of the appellant and put his case). The

Governors' lawyer was also present and advised us as to the law. The student's case was that his dismissal was "against natural justice", a phrase which had come into frequent use in the late 60's and which was a new concept in law to most of us, since no one had defined it satisfactorily, and it would appear to mean something different in each case. This particular case went through all the processes of law, right up to the Court of Appeal (and, I seem to remember, even to the House of Lords) and the Governors won. It was a "test case" and would be quoted often in the future when students in Colleges and Universities were dismissed for various reasons.

There were two other problems facing the Governors of Christ Church, and some other Teacher Training Colleges which conferred degrees. One was the difficulty of finding bodies or Universities willing to validate the degrees. The Government had decreed that in future all teachers must read for and be possessed of an academic degree before they could be appointed to a maintained school. It seemed obvious to many of us that Christ Church and Kent University which were so close together in Canterbury, should come together academically. And it might well be that the College could offer courses that the University could not, and vice versa, and that therefore it was sensible for Kent University to confer the degrees on Christ Church students. The negotiations for this quite drastic change in relationship between the comparatively small and unimportant Church College and the important and growing University were difficult and lengthy, most of the problems being legal and academic. They were conducted by Maurice Vile, then a pro-Vice Chancellor of Kent for the University, and myself on behalf of Christ Church, with supporting staff and governors on both sides, in the utmost cordiality. It had fallen to me to lead our team because there would have been a conflict of interest (apparent rather than real) in the fact that Geoffrey Templeman was both the head of the University and Chairman of Christ Church. In 1978 the negotiations were concluded and approved by all the bodies that had to approve, including the Department of Education and Science, and from that year onwards the University of Kent at Canterbury, to give its full name, assumed responsibility for validating the degrees awarded to students at Christ Church, and at Nonington, another Kent training college, for mature students.

In 1984, although I had retired in 1980 from all my educational responsibilities I was greatly honoured to have conferred upon me in a

Degree Congregation (ceremony) in Canterbury Cathedral by the late Jo Grimond, later Lord Grimond, the University Chancellor, the Honorary Degree of Master of Arts in recognition of the work I had done in the County, in the College, and in the University, where I had also served in the School of Continuing Education. I was also greatly honoured to be asked to give a short address to a crowded Cathedral of students receiving degrees, their parents and friends, on behalf of all of us who were receiving honorary degrees. What I said can be found in an appendix. The exciting story of Kent University's birth and growth from 1965 when the first undergraduates arrived on site, until today, is told in a remarkable and most readable book by Graham Martin, *From Vision to Reality*.

The late 60s and the early 70s were also a time of some discontent among the members of the National Association of Teachers in Further and Higher Education (NATFHE) with its eighty thousand members. The other problem concerned "contact hours", the number of hours in the week that Staff in the Colleges were in contact with students either in lectures or in tutorials. NATFHE was fighting for a lowering of the number of hours to twelve or thirteen, so that teachers could spend more time on preparation of courses and research. The Colleges were sticking at fifteen hours. I suppose there was some advantage in the fact that I was an independent person when I undertook the negotiations on behalf of the Governors when, together with two other governors, we met the Staff Union members. These negotiations too were conducted in a perfectly friendly atmosphere with no sense of confrontation or resentment. Nor was it easy sometimes to refuse sabbatical leave to staff who wanted to do a year's research on some abstruse subject in Biblical studies or archaeological investigations, but where it put undue pressure on other staff who would have to "fill in" or where the teacher concerned had already had more than his fair share of leave, it was necessary to be firm in refusal.

Adjoining Rochester was the village of Borstal, famous for the setting up of the first prison for the reformation of young offenders in 1908. These institutions are now (since 1983) known as Youth Custody Centres. One of the assistant Governors of the Rochester Borstal was a Reader in the Diocese and he gave me the opportunity, supported by the Chaplain, to visit and talk with the boys. One Good Friday I took the morning service in the prison Chapel. It was an interesting experience. The boys sang well and listened intently when I talked about Jesus the Scapegoat, for some of them were probably scapegoats, suffering for the sins of others, who had been unlucky to be found out and convicted. After the service I spent an hour talking with the boys in their recreation room. Some were highly intelligent, and I remember one coloured boy in particular who was very articulate and engaged me in a lengthy debate about God. Some of them had been very violent before their incarceration, and most of them had been convicted of stealing cars and dangerous "joy-riding". It was the period of the "bovver boot", and some of them had been convicted of almost murderous use of the boot. They all came from some family and in conversation with the staff afterwards it became clear that crime is very much a family thing, and that most of the boys came from families where the father was a criminal and had served "time" in prison. The Chaplain was doing a remarkable job, as were the staff, and their record of "non-returners" was good, but today I am not so sure - there is much greater poverty among the kind of families who produce problem children, and the rise in the number of the unemployed has had the undoubted effect of raising the crime rate.

For many years I have been an advocate of specialist ministries, not as an escape from the often boring chores of the parish round, but because certain men and women have gifts which are best used in special ways and in special circumstances - the teacher, the Hospital Chaplain, the industrial Chaplain (one of Rochester's industrial Chaplains became Chaplain at Heathrow Airport - not a ministry which comes easily to the mind) even the Company Chaplain as well as the more obvious Chaplain to the Forces or to Colleges and Schools and Universities. The prison Chaplain and the Chaplain to a Borstal or Youth Custody Centre has a very special and a very difficult ministry, but one which is full of great hope and great possibilities. It requires a very special kind of person, sympathetic but firm, non-judgmental, but who knows in his own mind what is right and what is wrong, understanding and gentle but not sentimental, one who is not easily "bamboozled", for the young criminal is an expert in "pulling the wool" over the eyes of sympathetic adults. I take off my (metaphorical) hat to them all, and if I had known in 1965 what I now know about individualism, and the need for specialists to have their own unique approach to ministry, I would not have worried quite so much when the individual members of the "team" of which I was to be "leader" made it clear that their particular little sphere of work was inviolable!

I hope it has been made clear how grateful I have been for the many and diverse opportunities which I was given in Rochester! I owe them to David Say, my Bishop for sixteen years. In 1988 I was asked to write a personal tribute to Bishop David Say for a Parish Magazine. This is what I wrote.

THE MAN WHO ALWAYS HAD TIME
A personal tribute

In 1964 Bishop David Say of Rochester invited an insignificant parish priest in the Diocese of Guildford to become Diocesan Director of Religious Education and leader of a team which included a Youth Chaplain, Industrial Chaplains, a Children's Adviser, a Moral Welfare Organiser and others. It was either an act of tremendous faith on his part or a blind gamble because although this forty-seven year old clergyman had nearly a quarter of a century's parish experience, had sat on numerous Diocesan Committees, and had served as a Schools' Inspector he was not at heart a "diocesan" person. However, the invitation accepted, I arrived in deep snow on January 1st, 1965, with my family and there followed nearly sixteen years of happy and fruitful relationship with the clergy and people of Kent, supported at every turn by a Bishop for whom I developed the deepest respect and admiration. David Say was and is a true "father in God", an understanding "boss", and a thorough professional. So many of my fellow clergy (and not a few Bishops!) are unprofessional, not answering letters, unprepared in conducting worship, unwilling to learn the art of chairmanship, that it was a joy to serve under David Say. I had already ministered under seven diocesan Bishops and I had some strong views as to what kind of man a bishop should be.

Every Bishop has a public "persona" - David Say is "every inch a Bishop" - an imposing upright figure at ordinations, confirmations, civic services, dedications (what a mercy he did not wear a *tall* mitre) enjoying not a little those glorious occasions when a bishop is expected to preside. But every bishop is first and always a priest, and I remember him best, quietly and simply and humbly celebrating the Holy Communion for the "two or three gathered together" at 8 a.m. in the Cathedral crypt each week.

I saw him often too, taking the chair at numerous diocesan committees, never hogging the debate as I have observed some other diocesan bishops, who shall be nameless, doing. He listened. What a gift that is! He had his own views and no doubt his own prejudices, but he never imposed them on others. If his view prevailed it was through reason and persuasion.

In the sixteen happy years I spent in Rochester I sat in the Bishop's study on scores of occasions, discussing the next step in education, the opening of a new school, new steps in lay training, changes in liturgy, the role of the Reader. He is a man who always had time. A note would arrive in the Diocesan Office, written in that tiny script, seemingly out of character for such a big man, but completely legible - "Come and see me at...on..." If the subject under discussion needed an hour, an hour was available. Never once did the Bishop say "Sorry, we must end there. I am very busy and booked up today."

Of course, if you stay up until the early hours of the morning writing your (excellent) sermons, you have more time in the day for your prayers, your visitors, your pastoral care of your flock, your House of Lords speech, and your letters written in your own hand. In the years since I left the diocese with a sick wife, David Say has kept in touch.

So I think of him as "the man who *had* time; the man who *gave* of his time to all unstintingly; the man who *made* time" yet perhaps for twenty-seven years the busiest man in Kent. Before opening a new School, for example, he would ask to be briefed on its history and ethos. At the opening he would keep to his brief, having taken time in his preparation, and afterwards at the "do" he would mingle with children, parents, staff, governors and "bigwigs", perfectly at ease. His time had been well spent.

As I said, when I was a parish priest I had strong views about what made a man an ideal bishop. David Say measured up to my ideal. I shall always be grateful to him for his wisdom, his pastoral care, his friendship. He is a good Bishop and a great man.

In his retirement, as an assistant Bishop in the Canterbury Diocese, and facing his eightieth birthday in 1994, he is still a very busy man, but he still has time to write to me. The fact that my years in Rochester were so full of contentment and fulfilment I owe to him. Few other bishops would have so encouraged this individualist or allowed him the freedom to experiment and be himself. Thank you David.

CHAPTER 11

EDUCATOR

"I don't know, Ma'am, why they make all this fuss about education;
none of the Pagets can read or write, and they get on well enough."
Attrib. to Viscount Melbourne (d. 1848) (To the Queen)

"Do you know Carter, that I can actually write my name in the dust
on this table?
Faith, Mum, that's more than I can do. Sure, there's nothing like
education after all."
Caption to a cartoon in "Punch", 1902.

"A school is an organisation in which several responsibilities are
involved... to the parents for their children's safety, welfare and
progress... to the ratepayer, the taxpayer, to professional standards - a
whole complex of interacting responsibilities is there. Furthermore
the organisation is run by grown-ups, with their special needs and
limitations, prejudices and capacities."
*John Blackie, formerly HM Chief Inspector of Primary Schools in his
book "Good Enough for the Children?"*

The word I have used at the head of this chapter to describe part of
myself in an ugly word, defined in the dictionary as a "specialist in
education; one versed in the theory and practice of education." When
I took up my work as "Diocesan Director of Religious Education" I
was certainly not a specialist nor had I read many books on the
"theory" of it all. I had been sent by the Bishop on a residential
course for Directors, organised by Eric Wild, Secretary of the
National Society (founded in 1811 "for the Education of the Poor in
the principles of the Established Church") and Secretary of the Church
of England Schools Council, as it was then called. It was a valuable
conference but it was principally concerned with what Eric Wild (later
to be Bishop of Reading) called the "nuts and bolts" of administering
the two kinds of Church Schools, "Aided" and "Controlled", which

had been established under the 1944 Education Act. Henceforth in dealings with Local Education Authorities, the Ministry of Education as it was called in 1965, managers and governors and trustees, the 1944 Act and the Diocesan Education Committees Measure were to be my twin Bibles. (I almost said my Prayer Book, as well, because unravelling the complexities of the laws of education needed much earnest prayer!) Another necessary volume in the Director's library was Volume 12 of Halsbury "Laws" (Ecclesiastical Law) which, with its 1164 rules and regulations, was akin to the Old Testament with its detailed instructions to the faithful, for Ecclesiastical Law impinges on the Law of Education at many points.

The Bishop had written, "I do not want the Director to be too much involved in the detailed work of buildings and trusts." But this was a pious wish, because Religious Education goes on in buildings and is often controlled by trusts, and it was soon to be made clear that if a particular school was to survive so that religious education might take place, it had to be rebuilt to save it being closed down. So I was, involved with lawyers, LEAs, the Ministry, architects and builders, willy-nilly. The Bishop came to understand this in due course, though it took time to persuade him, and he thoroughly enjoyed meeting children, parents and staff of the schools which I was responsible for rebuilding or enlarging, nineteen of them all told, when we had grand opening services and ceremonies, in the new buildings.

Shelley wrote, "I love snow"; the Hoffman family were not quite so keen! On January 4th, 1965 I had been instituted and inducted as Vicar of Shottermill in the midst of a snow storm and in six inches of snow. *1951*

On January 5th, 1951 I was installed as a Canon of Rochester at Evensong, in deep snow. Only two friends from Shottermill were able to be present in addition to my family. The 75 miles from there to Rochester had become too much for anyone else in such atrocious weather. I had married Cyril (Bill) Harding to Ruth Bennett in August 1952 before he and Ruth left for work in Rhodesia. Cyril had seemed greatly to resent the requirement that he and Ruth should come to the Vicarage on several occasions for wedding preparation, though he came from a strongly Christian family. He had sat, silent and resentful, on my study couch. Several years later he returned to the parish and came to see me - "I want to apologise for my attitude when you married us - I have never forgotten what you said. It has *1965* helped us in our marriage and we want to play a full part in parish life." They did. His sons joined the choir. He became Churchwarden and forty years later he and Ruth are still pillars of St. Stephen's. I was thrilled to see him there.

Gwen Fryer had made an equally hazardous journey from Hastings. She had been a Surrey County Youth Officer, had helped with the Sunday School and Captained the Guides. For several years she had lived at the Vicarage. I was much affected by their presence and it meant a great deal to me that they represented in their own persons the care and affection of the many people of my former parish.

The stall which I was given in the Cathedral Choir bore the name of *John Fisher* who had been Bishop of Rochester from 1504 to 1535. When King Henry 8th was contemplating divorce, Fisher, who was the Queen's confessor, protested. It was he who in 1531 secured the insertion into the Act the important words, "as far as the law of God allows it", acknowledging Henry as "Supreme Governor" of the Church of England. He refused to take the oath demanded by the Act, and was tried and beheaded for attempting to maintain the Pope's supremacy.

A few stalls away one was bearing the name of *Nicholas Ridley* who had been Bishop of Rochester from 1547-1550 when he became Bishop of London. He had been much influenced by the Protestant teachings of the Reformation. When Mary Tudor became Queen after the death of Edward 6th (who had approved the 1549 and 1552 English Prayer Books, with their Protestant slant) in 1553, she was at first lenient towards her Protestant clergy, but after her marriage to the Roman Catholic Philip of Spain in 1554 she tried to impose Roman Catholic doctrines once more and the supremacy of the Pope was reasserted. Nicolas Ridley, Thomas Cranmer, Archbishop of Canterbury, John Hooper, Bishop of Worcester and a noted preacher and theologian, were burnt at the stake in Oxford for heresy, as elsewhere were two hundred other bishops, scholars, and lay men.

Fisher and Ridley, both Bishops of Rochester, died for their beliefs. How sad and indeed how wicked, that one died under a "Protestant" King, and the other under a "Catholic" Queen. "How these Christians love one another!" Originally spoken in wonder, those words have often since been spoken in scorn and cynicism. It is almost unbelievable that the hatreds and misunderstandings of the 16th century which caused so much sorrow and suffering so long ago are still unresolved. Anglicans and Roman Catholics still cannot agree, are still suspicious of each other, still cannot kneel at the altar of Christ's sacrifice together. Every time I sat in my stall under the name of the martyr Fisher, a few feet from the stall of the martyr Ridley, I prayed for unity and resolved to do all that I could to foster understanding between our two Churches. As I remarked in my memories of being a Vicar, it is still difficult, and unity looks to be still far away.

After the installation, the Board of Education held a great "reception" and welcoming in the large Hall of the City Council chamber when I met my new colleagues and was introduced to representatives of the local Education Authorities and other Churches, Heads and clergy and members of the Diocesan Board of Education. It was an impressive and moving event which I owed to the organising ability of Joan Quaife, the Children's Adviser, and Maria Gross, the then "Moral Welfare", (now "Social Work") Secretary. The Youth Chaplain, Michael Upton, and the three Industrial Chaplains were also present.

The next morning, the Feast of the Epiphany, I attended Holy Communion in the Cathedral (indeed I think I was the celebrant) and later began work in my office in St. Nicholas Church. My predecessor had been Canon Reginald Soar, a much respected part-time Director and a Vicar in the Diocese. He had handed over two cardboard boxes of files, all that he had on the nearly one hundred schools and one hundred trusts for which the Board was in some way responsible. It was little enough to go on, so there was a clean slate. I was allocated half a day's help from Judy Young, the Archdeacon's Secretary, though I discovered later that most of her salary was paid from Board of Education funds. Once more I had to protest, and as the office work increased I was allowed to appoint a full time secretary to be shared between myself and the children's Adviser, Joan Quaife, who had an office on the same floor of the building.

Over sixteen years we had a succession of four marvellous Secretaries: Ruth Barnard, Janet Green, Jill Fennell and Norma Proctor. I worked them hard and when I started writing study material for the parishes and Readers they typed between them thousands of pages of words on to stencils which then had to be transformed into cyclostyled booklets, on a succession of temperamental copying machines. We began work at 8.30 a.m. and I always tried to answer letters on the same day that they were received unless some research had to be done to find the answers. In the early days my Secretary and I had to "learn the ropes" together. Unlike modern Vicars I had never had a secretary. I had typed all my own letters on a typewriter my mother had given me on my 19th birthday. I had answered the telephone myself and had not heard of such marvels as the answerphone. (If there is anything that annoys me more than the answerphone when I am trying to contact a clergyman, a friend, my children, an office, a firm, I do not know what it is!)

In all correspondence I had to remember that I was the servant of the Church and even when annoyed by something a Head or incumbent had written I had to remind myself that "a soft answer turneth away wrath" and I would spend time in working out a detailed and polite answer to the irate epistle. There were not many of such letters, but I soon came across one of the misunderstandings that the clergy had regarding "their" Church school. In simple terms, the law of education said that if a Church school ceased to be used for the purpose for which it was founded, it should be sold, and the proceeds of sale should be applied to the development of other Church schools in the same area of the Diocese. Incumbents and Church Councils who saw their schools being closed understandably said, "it was the folk of this parish who provided the money to build the school in the first place. Why should we not receive the proceeds of sale and use it for religious education in the parish?" The only answer was, "I'm afraid that the law does not allow that."

It was something that I had experienced in Shottermill. Sometime in the late 50's I received a letter from the Director of Education in the Diocese of Guildford regarding the Old Church School now used as a parish Hall. It said that the old school must be valued and that the parish must buy it back from the Diocese. The parish of Haslemere next door had received a similar letter regarding one of its old schools. Fortunately, I had a document in the Church records dated in 1928 which gave the Church Council the right to keep the old school as long as it was used for the benefit of the children. We took Counsel's opinion and he agreed that the fact that we held Sunday Schools, youth clubs and other children's activities in the Hall fulfilled the requirements of the law, and the people in Guildford Diocesan office had no claim on it for other Church Schools in the Diocese. I was therefore able to say to Rochester Clergy that in certain cases parishes could continue to have the use of their old schools where they had been closed in past years, but that the new laws made this impossible where a school was currently under threat of closure. Only where there were specific trusts (those things the Bishop did not want me to spend too much time on) which specified the rights of Church Councils to, it may be, part of the playground, perhaps as a car park, was I able to exercise discretion, and be glad that the priest and parish had no cause to feel a grudge against the Board of Education and "those chaps in the Diocesan Office".

The Rochester Diocesan Board of Education was an incorporated body, subject to the Bishop and the rules of the Board of Trade and in no sense subject to Councils or Committees of the Diocese. This was a great strength to us, and caused some difficulty with some members of the Diocesan Board of Finance who thought that they should have control of the Board's funds. I was much envied by fellow Directors whose Committees were subject in financial matters to their Diocesan Boards of Finance, and who were sometimes refused the funds needed to develop an Aided school. For some unknown reason my Board met in London, in the offices of the National Society. This seemed to me to be ridiculous as most members had to come to London from parishes in Kent, so I arranged early on that future meetings should be held in the Diocese, mostly in Rochester and sometimes elsewhere.

As Boards and Committees go, the Rochester Board of Education was probably the most highly qualified and experienced of them all. Chaired originally by a senior incumbent (who had no Church School in his parish) later Chairmen were either Archdeacons or Bishops, appointed by the Bishop of the Diocese, who would himself from time to time attend our meetings. Members included several heads of Secondary and Primary Schools, representatives from the LEAs, the Deaneries (sometimes lay, sometimes clerical) the diocesan Children's Adviser and youth Chaplain, and an industrial Chaplain, as well as appointees of the Bishop. The Board of Finance was represented and the Diocesan Secretary (a member) and his accountant, who looked after the Board's Finances, would attend. The Children's and Youth Councils were in a sense subsidiary to the Board as their interests and responsibilities coincided, but they planned and acted autonomously. Because of the unique legal position of the Board, its Chairman was *not* an executive officer as many chairmen are, though one of them tried to behave as though he was! The Secretary (the Diocesan Director) was legally responsible not only to the Board of Education, and the Bishop, but also to the Board of Trade to whom its yearly accounts had to be submitted. No one had told me this when I took over from Canon Soar, and I was in deep trouble with the Board of Trade (now the Department of Trade and Industry) for not submitting the accounts over a period of two years. Fortunately the Permanent Secretary at the Board of Trade was a personal friend, a New Zealander whose father had been Pat's father's Churchwarden when he was Vicar of Wanganui, and Maxwell Palmer Brown had been Pat's first "boyfriend". Though I did not use this connection in our negotiations, it eased the problem, I was given time to prepare the missing accounts, and all was well.

The most valuable role that the Director played in his capacity as a "Church Schools man" was in relation to the three local Education Authorities where the Board had the right of representation, Kent, Bromley and Bexley. Of the ninety-one schools that survived, twenty-five were "Aided" (i.e. the buildings owned and maintained as to 25% by the Church) sixty-six were "Controlled" (i.e. owned by the Church but maintained by the Local Education Authority). The LEAs of course paid teachers' salaries and day to day expenses such as cleaning, heating and lighting. Four schools were in Bexley Borough, nine in Bromley Borough, and seventy-eight in Kent. Kent County Council was particularly aware of the existence of Church Schools, since if account is taken of Roman Catholic Schools in Kent, and those in the Canterbury Diocese, more than a third of the Kent Schools are Church Schools.

I was a member or the Education Committees of both Kent and Bromley, and the Board had a representative at Bexley. In Kent I sat with Clifford Pollard, a priest who represented the diocese of Canterbury, and a Roman Catholic priest. The sight of our three clerical collars side by side must have been daunting if not intimidating, for we played a full voting part in all the Kent Education Committee's deliberations and were not afraid to make our views known on all aspects of education in Kent, particularly where Church schools were concerned. This raised the question of my title. I never regarded myself as exclusively concerned with "religious" education, except in the sense that the whole of life can be held to have a religious dimension. In any case it is quite wrong to separate religion from life. It could even be said, I suppose, that the quality of the religious education given in a school is as much related to buildings and equipment as it is to teachers' own convictions. I saw no contradiction in fighting the LEA and the Ministry for funds to replace disgraceful outside lavatories in many of our primary schools of Victorian vintage and fighting to rescue "Scripture" from Victorian methods of teaching it. So, without any implication of unacceptable "Empire building" I preferred to be called "Diocesan Director of Education".

The 1960's and 1970's were a time of great upheaval in education, and the surges forward and the retreats were related to changes in Government and the ideals and prejudices of the political party in power, each, it seemed, determined to undo what the other had achieved.

Soon after the epoch-making 1944 Act, Attlee's Labour government had been in power from July 1945 until October 1951. The Conservative governments of Churchill, Eden, Macmillan and Douglas-Home from October 1951 to October 1964, when Wilson's Labour government came to power, until the arrival of the Conservative Heath in June 1970. He was ousted in March 1974 when Wilson returned, followed by the Labour Callaghan in 1976, in turn ousted by Mrs. Thatcher in May 1979. Education has been a football, kicked from end to end by the party politicians, and many would doubt whether the result has been of benefit to the children or to society. It is a matter of debate as to whether educational theorising or attempts at "social engineering" through education have done the more harm.

We were in the midst of the battle. The Labour Government circular 10/65 had laid down the principle of comprehensive education and so began the "destruction of the Grammar Schools" but Kent and our London Boroughs were Conservative controlled and resisted the change as far as the law allowed, which meant delaying change as long as possible. We had two Secondary Schools which would be affected by the "comprehensive" principle, and many schools which would be affected by the new idea of a "Middle School" which would decapitate the Junior School and necessitate new buildings for middle age ranges eight to twelve or thirteen. I was myself in favour of the theory of comprehensiveness, for I was aware that the Secondary modern schools had lost out in every way over against the Grammar schools, in the quality of buildings, in the expertise of the teachers, in funds available, and, in the case of our large mixed Secondary school of St. George's Gravesend, the refusal of the Kent LEA to allow the School to develop its educational provision to "A" level. Without subscribing to any party political doctrines, I also believed that the division between Grammar and Secondary modern was socially divisive and eventually dangerous.

Much discussion was proceeding in the 1960s about the design of the many new schools that were being built. I was at that time a supporter of the "open plan" system in which the (primary) school was seen as a community, and where the classrooms were not divided from each other by thick walls. One of the first new buildings with which the Board was concerned was the replacement of Lady Boswell's School, Sevenoaks, and the design was traditional, a corridor of entirely separate classrooms divided from each other by solid walls. The inspectorate of Kent had objected to this old fashioned design but because of the independent and Aided status of the old school dating back to 1809, they were unable to refuse either architectural or educational approval.

When the new Aided school on the Isle of Grain was taken over and put into use, matters were very different. It had been planned in conjunction with the LEA of Kent which at that time favoured the "open plan" and the architect was Alastair Macdonald, son of Ramsey Macdonald, and famous for his designs for the great cinemas of the 1930's. Within a week of the opening I received in the office a "round robin" letter from all the staff at St. James' Infant and Junior School, Isle of Grain, saying that they could not teach in the new "open plan" building. Presumably they had sent similar letters to the Chief Education Officer in Kent, John Haynes, and his Inspectors. Teachers were competing with each other for the attention of their children and it was plainly impossible for one class, openly in sound and sight of other classes, to be having a music lesson when other classes were quietly trying to do their maths or English composition. Many meetings and consultations took place between all concerned and reluctantly the Kent inspectorate agreed to the erection of folding partitions between the classes. This did not entirely solve the teaching problems but it made life possible for staff and children, and when the partitions were pushed back, activities where the whole school was involved were certainly more possible than in a school like Lady

Boswell's. So the open plan had its advantages and henceforth, when we were planning new buildings, a compromise was reached, though as the years passed the County and Boroughs abandoned open plan as a doctrinaire principle and reverted largely to the single classroom idea. It had been a theory which did not work in practice, and a cynical comment would be that it was only invented to save money. Classrooms were getting smaller because of the restrictions imposed by the Ministry on expenditure. For example each classroom at Lady Boswell's, Sevenoaks, was 635 square feet. In later years we were restricted by financial stringencies to as little as 530 square feet.

Early in my time at Rochester, and mindful of the bishop's admonition about buildings, I sat down to consider how the diocese, and myself in particular, could help in the realm of Christian education. I identified several areas:

(1)   Assembly, which was still a statutory requirement in every school and was at that time mostly well conducted.

(2)   The actual content of "RE" as it could be taught (a) in the Aided School, where full "Church teaching" could be given, (b) in the Controlled School where children might be withdrawn for two periods a week to receive specific Church teaching, but which for the rest must follow the "agreed syllabus" of the LEA.

(3)   Help for the teachers themselves in the content and method of RE.

(4)   How "the Church" might help the teachers of RE in the maintained schools (i.e. "State" or County or Borough Schools).

(5)   Help for Managers and Governors in interpreting the law of education in their particular school, and in their relationships with the LEAs in regard to buildings and staff, as well as admissions (often an issue for popular Aided schools) and appointments.

Though I had attended many Primary School assemblies, one or two in Secondary Schools, and had conducted not a few, my interest and concern was re-awakened by a fourteen year old schoolgirl's essay which Pat brought home one day from her School. The girl had been a nuisance at one assembly and had been turned out ("asked to withdraw") by the Headmistress. As a salutary penance and "corrective discipline" she was told to write an essay with the following title:

"*The Purpose Of School Assemblies*.
Why we should behave ourselves.
Why attention and respect are necessary."

I give the essay in full:

"The purpose of School Assemblies is to teach us about God and Jesus. I suppose the purpose of them as well is to tell us all the good things the Saints, Disciples etc. have done and hope we will follow their example, but I doubt if anyone will, because the way of life's different today. If you try to teach about Jesus people will think your Dad's a Vicar or you're a crank. Because Christianity is dying out. Still, some people believe in it. Most don't. I suppose it used to be a kind of craze going to Church because nearly everybody did, once upon a time. But now there are a lot of strikes and demonstrations, people would rather go to one of them than go to Church.

We should behave ourselves because teachers tell us to, not because we want to. We have to sit like stuffed dolls until... has had her say, all about her friends who have been transformed into a Christian and such like. And if anyone does not agree with what she said, well, what do they do, what *can* they do? NOTHING. If anyone gets up in assembly and says 'I think you're wrong', well, I dread to think what will happen. So... rambles on day after day, week after week, month after month until we leave school. No ones ever told her, I don't suppose, that she does most boring assemblies, and I doubt if anyone will because the members of staff are just as bad, too scared, but sitting there listening to someone else's life story that no one particularly wants to know."

That was written by an obviously quite intelligent adolescent girl, as can be seen from the lack of spelling mistakes and her ability to transfer running thoughts to paper, and it should be said that in that school attempts *were* made to vary assemblies. The girls made up their own, and other teachers conducted them from time to time, but I took note of the warning contained in the essay against a certain type of assembly not uncommon in schools.

The Newsom report of 1963 had recommended overtly Christian content in all assemblies. It actually spoke about "worship" of God - "Corporate worship is not to be thought of as an instrument of education, but as a time in which pupils and teachers seek help in prayer, express awe and gratitude and joy, and pause to recollect the presence of God."

But the Plowden Report of 1966 (the Committee was heavily weighted with secularists) declared that:

"The act of worship has great value as a unifying force for the School, and it should illuminate personal relationships and introduce children to aesthetic and spiritual experiences." No Christ, no God, no prayer there.

There had undoubtedly been changes and developments in social and religious attitudes in the 60's - "Honest to God" had shaken the Church in 1963 and increasing numbers of children from "ethnic minorities" were attending all types of school, so it was inevitable that the Christian assembly must be modified to take account of the needs of children of other religious faiths.

In various papers and lectures I tried to stimulate thought and discussion as to what the assembly was for, how it differed from worship in Church, how it could be related to life at school and life at home and in those places where children met out of school. I gave the teachers lists of books useful for assemblies, and lists of new hymns which children had come to enjoy singing. I discussed in detail its form and content, the readings, the prayers, the hymns, the use of drama and dance, what was suitable for different age-groups and whether it should be compulsory or not. One problem in commending the idea that every child must attend was the fact that half the staff refused to attend - "if they don't take part, why should we?" I tackled various practical questions such as the time allotted to it - "We are not clocking in or opening the shop" - the 1944 Act had said - "The assembly is not an opening ceremony". Should the teachers be ranged down both sides of the Hall as if they were keeping an eye on prisoners? Were the books being used (if any) tatty, with pages missing? What kind of introductory and concluding music? Should the school use the radio services for schools? Should boys whose voices are breaking be expected to sing? Should pupils be encouraged to write their own prayers? (Of course they should.) What version of the Bible should be used? Should readings from other "holy books" or from other authors be used? (Of course they should.)

The debate has gone on. As I write in 1994 the present Secretary of State for Education is recommending a specific Christian assembly in all schools with appropriate recognition of other religions, and a tightening up of the Christian content of religious education. The basic difficulty remains: Governments may enact compulsions, but no one can compel me to be religious, no one can force me to pray, no one should force me to sing hymns to a God in whom I do not believe. And, reading again that girl's essay, are there not certain prerequisites to an effective and worthwhile assembly? Respect for the person taking it, discussion with those who are the recipients of what is being said and done, participation, *willing* co-operation, and most of all a new kind of life in the Church itself?

With regard to the content of religious education in the various types of school, Kent County Council had appointed a religious education inspector, or adviser. My opposite number in Canterbury, Clifford Pollard, and I worked closely with him in producing material for *all* schools in the County except Roman Catholic schools, and we encouraged all our Church Schools to use the Agreed syllabuses, supplemented by the specific Church teaching which was being given in the Aided schools. We held various conferences and seminars for the whole of Kent and produced three booklets: "*A Handbook of Thematic Material*" - this was to take note of new thinking in all teaching, using themes as a basis of the integrated teaching which educational "experts" were recommending on their understanding of the works of Piaget his colleagues. In 1969 Kent had adopted the Agreed Syllabuses from the West Riding, and Lancashire, rather than re-write its own, so there followed our second book: *Christians in Kent* (1972) which proclaimed itself as, "Not a text book but information and suggestions for developing work along the particular lines chosen by an individual school." It was divided into several sections... Historical, Christians at Worship (with two great Cathedrals in the County, and hundreds of ancient Churches, as well as the Chapels and Churches or the Free Churches, there was a wealth of material here. The Roman Catholics did not feel able to participate in this study) Christians Serving. This book included "work and activity cards" which I had prepared on the theme of "Visiting our Local Church". These books were greatly welcomed in all the schools and became much used.

The third book we called *Teaching the Parables*, an experiment in Curriculum Development. In the Introduction the Chairman of the Kent Education Committee remarked:

"*The Handbook of Thematic Material* was distinctive in that it brought together the work of a large number of teachers in all parts of Kent... and since its first publication has found its way into schools and Colleges not only all over the British Isles but also in a number of countries overseas. When therefore early discussions took place about the way in which the present book should be compiled it was soon decided that the teachers of Kent should again be invited to make a major contribution. About fifty accepted the Council's invitation to take part and what now appears is their work."

I wrote a long introduction on the *Use and Interpretation of Parables*. Twenty three of our Lord's Parables were chosen and different schools were asked to prepare lessons on them (a) in traditional form (b) with a thematic approach. The teachers were then expected to give a lesson on the parable they had chosen, and to make comments at the end of their exposition as to how the lesson had gone. Both Secondary and Primary Schools took part, along with Aided and Controlled Church Schools. Like the other books this was a great success.

The importance of all this was that the teachers were involved in producing their own material and evaluating for themselves the results. It was not something imposed on the teachers from above by people who did not have to stand day by day in front of a class, that "old fashioned" approach to teaching!

One of the joys of my time at Rochester was in the way that what I had to give was received by all types of teacher in all kinds of schools. I always greatly appreciated the opportunities that the LEAs gave me to lecture at their conferences on subjects like the Assembly, RE and the relationship between Christianity and other religions. This wide interpretation of my brief as Director enabled me to meet and work alongside many whom I would not even have met if my brief had been restricted to the ninety-one Church schools of my diocese. I valued too the friendship and advice of my opposite number in the Canterbury Diocese, Clifford Pollard, a man not perhaps as outspoken as myself, but a sound practitioner and wise counsellor, much respected by the officers and staff at "Springfield", the education offices in Maidstone.

Because we had far fewer schools in Bromley Borough my problems there were lessened, but I was privileged to chair the Committee which revised their Agreed Syllabus of RE. This was a salutary experience and a lengthy one because not only were many diverse views about RE in school apparent, but I had asked that leaders in the non-Christian faiths should be represented. Whether this had any legal force at the time I do not know, but it seemed to me that we should not be an exclusively Christian body, representing, as all such Committees must by the then Law, *only* the Churches, the teachers and the local Council, but also those of other faiths whose children attended our schools and probably chose to attend assembly and were not withdrawn from RE lesson. Indeed, when one of our Aided Church Schools, Holy Trinity, Gravesend, set in a predominantly Pakistani area of the town, had to accept an intake of 50% of children of non-British origin I was interested to learn that their parents on the whole *wanted* them to take part in both Assembly and RE lessons. Later the Government did lay it down that representatives of other religions should take part in preparing agreed syllabuses.

One of my difficulties in the Aided Church School in particular was the attitude of some incumbents of parishes who did not take full advantage of all that the Aided School was allowed under the law, which was Church teaching to every child, every day. More than one Vicar said to me when I suggested that he take assembly regularly, and should teach the Anglican understanding of the Christian Faith, "I'm no good with children." It is always possible to learn, and in any case what an opportunity for co-operation between Church and School! The other area of possibilities in which I encouraged the clergy of the diocese was in their relationships with the County schools. I discovered with pleasure that many heads of County Schools would have welcomed local clergy into their schools, not just to take an occasional assembly but also to teach within the Agreed Syllabuses. They would not of course have been able to give denominational teaching, nor make any attempts at proselytising, but just to make contact with the children of their parishes whom they would see every day in the streets if they were doing their own pastoral work properly. Some clergy were very good at this, but sadly, others were not.

I reminded the parish clergy how important it was, if any children did come to their acts of worship on a Sunday, that the hymns should always include some of those with which the children were familiar at school, and liked singing, but which were probably not in *Ancient and*

Modern; also that in school, children were used to hearing the Bible read in modern translations, and that prayers should also be familiar, and moreover that in school children were learning by acting and dancing and that provision should be made for them on occasion to present *in Church* what they had enjoyed at school, for example the acting out of some of the parables, or Gospel readings, where different readers took the part or the individuals in the story. The trial and crucifixion stories lend themselves to this kind of presentation, and in my experience the adult members of congregations welcomed the young people and were much helped by a new approach to understanding their own faith.

When it came to helping managers and governors in their work as those responsible for the smooth running of their schools, we organised a series of meetings and discussions to let them know the latest thinking of the politicians about their schools, and introduced to them the myriad of directives and administrative circulars which poured out of Elizabeth House, the new Headquarters of the Department of Education and Science. These were usually held in the first new school building for which I had been responsible - St. Mary's Swanley, a primary (juniors only) school for which I had been able to work what was considered to be something of a miracle, turning a controlled school, (with limited Church "Control") into an Aided School where the Church managers were in the majority and where the local Vicar could come in and teach daily, and celebrate the Holy Communion weekly and where the children could hold their assemblies in Church without incurring official wrath. In this I was much helped by the successive incumbents of St. Mary's and in particular by Roy Fidge the Headmaster whom we had appointed when he moved on from a small controlled Church School at Foots Cray. It was in his school that we frequently held Teachers Meetings and Managers and Governors Meetings. Often the agenda was purely practical, the provision of new buildings, enlargements, replacing outside lavatories, diocesan help for the upkeep of the school facilities (in an Aided School at that time the managers had to find 25% of maintenance of buildings, the rest paid for by the DES but for which local LEA approval had to be sought within an overall budget allowed to the LEA by the Department in London.)

When important documents arrived from London or Springfield or Bexley and Bromley, my ever patient secretaries would reproduce them and where needed copies would he sent to every school. Meanwhile, correspondence piled up as we planned new schools, or mounted conferences, and the meagre files bequeathed to me by Canon Soar began to grow. No doubt much of the paperwork was superfluous, but I was convinced that every query and every request from teachers, managers and incumbents should be scrupulously dealt with and a permanent record retained. When I left Rochester there were several filing cabinets full to the brim. I hope my successor had all the information he needed!

In my "newboy" days, and mindful of the Bishop's brief that I was to be "the leader of a team..." early in 1965 I felt it would be helpful if the whole "team" went away together for a residential weekend in a retreat house and I thought it would be more helpful to go to the Canterbury house at Westgate rather than to our own conference centre, Graham Chiesman House in Chislehurst, now regrettably closed. So I planned a weekend convenient to us all and we went. It was a failure. The key words in the Bishop's letter were "leader" and "team"! I soon discovered that most of the "team" didn't want to be "led", not by me at any rate, and they had no intention of being part of a team. They were individualists, who had probably come into their specialist ministries because they found it hard to work in a team. The men were all clergy until the arrival of a layman as training officer in about a year's time, and clergy are not notable for teamwork, and the Vicars with whom they had served had probably been individualists too, if not autocrats like Prebendary Bromley, in Weston, Bath. They had also been trained in various modern (of the "Tavistock" type) techniques of conferences and relationships which frowned upon the idea of having anything planned or "cut and dried". They resented the fact that I had drawn up an agenda of possible topics for us to discuss, including areas where we might act as a "team". The women, Joan Quaife, the Children's Adviser, and Maria Gross, the Secretary for Moral Welfare (later to be called Social Work) and whom I had known very well when she was in charge of a Mother and Baby Home of which I had been Chairman in Haslemere, were not so antipathetic to a set agenda as the Youth Officer and the Industrial Chaplains. "Each meeting must set its own agenda," they had declared. They were not on the whole traditional clerics, so they didn't say, "We must wait upon the guidance of the Holy Spirit." If they had, I might well have replied (rather frostily?), "I have myself already waited upon Him and this is what He told me we should talk together about."

I met this attitude frequently later on when I joined the Youth Chaplain and the Training Officer in parish conferences, and I came to see the force of it, and learned from it. It worked extremely well in some of the parish meetings and conferences which I conducted over the years. People came expecting to be told what to think and what to do, so after the initial period in which we "got to know each other" I would divide them into groups and say, "Go away and answer the question,'What is the Church for?', and report back in half an hour's time." In this way PCC's and other groups *did* set their own agenda. But for this weekend I thought an agenda was essential, and in turn we contributed thoughts on our own particular place in the Diocesan family and the contribution we felt we ought to be making. Because the whole event was set in the context of prayer and worship in the Chapel, the atmosphere finally thawed, the interfering Director of Education was seen as a colleague and not a threat. It is a strange fact about the clergy that we often feel threatened by other clergy, and among us jealousy is the main besetting sin. There was in fact little that we could do together as a "team", though we three who were responsible to the Board of Education and its Youth and Children's Committees found more to share with each other than I did with the Industrial Chaplains. They did invite me to give a paper on "Work" at one of their regular meetings, which I did, though the premises on which I based my thesis were questioned by some of them; and I was invited from time to time to accompany them on visits to the factories in the Medway area.

My relationships with the Chief Education Officers of Kent and the two London Boroughs, and with the Education Officers of the various districts in Kent, as well as with the Chairmen of the Secondary and Primary and Further Education Committees of the County Council, were usually cordial (though Bexley and Bromley could be "difficult") - even after one passage-at-arms with John Haynes, CEO of Kent, which took place in my early days on the Kent Education Committee. We were examining the accounts and County budget for education when I noted that the Methodist Church in Kent had been given £700 for its Youth work, but Rochester Diocese nothing. I took it upon myself to find out from Michael Upton the Youth Officer, and the parishes, how much Anglican Youth Work was proceeding and I estimated from the returns that, including Sunday Schools and Youth Clubs, some 20,000 children and young people were in some kind of contact with the Anglican Church in the Rochester diocese. When the allocations to voluntary bodies came up for approval by the full Council I raised the question as to why the Methodist Church and the Canterbury diocese had received allocations for their work with young people, but the diocese of Rochester, which was doing the most, had received nothing.

John Haynes was furious that I had raised this question in public and had not seen fit to consult him privately before the meeting. I was new to the job and had not realised that most of the decisions about education are made, not in meetings, but by the ruling political party, behind closed doors, well in advance. No doubt I should have raised it with him in advance. So furious was he that he took it upon himself to complain about me to my Bishop, who called me into his study some days later to say: "I have just had to do something I have never done before. I have had to go down to Springfield to mend fences between the Diocese and the County Education authorities." I was taken aback and the Bishop then recounted John Haynes' version of the event. I was given no chance to put my side of the story, and I felt aggrieved that the Bishop had not called me in *before* he went to see the CEO. It might not have been necessary to go at all. The upshot was twofold. The Rochester Diocese received grants for its Youth work in future, and I took a little more care in the preparation of my contributions to debate in Springfield and County Hall.

I must have redeemed myself over the years because most of the top education officers and Chairmen of Committees came to my "Farewell" in the Cathedral and made speeches of thanks for my contribution to education in Kent! When my great friend among the Officers in Kent, Bill Moore, had retired from being the man in charge of all primary schools, I had sent him a book signed and illustrated by all the Church Primary Schools in the Diocese. He replied in October, 1970:

"I write to record the deep appreciation of my wife and myself for the Address and Book of Church School signatures upon my retirement... any long work of a pastoral nature with people must induce humility and your most imaginative gesture so boldly and splendidly carried out, is indeed a 'comfortable word' to one who begin life in a Rochester school house. The delightful writing of the children will be especially evocative and rejuvenating. One's keenest sense is of the work still undone (you and I could list some of them from Northfleet to Tunbridge Wells), but my conviction of the great importance of Church Schools is not merely part of Churchmanship (though I hope it *is* that), but a rooted belief that islands of divergence and of varied freedom are vital and good for us all and a real strength of our system."

In the next ten years we *did* do the work undone, from Northfleet to Tunbridge Wells. It *was* a matter of mutual respect and co-operation that we were able both to improve most of the schools materially, and also to enlarge many of them so that the number of children in contact with the Church and receiving *related* religious education was nearly doubled. It would not have been possible without the support of Bill Moore and his successors in the County. I was grateful too to have been involved in the training of teachers of RE, not only in the Church Schools but in the maintained schools as well.

The two most important development projects with which I was associated were the enlargement of Bennett Memorial School for girls, Tunbridge Wells, and of St. George's, Gravesend a mixed school. We battled to make these two schools five form entry comprehensive schools, teaching children up to "O" level, "A" level and university entrance. It is a long story of battles with the LEA and the Department of Education and Science to "get into a programme" of development, of planning vast new buildings and finding the Church's share - by that time only 20% was demanded, the rest paid for by the DES - commissioning architects and overseeing the work. I know that some in the diocese thought that I was spending my time on buildings rather than people, but this was not so. Because Pat was also at work I was able to give much of my time to building projects without affecting the time I spent in religious writing (more of that later) and visiting the schools and parishes. The creation of these two schools as two of the most popular and successful schools in Kent is a saga on its own, for which there is no space in these memoirs, but the outcome was clear - the Church had two Secondary Schools, with young people from 11 - 18 being educated in the totally committed principles of the Church of England. Application lists were twice the number of available places, and Bennett Memorial has now attained a status for which I fought without success in the 70's - it too takes boys. So the time I spent on buildings has been well rewarded - two thousand boys and girls are within the orbit of the Church and are being taught the full Christian faith without any shame or reluctance on the part of either the Diocese or the LEA.

"To be a leader." What did the Bishop expect of me when he wrote that phrase? "A person who rules, guides or inspires others," says the dictionary. Leadership: "Administration, directorship (that sounded bells) domination (the industrial Chaplains rejected that) guidance, management, authority, command, influence, initiative, supremacy, pre-eminence..." The synonyms were endless. At this time (October 1993) of Political Party Conferences the whole question of leadership is being hawked around the newspapers and TV screens. John Major's leadership is said to be in decline, John Smith's leadership is "on the up and up" (Smith died in 1994). Paddy Ashdown's leadership is much admired. What do people expect of a leader? I suspect that most people want to be told forcefully what to do. If the Labour Party conference is any guide, they want to be shouted at, ranted at, cajoled and threatened in equal proportions. I began to research into the problem when a parish asked me to conduct a conference on Leadership.

Some such conferences had been held in the diocese, mostly based upon managerial techniques and group work ("'T' groups" they were called) in terms of the Executive, the Planner, the Policy Maker, the Spokesman, the Ideologist, the Father-figure, the purveyor of rewards and punishments. These secular-style conferences had much to teach the Church, especially about communication between people, and about the quaintly called "feedback". But is there specific "Christian" understanding of what leadership means? And if there is what does it say to the whole Church (e.g. the Synod) to Dioceses - what is the Bishop's leadership role, in Deaneries (the Rural Dean and Lay Chairman), in parishes (the Vicar)? Was it a failure of leadership that led to the failure of the General Synod to approve the proposals for Anglican-Methodist unity? Who gives the lead in the realms of Women's Ministry, Unity, Morality? What kind of leadership could a Director of Education give? I remembered a member of my PCC saying to me when I had decided on a certain way forward in the parish, "You're a dictator, Vicar, aren't you?" Was I being a dictator or a leader of a reluctant group?

So, as I was wont to do when facing such questions, I went back to the Bible, and wrote a series of study books beginning with *Leadership in the Bible*. I examined Moses' role in leading the children of Israel out of Egypt. This was a fascinating study and I concluded that the man who "saw God", "spoke with God", whose words were the "oracles of God", was "filled with the Spirit of God", was a meek and humble man, conscious of his own inadequacies. Though his word often fell on deaf cars he remained loyal to his people and faithful to his God. In the wilderness he was able to supply the "expertise" necessary to get water from the rock. Leaders then, in the Christian sense, must be in constant touch with God, and must have a love and care for people, as well as a knowledge of their weaknesses, with no place for pity and self-concern. This was a far cry from management techniques. In the study I went on to look at Joshua and the Judges, Samuel and the Kings, David, Elijah and the writing prophets. I then went on to analyse the leadership of Jesus and of St. Paul and the apostles. The next booklet was concerned with *Leadership in the Church*, and the final one with the title *Leadership of the PCC, especially in Stewardship.*

Whether I was successful in applying all the principles I had learned from my study it is not for me to say. I hope that some of them came through in my activities in the schools and the parishes, and later in the wider Church. But I always had to remind myself of Paul's confession to the Corinthians of his concern, "lest when I have preached to others, I myself should be a castaway." The most effective leadership is not loud, it is quietly effective, it is not assertive, it is firmly present but often not overtly expressed; it takes account of people's needs and worries; at all times it seeks and accepts co-operation, and it is not averse to taking advice; it encourages every member of a team to make his own particular contribution; it may sometimes be critical but it is never destructive.

As I became better known in the diocese I received many invitations to preach, to conduct quiet days, to take parish retreats and weekend conferences. When my morning's work in the office was complete I would retire to my study on the first floor of White Friars and begin my research into the subject I had been given. I would get out all the relevant books and begin to make notes. Then I would sit and think and pray. As we always had an evening meal when Pat came home, my lunch was meagre and my lunch time short. I have always composed best at a typewriter, and from 1.30 p.m. until 4.30p.m., unless I had a school visit to make in the afternoon, a managers or Governors meeting perhaps, I would type away on the themes that parishes or teachers had requested. In this way I wrote the study papers for the ecumenical *Mission to Medway* in 1969. *Man and Ministry, studies in Clergy-lay relationships, Humanism* and *Christian Humanism* (1968), which arose out of a public dialogue which I conducted in Tunbridge Wells with H.J. Blackham, the prominent humanist. *Anglicanism*, a lecture given at an ecumenical gathering at the Roman Catholic Priory at Aylesford. Various Lent lectures were given in several parishes on *The Christian Use of The Old Testament; Prayer; New Moves in the Church*; *The role of the Christian in the World*; *Art, Education and Religion*; *Ecclesia*; *Opportunities for the Church in the Parish*; *Questions People Ask*; *What Can We Then Believe?*; *What Did Jesus Teach?* Then there were conferences on *Home and Family, Stewardship, What is a Living Church?, Off-Centre*, an examination of some of the beliefs of the quasi-Christian sects and *Some Modern Moral Problems*.

The Dean and Chapter asked me to address them at one of their day retreats on *The Cathedral* and how I saw its role in the Church today. A woman's Luncheon Club wanted to hear about *Superstitions,* youth workers on *What is happening to our young people* and social workers on *How the Church can help in Community Care, The faith of a caseworker, The changing situation in Social Work*. Teachers wanted help with other beliefs: *Why Christianity?* I gave a Lecture at Bexley on *Everyday Life in Old Testament Times*, *Church Schools and State Aid* in Tunbridge Wells; *RE in Primary Schools, Agreed Syllabuses Past and Present, Why do Some Children Dislike Religious Education?* - which arose out of a study of RE and children's responses to it in Pat's School at Walderslade. I often talked to meetings of Sunday School teachers. A Survey of the Middle School was given to clergy in my old Diocese of Guildford, and I talked to the Heads of Public Schools in the Southern Division of the Head Masters Conference on the broad subjects of "*Religious Education*", and "*Humanism*".

I think the most worthwhile studies I produced were for groups in Parishes - books on "*The Creed*", "*The Lord's Prayer*", and the "*Ten Commandments*", (the old confirmation course of study - "what everyone being confirmed ought to know!") and *Religion and Healing*, as I came to be more and more convinced that the Church was not obeying its Lord's command to "Heal the Sick". When the various Synodical Reports on *Church and State, Marriage and Divorce,* and *Christian Initiation* were published I produced synopses of their arguments and conclusions, with study guides. These seemed to be appreciated by the parishes who bought them for group study at very low cost, just enough to reimburse the Diocese for the reams of paper used. Some of these summaries, running to twenty or thirty pages sold several thousand copies and I can never be grateful enough to my secretaries who typed them all, and who stood at a long bench stapling them together, hour after hour.

The fullest subjects I dealt with were *The Prophets*, a complete one hundred page study of every one of the Major and Minor Prophets, their original messages and their message for today, in terms and language which I hoped the ordinary churchgoer might find helpful and understand; and *A Study in Sacrifice* (... in the Old Testament, in the New Testament, in the Holy Communion, in Christian history etc., running to eighty pages).

I also valued greatly the opportunity to write about prayer and worship, and appreciated the chance to conduct Retreats at Stacklands, the Retreat House in the diocese, on *This is our God, The Prayer that Spans the World,* and other themes.

So perhaps I was exercising some kind of leadership, if not of the team that the Bishop had envisaged, but by enabling the teachers, Sunday School teachers, and ordinary Churchgoers (and perhaps some of their clergy) to understand their Faith and how it could be put into practice.

As I have remarked, probably more than once, the church seems to go on endlessly discussing the same subjects, particularly Baptism and Confirmation. It had been a major subject for debate in Lincoln Theological College and in all the parishes and dioceses I had served. It raised its head for me again at Rochester, and in the following way.

In 1969 I had been elected by my fellow clergy as a "Proctor in Convocation", a clerical member of the then Church Assembly, the Central body set up by the Convocations in 1919, and superseded by the "General Synod" in 1970. There were originally two Convocations, of Canterbury and York, consisting only of prelates and going back to Anglo-Saxon times, but at the end of the 13th century they were composed of Bishops, Abbots, (until the Reformation),

Deans, Archdeacons and representatives of the clergy of each Diocese and Cathedral Chapter. At first the Bishops and Clergy sat together, but since the 15th century they have sat as two separate "Houses". For some centuries these assemblies were the means by which the clergy taxed themselves, and they legislated for the Church (and in many ways for the people) by "Canon". By the "Submission of the Clergy Act" of 1532, the Convocations surrendered their powers to Henry 8th. When the Church Assembly became the General Synod the Convocations lost their remaining powers but continued to meet separately.

In my view the old Church Assembly was much more effective, and represented the mind of the Church more truly than the General Synod does today. Churchmanship and the "party line" were much less in evidence in the Assembly. When the Assembly became the Synod there were new elections and as an "independent" member I was squeezed between the "high" and the "low" factions among the clergy and lost my seat, but not before I had been appointed to the "Archbishops' Commission on Christian Initiation".

The Commission was set up as a response to widespread failure of the current practice of Confirmation as a sort of educational hurdle to be surmounted (with consequent massive "fall-out") and equally widespread concern about infant baptism - should it be offered to all, or as many rigorist clergy believed, and were applying in practice, only to the children of existing regular worshippers? Enormous changes had also taken place in educational theory and practice since the last report on the subject in 1954 and this must of necessity be taken note of in parishes when candidates were prepared for Confirmation and Communion.

The Commission was chaired by the Bishop of Ely and its terms of reference were:

"... to comprise Bishops, Clergy and Laity to consider the pastoral and theological problems concerned with Confirmation and admission to Holy Communion in the light of...

(a) ... the series of Reports from *Confirmation Today* (1944) and *Baptism and Confirmation Today* (1954).

(b) Subsequent changes in the conditions and customs of parishes.

(c) Evidence from the parish clergy and educationists familiar with modern teaching methods: and to report."

Perhaps it was a pity that we were not *specifically* asked to "make recommendations", though we did, sixteen of them, because the Church might have taken the Report more seriously in its main thrust that Baptism is the sole requirement for admission to Communion, but that preparation for that event should take place through the whole of childhood within the Church. Also that some adult commitment to the Christian life should be expected from all. Many parishes were already anxious to admit children to Communion where whole families worshipped, and many Clergy were anxious to follow the Roman Catholic pattern of confirming children at seven or eight, rather than at the disturbed and disturbing period of adolescence. It is interesting that at this time the Roman Catholic Church was seriously considering the *raising* of the age of Confirmation.

We were a very "mixed bag", the fourteen members of the Commission, and wonder of wonders, we even had two women among us, a Headmistress and a Vicar's wife! Three were active incumbents and several others among us had been, including myself. There were two professors of Theology, the head of a large Public School, an Archdeacon and a college Chaplain, as well as the Bishops of Ely and Sheffield. We were assisted by consultants from the Church in Wales, the Roman Catholic Church and the Methodist Church, and a lecturer in Divinity from the Anglican Teacher Training College, Christ Church, Canterbury. I suppose that I was chosen as having some insight into modern methods of education as well as having been concerned with Baptism and Confirmation as a parish clergyman for nearly a quarter of a century.

We had twelve day meetings and two residential meetings and other gatherings in smaller groups to consider various parts of our mandate. I was particularly concerned with the previous reports and it soon became clear that most of what we might want to propose had already been mooted several times before, and that the Church had been too frightened to be radical in its baptism and confirmation practice. It seems to be the fate of reports to be pigeonholed, but the years roll by and times and practices do change. Though our report was "taken note of" after presentation to the General Synod and debate and discussion in the dioceses (overwhelmingly approved in the Rochester diocese - I wonder why!), it has never been implemented. Parts of it are now common, like the use of chrism (holy oil) and the giving of the candle in Baptism, and in particular the administration of

Baptism in a main service of the Church. As we recommend, more laity are taking their part in Confirmation preparation in many parishes but our main proposals have not yet been adopted, that Confirmation be not required as a necessary preliminary to Communion, and that members of other Churches, who had been duly baptised with water in the name of the Trinity, who wish to become members of the Church of England should not be required to be confirmed. We also proposed to enhance the importance of first Communion, that where possible a Bishop should be the celebrant. One day, I have no doubt, all our proposals will have become common practice!

CHAPTER 12

TRAINER

"One who schools race horses; a certain kind of shoe; a piece of equipment, e.g. a simulated aircraft cockpit."
Collins Concise Dictionary 1982

"A person who trains athletes."
Ditto
(We were taught in school not to define a word in its own terms! What does this person do when he "trains" athletes? Feed them?)

The Dictionaries are seldom helpful when you wish to define a sphere of work. I had been involved in "training" the laity in the parishes for several years, i.e. helping them to understand their Christian faith, and how to put it into practice, when in January 1974 the Bishop invited me to become "Warden of Readers." Here Collins was a little more accurate: "Warden: a person who has the care or charge of something, esp. a building, or *someone*." (Ignore: "One responsible for the enforcement of certain traffic regulations, e.g. traffic warden; a person employed to patrol a park; US chief officer in charge of a prison.) The word also means to be a guardian to someone. So I understood that the Bishop was asking me to train those laity who had been put forward by their incumbent (and also the Church Council, one hoped) to assist them in "reading" the offices in Church, as the original founders of the Office of Lay Reader had intended when it was initiated in 1866. The ministry of the Reader had enlarged over those hundred and more years, and most were now licensed by the Bishop to preach as well as to "conduct religious services." I took it that I was also to "guard" their office, and defend their role in the Church against those who rejected the right of lay men and lay women (women had been admitted to the office since 1969) to speak in Church, and there were such. I sometimes had to guard them against their own incumbents who, having nominated them for the work would not let them fully exercise their ministry.

In his letter the Bishop had written:

"I have, as I hope you realise, been trying for some time to enlarge your sphere of responsibilities in the Diocese. Circumstances beyond my control have made this difficult.

However I now have the opportunity of asking you to take on an important piece of work for me and for the diocese and one which I hope may appeal to you. I would like you to succeed Harry Gripper as Warden of the Readers. My reasons for asking you to do this are briefly as follows:

(a) The Readers are an increasingly important and competent group and their leadership cannot revert to a parish priest. The Warden must be known to be someone involved in Diocesan Affairs and with a knowledge of the diocese as a whole.

(b) Preaching continues to be an essential part of the Reader's life and whoever is Warden must not only accept this but be known as a first class practitioner himself.

(c) It has been strongly represented to me that there was great gain and convenience in having the Warden in Rochester and associated with the Cathedral.

(d) Harry's greatest work was in raising standards and attracting educated people to the task, many of them graduates. I know you would not let this slip back.

(e) The job is essentially a pastoral one and one which includes a real sharing in the Bishop's oversight. Readers are conscious of being Ministers and they expect to be accepted as such. They want a Warden who will be their professional leader and adviser. They do *not* want a do-gooder.

(f) The new Warden must be someone who will accept and encourage women and treat them equally with the men in all respects.

For all these reasons I want you to do this if you will. I believe it might give you a responsibility for men and women that you do not have in quite the same way at the moment and I make bold to say that the last nine chastening years have prepared you in heart, mind and temper for such final responsibility.

This has the full backing of my episcopal and archdiaconal colleagues.

Yours ever, David."

It took me only a short while to decide that I should accept the new work. I greatly respected my Bishop's judgement and what is more, his confidence in me. I had no idea how the post of Warden would deepen and develop, or whether I would gain the confidence of the men and women who would be under my care. The Bishop was correct in calling the work "pastoral" and in the coming years I was often made the confidant of men and women whose lives were being made difficult by illness, family problems, or strained relations with their incumbent.

There were a few Diocesan Readers, and a few who were not licensed to preach, but the majority were fully licensed (at a special service in the Cathedral) to the incumbent of the parish in which they lived or worshipped. As Curates became rarer birds the need for a Reader in a parish had become more urgent, especially where there were two or more Churches and only one priest. Readers were not allowed to celebrate the Holy Communion, but they could conduct Mattins and Evensong, and in certain circumstances, with the Bishop's permission, they could administer the Reserved Sacrament. The previous Warden, Canon Harry Gripper, one of the Residentiary Canons of the Cathedral, was principally concerned with the Reader's academic understanding of the Faith and under him the training consisted in writing twelve essays, and reading a sermon to him in his study. He assumed (usually correctly) that anyone who put himself forward and was approved by his Vicar and congregation would have not only a deep religious conviction that this was what God wanted him to do, but also that he had the necessary intelligence to learn how to do it. So the roll of the Readers included some highly qualified businessmen, University Professors, a Metropolitan Stipendiary Magistrate, a Consultant Surgeon, Head Teachers, top civil servants and many more. High academic qualifications however do not guarantee that a man can interpret his faith in an acceptable, interesting, or memorable way to the ordinary non-qualified person in the pew, and I was asked quietly by more than one incumbent to widen the training, especially where the conduct of services (i.e. the way the lessons and the prayers were read) and the preaching, as the Bishop had indicated, were concerned. In the early days this affected Mattins and Evensong principally, but as those two services became rarer and the mid-morning Sung Eucharist became in most Churches the main Sunday service, it was the Reader's part in conducting parts of services according to the Alternative Prayer Book (Rites A and B) that took on a new importance, as well as the rather specialised type of preaching needed at a "Family" Eucharist.

In this particular piece of work I became one of the Bishops's "Examining Chaplains". I interviewed each applicant for Readership and talked with his incumbent about how he (or she - more and more women were being nominated, and at the end of my seven years stint I had trained an equal number of men and women) would be used in the parish, whether he or she would be fully acceptable to the congregation, and whether the incumbent would be willing to take part in the training. The response to this last point was mixed. There were those who wished to do all the training of their potential Readers themselves. This was not acceptable, as there had to be a set course followed by all Readers and much of the training in future would take place in groups, and not as under Canon Gripper, individually. Other incumbents wanted no part in the training for a variety of reasons - "I just haven't the time", or "He wouldn't take it from me." At the extremes of churchmanship there were those who questioned whether their man would be given training which reflected their particular point of view - the fundamentalist evangelicals were suspicious of me as a modernist liberal; the Anglo-Catholics were suspicious of me - as a modernist liberal. I was neither modernist nor liberal. I had always tried to be what Eric Abbot at Lincoln had advised me to be a generation ago - an "evangelical Catholic", concerned not with the minutiae of theological speculation but with the basics of the Gospel, the Good News, as proclaimed within the Catholic, universal Church; its doctrines Bible based, its sacraments as taught by the Church over the centuries. This did not exclude the ecumenical dimension for which I constantly worked.

The course which I prepared and planned reflected these convictions. I kept the principle of essay writing, having agonised for a long time about the value of the essay which could become, as it was not an examination-type memory exercise, merely a copying out of what the textbooks said. But at least to write an essay demanded that the books were read. I had prepared a long list of books in two categories - the "absolutely essential", and the "additional recommended". Candidates were also given a long list of questions which gave them a choice of subject in the various categories - the

Old Testament, the New Testament, Church history, Moral theology, ethics, Liturgy and Worship, preaching, evangelism, etc. I marked each essay and wrote a comment when I returned it. This was a very time-consuming burden which I had placed upon myself. If there were a dozen men and women in training it meant that I had committed myself to reading nearly one hundred and fifty essays! There were problems:

"Dear Warden,
I write to say that I reject entirely your comments on my essay on Genesis. I believe the Bible story to be true as the Word of God. Adam and Eve were real people and the world was made in six days and what you say about 'myth' undermines the faith that I have been taught since childhood."

So wrote one "trainee". I was amazed that his Vicar supported him. I had thought that such extreme fundamentalism had died out years ago. In my comments on his essay I had tried to define "myth" as something that conveyed the truth in picture language and said that the word was not used to imply that Genesis was untrue, but that it conveyed the truth about the origins of the world and of humanity in language that those who lived one thousand years before Christ would understand. We met to discuss the matter and I think we came to an amicable conclusion. Eventually the trainee was licensed, but he proved to be a difficult man in the parish and six months later the Vicar confessed to me that it had been a mistake to license him. This was some kind of justification for my own conviction that the man should not go forward to licensing, but the Vicar had said, "I don't accept your ruling, I shall appeal to the Bishop." I had pointed out that in this respect I was the Bishop's examining Chaplain and though he could certainly appeal to the Bishop, I had the Bishop's confidence to make appropriate decisions. If I had refused, I knew that I would have created unbridgeable gaps between myself and the parish and would have had to face the consequences of widening distrust in the diocese. Perhaps I should have been firmer!

In previous chapters I have written that I consider preaching to be a vital part of the priest's ministry - "Preach the Gospel, heal the sick." I had preached my first sermon when I was still a student. Preaching is different from teaching, though it must contain the element of teaching. With others, Douglas Cleverley Ford had founded the "College of Preachers" in the early sixties and I had been associated with it since its inception when George Reindorp sent me to one of its conferences. We had each been asked to bring with us a tape of a sermon, and the one I took was called *The Symbolism of the Tape Recorder*. I had had the flu and was confined to bed one Sunday, so I recorded the sermon to be used at Evensong while my Deaconess took the service. It was a novel experience for the congregation to listen to a disembodied voice on one of the early large tape-recording machines, but I suppose it was no different from listening to a radio sermon. The theme was a pre-Lent one - "Method, Order, Discipline", and the simple message was that as you only get out of a tape recorder what you put into it, so you only get out of life, of religion, what you put into it but that the religious life, like ordinary life, needs method, order and discipline. The sermon and the method of its delivery in spite of a rather thick flu-ey speech seems to have impressed Cleverley Ford and the other clergy at the conference and I was asked to be a member of staff at some of the College of Preachers conferences for Readers which were held regularly at Haywards Heath. My interest in form and content and presentation of sermons, the use of the Bible and of illustrations, grew.

In time I became somewhat disenchanted with the type of conference mounted for Readers by the College, so I planned and presented my own with valued and expert help from local clergy (a) in the theology and Biblical Study behind the sermon (b) in form, content and presentation of the sermon. An Old Testament scholar, Joe Robinson, now Master of the Temple, often helped with a lecture on the Old Testament, two Rochester parish priests, Denis Runcorn and Peter Morris, later to publish their own sermons in Cleverley Ford's Series of *Sermons at the Parish Communion*, came to help regularly and taught us all much. Canon Martin Baddeley from the Cathedral, later Principal of the Southwark Ordination Course, also helped us from time to time.

Each year we held such a Preaching Conference for Readers and Trainee Readers at Graham Chiesman House, the Diocesan Conference Centre at Chislehurst. It lasted from Friday supper time to Sunday teatime, and included lecture sessions, group study, chapel worship, question and answer periods; and in groups, preaching of a ten minute sermon by every member, followed by group criticism and self-criticism. Books and printed lectures were available with the help of the SPCK bookshop which had its premises in St. Nicholas Church, alongside the diocesan office. Because I was aware of the dangers of the "Don't do as I do, do as I tell you" syndrome, I made available a selection of my own sermons, and was prepared to be criticised and analysed as much as those who were submitting themselves to criticism. Some of the sermons we heard were brilliant, and it was easy to spot the Reader who would be listened to with interest and excitement even; sad too, to see the reliance of some on the Biblical commentaries, where bits of the sermon were copied word for word from a book, making no contact with the life of the listening congregation, containing no relevant illustrations, issuing no challenge, offering no strength and comfort of religion.

To help the Readers I wrote a small booklet which I called *Ten Minutes to Wake the Dead*, a title I borrowed from a book by the greatest of modern Scottish preachers, Professor J.S. Stewart. In another booklet *The Reader Speaks* I dealt with voice production in Church, the reading of the office, the prayers, the lessons, and the presentation of the sermon "voice-wise" as the horrid modern phrase would have it. Readers were often asked to speak at Family Services, so I produced another "slim volume" called *On Talking To Children*. I had taken over for a period the training of the Students of Rochester Theological College, housed in the huge old Deanery, in the conduct of services and voice production, and had used the tape recorder extensively in this exercise. It surprises most or us to hear our own voice, and I was able to demonstrate some of the more obvious traps into which all of us fall from time to time when we speak in public - dropping the voice at the end of a sentence, speaking too fast or too slowly, pious and parsonical tones, over dramatisation, under emphasis, over emphasis of the wrong words. Twice a year we held a day conference for all the Readers in the Diocese and one year I took *The Reader Speaks* as a theme and I illustrated some of the things we ought *not* to do in reading the Bible in Church, by playing a record of Laurence Olivier reading the Psalms. In my opinion he committed all the faults I have listed, including declaiming some of them as if he were playing his film part of Richard III. I said all this and was rebuked by more than one Reader afterwards for daring to criticise "our greatest dramatic actor"!

These day Conferences of all the Readers - some one hundred and fifty of them in the 70's were usually very happy occasions. We would invite a well-known speaker to address us on some Biblical, Theological, Moral or Evangelistic topic, or some current matter of moment for the Church. Sometimes the speaker would be too abstruse and intellectually in the clouds and the audience got restless. On one occasion I got restless too. I had invited a prominent priest to speak about what mission and unity might mean in the parishes from which the Readers came, and all we got was an almost incomprehensible talk on the works of Alexander Solzhenitsyn the Russian novelist who had rebelled against Stalin and written a famous book *The Gulag Archipelago*. I had advertised the chosen subject and I was inwardly furious that the speaker had not taken any trouble to prepare an appropriate address, but had gone to his desk and picked up a few pages of a review he was probably writing for some publication or other. He was not a particularly busy man I would guess and I was reminded of the course of sermons on *God and the Human Family* at Shottermill where only the busiest man of the seven chosen to preach had taken the trouble to do his homework thoroughly - Bishop George Reindorp. I think it was the only time we were let down in that way, and many will remember the talks given by Professor C.F. Evans of King's College, London, one of my former tutors at Lincoln; and by that remarkable Bishop, scholar, missionary, writer, ecumenist, Stephen Neill. As I sat alongside Bishop Stephen as he spoke, I could see his notes and it was clear that in his crowded life he had taken time off to prepare his material just for us. A truly remarkable man.

As I encouraged more women to offer themselves for leadership, some very highly qualified people, including some wives of the clergy, joined the list of trainees. I realised that women had special gifts to offer and encouraged them to follow out the line of those gifts - it may be in Hospital visiting, in work with children and other women or in old people's homes. This was another area of training which we developed, and Readers were required to attend post-licensing sessions at one of the hospitals; one on social work, and another on pastoral care. Others were: "How to conduct a study group", and "The use of the media". It was no surprise therefore when several Readers expressed to me their dissatisfaction with the limits placed on their ministry as "mere" Lay Readers. The word "lay" had been abandoned by the Church in the mid 70's, and to fulfill their desire to widen their ministry, many of the men began to offer themselves for the non-stipendiary ministry, and many of the women offered themselves for training as Deaconesses and later as Deacons. I have no doubt that some of the women will proceed to ordination as Priests, just as some of the men I trained have become Priests since I left the Diocese. (Since writing those words I have learned that many of the women Readers I trained *have* been priested. I am so pleased for them.)

What did surprise me, and it should give pause to those who shudder at the thought of "women in the pulpit" as much as they recoil at the thought of "women at the altar", was that in general the women were better preachers than the men. Each trainee was required to write a sermon, discuss it with their Vicar, and preach it at a Sunday service. It was to be tape-recorded and sent to me for criticism. The words "critic" and "criticism" are often misunderstood. They come from a Greek word which means "able to discern", and are not, as we seem instinctively to believe, bound up with *adverse* comment. A critic may say *good* things about a book, a picture, music, a sermon, as well as cruel things. There were sermons that I did not "carp, animadvert, censure, condemn, disapprove, disparage, find fault with" (that shows that even those who write dictionaries instinctively put the bad interpretation first!), but rather, which I found worthy of praise and approval. Many of the women's voices were often clearer than the men's, their message was simple and direct, their illustrations were related to their theme, their conclusions short and creative. I am not implying that all the women were "good" preachers any more than I am saying that all the men were "poor" preachers!

The sermon which has done most to improve preaching, certainly in the Church of England, was written as a humorous sketch by Alan Bennett for the Review *Beyond the Fringe*. Along with the three other stars of the Cambridge University "Footlights" company, Peter Cook, Jonathan Miller and Dudley Moore, all of whom have since attained fame, Bennett had written the sermon for the Edinburgh Festival where it was first "preached" before the Review opened in London at the Fortune Theatre in 1961. One suspects that it grew out of painful experience at public school where Bennett, now a famous playwright in his own right, and author of the TV series *Talking Heads*, must have listened to visiting preachers in some mental pain. Cleverley

Ford had used it in his Preaching Conferences, I had used it in mine, and Paul Welsby, the residentiary Canon in charge of post-ordination training had borrowed my copy of the record for his conferences, so some Readers and Clergy at least should have learned to avoid all the common footfalls:

the parsonical voice,

the meaningless text repeated twice (according to the rules of the Vicars' Union someone once said),

the irrelevant reference to the "original Greek word",

saying the same thing twice but in a different way,

poetic quotations, also irrelevant,

"er"ing and losing your place,

clichés - such as "as I was on my way here tonight",

words like "advisedly",

phrases like "the sort of question I should be asking you, as I ask myself",

personal reminiscences such as "Many years ago when I was about as old as some of you here tonight...",

ridiculous similes and metaphors - "Life is like a tin of sardines"...

"... All of us are looking for the key... roll back the lid of the sardine tin of life, but there is always a little bit in the corner... is there a little bit in the corner of your life...?" etc.,

"So now, as I draw to a close, I want you to...".

Finally, the repetition of the text which hasn't been mentioned again in the sermon, and has not been interpreted or expounded.

The part about the sardine tin may not be quite so exaggerated as it seems. I remember one student at Lincoln during a session on preaching, reading us a sermon for Whitsunday where the gift of the Holy Spirit was likened to air being blown into a bicycle tyre with a pump. Thank you Alan Bennett. You have saved many a congregation from embarrassment and boredom.

The number of Readers in the diocese grew to two hundred and fifty and their contribution to the worship and work of the parishes came to be greatly valued. The time had arrived when there were more Readers than clergy. This was not something of which the Church should be particularly proud, but it does indicate the increasing importance of the contribution of the laity, those who *are* the Church, alongside the work of the ordained ministry - the men and women of the congregations, dedicated, committed, loyal and enthusiastic, leaders, teachers, evangelists and preachers in their own right.

In all this I was not of course working alone. In London there was the "Readers Board" which issued help and advice from time to time. They also produced a series of suggestions for courses of Readers' training which I regarded as too academic and bookish, too theoretical and impractical, for use in Rochester, largely because they had been written by academic theologians and not by parish priests and those at the "coalface" or "grassroots". The Wardens of Readers from all dioceses met from time to time in London to share experiences, hopes and failures, and not all of us were priests. I regard it as essential that some of those who are in charge of various sections of the Church's work should be laymen or laywomen. We are a too clerically dominated Church. I was also greatly helped by several clergy and laity in the training of individuals where groups within a Deanery had offered themselves for Readership. In Gravesend in particular I had a highpowered and efficient group of "trainers". I thank them all.

I was interested to meet Readers from other Dioceses when I acted from time to time as a "selector" in conferences held under the auspices of ACCM, the Advisory Council for the Church's Ministry. Mature men were being interviewed for the non-stipendiary ministry, and among the candidates I met men Readers from many dioceses including Truro where I have landed up as an ageing retired priest. This was twenty years ago. The panel of selectors at these residential selection conferences included the Secretary of ACCM (now called ABM, Advisory Board for Ministry) or another "high up" from London; a layman, who would assess the candidate's acceptability to the lay people of his parish; a priest, who would try to assess his pastoral capabilities; myself, on the level of his education; and sometimes a woman, but not often enough, since the majority of the members of the church are women.

It was all a far cry from my own selection interview of half an hour with Canon Woolnough of the ginger hairs, sitting in a narrow room in Dean's Yard, Westminster, in 1934. Each member of the panel conducted an interview with each candidate within his own sphere of interest and made notes for use at the final selection conference when the candidates had gone home. There were group meetings when each candidate would take the floor and conduct a discussion on a particular theme, and we observed the men in social contexts, how they reacted to their fellows in agreement and disagreement, observing those who were dominant and those who were shy. We took note of the candidate who always reacted unfavourably to criticism, the one who never spoke, the one who talked endlessly about himself and what *he* was doing in *his* parish. Was this due to nervousness or sheer self-centredness? One has to be very careful in making judgments, even over a period of forty-eight hours. The interesting thing was that when all the selectors met for their own final conference, the recommendations were always unanimous. We had not compared notes at all during the conference but when we came to share our conclusions we found that all of us had come to the same opinion on the individual. This was not always in tune with what the incumbent had said about his man - some indeed, though they had agreed to the candidate coming to a conference, were lukewarm about the recommendation. Nor was it easy to have to write and tell A or B that they were *not* recommended for training as priest. Fortunately these letters were written from ACCM and not by us as selectors.

Before I left the Diocese the Bishop asked me in June 1980 to say how I saw the work of the new Warden whom he would have to appoint. I replied:-

MEMO TO THE BISHOP

The work of the Warden of Readers in the next few years.

Note: There is little doubt that the "peak" of applications for Readership has passed and I would anticipate that it will level out at about 30 a year between 20 and 25 new Readers being licensed each year, as a maximum and 15 as a minimum.

With deaths and removals, the number of Readers will be maintained at about two hundred and fifty unless there is a vast increase in the already steady stream seeking Ordination.

1. I would see the work of the Warden as first, *consolidation*.
2. Next, there will have to be some *development* of the training programme.

No one is more aware than I of the gaps in the present programme - e.g. I have never thought it my duty to enquire into the candidate's personal faith and commitment, accepting that by the time I interview him/her this has been established already. In this I have probably been wrong. But before a Reader can be a teacher of prayer, he must have learned to pray - how many have so learned in their Parishes?

The "apologetic" element needs strengthening. Readers perhaps more than any laity have immense opportunities to defend and expound the Faith. It is not enough to tell them to read Hans Kung. Some of this is now in the "Ethics" syllabus, but more needs to be done.

I am also conscious of the weakness of the "Worship" section. This is partly due to the rapidity of change which we have experienced, but partly due to the immense dearth of modern writings on the subject. We need an up-to-date *Liturgy and Worship*.

I hope my successor will continue and develop a wide Post-Licensing course and maintain the Preaching Conferences.

3. Though I have held many "Clergy and Reader" sessions in the Deaneries, the constant cry is to do more to help clergy/reader relationship and understanding, and to help clergy with Readers to know how to use and treat them!

4. The new Warden must be able to exercise a greater pastoral care of his flock. Of course, the prime responsibility is on the Incumbent, but the Warden must learn more quickly and more fully than I did of the problem areas. This cannot be organised or happen as the result of exhortation in circular letters; it must arise out of personal meetings and the creation of confidence in a *person*.

5. I hope the new Warden will be able to carry on writing what used to be called "monographs" (see Sherlock Holmes) to supplement *The Reader Speaks*, *On Talking to Children*, etc.

6. To touch finally on two difficult subjects:

   (a) The new Warden should be encouraged to choose (with great care!) a larger tutorial team than I have been able to muster.

   (b) He must explore, with Jim Ball perhaps, whether the central syllabuses are now in such a form that they can be used in the Diocese. As you know, I have set my face against them (after taking expert advice) as too daunting and too self-consciously academic, and because of the inherent dangers and difficulties of dual assessment at Diocesan and central level.

7. The Warden of Readers, like the Director of Education would be able to work best from Rochester, where all records are kept."

Most dioceses have, (or had -- whether they will survive in a time of painful financial stringency or not, time will tell) a "LAY TRAINING OFFICER". Rochester did not have anyone on its staff called by that name, though all the members of the team were engaged in lay training, and the Youth Officer was given a lay assistant with responsibility for such training, who was with us for a few years. Later on it was agreed that we needed a diocesan "Training Council" to oversee, coordinate, and promote training of clergy and laity. Meanwhile I tried to supplement the work of the team by promoting day conferences, weekend conferences (non-residential) and residential weekends for parishes. Sometimes an evening conference was mounted but this had limited value. Most of all there seemed to be a need for material for study in groups in the parishes, not conducted by someone from the centre but chaired and directed by lay people for lay people. Most of the material I wrote was of this kind, and covered all the Synodical Reports which had been "sent down" to the Deaneries and parishes for discussion and "report back"; then there were the three lengthy studies of the Creed, the Lord's Prayer and the Ten Commandments and the subjects I have already listed elsewhere.

I was aware that the most effective method of education was "learning by doing", but that cannot cover the whole area or education. I was aware that one can only learn to pray by praying, only learn to preach by preaching, only learn to visit the sick by doing so; but before those activities are entered into, some learning *about* prayer from books, *about* preaching by listening to sermons, *about* visiting by being told some of the pitfalls in practising the art, were not to be neglected and would undoubtedly assist the application of the theory. With this in mind I would retire to my study and picture the groups in someone's lounge, enjoying coffee and chat before the "leader" remarked, "I think it's time we started. Have you all read the section on tonight's theme? Mrs. A., Mr. B., what are your reactions?" To take one or two examples of material which was found helpful:- in the newspapers and on television a variety of subjects of deep concern to the moral life of society were being debated and by no means all the articles and programmes were positive or in my view helpful to the Christian. *Some Modern Moral Problems* was written to meet the situation. It covered the themes of Birth Control, Suicide and Euthanasia, Should Doctors tell? (this was related to a much publicised case concerning a teenage girl which was being hotly debated at the time), Industrial Action (at a time when strikes were still common), and Crime and Punishment (when Home Secretaries were making grand statements and prisons were facing disturbances among their inmates).

In 1968 I had written the study papers for a Stewardship campaign in parishes at the request of the lay stewardship adviser, Roy Whiteley. They were based upon the experiences or my former parish at Shottermill in our 1960 campaign and included not only the basic theology and philosophy of stewardship, but also a series of letters for Parish Magazines explaining these basic matters over a period of several months, and a selection of appropriate sermons called *All Life is Sacramental.* These booklets were in use for several years by parishes in preparation for their campaigns.

In 1977 I was asked to give a series of six Lenten addresses at Compline, at a church in Gravesend, called *The Cost of Discipleship.* This I did in the form of *Letters to my friend, John*, a sceptic about religion and the teachings of the Christian Church.

1. On taking up a Career. The first letter to John
2. The Cost of Discipleship to our Talents
3. The Cost to our Pockets
4. The Cost to our Time
5. The Cost to Ourselves
6. Epilogue. A second letter to John

People were always asking for help with their prayers and teachers of RE and Sunday School teachers were asking for help in teaching Prayer to children, so I devised a *School of Prayer* which covered sessions on:

The God to Whom we Pray
The Glory of God and the Dignity of Man

The Geography and the Geometry of Prayer
Praying together and praying for the Stranger
The Bible from which we learn to Pray
The World in which we Pray

On the Bible itself, another course for teachers and Sunday School teachers, which was also used in parish study groups, was entitled *The Most Valuable Thing*, (a quotation from the Coronation Service as the Bible is handed to the Monarch.)

A Modern Approach to the Bible
Inspiration and Interpretation
The Bible View of History
Miracle and The Bible
The Gospel of Fulfillment (a detailed study of St. John's Gospel)

Of course there was nothing startling or novel in any of these studies. I had always regarded my teaching work as interpretation, not innovation, so whatever I wrote was inevitably a distillation of other people's thoughts and work. In sermon preparation classes I was often asked, "Can we legitimately use other men's thoughts and ideas and stories, even quotations from them?"

My answer was, "Yes, as long as you make those thoughts and ideas your own and express them in your own way, and as long as, if it seems appropriate, you acknowledge your debt to your source."

After all, many of the great authors and musicians had done exactly that. Some had even plagiarised without acknowledgment. Shakespeare was the greatest of them, borrowing wholesale from Holinshed's *Chronicles* and Plutarch's *Lives*. One anonymous author describes Shakespeare's methods (in 1728 in a book called *Essay against too much reading*):-

"His being imperfect in some things was owing to his not being a Scholar, which obliged him to have one of those chuckled-pated Historians as an associate, and he maintained him, or he might have starved, upon his history. And when he wanted anything...for his Histories, he sent to him and took down the Heads of what was for his purpose in Characters, which was thirty times as quick as running to the books to read for it.

Then with his natural flowing Wit, he worked it all into
Shapes and Forms, as his beautiful thoughts directed."

I didn't have an associate. I had to go to the books! The
Musicians were not less ready to steal from others in their *Variations*,
Beethoven, Dvorak, Brahms, Rachmaninoff, all borrowed from past
musicians, weaving their work into their own. Few of us have original
thoughts and it was because I owed so much to so many authors that I
resisted the frequent suggestions that I should commercially publish
what I had written. Apart from the fact that most of my illustrations
were taken from contemporary life, and therefore would be out of
date when published, I would not want my publishers or myself to be
accused of plagiarism if someone found a phrase or a passage or an
illustration which had already appeared in print, and which I had not
specifically acknowledged.

Needless to say, all these writings were known as the "Tales of
Hoffman," though I doubt whether many in Rochester had ever read
the *Fantastic Tales* of Ernest Theodor Amadeus Hoffman, whose
stories inspired Offenbach's opera.

In November 1976 I received a letter from the Lord Chamberlain's
office in St. James' Palace in London.

"Reverend Sir,

I have it in command from the Queen to offer you the appointment
of a Chaplain to Her Majesty, and I shall be glad to receive your
acceptance of Her Majesty's gracious offer.

The appointment is at Her Majesty's pleasure and terminates upon
the holder attaining the age of 70 years, or upon preferment as a
Bishop, Dean or Provost.

The Duties of the appointment will be explained to you by the
Reverend Canon James Mansel, sub-Dean of Her Majesty's Chapels
Royal.

Will you kindly let me have your full name, degrees, etc. so that a
formal announcement can he entered in the London Gazette.

I am, Reverend Sir,
Your Obedient Servant,

MACLEAN, Lord Chamberlain."

This was not the first intimation I had of the honour which was being offered to me. In October 1976 I had received a letter from the Bishop of Sheffield marked "Private and Confidential" which said:

"It is part of my duty as Clerk of the Closet to make recommendations for appointment as Chaplain to The Queen. I write to say that I would be pleased to forward your name for appointment to one of the vacancies now existing. As you will readily appreciate the duties of the office are not onerous...They include an annual preachment in the Chapel Royal on a rota arranged by the sub-Dean... the office of Queen's Chaplain is an honour and a dignity which I am sure you would enjoy.

Would you let me know whether you are prepared to accept this appointment? On hearing from you I will inform the Lord Chamberlain who will complete the formalities of appointment, meanwhile I must ask you to treat this matter as strictly confidential.

Best Wishes, your sincerely,

GORDON SHEFFIELD."

Naturally I replied in the affirmative. I knew a little about the "scarlet cassock", and the silver badge which Chaplains wore, and about the annual sermon, because my father-in-law had been a Royal Chaplain as Vicar of Windsor. Life was returning full circle. I had begun life as a "humble Curate" in Windsor, had often been in the Castle, had sung with the "Pastime Singers", a group in the Castle headed by a member of the Choir of St. George's Chapel and on occasion had seen the two princesses, Elizabeth and Margaret, though I had not at that time spoken to them. I had met Princess Margaret at the opening of the school named after her in Windsor in 1943, and had chatted with her about that occasion when she came in 1966 to open an extension of the Diocesan Retreat house at Chislehurst. It would be an accolade beyond my dreams to have such a connection with Windsor again. I did not know the Bishop of Sheffield in his quaint role as "Clerk of the Closet", and I detected the hand of the Bishop of Rochester in choosing me for this distinction. It was certainly, an "honour and dignity" which I enjoyed, particularly my annual visit to St. James' Palace to preach in the Chapels there. Perhaps some explanation is needed here, because I am frequently asked, "But what does a Royal Chaplain *do*?"

Queen Elizabeth the Second has inherited the title "Defender of the Faith", and a legacy from the Middle Ages of thirty-six private Chaplains who used to accompany the monarch (not all at the same time!) on his/her journeyings, along with the Royal Physicians, cooks other household persons. Today the Royal Household consists of various departments, Secretarial, Privy Purse and Treasury, the Lord Chamberlain's Office, the Medical Household, the Ecclesiastical Household, a department looking after the Royal palaces, a Royal Mews Department of Equerries and Vets, and several others. Many of the appointments to these offices, like that of the Chaplains, are honorary. Apart from the annual sermon, we "do" nothing during our time as Chaplains. I ceased to be a Chaplain after eleven years when I reached the age of 70.

In the foyer or ante-chapel of the Chapel in St. James' is a board listing the famous musicians and organists from 1444 when the first "Master of the Children" was appointed. The ten choristers still wear their scarlet and gold Tudor dress when they sing, and receive their education at the City of London School. There are six men choristers and the Music is beautifully sung. Among the "Masters" of the past were Thomas Tallis, William Byrd, Orlando Gibbons, John Blow, Henry Purcell, Maurice Greene, William Boyce and George Frederick Handel. What a company! Most people will have seen the Children of the Chapel Royal singing at the Cenotaph service in Whitehall on Remembrance Day. They also sing at the Royal Maundy Service as the Queen goes to a different Church or Cathedral each year. The Choir of St. James' maintains the glorious tradition of Anglican Church Music as the names of those famous composers of great anthems and masses indicates. The two Chapels, one used in the winter and the other in the summer, are treasure houses of history. The Chapel Royal, with the gate house, is all that remains of the palace which was built by Henry 8th for Anne Boleyn in 1531. The rebuilt palace housed the imprisoned Charles I and in the Chapel he received Communion before crossing the park to his execution in Whitehall in 1649. Queen Victoria and Prince Albert, the Duke of York (later George V) and Princess Mary of Teck, were married there.

The summer Chapel, called the "Queen's Chapel", across the road was built for Roman Catholic worship and was finished in 1627. After the Restoration in 1660 Christopher Wren refurbished it for

Charles II's wife and it was used for Roman Catholic worship until
the time of William III.   Samuel Pepys wrote of his visits to the
"Popish Chapel of St. James."   When George V died Queen Mary
came to live at nearby Marlborough House and in 1938 it was restored
and given for the use of the Chapel Royal.   The Chapel Royal is not
open to the public except for Sunday Services and the Queen's Chapel
may only be viewed by arrangement with Marlborough House.   It was
a great privilege to be part of a thousand years of royal and musical
history.   For most of my time the Sub-Dean was Canon Anthony
Caesar who had been a master at Eton, and had played an organ
concert for me at All Saints Chertsey in 1948, which he couldn't
recall!   He had also played the organ of Windsor Parish Church in my
father-in-law's time as Vicar, so we had something in common to chat
about each time we met.

Pat and I were supposed to meet the Queen after my appointment
as a Chaplain, at a Royal Garden Party in Buckingham Palace
gardens.   The date and time were fixed and Pat had bought a new
outfit, and a hat, which she did not normally wear, for the Great
Occasion.   We were to travel to London by train from Rochester
Station in time to arrive at the Palace at 3 p.m. and had given
ourselves ample time for the journey.   We waited patiently for the
train but it never came.   That afternoon *no* trains on that line passed
through Rochester because there was an incident on the line further
back at Gillingham.   So we missed the Garden Party, and we missed
our meeting with the Queen.   I believe that the other Chaplain who
was to meet her also missed the occasion, the Reverend John Lang,
who was at the time Head of BBC Radio, now Dean of Lichfield, was
held up by the fact that his wife was about to give birth!   We did meet
the Queen on other occasions but what a waste of a nice new outfit!

The most memorable occasion was a gathering of all the Royal
Chaplains at Windsor, for Mattins at the Parish Church, lunch and a
meeting with many members of the Royal Family and a tour of some
of the rooms of the castle.   It was a moving moment for me to sit in
my scarlet cassock in the choir stalls of the Parish Church where I had
been so happy nearly forty years before, as a newly ordained Deacon
and "second curate".   The Duke of Edinburgh read the lesson,
beautifully as he always does, an example to many a clergyman and
Reader, and before lunch there were drinks with members of the
Family.   I was able to have conversations with the Queen Mother who

had been particularly kind to my mother-in-law when my father-in-law and first Vicar had died. She remembered them both and with great affection as Queen, often resident in Windsor, when Ralph Creed Meredith had been Vicar from 1940-1957; and with the Princess Margaret, about the future of the school named after her which was under threat of amalgamation or closure.

The Queen and the Duke were gracious as always. What a life is theirs! - making conversation with all and sundry, the interesting and the boring, the obsequious and the fawning; appearing to be interested, wishing to yawn and break away, but trained to accept the life as part of a historic duty to be a monarch to all; knowing that the folk who have been introduced to you are scared and tongue-tied anyway at the awesomeness of the occasion. And what sadness had been theirs in recent years, seeing one after another of their children's marriages breaking down after such hopes and dreams and expectations had been aroused. Royalty is a state to which men and women are born. It cannot be entered into by a marriage ceremony, and it is true that the pressures are greater than those upon any other family; and though we may guess that what has happened to the Royal children and the Queen's sister is only a reflection of what is happening to nearly half of British families, the breakdowns are especially sad because they take place in the glare of publicity and those who suffer are at the mercy of the unscrupulous manipulators of the tabloid newspapers.

Throughout her long reign the Queen has seen not only the breakup of her children's marriages, she has seen the gradual breakup of the British Empire and its metamorphosis into a shrinking Commonwealth, with Pakistan becoming a Republic in 1956, South Africa in 1961, Jamaica in 1962, Malta and Kenya and Malawi in 1964, Guyana in 1970, Zimbabwe in 1980. These and many others became independent, some within the Commonwealth, some outside it. Now that Australia may well decide to loose the ties that binds it to the Monarchy, other Dominions, Canada, New Zealand may follow. The Queen has also lived through the Falkland and Gulf wars and a series of crises in society, but has remained serene and calm through it all, an immense strength to her Ministers as every one of them testifies, and to her people. Though the mutterings about the "cost of the monarchy" and about the archaic nature of royalty continue, sometimes with justice, the Queen's personal position is secure and I am glad to have been one of her Household, however insignificant.

Life at Rochester went on in normal fashion. Pat's routine and mine were both fixed, but obviously the Bishop felt that it was time for a change. He offered me the chance to go back to parish life, but I felt that I still had much work to do as Director and Warden, and interviews for the General Secretaryship of SPCK, and as Archbishops' Appointment Secretary came to nothing. I plainly did not have enough experience in the world of publishing for the former, and I did not really approve of the terms of reference outlined to me for the latter. My work with Christ Church College and the University at Canterbury was also increasingly important and I did not want to give it up. I also believed that Pat's work at Walderslade should not be interrupted in her last year or two before retirement. She would be 60 in July 1976, but as it happened her Headmistress became ill and Pat was asked to continue as Acting Head.

The improvement of schools and the rebuilding of some was proceeding apace, and I was deeply involved in the revision of Agreed Syllabuses of Religious Education in Kent and Bromley. The provision of new ranges of buildings which effectively meant doubling their size was going ahead at St. George's Gravesend and Bennett Memorial School Tunbridge Wells, so that each school could accommodate and teach up to a thousand children,. providing "O" level and "A" level up to University entrance. This involved a great deal of time spent with architects, Kent Education Officers, and Ministry Officials, but it was time well spent, and it assured a continuing commitment to a specific Christian education for a large number of boys and girls up to eighteen years of age in two important towns in Kent.

Aided Schools were rebuilt at Brenchley, Chevening, Crayford, Grain, Holy Trinity Gravesend, Hunton, Lamorbey, Northfleet, Penge, Sevenoaks, Swanley, Tunbridge Wells, and major improvements were carried out at others. The Board of Education co-operated with the Local Education Authorities in improving and rebuilding many of the "Controlled" Schools, including a new Middle School, at All Hallows, and I make no apology for the time spent with the Heads and Governors of those schools, planning buildings with them and the excellent architects whom we engaged. The Church is concerned with the body as much as the soul and the conditions under which children are taught in Church Schools should be at least as good as, and if possible (as an example) better than, those provided by "the State".

When Pat retired in 1977, she did temporary teaching for a term or two in other Secondary Schools, and then she decided to give up teaching altogether. She had received a tremendous "send-off" from the staff and girls of Walderslade and we held a great luncheon in the garden at White Friars for staff and their wives and husbands, past and present. The Chief Education Officer, W.H. Petty, had taken the trouble to come to the school to say thank you in person for Pat's many years of service in a "difficult" school. It had been a time of increasing behavioural problems in schools, and teachers were beginning to feel the strain, a strain which successive governments do not seem to have come to terms with. In one of the schools to which Pat went as a temporary member of staff after official retirement, as a Domestic Science teacher, she had cause to reprimand a girl of about fifteen, and as a discipline, for what had been dangerous behaviour in a domestic science room; she told the girl she must stay behind after school. The girl, who was coloured, was on the School Council and there was a meeting that afternoon after school. "I'm not staying in for you," she shouted, "I have got to attend a meeting of the Council." "That's too bad," replied Pat, "you should have thought of that before". The girl raged and screamed at Pat, but was not allowed to leave. The next day she appeared, with a group of coloured friends, and prepared to assault Pat physically, and Pat was only saved from hurt by the appearance of another member of staff, a man. I mention the fact that the girl was coloured not for any racial reason but because of the difficulty which coloured children and adults have in believing that such incidents are *not* racially inspired, the belief that many of them have that they are always being "picked on", because of their colour. It illustrated another fact, that temporary staff have a worse time than permanent staff. Such a thing had never happened to Pat when she wielded the authority of a Deputy Head or Acting Head. As a "temp" she had no standing and no authority.

Only once had I myself had difficulty with children in class and that was when I was part of a team from the diocese taking RE in a local primary school in Rochester which had a large ethnic minority. I found it difficult to keep the children interested, and the coloured children especially were a problem, baiting the man with the clerical collar. It was a salutary experience because I had always regarded myself as "good with children", able to keep them interested in what can be the most exciting subject of all, if well taught. I had always had good relationships with the children I had taught throughout my parish ministry.

I call to mind only one other time when I found it difficult to make contact with adolescent boys and girls and that was when I served as a Chaplain on a Schools Cruise with several hundred pupils from Kent, on the SS Uganda. The fortnight's cruise was itself an exciting experience, taking us by air to Venice and thence by sea to a variety of places in the Mediterranean - Athens, Rhodes, Crete, Malta, Naples, but neither the Roman Catholic Chaplain nor myself had a very positive response to the services we held. We invited volunteers to plan and execute assemblies and we took part in all of their activities except the classes which were held aboard. We visited the few children who were confined to the sick bay of the ship and even joined in their "rock 'n' roll" sessions, but I detected a feeling among the young folk that they were being "got at" by the mere fact of having Chaplains on board. The Chief Education Officer, Bill Petty, and his wife were loyal attenders at the Communion services along with other members of staff and a few pupils, but the fact that we always ate at the "Captain's Table" was probably a barrier to communication with the young. However, I gained much from chats with them and learned something of the adolescents' attitude to the Church and to religion, and I visited places which would have been unknown to me in any other way.

On retirement Pat knew that she was not by instinct or upbringing a woman who could happily spend her days indoors cooking, housekeeping, dusting and mending. She was an excellent needlewoman, and loved making curtains and cushions, but when she retired she could not pass all her time in such exercises, so she decided to become a hairdresser, not for financial reasons, but as a social service. She took a six-month course at a College in Bromley during which she was warned that the occupational hazard of hairdressers was back pain, through standing long hours at awkward angles when working. But Pat had been physically fit all her life, had never had an illness except (was it?) chickenpox, just before our marriage. She had been a champion swimmer and games player so she took little note of the warning.

Her first thought had been to take up physiotherapy when she finally gave up teaching, and she was re-registered as a member of the Chartered Society of Physiotherapists (which she had belonged to in its former life as the Chartered Society of Massage and Medical Gymnastics, having obtained their Diploma while in training at the Bergman-Osterberg College in Dartford, a college for training PE teachers). But this venture had been a disaster. She had obtained a post as a junior in one of the Medway Hospitals but was completely at a loss in the use of modern electrical and other physiotherapy equipment which had not been invented in the 1930s when she was trained. She was given a series of manuals to learn from, but found it beyond her 60-year-old mind. The intelligence was there but not the capacity to study for hours. So she resigned.

The hairdressing offered a worthwhile alternative because she was interested in people and in the problems of old people and was extremely good at getting on to their wavelength. When she offered herself as hairdresser to the residents of some of the local authority homes in the Medway towns, they jumped at the chance of having someone who would not charge for her services except for the cost of petrol. At the height of her popularity in this new guise, Pat had fifty eight clients on her books in homes in Rochester, Chatham, Gillingham, Cobham, and elsewhere. She enjoyed every minute of it and so did they. But it took its toll. Many of the local authority homes were in Victorian or even earlier buildings, and the conditions were atrocious. Pat found herself lifting old ladies from bed to chair without help. She had to shampoo their hair over antiquated baths and none of them provided equipment for hairdressing or hair drying. It was this that did the damage, as she was of necessity forced to buy her own hairdryer on wheels. It weighed thirty-two pounds and she would lift it in and out of the boot of her Austin 1300 car, and often had to carry it on her hip up flights of stairs. Because she was such a physically fit person she did not realise the damage she was doing to her spine and after nearly two years she was forced to give it up as she was often in great pain, particularly below the shoulder blades.

So began the long sad saga of medical treatments and countless minor and major operations which ended in her death. When the pain became difficult to bear she was sent to various consultants in Medway towns. She was treated by a homeopathic specialist who proclaimed himself as a Buddhist. She was sent to one orthopaedic surgeon who told her that "it was all in the mind". She had several spells in the Brook hospital in Woolwich where she was, in theory, put to sleep for a week so that her mind might cast out all thoughts of pain. Unfortunately, the drugs did not work and after twenty-four hours, when I visited her, she was not in her room but walking in the Hospital grounds. She was sent to the "nuclear" department of the Hospital and given various types of brain scan, but nothing untoward was found. There was in fact nothing wrong with her mind!

It became clear that as Pat more and more had to spend her days lying down, the only posture that could relieve the pain, I would have to spend more time with her. Many friends were wonderful in coming in to sit with her when I was out, but I was unable to fulfil my duties as I would have wished, so with the utmost reluctance I had to inform the Bishop that I wished to retire, and move to the retirement bungalow which we had designed a year or two before, and had built with a Kent firm, Colt Houses of Bethersden, in Headley Down, Hampshire. I was sixty-three, and two years off my proper retirement age. But the Bishop and all in the Diocese Office and diocese were marvellously sympathetic and generous with gifts and words of comfort as well as undeserved letters of gratitude for what I had tried to give to the schools and parishes, to the clergy and the Readers. I was especially affected by the letters I received from officers and members of the Kent and Bromley Education Committees on which I had served. I had always felt that I was a "thorn in the side" of Bromley in particular, as I disagreed with much of what the ultra-conservative authority was doing with the schools and had said so often and forcefully. However, Joan Bryant the then Chairman, wrote:-

"Dear Stanley,
Thank you for your letter of June 11th 1980 in which you tell me of your resignation from Bromley Education Committee to take effect from September 30th, 1980. We in Bromley will miss you very much. I always found your contribution to our debates stimulating and interesting, even though I disagreed with what you said. Thank you for the work which you did as Chairman of the Agreed Syllabus Committee. This is a project dear to my heart and I know to yours also. I hope that you and your wife will have a very happy retirement and that your wife's health will improve.

With best wishes to you both, yours sincerely,
                                Joan."

Similar letters came from Kent. Perhaps I had not battled in vain!

When I had first mooted the possibility of retirement to the Bishop, he had replied in his own handwriting and with his familiar understanding and generosity:-

"My Dear Stanley,

Thank you for your letter. I am sad beyond measure at your news of Pat and I realise what this lack of progress must mean to you both. I hope Mr. Lettin will respond helpfully and sympathetically (this was the orthopaedic surgeon who was seeing Pat every three weeks in London).

Whilst I shrink from the thought of you not picking up the reins again I think that for Pat's sake you ought not to try if you are sure you will have enough to live on until you are 65. I can well understand your reluctance to return to Whitefriars (we had temporarily moved to Hampshire) and if you tell me that you want to resign at the end of July or September I shall be ready to face the consequences, albeit reluctantly.

What matters *above all else* now is that you should both be able to live quietly at your own speed and to allow time for the natural recovery for which we all pray. We shall be losing Martin Baddeley in August...and David Silk in September, so I look like having a trio of major appointments to fill. I shall be ready for a "definitive" chat whenever you wish and will come to "Cedarwood" on a Monday if you wish.

With love to you both, David."

The letter which I treasure most came from the young Vicar of the parish of Walderslade in which Pat's school was situated. Julian Reindorp (son of my former Bishop, George Reindorp of Guildford) wrote:-

"Just a note in case I don't see you again. Thank you for your kindness to me. One of the things I have enjoyed most in this diocese is the friendliness of the Staff.

But I really wanted to thank you for all your hard work behind the scenes. Your pamphlets have been invaluable as precise summaries on so many issues, and while I have tried to read much else, as I am sure you hoped, your writing has helped us to get a flavour of a subject without feeling that the subject is too big to handle.

I always remember William Barclay's comment about doing things by wearing out the seat of your pants. I suspect your clothing has taken a very great hammering!

Pat as you know so well, was a real breath of fresh air at Walderslade, and for the girls the youngest 60 year old ever when she retired. The group I asked thought she was in her forties - she thought I'd made it up when I told her...

Do give her my love, and thank you both for your very real encouragement to one young parish priest.

Our love and prayers, Julian."

Such letters bring tears to the eye, but strength and encouragement when life looks bleak and the future doubtful.

I returned to Rochester Cathedral for a great and moving "Farewell" and many gifts on September 22nd, 1980, and sixteen marvellousy happy years came to an end.

CHAPTER 13

MARRIAGE
(A DIGRESSION)

"It won't be a stylish marriage. I can't afford a carriage..."
Harry Dacre. "Daisy Bell"

"But love is blind and lovers cannot see the pretty follies that
themselves commit."
Shakespeare. "The Merchant of Venice"

"Marriage is like life in this, that it is a field of battle,
not a bed of roses."
R.L. Stevenson (d. 1894)

"Love and marriage, love and marriage - go together like a horse
and carriage." When the songwriter gave those words to Frank
Sinatra to sing they were largely true, even in Hollywood where they
originated, in spite of the reputation of the "stars" in the thirties for
multi-marriages. The Americans have always paid lip service to the
high ideals of marriage, even though their practice may be different.
The heir to the Dodge automobile fortune married a dozen times! But
the "ideal" couple of the thirties were Ginger Rogers and Fred
Astaire, who never really kissed in any of their films, though they
spent much time on the dance floor in each other's arms. The
Broadway musicals of Rodgers and Hammerstein were "squeaky
clean", always aiming at the highest ideals of marriage and family life
- "Climb every mountain." The horse and carriage were still well
harnessed together. The prince and princess were deeply in love and
would eventually marry and live happily ever after. The ideals and
ideas of "Romantic love" ruled, largely because of the influence of the
cinema. Before the war, and during it, more than sixteen millions
went to the cinema every week, and clean romantic comedies had far
more influence than the crime stories featuring Edward G. Robinson,
James Cagney or George Raft. At that time perhaps one in a hundred

marriages ended in the divorce court, even after A.P. Herbert's loosening of the ties in the Act of 1937. Today sixty or so years later there are approximately 395,000 marriages and 150,000 divorces each year. If the carriage is being drawn by a pair, at least one of the horses has broken away.

I am sure that, like most of our contemporaries, when we married in 1943 both Pat and I had the romantic view of marriage and had no idea other than its permanence. When we made promises we intended to keep them. That was how we had been brought up, and that was how we would bring up our children. Falling in love might be something that happened more than once, but when "Mr Right" appeared, eternal happiness was assured. Pat has appeared in these pages from time to time, but she may seem a shadowy figure, so...

I have no poetic words to describe my first sight of Myfanwy Meredith as she was when I first saw her in Church (surely that must hallow all future relationships?) She wore a smart tan-coloured suit with a wide-brimmed hat of the same colour. Beneath the hat were sparkling, laughing, dark brown eyes, a complexion and lips that needed no artificial aids, beautiful firm, even teeth, a smile and laughter never far from the (in church at least) demure expression. Her hair was very dark and shining. Her figure was perfect, as I discovered later, (not in Church!) and her legs a dream. You see how much influence the films have had upon me! The book of synonyms has not enough space to provide the appropriate words, or the feelings that I had when I first set eyes on her, feelings which I continued to entertain for forty-eight and more years of life with her. She was handsome, but that word perhaps implies a rather tall, horsey woman. Pat had learned to be an intrepid horse rider in New Zealand, and she *did* look handsome in riding kit in pictures of her taken there. Her personality was effervescent, ebullient, outgoing; she was full of fun. Indeed at the first Sunday evening supper at the Vicarage when I met her, I was overwhelmed by this fascinating girl who had just travelled round half the world to come home in a wartime convoy, shadowed by U-Boats, from which some ships had indeed been lost. Maybe "love is blind" as Shakespeare wrote, but at the time we fall in love, blindness is a virtue not a drawback. If the "pretty follies" appeared too soon, none of us would enter the state of holy matrimony; we should be scared stiff. She was lovely, and loveable. She was deeply interested in other people, and never spoke about herself or her achievements, which were many. Loveliness is as much in the character, which needs not fade away, as it is in the face.

Our courtship was a whirlwind one. We met in March, were engaged in May and married in August. Our loving was passionate within the bounds which our upbringing had set. We would have had no more thought of going to bed or "making love", as today's conventions have widened the phrase to include intercourse, than we would have thought of going to Church in a swimsuit. Many men, in Clacton where she was a teacher after leaving College, and in New Zealand, had asked Pat to go to bed with them, including her own cousin, but she had refused. She had too high an ideal of what it means to be a person of integrity. Later, when she was a teacher at Midhurst, the same proposals had been made to her (as a married woman, and married to a clergyman to boot!) and she had turned them down with some contempt. The fact that we were able to speak to each other of such things indicates, I hope, the level of trust and confidence which we had in each other all through our often stormy relationship. Penelope Mortimer has just written her autobiography, and speaks frankly of the problems she had with John Mortimer, (creator of "Rumpole") the rows and the infidelities on both sides, and she remarks that if you do not tell the truth in an autobiography, there is no point in writing it. The truth is often painful.

There were no infidelities in our marriage. I recall my aunt Mary, who was organist of a Church in Sussex, telling me with bated breath how terrible it was that their Curate had had a child only five months after his marriage. I was not tempted in that way. But there *were* rows. They stemmed from ignorance on both our parts. We were a very ignorant generation. We were ignorant of birth control. We were ignorant of premenstrual tension, we were ignorant of post-natal depression.

At Lincoln I had bought a bright yellow volume published by Gollancz called *A Marriage Manual* by Hannah and Abraham Stone. Such was the retarded sexual climate of those days, that books with that kind of title had to be wrapped in an extra brown paper cover in case visitors might see the title on your shelves and come to the conclusion that you were a sex maniac or interested in pornography. It was a harmless book, and bland in its technical approach to sex in marriage. It helped me very little. I know that after marriage we made love too frequently, with the consequence that we were often tired and irritable. Mrs. Short (who thrust Anne at me and gave me milk on Fridays!) had warned me of the dangers of too frequent intercourse but I had inwardly laughed at her. I wish I had taken more notice. We had our first child, Peter, 9½ months after marriage. It was much too soon. There had been no pre-birth preparations, no group work with other pregnant mothers-to-be as there is today. I had not been present at the birth as I would have been today, and for Pat it was the most frightening experience of her life. She was in a nursing home in Windsor, I was in Bath. Though she was pleased and proud to have a son, she was also resentful at the ties which would now bind her, resentful too that the old fashioned birth prevention method which the local GP in Windsor had recommended, had failed. In those days condoms were hidden under the counter in chemist's shops, though they were in view in hairdressers, but such was my own upbringing that I would have been ashamed to ask for a packet, and wrongly expected Pat to take any "precautions" necessary.

Peter was a bonny baby, eight pounds six ounces in weight, but born with jaundice. No one knew why this was, because Pat came home from New Zealand full of good food. New Zealand farmers had so much produce that they did not know what to do with it in wartime. Lamb chops were served for breakfast and thick rich cream and scones oozing with butter, with morning coffee. Peter was breast fed and Pat had too much milk which was in itself painful, but when abscesses also developed, life for her was agony. She had always been hyper-sensitive to pain, and was so all through her adult life. No one has yet discovered why some people feel pain more keenly than others, why pains which most people can cope with by taking an aspirin can prostrate others. But she bravely persevered with the feeding, for she was never, right to the end, a person who would give up trying, and when Peter was weaned, all was well. Money was short ("I can't afford a carriage") and baby food difficult to obtain in wartime. I would cycle down into Bath from Weston and queue for perhaps half an hour at Boots or some other chemist for Heinz baby food, or at the fishmongers on the hill into Bath for a piece of plaice or cod. Milk was no problem, but as rationing was tightened it became more difficult to buy butter or meat. We survived, largely with the food parcels sent from New Zealand and America. We sold some clothes, some books and some wedding presents to "make ends meet".

The rows I spoke of were of course childish and often ridiculous. I was working very hard under a Vicar who was very difficult to please - I have written about him earlier in these pages, but it created the tension which was so easily demonstrated when Pat herself was tense and frustrated at being tied to home and child so soon after marriage when she would have loved to have been out in the countryside on a horse. My mother had remarked often that she and my father had never had a cross word in their twenty years of marriage. I had not believed her, but I wish she had never said such a thing, because it made me feel very guilty when Pat and I had "words" about silly things like "should we have roast potatoes or boiled?" or more vital things like money. Pat had said jokingly that she wouldn't marry me unless she was allowed £50 a year for clothes and hairdos. This was a large part of my stipend when she was not herself working, but I knew what Pat had given up to marry me, and we came to a compromising arrangement and she was able to buy a few clothes and have a perm from time to time, though her lovely hair did not need it.

One expression of our love is in the letters we wrote to each other, at least once a day before and during our engagement, and even more frequently when we were away from each other. One which she wrote to me only a fortnight after we had met and fallen hopelessly in love, will tell more about her and about me than a whole chapter:

The Vic,
Windsor,
Thursday afternoon.

"Darlingest,

It's just hopeless. I've been sitting at Mum's desk trying to finish a New Zealand letter I started days ago but it hasn't progressed. You kept drifting along and upsetting it all and then just as I'd made up my mind it was quite hopeless I thought I might as well sit down and write to you, though I had intended not to earlier in the day, I don't know why. Perhaps because I've still got one of the songs I heard in 'Old Chelsea' in my head, which says, 'Never let a fellow know you're caring.' Anyway I was just about to start writing, if you can call my scrawl such, when you dropped my very blue letter in (at that time I was using bright blue notepaper - a gift!) Boy Mine! Are you? It's the nicest possible letter and I love you for telling me about the first Tuesday (the day she had visited me for the first time in my "digs") and you'd never, never be foolish to me.

I got back from school early today, feeling full of the joy of living, mainly because I'm on holiday now, and a little because of you! Blow you! T'other way round really. I had tea in the garden with Dad who told me what a lucky chap he was to have such excellent Curates. He's very thrilled with Philip (a newly appointed Curate for the hospital work) who incidentally is very nice I think, rather impractical. That looks a funny word to me. Is it correct? It's a long way to my room to fetch 'Dicky, my Boy, the Dictionary' - silly family joke. Enough of him. He said lots of nice things about you - I'll tell you some time.

Did you need a 'reference' about me from him, dearest? I'm not much good at anything, so I've often been noisy and mad just to draw attention to myself and get attention when other people could do it by their brilliant conversation and witty jokes. I've told horrid fibs but always owned up afterwards. Maybe I've flirted a terrific lot but I've always played fair and never said 'I love you' when I didn't. I don't know if I've got any good points. I hope I'm unselfish and generous. I know I'm affectionate and think my friends just perfect. I don't know whether that's a good point? Am also terribly impulsive but to some extent I've controlled that a bit. Excitable. I just went mad when we walked along Broadway (the ship had stopped off in New York to pick up convoy escorts) I used to be terribly tactless. I've cultivated a bit under the guidance of the head at Iona (the Presbyterian boarding school where Pat taught in New Zealand). She's a dear and paid me the best compliment I've ever had paid. She once said: 'Goodbye. Have a good holiday; you have a wonderful capacity for enjoyment.'

Heavens! (Is that swearing?) What a lot of twaddle about me. What of you, darling Boy, I don't know why I like you such an awful lot, it's just I like what you say, I love what you write. I love your voice. I shouldn't tell you that - I expect all your doting parishioners do, and most of all I love you for not being a snob. I'm a bit of a socialist, dear, and I've always had a terrible horror of snobs. Must stop. I could go on for hours. I've just had that unnecessary meal, from my point of view, dinner, and I must help young Ann wash up

as Peggy's in bed with the dickens of a pain - notice I didn't swear
and it's a bad enough one to swear about. (Peggy and Ann were the
Vicarage maids. Maids were an absolute priority in Meredith's
Vicarage and Pat got into trouble for having a normal friendly
relationship with them, as they were not on the same social level.
That was why I had approval as not a snob! Peggy became our
chidren's nanny and a close personal friend.)

Poor kid! Ann and I have just been up in her room yelling with
laughter - can't imagine she feels like being cheered up by us. I get
an horrible pain too sometimes. Ugh! I hate to think of it and ye old
gynecologist (spelling??) charged me £3.3.0. and told me I ought to
have an infant. Says I: 'Oh dear. Trouble is I've been once round the
world looking for a husband and now I'm off again and I seem to have
arrived here too late (his engagement had just been announced in the
paper) what do you suggest I do about it?' He's a dear and was quite
amused and the next time I went he only charged me £1.1.0.
Anyway, says I to Peggy - 'the only thing is to have a baby,' so we
fetched her one of Richard's baby animals (Richard was her young
brother, eighteen years younger than Pat, later to be Headmaster of
Monkton Combe School) and put it in bed with her. Quite stupid! but
it wasted a lot of time.

Oh help! It's a terrible long time till Sunday. Thank you again for
a lovely, lovely letter.

Bestest love, your Pat.

PS. I'll try to 'say a prayer' but I've rather lost the habit. You'll
have to be patient. Am I worth being patient about?"

(Having an infant on June 8th 1944 did not end *Pat's* pains.)

Four days later I had this letter:

"My darlingest Boy,

'Whoopee! Whizz-bang!' I used to say in N.Z. I had fifteen
letters this morning so they all have to be answered and here sit I
scribbling another book to you. No, it won't be a book, merely a few
lines to remind you I exist and to tell you, strange as it may seem, that
I love you better than anyone on this earth and that you are a beastly
nuisance because Peggy is still in bed and I must be up and doing the

work instead of writing to a lad who calls himself proud, fearful, and selfish. I haven't noticed it yet darling, I'll tell you when I do.

Last night was just perfect. Do you mind me sitting at (or on) your feet, calling you dear and looking all possessive, for it shall be stopped if you do. Heavens how unlike me this is, being willing to do just what you want. I've always gone round before saying what *we* would do, and then sulking if we didn't, nearly as bad as that anyway.

Darling, don't get all het up about my stupid middle getting topsy-turvy. I don't get pain a tenth as bad as Peggy's, poor kid, but I do get a bit cross, a bit tired and have to have a dozen or so aspirins. But I still trot off to school, cursing at being a woman, and take gym and games, bend, stretch, skip, jump, etc. etc. They took out my appendix and puddled around inside and said it was a very good inside, so that's that. Now shall we talk about your catarrh? Ha! ha! (There were many more pages and it ended...)

Must stop and work, darling. Do you love me? All the bestest love in the world, yours always. Pat."

Six days later, after several more letters, I received the following. I quote it because it explains how I had been putting my "religious" foot in it, and it also explains Pat's continuing attitude to "the Church" and to "religion" all through our married life.

> c/o Mrs. Beard
> 142 Red House Lane,
> Aldridge.

"My own darlingest Boy,

Your very wonderful letters arrived this morning. It doesn't matter a tap if they come both together. What matters is that you found time to write them when I know you're busy; and that you did go to the Post Office to try and get the first one here yesterday... (some local news of her friends with whom she was staying).

I fully intended not to write to you again, hoping to make you miss me a little bit more but it's no good...(some references to Iona College).

Stanley, there's too much in your letters to attempt to set out my reply but I will try when I get home and can be on my own for an hour or so. At the moment I can't set my thoughts out. All I know is that the days seem empty when I can't see you. The picture isn't enough. And that I think, think, think about you, about us.

On my own again, dear, for a little while, but probably I shall be interrupted so don't take anything I say to heart because I haven't really thought it all out. Religion. Don't preach at me much dearest, just let me try and get my own ideas. At home, I've always had a horror of being like Mother, not *thinking* much, just blindly conscientiously *doing*, because of her devotion to my father. It's alright because it satisfies her and she had no other interests. Dad married her because she wasn't bad looking, came of quite a good family, would do as he asked, and help him a lot. You see what I mean by 'a piece of furniture'. He is also conceited enough to think that she did rather well to get him and got the best of the bargain. He is a parson and a good one, but the unselfishness he preaches hasn't been shown to her much. She doesn't realise it of course and is perfectly happy, but I shouldn't be. That's why I keep pressing the point about the piece of furniture and your love for me. I know you don't think like this but I suppose it's just because I've seen Dad and Mum that I'm a bit scared. You see, my darling, I love you with all my heart and would try to be what you wanted but I don't want to be loved by you unless it's 'all or nothing'. Sometimes you make me feel as if I were applying for a job and had to prove myself the right person by references, testimonials, from my father and such. Well, I'm not. If I were just applying to get married I could have my choice of several any day. That's conceited, isn't it? It's the same for you I know. What I want is someone I can respect and love, who loves me for what I am, not for what sort of decoration I'd make to his house. And because I loved and respected that person, wouldn't it follow that I'd love his work?

Sweetheart, I've never been unhappy, nor likely to be. It was all a great adventure being a rebel, and I've only been rebelling against snobbishness, not against religion, or if it was, it was only against a religion which allowed one to be a snob. I couldn't square the two (Dad's religion and his behaviour). I love people for what they are and what they make of life, not for what they were born (Ralph Meredith's father was an Irish Baronet) . I could love you as much if you were a shop boy, provided you lived for truth and right. The thought of being married to you is wonderful and somehow I don't think we'd be misfits, but I'm not going round getting testimonials for *you*.

This is all involved and I'll get it sorted out one day. Perhaps I could tell you better than write it. That's another reason I love you. I call talk to you, but dearest, please don't preach at me. Mick's letters have sickened me such a lot - his hearty way of saying we can show God to the *working class* by doing little deeds of kindness, mowing their lawns and so on. Glory! who does he think he is? We are all working class. Does he imagine that the old Woolwich curates are the only people in the world doing little deeds of kindness? I can't bear folk who skite (New Zealand word) about all the good they do. This is all wrong about Mick I know, but it's the way he writes. Enough of this. I'll get it all clear one day and tell you. (Mick was her brother, a curate in Woolwich. They had been close as children but had grown apart. Later Pat grew to appreciate his virtues.)

Somehow I want to see a *practical* religion - what I try and teach through games and so on - unselfishness, team spirit and so on. I hate sentimental women without anything to do who see in their padre a Christ and worship the priest; the 'faithful' who roll up to Church day by day. My friend Nora (with whom Pat was staying when she wrote this letter) has just had a mad letter today from a religious maniac. Oh, my hat! Blow it, I've started again. Let's talk of something else. (here there was more about the very 'ordinary' friends she was staying with - she had lodged with them in Clacton. She concluded...)

Nora and her mother are two of the most wonderful people I know. Amazing, as I don't suppose they've a wonderful family tree like the Merediths, says she bitterly. Oh, Stanley. Please love me for myself, always, always. I do you.

Miss me darling? all my love. Your Pat."

Our exchange about religion and the role of the parson's wife continued. Pat had agreed to marry me, but did not want to announce the fact yet, until we had clarified our mutual expectations. Pat wrote again, the same day:

"It's nearly midnight and that means I'll see you today, or at least as soon as it is 12 o'clock I shall. I feel rather mean. I've had four lovely letters, including the one I shall get tomorrow - today I mean! and only sent you two, and far from lovely, so when I came to bed I couldn't decide whether to curl up the ends of my hair because I'd be seeing you in less than twenty-four hours, or whether to write you a short letter to tell you how lonely I'd have been without you and your letters. Stanley, I think my second letter was a bit sniffy and if it was, I hate myself. I somehow felt your second was rather preaching and all your talk about not forgiving yourself if you made me unhappy was insincere and what you really meant was you'd never forgive yourself if you married a girl who let you down and ruined your chance of being a Bishop or some such thing, and your expression 'There is a real vocation in being a clergyman's wife' sounded to me as if you expected me to feel suddenly that teaching wasn't the job for me, that my vocation is to be a clergyman's wife - 'heavens, must scoot round and see if I can pick one up,' and I couldn't help wondering if you'd thought all that out before you asked Frances to marry you, and I fancied not. I fancied it was absolutely spontaneous with her, and because you loved her, not because she'd be a useful Vicar's wife, not that she wouldn't, for if she loved you she'd want to be. Anyway, to put all this in a nutshell, I didn't write yesterday because I was a bit pipped, and now I'm sorry for I've read and re-read your letter and thought that I'd read the wrong meaning into it all, especially after this morning's letter which was lovely.

Are we really going to *Hiawatha* and a show? Oh boy, oh boy, oh boy! Whizzbang! Whoopee!

(There followed more about her activities with her friends and then...)

"Stanley, dear - confession to make - get it over quickly. I didn't go to Church either on Good Friday or Easter Day, but there was this difference, that I wished I had and something seemed missing. Golly, that's over! I feel better.

(Five more pages and Pat ended...)

Goodnight and good morning!
As always, all my love, boy mine. Are you?
Your Pat. Am I?"

These few letters from a series which would make a book in themselves, reveal a remarkable woman of character overflowing with love who retained her outgoing and sensitive enjoyment of life until the agonies of her illness changed them. To the end of her life at the age of seventy five, even in the midst of her greatest pains, she was always more interested in other people than in herself. She was nearly twenty-seven when she wrote them, but she continued writing to her friends, many of them still friends in New Zealand after forty years, in the same delightful, often humorous vein. She had been "a breath of fresh air" to a solemn young curate, as she was to all the children and staffs of the schools in which she taught, right up to her retirement, as the letter from the young Vicar of Walderslade told me.

They also uncover a problem of the Church's ministry about which I have already written briefly. It was expected of a Curate's wife, and of the Vicar's wife, that they become unpaid ministers in the parish upon marriage, right up to the end of the 1939-1945 war. After that time, many clergy wives rebelled, not only because money was short and a second income in the family was essential to fight poverty and deprivation which could be very real on a curate's pay in the 50s and 60s, but also because many of them were professional people who wished to exercise their own profession, as Pat did. As she had remarked, being a teacher was her vocation, not being a Vicar's wife. The laity often misunderstood this and were resentful because the clergy wives of the post-war period did not behave as their predecessors had done.

Those letters also illuminate another difficulty and dilemma unique to the Church's married ministry. No one expects a solicitor's wife to behave as anything other than a wife. She is not expected to take part in his activities at law. A doctor's wife, though she may act as his receptionist or secretary, is not expected by his patients to do anything other than be a wife. The judge's wife does not have to sit in his court every day. But the clergy wife *is* in many cases expected to attend Church, to be a member of the PCC, to take part in all Church activities, to run the Mother's Union, superintend the Sunday School, do the flowers, join the Lenten study groups. Many clergy wives today do not accept some of the tenets of the Christian faith that their husbands profess and preach; some find the worship in their husband's Church unhelpful and do not attend. This creates a quandary for the couple at the Vicarage, and leads to arguments and unhappiness. Many in the parish wonder why the Vicar's wife does not wish to live up to *their* ideal of her. In the case of the Curate, many Vicars behave as Prebendary Bromley did at All Saints' Weston, with resentment and undisguised dislike of the reluctant clergy wife. It may well be that the increasing numbers of breakdowns in clergy marriages can be attributed to these facts.

In the book by Mary Loudon already mentioned (*Revelations*) the Reverend David Perrett, Vicar of Ollerton, Newark, Nottinghamshire, a former Methodist who was very happy in his first Curacy, has some passionate and often vitriolic things to say about the treatment of his wife when he became an incumbent..."the congregation treated my wife abysmally... she's been used as an avenue to get at me. So she's said 'I'm going to exercise my Christian ministry in a secular setting in an old people's Home, doing what I think I can do best, and stuff the Church.' But her faith has suffered incredibly...and there have been times when I have had to say that my marriage is a darn sight more important than the Church and it comes first." Pat's treatment was not as extreme as that given to Dorothy Perrett, but it is certainly time for "the Church" and for people in parishes to recognise that the Vicar's wife can have, and has a right to, her own divine vocation.

Pat had always vowed (largely because of the circumstances in her own home and of the subservience of her mother to her father's profession) that she would "never, never, never, marry a clergyman". But she did, and as her letters said, she would try to love his work because she loved him. She remained adamant that her vocation, and it was a vocation, was to teaching. She hated hypocrisy of any kind as well as "snobbishness!" and she did not want the duplicity and pretence which she had detected at an early age in her own Vicarage family to be reproduced in ours. For example, her father had been a great champion of Church Schools, and had for a while acted as a local Secretary for the National Society, the central authority for Church Schools, but as I have already remarked, he did not send any one of his three children to a Church School. Whatever his financial state, he always found the money to send them in their primary years to private schools. Pat was adamant that if you believed something you should live it out in practice. This was the source of the adolescent rebellion she spoke of. Our children went to the local village schools.

Each Sunday at Weston, Pat would push the pram down the hill to attend morning worship at All Saints, leaving Peter in the pram outside in the sunshine, or in the porch if it were raining, and ask someone at the back of the Church to keep an eye on him. When Jill arrived on October 16th 1945, this became impossible. There was a gap of only sixteen months between the two children, and as with Peter, Pat had had a bad time during her pregnancy and with the births of the two babies. "All these PE types," declared our local GP in Bath, Mary Watson, "have been so over-developed inside, that they are bound to have a bad time." In PE Colleges of the 30's the programme of physical training was so constructed that all the wrong muscles were over-developed, and the birth complications had become so common among PE specialists, that a survey was made which gave rise to a change in the programme of teacher training. Gymnasts on the international scene are subject to the same troubles physically in later life.

After a year or two Pat returned to teaching and our finances improved - Peter and Jill were looked after by nannies until they went to school themselves, and they made lots of friends. Pat had bought a bicycle at Windsor so that we might enjoy the countryside during our courtship and engagement, and with a sort of chair on the back of each of our machines we went about as much as we could as a family in the lovely county of Somerset, sometimes putting the bikes on a train and going a few miles into the country. We had no car and did not particularly envy those who had, though the Stares family opposite were generous in the use of theirs, within the limits of wartime petrol rationing. David Stares was the same age as Peter and was his great friend. Also kind to us, especially when Pat was overwhelmed by the burden of a house and two children, were the Bones, a lovely Churchgoing couple in Bath for the "duration". Neville, Jill's godfather, worked for the Admiralty Department then based in Bath. Pat could always go and talk to Madge and unburden her woes, and we remained friends until their deaths.

In her letters Pat had promised complete loyalty to me and to my vocation, and she never wavered from that loyalty. She always followed me into my new work; with regret I am sure, because she had the wonderful facility of making friends wherever she taught, and would miss them greatly, but never with resentment or complaint. We discussed it, certainly, and probably had arguments about the pros and cons of each curacy as it came up; but she went with me from Windsor to Weston, Bath to Chertsey, and from Chertsey to Shottermill, from Shottermill to Rochester, meeting the criticisms levelled at her in each parish as a non-active clergy wife with her own life to lead, with patience and forbearance. Any differences of opinion that we had, and there were many because each of us was "strong-minded" (if not stubborn) were resolved in the end, and we kissed and made up. I love the way Tennyson puts it in *The Princess*:

> "As thro' the land at eve we went
> and pluck'd the ripen'd ears,
> we fell out, my wife and I,
> O we fell out I know not why,
> and kiss'd again with tears.
> And blessings on the falling out
> that all the more endears,
> when we fall out with those we love,
> and kiss again with tears."

The physical passion passed, but not the deep, deep love, the kind of love that St. Paul spoke of in the famous hymn (1 Cor. 13) - I can hear Pat saying "don't preach!" - I give it in J.B. Phillips version:-

"This love of which I speak is slow to lose patience - it looks for a way of being constructive. It is not possessive; it is neither anxious to impress, nor does it cherish inflated ideas of its own importance (Pat would approve that!). Love has good manners and does not pursue selfish advantage. It is not touchy. It does not compile statistics of evil (How often we drag up the past sins of others when we try to justify our own!) or gloat over the wickedness of other people. On the contrary, it is glad with other good men when Truth prevails. Love knows no limit to its endurance, no end to its trust, no fading of its hopes. It can outlast anything. It is in fact the one thing that still stands when all else has fallen." How true that was of our life together, especially of the last ten years of increasing pain and suffering, despondency and disheartenment which stemmed from the spinal injury, and which in itself raised unfathomable mysteries as to why such a good person, having taken up a loving social service, should have to suffer what can only be called the evil consequences of doing good. Those faded letters with their distinctive and actually very legible, exuberant handwriting, and their loveable phrases - "I must go and have my wig washed", bring to life the person who is not dead and whose charm and loveliness of person and character lives in the minds and memories of a myriad of her friends.

Perhaps part of the secret of our relationship was the ability to share thoughts and hopes, desires and fears, and the willingness to say truthfully to each other what we really felt when there had been tensions or arguments. In a recent article one man tried to analyse the cause of a broken relationship which left him as a single father-:

"I assumed she'd know how I felt. I was very happy but I didn't show it. I spoke about some of the negative aspects, for example, financial problems, and she took it to mean I didn't want the baby. I should have said I really want to be a father, I want to be there to care for the child, change nappies, do my part. I should have said those things to her."

He was unable to communicates his feelings. Modern counsellors spend a large part of the time with their clients emphasising this aspect of the absolute necessity of communication between partners, whether married or co-habiting. "That is the importance," Bishop George Reindorp used to say, "of the Double Bed!"

A similar difficulty arises with many individuals when they have to learn how to cope with a bereavement. Many men in particular find it difficult to talk about the death of their loved one. One such man wrote of how he put away all photographs of his wife: "I couldn't bear to look at any of Sheila's photographs until a few months ago...it hurt too much. I'd just sit in the house alone. There's not a sound. It's awful. I got to the stage where I didn't want to go home. I'd walk the streets delaying my return." At work he found it difficult to talk to anyone about what had happened (his wife had died suddenly of liver failure, a week after being admitted to Hospital). He had not been warned that she might die and still lives with the guilt of not being at her bedside after thirty-three years of happy marriage - "the fact that I left her to die on her own haunts me to this day." He went to counselling sessions and learned to talk about his wife - "Talking does seem to lighten the burden. The fact that I met other people feeling like I did made me realise I was not alone."

The circumstances of Pat's death which I shall shortly write about might well have been a reason for myself remaining silent about her, but because we had such a close relationship and had always been able to talk about love and life and death without embarrassment, after her death, I was enabled to speak freely of her to my family, to my friends, and even to a congregation in sermons; and I brought out *more* photographs!

It has been interesting to me to observe the drastic changes in attitudes to love and marriage and the family over the last fifty years - how that families are smaller, how the State provides so much more for mothers and children than it did in the 1940s - free cod liver oil and orange juice was our lot. There have been so many changes: the advent of the contraceptive pill in 1960; the disappearance of the extended family, with granny living in the home and influencing the children; the decline of the maiden aunt; the emergence of the working mother outside the home - Pat was in a minority when she went back to work when Jill was two years old; the complete change in the status of women; the advent of television - we did not possess a TV set until 1957, when Jill was twelve and Peter was thirteen plus; and in particular today, we have to examine what has been the influence of the video, and video games, and of the computer. All these factors have contributed to the decline of the Church's influence on the family ("don't preach!" says Pat!) and perhaps have contributed to the increase in juvenile crime. There have been other influences too, and unemployment, especially among the young, is undoubtedly one of them.

I began these memoirs with a few thoughts about my father. I like to think that in the building of the character of my own children the fact that I spent more time in the home than most men can, helped them to a balanced view of life. I don't think that Peter gained much from going away to boarding school, which he hated. Jill *did* gain much from going to a day school, and returning home to stability and concern each night. The holidays we had together, always by the sea, have helped to cement relationships which were of their own period, namely halfway between the "children shall be seen and not heard" days of my own childhood, and the (to me) lovely modern world in which mothers and fathers talk about everything to their tiny children and ask them what *they* feel and what *they* think, and what *they* would like to do. This I totally approve of, and wish I had known how to practice it with my own children. I much regret, as I know Pat did, the frequent lack of communication.

Perhaps my children would say that little communication took place because we were too busy. That is true. We each had an exacting and time-consuming job, but we put no restraints on them and they were not *made* to go to Church. All their friends were welcome to our house, and we always took away on holiday *their* own choice of companion - or at least Jill's. One of the drawbacks of a boarding education is that it leaves the child without local friends for two thirds of the year. That was why Andrew Rowland was such an important friend to Peter. He and his sister Mary, friend to Jill, spent long hours in our house playing Monopoly, and in the garden playing cricket, long jumping, high jumping and the rest, and the boys firing airguns. In return they spent long hours in the Rowland home, where Mrs. Rowland was always thought of, apart from her skill at making chocolate cake, as the sort of parent they would have loved to have had. Perhaps the Rowland children thought the same about Pat. No, I am sure they did!

In time, both Peter and Jill left home for "higher education" and we only saw them in the holidays. Peter went to sea and Jill became a teacher. Pat and I were thrown closer together, and in our last few years at Shottermill as Pat approached the menopause, the effects of pre-menstrual tension became more marked, as I see now, though at that time I still did not always recognise the symptoms. Rows about little unimportant things always took place on these particular days and I had to learn not to lose my own temper when Pat was irrational in conversation or did irrational things, like disappearing in the evening without telling me where she was going, and not returning till nearly midnight. The thought of leaving her beloved Midhurst Grammar School and the host of friends she had made there among pupils and staff was hurting from the time I accepted David Say's invitation to go to Rochester, but she understood that I needed a change and with her usual loyalty she bore the hurt and fulfilled her promise - "Whither thou goest, I will go." What a remarkable woman Ruth the Moabitess was! She lost her Israelite husband, as had her sister Orpah, and both were childless. She returned with Naomi, her mother-in-law, to Israel: "where thou goest I will go, where thou lodgest I will lodge; Thy people shall be my people, and thy God shall be my God." In a foreign land she found happiness. (Ruth c.1)) I think Pat found much happiness in Rochester, in spite of her Headmistress's attitudes and demeanour.

All this has been in the nature of a "flashback" beloved of a certain kind of film maker. It is now almost time to return to the theme of retirement, illness and pain, and eventual triumph, but before I do that

I must confess that since her death I have often pondered on why our marriage of nearly half a century survived and was in fact rejuvenated when so many other marriages failed and collapsed in a welter of recriminations and sadness. On my side of course there was the fact that I was a priest and it would have been unthinkable for me to abandon all the principles which are inherent in the priesthood, and that the damage done to the Church by the break-up of a Vicarage family would have been immense. Pat too, with her own Vicarage background would have felt the same. Not perhaps a worthy motive for maintaining a marriage, but there was much more to it than that. We belonged to a generation where promises made, in particular those promises made solemnly in Church, were felt to be binding. For these reasons if for no others we would have made all possible efforts to sustain a marriage, but there was even more than this. There was our concept of love. We were fortunate I suppose that "love" implied to us more than sexual attraction, more than the superficial trivialities of the popular songs of the thirties and forties. Though the fires of sexual attraction, which were fierce in the early years, dimmed, though they never died, love meant much more. More than "never needing to say you are sorry". On the contrary, love is deepened when you can say you are sorry, and it often takes a great deal of courage to say so and to ask forgiveness. Then too, there was a large element of "the attraction of opposites". I was a duffer at all physical activities. Because of the lack of sight in my right eye, I had hated soccer, cricket and rugby football and the PE lessons at school. Pat was a very physically orientated person, good at swimming and all games. I was an avid reader and might be called an academic, "cerebral" rather than "somatic". Pat was completely uninhibited, outgoing, demonstrative, extrovert, whereas I was often withdrawn, undemonstrative, even shy, though I had managed to overcome much of my diffidence and apparent lack of confidence by an assertiveness and even aggression when I was cornered in argument or criticised. We loved each other and admired each other for these opposite traits in their better and more gentle manifestations.

In other ways we shared the same likes and dislikes and that cemented love. We had the same sense of humour and laughed at the same jokes. We loved the same friends, appreciated the same pictures and furniture and flowers. We loved our children, though sometimes, like many mothers, Pat had passages at arms with her daughter.

Children complete, cement and perfect a marriage, and because caring for them, coping with their growing pains and problems, is a mutual thing, our children drew us together.

Loyalty was another significant and primary element in our relationship. To both of us the promises of the marriage service which we had taken part in on August 17th, 1943 were not only restraining. They were compelling. "Keep thee only unto her/him, so long as ye both shall live," meant exactly what the words said in their stark simplicity. Each of us could appreciate the attractions of others. Clergy are not immune to the allure of a pretty face or the turn of a comely ankle, nor are they spiritually inoculated against the woman who wishes to flirt. Nor are PE mistresses exempt from the advances of the male philanderer or the handsome athlete. We were so satisfied and happy in each other's company that we were both able to resist such blandishments. Is it because so many young married people do not allow themselves to resist, that so many marriages die and love flies out of the relationship? ("Don't preach!" - I hear that phrase again.")

One other component of our marriage gave it a stability which some other unions lack - we each had our own income. It has always seemed to me to be tragic when a wife has to beg her husband for money, when he scrutinises all her expenses and criticises her for her improvidence. Though I have never approved of the joint bank account, I have always taught that where a wife does not go out to work she has earned her husband's salary equally with him, by enabling him to go to work, by caring for him and his home. All her working life, Pat earned more than I did, and when we retired her pension was greater than mine. So many modern marriages seem to collapse because of money problems. Apart from the early years when shortage of money was a real matter of argument we had come to a loving arrangement about who would pay for which part of our expenditure, so the disagreements became few and the agreements were many.

I would like to be able to say that our marriage was underpinned by a shared religious experience, but I can't, because it wasn't. In the early days we had prayed together at our bedside at night, and I had even read my sermons to her for criticism and comment, but somehow when life becomes fuller and we are at our children's beck and call, even such important practices seem to get neglected. Pat often accompanied me on my visits to parishes to preach, but she was not a regular communicant and confined her reception of the Sacrament to the festivals. All her life she was suspicious of the formalities of religion, and I guess that from time to time she detected in me what had so offended her in her father, a hypocrisy, even a pharisaism which failed to put the theory into practice. Her own ideals of behaviour, of courtesy, good manners and self-giving were high, and she lived up to them always. When a Bishop came to the Vicarage after a Confirmation one evening, and being shown into the drawing room, proceeded to wolf the sandwiches without so much as a "May I?" and without offering them to others, Pat was much displeased and the episcopal image sank to a new low! She would have approved the sentiment in the story of the old shopkeeper, commenting on the Church in the terms of a sales representative selling his wares: "Christ, he's alright. Christians? They ain't up to sample."

Underneath however, there was a basic religious understanding between us. I too believed that religion must be "practical" as she had written to me all those years ago. I know that she did pray every night, because she told me that too, but her faith was sorely tried by those same doubts which all who suffer have when they pray and when they know that many are praying for them, and no healing, and even no improvement, takes place. I gave her all the slick answers which I had put down in the booklets I had written not long before in *Religion and Healing* but they did not satisfy her or enable her to cope with her pain one whit better.

Perhaps, if she had not been prescribed so many drugs, perhaps if her memory and her resistance to pain and disease had not been so drastically reduced by a totally unacceptable number of shots of ECT, electroconvulsive therapy, she may have been helped more.

CHAPTER 14

RETIREMENT

"An elegant sufficiency, content
Retirement, rural quiet, friendship, books."
James Thompson (d. 1748) (author of "Rule Brittania")

"For solitude sometimes is best society,
and short retirement urges sweet return."
Milton (d. 1674) Paradise Lost.

My lovely and captivating wife made many sacrifices when she promised to marry me. The greatest of them was to abandon her intention to return to New Zealand when she had fulfilled her obligation to return home to visit her parents in dangerous wartime. She had loved her childhood there from the age of eight when her father was Vicar of Wanganui. She had loved even more her time there as a PE teacher at Iona College, Havelock North, in the semitropical North Island, from 1939 to 1943. Before leaving, she had been offered the most important PE post in the dominion, as Organiser on the girls' side of all Physical Education, alongside the boys' Organiser, Philip Smithells, who had expressed not only his admiration for what she had accomplished at Iona but also his love for her. We had always agreed that when she retired from teaching in England we should together make an extended trip to New Zealand, to see all her friends, and for her to show me the wonderful scenery of that delectable land. In her school holidays she had stayed with members of staff and with the parents of pupils, and had made a multitude of friends. At one time in the 50's she had persuaded me that we might emigrate and I had made enquiries from various New Zealand Bishops about vacant benefices. The only one that had been vacant and offered to me was the parish of Bluff at the extreme end of the South Island in the diocese of Dunedin. It was then a very remote parish, of a small town and an island, though now it is a flourishing oil terminal, as I discovered when I visited New Zealand in a nostalgic pilgrimage after Pat's death. But it offered only £200 a year and the obligation to provide our own house when we got there. Understandably, in spite of the attraction of living in New Zealand, we did not proceed with this venture.

The Bishop had generously said that I might have a six month "sabbatical" to enable us to go to New Zealand when Pat retired, as we thought in 1976. I had been in my job without a real break for eleven years, but, as we realised with hindsight, we foolishly did not take up the offer. Instead Pat decided to carry on teaching for a while and then made the fateful decision which had such disastrous consequences, to take up hairdressing. We were forced into a premature retirement because of her illness and we never did go to New Zealand together.

At least we had a house to go to, two houses indeed! One of the saddest things that can happen to a clerical family is an enforced retirement when there is nowhere to go when the Vicarage has been left. The Church of England Pensions Board has made remarkable strides in providing housing for retired clergy but not everyone wants to live in a clergy retirement home, along with other clergy and churchworkers. The Board has since made provision for clergy to move to their own homes at a chosen site, by the offer of a loan and mortgage on a house.

We had bought "Zansizzey", a small, 1928 vintage bungalow in Trevone, near Padstow in Cornwall in February 1976 for £14,750 with legacies from Pat's relations and the sale of a shop which I owned with my two sisters in Hayes in Middlesex. We had spent a few days after Christmas there in 1976 to see if we could stand the climate, which was notorious for its Atlantic winds and heavy rainfall, and we decided that we couldn't. A piece of land had been purchased in Headley Down in Hampshire. We let "Zansizzey" as much as possible and designed, and had built, Pat's "rabbit hutch" as she called it - a small wooden bungalow which had all we needed, a large lounge, a large kitchen, a small study, two bedrooms, a utility room, and a second toilet (absolutely essential when visitors are staying) with a bathroom and toilet. It had trees and quite a large garden, mainly grassed. We had designed it with built-in cupboards in most rooms and did not need any of the large bedroom or dining room furniture which had filled our huge mansion in Rochester. We sold as much of the White Friars furniture and oddments as we could, and gave away the rest. With regret I got rid of two thousand or more books, and put files with two thousand sermons into the dustbin. That sounds like a lot of sermons, but as a Vicar preaching twice each Sunday, I had typed out at least one hundred and thirty different sermons each year for fourteen years and had kept every sermon of the ten years curacies before that. I came to regret this destruction when, through Cleverley Ford, Mowbray's offered to print a year's selection of them in one of his series for the Parish Communion, but as they only offered me £50 and a tiny royalty on each book sold, I turned down the offer. A pound a sermon seemed too little to accept for the sweat of research and study and the careful honing of words, and it would have taken many more hours to put them into such a form as would have been helpful to any clergy who might buy the book. I kept a few dozen basic theological works and commentaries, as the bookshelves in my "Cedarwood" study would be small. Of course I have subsequently needed some of the volumes I gave away!

James Thompson's 18th century version of a rural retirement with "an elegant sufficiency, quiet, friendship and books" was to be largely true for us. Money was not a great problem. The Diocese and the Pensions Board had been generous to me, and Pat had a reasonable pension as a former Deputy headmistress - not "elegant", but sufficient. Our little Hampshire bungalow was in a quiet cul-de-sac, and we had friendly and hospitable neighbours in Betty and Claud Chambers. It was from them that we had bought half their garden to build on. On the other side was an ex-headmaster of a Church Secondary School in Farnham. When we had decided to retire to Hampshire with its vast tracts of National Trust land on which we had intended to walk daily, we had agreed that we should try to be near Shottermill where we had many friends from our time there at the Vicarage, and to be near enough for me to help at St. Stephen's if I were wanted, but far enough away not to be a nuisance to the present incumbent.

This was achieved. Headley Down was only six miles from St. Stephen's, but it *was* six miles! London was on the direct line from Portsmouth via Haslemere, our old and familiar railway station. This was to be important soon, as Pat was sent to various Hospitals in London for a series of different operations and treatments. I was asked to take services at Shottermill from time to time and it was a joyful pleasure to renew friendships with former parishioners.

Though we had left the Vicarage sixteen years earlier, and though many of my former congregation had died, we were delighted to find that many loyal parishioners had survived and continued to live near.

We made friends again with Ken and Mary Allport. Ken had been Pat's opposite number at Midhurst, and Mary, the School Secretary, and with Darrell and Jane Stirling. Darrell had taught at the Secondary Modern School where Pat had begun teaching, when that school was first opened. I had a particular affinity with Darrell as the years went by and Pat became more incapacitated, for Jane Stirling had had a heart attack which partially paralysed her, and Darrell had looked after her, an invalid wife, as I had Pat, until Jane died, shortly after Pat. Another great friend upon whom we came to rely was Hilda Sutton who had been a Domestic Science teacher with Pat at Walderslade. She now lived at Eastbourne and came to visit her regularly.

May Williams was organist at St. Stephen's and Pat was delighted to renew with her the friendship which had begun when they got together on a Thursday evening when May's husband Archie was at the Vicarage for a Men's Society meeting. May's son Gavin had been organist at the Church in my time. A brilliant musician I had recommended him to Douglas Vicary at the King's School, Rochester, as Music Master. He was appointed and remains in that post still. There were many more friends who came to tea regularly and made life bearable for Pat. She continued to exercise her exuberant charm in spite of the pain she was enduring. Few who came knew that she had taken a number of drugs before they came in order to be her old self, if only for a brief while. The number of visitors increased as we came to make more friends in Headley and Headley Down.

Without consciously working it out, it appeared to me that retirement would require activity in certain well-defined areas. First we must make "Cedarwood" into the kind of home in which we could live together in comfort and quiet peace. To do this we purchased a whole range of comfortable furniture, including a seven feet long settee on which Pat could lie on her back, the only position in which she had any relief from pain. All the other chairs must be fairly upright and not low slung. These were much appreciated by our guests, many of whom had their own back troubles. I sold the Austin Allegro which had been my "office car" and which I had bought from the Diocese, and replaced it with a "Maestro" which had a wide back seat on which Pat could lie. Later I removed the front passenger seat from the "Maestros" which followed the original one, and shaped a large board to make a bed base, on which we put a mattress from a long garden chair. Borne up on shaped wooden struts this was a most successful innovation and was greatly approved by Jason Brice, the eminent neuro-surgeon at Southampton General Hospital who tried so hard to cure Pat's deteriorating spine. Much more of him later.

Lying on her back as she did on every possible occasion, especially in the Hospital waiting rooms and clinics and in the hairdressers, caused many a person to say to me in a stage whisper, "What's wrong? Is she all right?" Pat had no qualms about lying down in public places such as those, though she always asked permission, and she took with her everywhere she went a thin folding mattress which she had herself cleverly made for the purpose.

Getting "Cedarwood" properly furnished for a semi-invalid, renewing old friendships, and making new friends were practical and social priorities. Above both of those was an even greater need - to make contact with anyone in any branch of medicine who might be able to help her. Medicine is no longer a unified discipline, if ever it was. "Alternative medicine" was a phrase being much bandied about in newspapers, and on the television and radio. We knew little about the alternatives when we moved from "White Friars" to "Cedarwood". Even the Buddhist "Holistic" doctor had been recommended to us from within the "mainstream".

We made contact immediately with the group of Doctors in Grayshott, but our reception was not a welcoming one. My proffered handshake was ignored at my first meeting with one of the doctors. None of them was particularly interested in Pat's case, though when she was confined to bed from time to time, they would call if asked. I began to be rather incensed at this treatment and we decided to change our doctor. Though no reason needs to be given on either side when this happens, I felt it only right and polite to telephone the senior partner in the practice and explain the reasons why we were changing. I mentioned one of the doctors, with whom our relationship had not been easy, by his surname, only to be told in fierce tones that I should have referred to him as "Doctor". We were both professional men and at that time we clergy always referred to each other by surname. I told him so, and said that I would be very happy if he called me by my surname. I did not mind if he did not use my title, and that I had hoped for such a friendly relationship that we could drop titles. He was extremely rude and crashed the phone down.

We enquired from the Rector of Headley the name of his doctor and he told us of Paul Beech. The Rector's wife worked at the reception office of his surgery and was very happy there. We went to see Doctor Beech and at our first meeting we explained something of Pat's medical history and then he examined her and gave us a whole hour of his time. He became a valued adviser and friend. Later we were happy to call each other by our Christian names. Whenever we went to see him, which was frequently, he always shook hands, both when we went into his room, and when we left. Paul Beech advised Pat to take up swimming again which she did, both in the pool which had been built by public subscription in Shottermill after we had left, and at Alton, Farnham and Aldershot. The swimming was a valuable therapy and Pat enjoyed it. She had always been a keen swimmer and at the age of eight in New Zealand had swum a mile, non-stop. The other great therapy was music to which she would listen when I was out, and in the middle of the night when she couldn't sleep. Classical and light classical, musicals, soloists and in particular the records of Aled Jones, the Welsh boy soprano. She was so taken with Aled that she had a brief correspondence with him which gave her much pleasure.

And books! We spent a small fortune on paperbacks, beginning with Catherine Cookson, and running through all the popular romantic novelists (though not Barbara Cartland!). This too was a real therapy, and reading two or three books a week, her mind was relieved of the thoughts of her pain. Library books were too heavy for her to hold.

On arrival in Headley Down I wrote to David Brown, the Bishop of Guildford and asked for permission to officiate in his diocese during my retirement. I said how pleased I was to be back in a diocese where I had already spent seventeen years, and explained why I had to retire. I remarked that I had received a warm welcome from my old parish and that I would be pleased to help in any way that I could. The answer I received was short and cold. There was no personal welcome to someone who had spent long years here as a parish priest and had served on many diocesan bodies. I assumed that he knew David Say and could have asked him about me and that "permission to officiate", i.e. to take services and preach, would have been given automatically by the Bishop himself. Not so. Instead I was told to contact the Rural Dean, whose approval must first be given and indicated on the appropriate form.

I understand the principle involved here - that an unsuitable person or one past his "sell-by date" might well want to "officiate" and not be very welcome, but it seemed strange to me, and hurtful, that a priest of sixty-four who had spent sixteen years in a responsible position in another diocese, as well as seventeen in this one, should have to be approved first by someone who did not know him, and who had made no effort to contact him. I sent the form to the Rural Dean by post, and he still did not call on me. In fact no Rural Dean called on me until I wrote a letter to David Brown's successor, (who was *not* pleased at episcopal and Deanery oversight being called into question), complaining at the treatment of the retired clergy. It must have struck home, because within two days the then Rural Dean, *and his wife* called on us. Not until I had lived at "Cedarwood" for twelve years was I invited to join the local clergy in a Chapter meeting, and in all that time no other Rural Dean, no Archdeacon, no Bishop, no Bishop's officer for retired clergy, ever deigned to call, though I was invited by post to meetings of retired clergy in Guildford or Woking. If my seven thousand colleagues of the retired clergy are all treated in similar fashion (which I cannot believe is so) what a sad commentary on the pastoral care of retired Anglican priests!

Nor was this the full story. I was soon asked to take services in the area, mostly in Headley Down where the little ecumenical Church of St. Francis had a delightful priest in charge, Harry Dickens, a former businessman. I "officiated" at the Parish Church in Headley, and during interregna, at Grayshott, at Churt, at Camelsdale, the Bourne, Frensham, Rowledge and Thursley but when I was invited to the institution and induction of new incumbents at some of those parishes, only once did the Bishop taking the service come up to me either before or after the service and say a word. That Bishop was one with whom I had served on Guildford diocesan committees twenty-five and more years previously, Kenneth Evans, Bishop of Dorking, and he was most welcoming. I regret to have to say also that very few of the clergy gathered for these occasions, except those who already knew me, took the trouble to come up to the unknown man in the scarlet cassock and introduce themselves and ask who I was.

This off-handedness on the part of the hierarchy and my fellow clergy was not paralleled in my reception by the laity of the parishes to which I went. They were universally welcoming, and where I was officiating during an interregnum, the Churchwardens were exemplary in their arrangements, without exception. This was an encouragement and a heart-warming attitude, but other clergy among my friends who have retired tell me that their experiences are not dissimilar. Retired clergy are not consulted *by right* on any matter that is facing the Church at any one time - the Ordination of Women for example. Rarely is our expertise called upon, rarely are we invited to give our opinion or advice, unless as in my case now, we have a kindly and cordial incumbent to befriend us and use us in the capacities for which we have skills and "expertise".

Because we lived in the parish, the clergy of Headley and Headley Down were an exception, as were their congregations. Dick Woodger, the Team Rector of Headley was notably kind and sympathetic at the time of Pat's death, and conducted her funeral service sensitively with a short and helpful valediction.

We kept only one car when we moved, and Peter took Pat's Austin 1300 for his own use, because his own car had failed him, and in the first year or so Pat was able to drive the Maestro on her own to visit friends and do her shopping. For this purpose she had special back cushions and was given a "Disabled" sticker, which enabled us to park conveniently near shops. We had long ago given up going to the theatre and the cinema, though we had enjoyed such visits in our earlier years at Rochester. When the English National Opera set up their permanent home at the Coliseum we went to almost every opera they mounted, though Pat did not enjoy all of them, particularly where there was a great deal of noise. We had once attended *Rigoletto* at Sadler's Wells and Pat had to leave hurriedly in the dark and noisy storm scene. Nor could she endure plays or films with loud bangs or guns firing. Whether this was a consequence of some early experience we could not discover.

As the illness progressed I became nurse and physiotherapist! I would rub her feet for minutes on end, which seemed in a strange way to help other parts of her body. An infrared lamp gave heat to her shoulders where most of the pain was seated, though she liked the lamp to be so near to her body that sometimes a burn resulted. I had to learn how long and how close the lamp should be. Then there was an electrical device which had been introduced to us, which passed small shocks across the points where the pain was seated. I would massage her back for hours with pain killing ointments, and various pain killing sprays, such as are used to ease tennis players' strains and injuries, gave her some small relief. In the next chapter I shall deal with the treatments she received in her illness at greater length with my own conclusions and observations. Meanwhile together we learned to deal with the opportunities as well as the difficulties of retirement.

Until retirement Pat and I had lived largely separate lives, being with each other only in bed, for a day or so at weekends, and in the evenings when I had no commitments. We had always made sure that we had a few days together after each festival, going away if possible, usually to the Cotswolds, once to Paris, and twice to Switzerland. We loved these times together, especially the walking among the mountains in Switzerland. We had also had a holiday in France when Jill was teaching there. Most of all we had loved the three weeks in the summer with our children, during which we enjoyed the bathing and the surfing somewhere at the seaside, usually at Bude in Cornwall.

Now we were together most days for twenty-four long hours. As the books of advice tell you, this is one of the real problems of retirement, and needs a radical adjustment in relationships. What do we have to say to each other? Do we make the effort to talk to each other all through the day even though it may be only trivialities that we share? Our discovery was that one can spend long periods in companionable silence! One does not *have* to talk, and in any case people who love each other and have been married for a long time know what each is thinking. Words are not *always* necessary. But they are *sometimes* necessary in such situations as ours. We had to discuss treatments and their results. We had to plan each day ahead, and whether walking or swimming or shopping was to be the order of the day, and whether Pat would be well enough to accept invitations. These were the trivia of married conversation. We could now watch television and listen to the radio more than we had previously done and here was a fruitful source not only of time-passing but of exchange of ideas.

Pat had asked me, early in our first exchange of letters in 1943, to teach her how to type. Always willing to learn new skills she had bought herself a manual and had taught herself while we lived in Rochester. Now she was able to write long letters to her friends, particularly those in New Zealand. Her illness had not affected movement in her arms and hands. She enjoyed cooking and needlework and with infinite patience and the tiniest of stitches she embroidered cloths for all the chests of drawers, the sideboard and tea trolley, and in so far as I could, I helped her in all her activities. We had now learned to do things together, instead of separately, each in his own little world. Though I was happy to continue my own ministry as far as I was invited to, I realised that I now had a new and completely different role in life.

We had planned the garden at Cedarwood to give us the least trouble, and it was mostly lawn, but there were several flower beds and a large patio with many tubs and boxes of annuals. Gardening became a new interest and we spent many happy hours in garden centres deciding which plants to put into which parts of the garden. It was a time when garden centres were expanding their range of activities and "Forest Lodge" a few miles away had installed a coffee lounge and restaurant, sections for books and cards, toys, pottery, dried flowers, as well as "garden requisites". A weekly visit to Forest Lodge for coffee and a browse became a "must", and a further therapy was discovered - dried flower arrangements. Pat had always belittled any suggestion that she was artistic, but she was in fact a very artistic person, with an eye for form and colour. She had shown this already in her choice of clothes. In the house the curtains, carpets and furniture always blended in a restful and pleasing way. Now the rooms were filled with flowers in the summer and dried flower arrangements in the winter.

Physically too we discovered a new level of relationship. The kiss and the embrace became more important than it had been for years. How we married people take each other for granted! But living together every minute of the day could be a strain and it took a lot of hard work to maintain an even keel. I had to remember not to say "Pull yourself together!" when Pat complained about her pain, or when she bewailed the diminishing of her powers. She had to learn to release me for an hour or two so that I might continue with my ministry, though as time went on, as I shall tell soon, I began to fear what might happen if I were away from the home for too long.

"Don't leave me alone!" she would cry, and when the anti-depressant drugs had not worked, "You don't really love me!"

What then was the basis and motivation of our marriage? One small part of it was our mutual love of Cornwall, John Betjeman's Cornwall, comprising mostly the north coast from Morwenstow on the Devon border, westward to Perranporth and beyond, to Land's End and Cape Cornwall. Cornish nationalists say that all that part of the peninsula west of the river Tamar is a separate kingdom, owing no allegiance to England, some of them even claiming exemption from English law and English taxation. Whatever your view about that, it cannot be denied that Cornwall as a County is "different", different even from South Wales, and from Brittany to which many writers compare it, and which have the same volcanic origins. I would go further and say that it is "unique", even magical, and not only because of its holy wells and pixies and the Arthurian legends based in Tintagel and Dozmaré pool where the great sword Excalibur was returned, but also because of its rocks and cliffs, its ever changing seascapes, its sunsets and sunrises, its rainbows and its fascinating cloud formations. Nowhere in Cornwall is more than a few miles from the sea, which can be seen from the moors and from many inland parishes. In more than one place the English channel and the Bristol channel can be seen on either hand glinting in the sun. So we explored Cornwall and its varied countryside.

There is such a difference too between the north coast with its jagged ramparts of cliffs facing the stormy Atlantic, and the softer, gentler channel coast in the south, with a climate so mild that parts of it are even called the "Cornish Riviera". In the south the bays are warmer and the tides wind in and out of wooded creeks and valleys. As I have already told, Pat and I fell in love with the bleak north coast on our none too happy honeymoon at Morvah, and though for some years we took family holidays in Essex and Dorset (always by the sea) we had always determined to return to Cornwall. When we bought "Zansizzey" in the still unspoilt village of Trevone in Padstow parish it was a rather basic little bungalow with no garage and no central heating, and the only "back parts" a coal hole. It had a lounge ten feet by eighteen feet which, by the way in which the furniture had to be arranged, meant that visitors sat opposite each other rather as in a railway carriage. Over the years, and planning it was a real therapy for Pat, we installed central heating, had a garage built, turned the "coal hole" into an additional lavatory, extended the rear portion to make a utility room, enlarged the lounge to a decent size, put in double glazing and turned the back bedroom into a sunroom. With the addition of a caravan in the garden it made a wonderful holiday home, and for Pat and me an ideal retirement home. Until, that is, we spent those few days here in December and decided that it was *not* the ideal! However, in all the ensuing years, we spent weeks, and later months, in the glorious summer weather which Cornwall has to offer - if you stay long enough.

Swimming and surfing, walking and lounging in the garden filled our days while Pat was still able to enjoy such activities. Constant visits to discover new delights in the National Trust houses of Trerice and Lanhydrock helped to answer the question "What shall we do today?" We watched Padstow grow, and it became more and more "tarted up" as David Say remarked when he visited us here one day. Once upon a time the railway came as far as Padstow, but now the track is called the "Camel Trail". Betjeman called the five and a half miles from Wadebridge to Padstow "the most beautiful train journey I know." He writes, before the Beeching axe descended, "See it on a fine evening at high tide, with golden light on the low hills, the heron-haunted mud caves flooded over, the sudden thunder as we cross the bridge over Little Petherick creek, the glimpses of slate roofs and a deserted jetty among spindly Cornish elms, the wide and unexpected sight of open sea at the river mouth, the huge spread of waste of water with brown ploughed fields coming down to the little cliffs where no waves break but only salt tides ripple up and ebb away. Then the utter endness of the end of the line at Padstow - two hundred and sixty miles of it from London. The smell of fish and seaweed, the crying of gulls and the moist west country air and valerian growing wild on slate walls."

This is not a guide book, but you can see why we loved Cornwall. We walked the same line alongside the river when it became a Camel Trail, until Pat could walk no more, and I would park the car by a creek and walk it myself while she stayed on her bed in the car and read her book or listened to the radio. I walk the trail still, most weeks, from Padstow to Wadebridge and back, nearly ten miles all told and the river and estuary sights are always new, though now the trail is also a cycle trail and hundreds of hired bicycles rush past you in the summer, going in each direction, and since no one rings his bell as he passes, you take your life in your hands as a pedestrian.

The northern coast of Cornwall is almost treeless because of the strong salt winds, but wild flowers, the thrift and the gorse, the vetch and the mallow, and the delightfully named Hottentot Fig, Sea Beet, and Sea Radish, grow on the cliffs and the rocks. On the sand dunes grows the marram grass, so eroded by the feet of countless tourists, that it is having to be replaced at Constantine Bay, together with the sea campion, sea holly and sea kale. Inland, along the headlands we found the lovely feathery tamarisk, the corncockle, and the tiny orchids; the ubiquitous escallonia (of which we have a hedge in the garden) and the Valerian. There are more than a hundred wild flowers to be found on our coast and in our walks Pat and I delighted in discovering them.

Along the Camel Trail we would also observe the many sea and river birds, the oyster catchers, the sandpipers, the herons, the curlews and the waders, even the mute swans. Inland came the many types of seagull, and on the rocks and seashore, if one was lucky, one might see the puffins, the razorbills and the guillemots. Trevone (though "not many people know this") was the first nesting place of the fulmars in Cornwall in 1944 and now there are hundreds of pairs along the Cornish coast, coming in from years at sea to nest in January. Pat and I were never great bird-watchers in the professional (or amateur) sense, but we delighted in observing them and trying to identify them by name while she was still able to walk the coastal paths.

Inland there are many more trees and woodlands and the Forestry Commission has planted several of their ugly pine forests. One of our haunts was Hustyn Woods and St. Breocke downs (now the site of a windfarm), where we would take our portable mattresses and a picnic and spend the summer afternoon hours, reading and talking, and I would take a walk. Another National Trust property, Trelissick gardens bordering the River Fal, gave us endless enjoyment too. Pat had become a life member of the Trust in 1969 when she had had a salary windfall of £50, and I had been a member for many years, so our visits to Trust properties were frequent. At Trelissick it was a relief to see the deciduous trees so lacking from Forestry Commission woodlands, and so rare or non-existent on the north coast - there were the beeches, the oaks, the ash and the sycamore. We do have two sycamore trees in our "Zansizzey" garden but since they grow so rapidly and shed such a wealth of leaves and seeds they are not our favourite tree. Trelissick also boasts yew trees, Japanese larch, Douglas firs as well as masses of bright yellow gorse attracting the butterflies. At Lanhydrock, which we visited regularly, many of the trees in the great Avenue first planted in 1648 with sycamores, and later beeches, were blown down in the great gales of a few years ago, and here, unlike at Trelissick, the house is open to visitors and we would take our visitors to the house and demonstrate our own ignorance of Cornish history when they asked pertinent questions.

One of the sadnesses of Cornwall is the almost total disappearance of the mining industry. In former days there were hundreds of mines at work, digging out of the earth the valuable tin, copper, silver-lead, arsenic and other minerals. The County is littered with derelict mines, with their tall brick engine-house chimneys. One of the saddest sights is the "Moonscape" of china clay waste on what used to be the moors behind St. Austell. "Stretching far and wide, dominating and despoiling, the extraction of china clay has developed from a rural industry to a technological one that grows by leaps and bounds. Industry on this scale, ripping open scores of square miles of country may be profitable, but it is beginning to obscure the image of the other Cornwall - the true Cornwall upon which depends the whole long-term economy based upon tourism." (G.R. Gardiner)

For several years we let "Zansizzey" in the summer to some of these tourists. On the whole they treated the property with care, and the income helped to pay many of the bills resulting from Pat's various treatments and visits to specialists. Now it is my retirement home. Pat did not like the climate in winter. I love it, summer and winter, spring and autumn. The rains do not worry me. Indeed I love them, a throwback I suppose to my childhood when I would watch the raindrops running down the windows of "The Homestead" and when, dressed in wellington boots, sou'wester and shiny black raincoats we would splash home from school through the puddles and the rain to eat toast made on a brass toasting fork before the open coal fire of the kitchen range. That at least we always had - a warm house, since father was a coal merchant!

Though I am too cowardly to set sail in them, I get an almost sensual pleasure from the Cornish gales and deluges, and now, while I am still able to, I leave the house every day, whatever the weather and walk the lanes and headlands. If you live in Cornwall you must ignore the weather and if it is raining as it often is, you must abandon the pathetic little "showerproof" anoraks and put on a good completely waterproof coat, hooded and windproof, that reaches below the knees, strong waterproof trousers and take a stout stick, defying the elements and glorying in the wind and the rain on your face!

In my now solitary retirement in "Zansizzey" I am so pleased to be used in the work for which I was ordained. Rarely do I have a Sunday free when I am not taking services in one or other of the many churches in the district. Cornwall's Anglican Churches number more than three hundred, and many clergy have two and sometimes three parishes in their care where once each parish had its own priest. Cornish saints' names abound in all the parishes, and on successive Sundays recently I took services of the Holy Communion at St. Petroc's (Padstow), St. Saviour's (Trevone - a lovely little church, made of Cornish stone and opened in 1959), St. Mawgan, St. Columb, St. Ervan (the church where John Betjeman had a converting spiritual experience as a schoolboy drafted in all unwillingly to say Evensong with the aged Vicar) and St. Wenn. Recently I have helped at St. Mary's (Wadebridge), St. Breocke, and Egloshayle - those last three, together with one more, Washaway, are now joined as one parish under one priest. The benefice had no priest for more than a year, such is the state of the Church of England in the countryside, and now the forecast is that the number of parish clergy must be reduced yet again. That to me is a sign of faithlessness, but it is also a warning that groups of parishes like that just mentioned have of necessity to swallow their prides and prejudices and must be prepared to close buildings, and worship together. How weak the Church is when it is so divided within itself. With a congregation of fifteen here, ten there, thirty elsewhere, perhaps forty in another place, how effective can we be? But if, putting aside their partiality and their preconceived notions and prejudices of churchmanship, those ninety-five worshippers would come together, what strength would be theirs!

There is so much in all this of which we should be ashamed. As I was thinking back on the family holidays we used to have in Cornwall in the fifties and sixties I remembered one occasion when we were holidaying at Bude and went to Church one Sunday morning at a neighbouring church at Poughill, for a CSSM family service. As we were trying to make our way in with the crowds, we observed an elderly lady leaving the church, brandishing an umbrella, and shouting to all and sundry, "I have been attending this church for forty years, and now they won't even let me sit in my own pew!" "My own pew"? How long does it take for some of us to learn "what it means to be a Christian"? Such are the attitudes which are an offence to the Gospel and alienate the ordinary non-churchgoer.

In retirement I am grateful too for the opportunity to baptise, marry and bury and on occasion to visit the sick and the bereaved. Grateful too for the welcome from local clergy, so lacking from some of them in my retirement in Hampshire. What a joy it is to one who was once in love with a non-conformist girl who used to take me to the Methodist Central Hall in Uxbridge (now no more) for Sunday evening worship, when I should have been singing in the choir of St. James' Gerrards Cross, that I am welcomed to take services in the local Methodist churches in Padstow and Trevone. Perhaps one day the two congregations, Methodist and Anglican who meet in Trevone in buildings fifty yards apart, will learn to worship together. That would rejoice the heart of our Lord who prayed "That they may be one, even as You Father, and I, are one." Perhaps part of my ministry in retirement will be to work for that day. I certainly pray for it.

In retirement I have also had time to cogitate, at a distance of time from my own involvement, on "the state of education" today. All are agreed that much is wrong, that some standards (not all) are in decline, and that moral guidelines and benchmarks have been removed. It is also widely agreed that young people today are often deeply concerned about their fellows, their environment, about preserving wildlife, and about world peace. There are good schools and many good teachers, as well as some inadequate ones, and though many, myself included, have bewailed what we do see as a falling off in educational standards, we have to admit that more pupils are being trained to a much higher level than we were in the kind of schools I have described in Chapter 5. I have come to believe that the very large school is a mistake, unless it has more than adequate buildings, and a higher than average ratio of teachers to pupils; and that mixed ability classes, though fine as an ideal, just cannot achieve what the tripartite system could achieve given the resources and the manpower.

Nor can we ignore the influence that the disintegration of the family has had upon our schools. Britain has the highest divorce rate in Europe. Lack of stability and discipline at home, means lack of stability and increasing indiscipline at school. Where teachers themselves live broken lives they cannot fail to offer their pupils inadequate schooling and guidance. Where children go home to empty houses, or to constant family upsets, they are incapable of good work the next day. In a society that is, to say the least, indifferent to the Christian faith it is wrong to expect the churches, or the teachers of religious education to shoulder the whole burden of moral guidance and spiritual direction.

Eric Anderson who has just retired as Headmaster of Eton has written, "Particularly worrying is the anti-educational effect of TV. It is arguable that the most insidious influence on the young is not violence, drugs, tobacco, drink or sexual perversion, but our *pursuit of the trivial* and our *tolerance of the third rate...* we seem content to let our children spend their formative years under the influence of a succession of cops and criminals, of Nintendo and Ninja turtles, of Michael Jackson and Disneyland." He goes on to say, "We have lost our moral map...as guardians of civilised values we must, like Old Testament prophets, tell people truths that they do not want to hear, that there are higher standards than those which most people find good enough and that the effort to reach them is worthwhile. Our words may fall on deaf ears, but that is no excuse for not speaking out."

I do not myself despair. Faith and hope are as much cardinal virtues as love itself. Like Christian in Bunyan's *Pilgrim's Progress*, we have to go through the Slough of Despond, and up the Hill Difficulty before we attain the promised goal.

CHAPTER 15

PAIN

"There was a young lady of Deal,
Who said, Although pain isn't real,
When I sit on a pin and it punctures my skin,
I dislike what I fancy I feel."
Anon. after Edward Lear.

"And God shall wipe away all tears from their eyes. And there shall
be no more death neither sorrow nor crying, neither shall there be any
more pain, for the former things are passed away. And he that sat
upon the throne said, 'Behold I make all things new.'"
Revelation 21:4

After our move to Cedarwood Pat had been sent to the National
Hospital for Nervous Diseases by a specialist who had presumably
been told by the Rochester doctors that it was "all in her mind" and
with the ECT (now a totally discredited treatment, and indescribable
in its cruelty) and strong drugs, the mental depression had been so
deepened that one evening in 1981 she got into the car and drove off
with the intent of committing suicide. I thought she had gone to visit
friends and did not expect her back until late. She *did* return but not
before I had found the letter she had left behind. Plainly she had
decided that she could not go through with the act, though she had
purchased hosepipe and tape. It was a loving and beautifully coherent
letter, thanking me for thirty-eight years of happy married life, telling
of her love for Peter and Jill and all her friends, but saying how she
could not face the pain any longer.

After a long talk we went to bed, shedding many tears. Only the
letter itself can convey what Pat felt at this time and it seems an
appropriate passage with which to begin a chapter on pain, sad and
poignant though it is.

"Darling,

I'll make a hash of this last bit of our marriage I've no doubt, but be my pain mental or physical, or some of both, I don't think we can go on like this for endless more years, and you are so young, handsome (truly), and wonderful in every way. You've got time to build a new life. Thank you for 38 years of marvellous love and care and patience. I know all my friends envy me my husband. Not one of them has one who suffered so much from, and for, a basically selfish wife. I just never thought it could be like this, for you've given me all I ever wanted, from a home by the sea to our so warm and cosy bungalow. You've been so marvellous at being so caring and devoted and making my friends so welcome, and in fact doing just everything and anything I wanted. It's not too late for you to start again, but this time get someone to spoil you for a change! All, all, my love as it always has been. There could never have been anyone else who would have given up so much. When you feel you can, would you thank the people on the enclosed list for all their love and care? (there were 40 names on the list. What friendship! SH) and thank Jill and Peter for being such super children. I've been so very very lucky. I love you, love you, love you, and thank you, thank you, thank you.
                    Pat".

There followed a little drawing of a heart, pierced by an arrow, Pat/Stanley. It was the sign of our deep affection which I used childishly to draw on the ground with a stick when we were out walking. This letter speaks more of our love and our marriage than could ever be written down in a whole book. It was written in 1981. Pat was 65.

Through clouds and sunshine, through much pain and much sorrow, and some relief, our love survived another ten years. My faith tells me that it survives still. When faith wavers and hope dies, there *is* only love.

Pat had seen her first orthopaedic consultant in February 1979. Twelve years later she had seen, or been sent to, no less than thirty general practitioners, consultants, surgeons, physicians, anaesthetists, acupuncturists, a hypnotist, and a number of osteopaths. As I look through that long list of the medical profession and of others on the fringe, I must confess that it appears that Pat was a hypochondriac, one who has a chronic anxiety about the state of her health. Nothing is further from the truth. Her state of mind was quite clear. She had severe back pain, and she was convinced that it was caused by a *physical* injury.

It has taken a long time for certain members of the medical profession to restrain themselves from ascribing many types of pain to mental causes alone. Certainly it is clear that some anxiety states do cause physical symptoms and that there is a cross-relationship between the way the anxieties of the mind affect the body, making it tired and listless, forgetful and subject to states such as asthma and eczema, and the physically caused pains of the body resulting in depression, mental disturbance, tension and disorientation.

The tragedy in Pat's case was that in the early days of her examinations by the doctors they could find no physical cause for her pain. GPs had an inadequate knowledge by which to make a proper diagnosis and they took the easy way out of saying, "*I* can find nothing wrong with you," and followed it, perhaps all unconsciously, with the apparently logical but unspoken conclusion which is itself a non-sequitur, "Therefore there *is* nothing wrong with you." Even consultants tended to say the same. It was because we lived in three different places during those twelve years, Rochester, Hampshire and Cornwall, that the number of doctors seen seems so large, and if the various consultants seen in London, Southampton and elsewhere are added, the reason for the multiplicity of treatments becomes clear.

The Secretary of State for Health said in 1976:

> "Backache is a major problem bringing discomfort and disability to very many people. It is also clearly a serious economic problem. Both the nation and those who suffer from this group of diseases would benefit if they could be prevented or if treatment were more effective."

The setting up of pain clinics did follow this statement, but it has taken a long time to set them up, and there are few effective ones under the NHS. It is estimated that today ten percent of the adult population suffer from chronic and continuing pains in some part of the back, and that each day some twenty percent of the working population is unable to go to work because of pain. This sounds a very high proportion, but is testified to by the Back Pain Association. In 1979 the Association wrote that the back pain epidemic cost £300 million a year in medical care, sickness benefit and lost production. In 1989 the figures had multiplied several times. "The cost to the individual and his family in personal suffering is impossible to estimate... yet astonishingly little is known about the cause of back pain and how best to prevent it or treat it."

Much research is now going on in a field which has none of the "glamour" of research, into the causes of cancer, for example; and the astounding figure of only seven pence out of every £100 spent on medical research into the study of diseases of the back in 1976 must surely have been multiplied many times over by now. Research is now proceeding into all the areas which one or other of Pat's consultants mentioned in their diagnosis as the years went by - weakness of the neuromechanisms of the back (a specialism of Jason Brice FRCS, of Southampton General hospital, who tried so hard and did so much for Pat through minor and major operations, manipulations and injections); ankylosing spondylitis (ankylosis is abnormal adhesions or immobility of the bones - of the spine and shoulder in Pat's case - caused by the growth of fibrous tissues; spondylitis is inflammation of the vertebrae, the bony segments of the spine); osteoporosis, or brittleness of the bones due to loss of protein from the bone matrix, and almost inevitable in the bones of those in "old age".

The word most beloved of the doctors was, "Of course you must expect all these problems as you get older." Then there were advanced X-ray and scanning techniques of increasing complexity. As the continuing back problems of prominent people like the Prince of Wales began to be featured in the picture pages and articles in the daily press, interest grew and less was ascribed to "the mind", and more to the physical and neurological causes. After all, there are at least two thousand nerves deriving from the spinal column, all of which send messages from the brain right up to the ends of the hairs on the backs of our hands, and if there is pressure on any part of a major nerve, (of which there are thirty-one pairs, cervical, thoracic, lumbar, sacral and coccygeal, emerging between the vertebrae) for example by the "squashing" of a disc or the displacement of it, then the patient is bound to feel pain, and the source of the pain is almost impossible to pinpoint with accuracy.

In 1979 and 1980 there were many articles in the newspapers about the "new approach" to back pain by one of the most famous orthopaedic surgeons of the post-war period, a man called Cyriax, who in the late 1940's had written the definitive textbook on the subject. On the principle of "going to see the top man" we wrote to him and asked for a consultation. In his house near Regents Park, in a room dark and crowded with strange furniture and stranger still decorations, he gave Pat a short examination. "You need to forget about yourself, my dear. Go and find something to do." This was the first of our "private" consultations, and as can be imagined, it was a great disappointment. Pat was the last person to say such a thing to. She had been active all her life, "doing", things for others without thought of self, for more than forty years. Indeed it was because she had been *doing* things for others that she was in this state. It made us rather cynical about the reputation of the famous.

Cyriax had a younger colleague who was also growing a reputation, so we thought we might get better treatment from him. He was much more sympathetic and seemed to understand that there was a physical cause, stemming probably from a neurological source, and we went regularly to London for a course of injections only to discover that they were the same injections which had been originally given by Alan Lettin, an orthopaedic surgeon recommended to us by St. Luke's Hospital, the Clergy Hospital, in London's Fitzroy Square. These had given some relief but had been suspended by the surgeon himself because he felt he was achieving nothing.

The first hope of a break-through came in an unusual way. In her early days Pat had been a keen, though not particularly expert, tennis player, and when she was reading in the newspaper about the Tennis Tournament at Wimbledon at the end of June 1980 she came across the name of Jo Durie, later to be Britain's number one player. The report said that Miss Durie had had severe back pains from a spinal injury and that she had had a successful operation. She is still one of our leading tennis players after fourteen years on the back-punishing circuit. Pat wrote to her, and asked her if she could let us know the name of the surgeon who had performed the operation, explaining her own PE background and her current problems. A reply came from Jo Durie in the midst of her busy Wimbledon week, in pencil on a scrappy bit of school notepaper. It gave the name of a Mr. Helal of the London Hospital, Whitechapel, with a high recommendation.

We went to see Mr. Helal and he was the first to suspect damage to discs and a deteriorating vertebra. "Have you ever been X-rayed leaning backwards?" he asked. "No." X-rays were taken and the diagnosis made that small amounts of bone needed to be chipped off one or two vertebrae to relieve the pressure on discs and nerves. The operation was performed in a North London Hospital and many further outpatient visits were made, Mr. Helal confessing that he was primarily a hand and foot surgeon. Pat and he got on well together and found many points of contact. Pat was always able to find a point of contact, even with the most remote stranger, and with folk in every level of society. The contact here was that Mr. Helal lived in Cheshunt, opposite the Old Vicarage where Pat had spent her adolescence from the age of fourteen when she had been dragged back there in tears from her beloved New Zealand. Though not entirely successful, the operation clearly relieved some of the pain and apart from the abandoned suicide attempt Pat and I were able to live a fairly normal life within certain constraints until early in 1983.

It is in the nature of the human body that the ageing process tends to undo previous successful treatments, in that new areas of deterioration appear. The pain returned and our Headley Down GP, Paul Beech, was greatly concerned and put us in touch with another local surgeon who performed a small back operation in the region of the scapula. Like all such operations and the many injections of marcain and other drugs acting as painkillers, this gave some relief, but it was not permanent. Willing to explore every medical possibility, Pat agreed to see a hypnotist at his clinic in Basingstoke as a private patient. His simple advice (at considerable cost!) was that she should practice a form of meditation, lying on her back and counting downwards slowly from ten thousand. This was clearly a form of self-hypnosis and for the time that it made her drowsy it was successful in banishing the idea of pain from the mind, but it was of course no cure for the basic cause. The "thoracic rhizotomy" performed in Basingstoke, an operation to cut the roots of the nerves deriving from one of the higher dorsal vertebrae, was the first of several such operations performed by various surgeons to eradicate the pain in the shoulders or in the region of the scapula, but as it was explained to us in simple terms, the effect could not be permanent because the nerves were clever enough to find a new route when one their number was cut. This is a wholly unscientific explanation, but it does make clear the reason why none of the surgical treatments was permanently successful. As Jason Brice was later to say: "I could easily get rid of all your pains if I could cut your whole spine out!"

It was a friend who pointed out to us that the solution to Pat's suffering and physical torture might not be with the orthopaedic surgeon, although his branch of the discipline was concerned with disorders of the spine and joints, and repairing injuries to them, but with neurosurgery which is specifically concerned to deal with the nervous system. Dr. Browne at Alton had made a small attempt to get at the root of the trouble (the word Rhizotomy comes from the Greek word for "root", rhiza) but from 1983 until her death Pat was in the hands of Jason Brice, the top neurosurgeon at Southampton General Hospital whom Paul Beech recommended to us unreservedly.

It would take too long to retell all the details of the other treatments Pat had, usually at the suggestion or endorsement of a friend. There was the doctor in Colchester where we went by train along the notoriously late and disrupted line from Liverpool Street, and then by bus to his home, for Pat to undergo a manipulation which in fact left her exhausted and in great pain for weeks after. Jason Brice also performed manipulations later on, to stretch the spine and relieve pressure on the discs. These too were painful so they were performed under anaesthic and were only temporarily successful. A course of water-therapy was undertaken at Lord Mayor Treloar's Hospital, Alton. Acupuncture was coming into its own as an "alternative therapy" and was beginning to be approved of by the more orthodox among the medical doctors, and Pat had several sessions of needles with a doctor in Dorset where her mother lived and who was recommended by a friend. Another friend had approving words to say of an acupuncturist, also a qualified doctor, in Guildford. None of these sessions of acupuncture achieved more than temporary effects, though I suspect that Pat had made up her mind that they *were* going to help. They did help for a few days, but then the pressure on the nerves re-asserted itself and it was "back to square one". We abandoned other forms of treatment and put ourselves solely in the hands of the neuro-surgeon.

Jason Brice was marvellous. Brusque and rather offhand and forbidding at first, he and Pat became friends and were soon exchanging reminiscences of their grandchildren. We originally saw him in his clinic in the General Hospital, and he performed his first big operation on Pat there. He had done two smaller ones for her in private hospitals in Milton on Sea and in Chalybeate, a private Hospital opposite the General Hospital, and also two smaller ones in the General where she would come in for a night or two. He was most generous in his time and patience and over the eight years in which she was under his care we saw him no less than forty times.

At the end of the series of operations Pat had the marks of one hundred and thirty eight stitches in her back, and three long scars, one down the *line* of her spine and one on *each side* of her spine, running from the shoulders to the buttocks. How she suffered without complaint so many painful operations over so many years I cannot guess. I continue to marvel at her determination to get better. It was in no sense masochism, self torture, which some folk seem to enjoy, because she was in fact highly sensitive to pain, but she longed to get well so that we could live a normal active life. In between the operations she was taking many pain killers each day, and as a result of one of Brice's operations which went wrong, she became incontinent and was on a set of different drugs for that. For the depression which always followed long bouts of pain she was on anti-depressants. Various other problems derived from the continuing low state of health in which she was endeavouring to live a normal life - diverticulitis, bacterial infections after operations (almost inevitable in certain circumstances and in no sense due to negligence on the part of the Hospitals) infective diarrhoea, sciatica, which put her to bed for long periods, often unfortunately while we were in Cornwall, which we visited annually for several weeks, and in the last two years, for several months at a time.

When we were in Cornwall we kept in touch with Jason Brice by telephone, and with the local doctors, including our excellent Padstow GP, Mike Rees, and various physicians and pain killing specialists in Newquay and Truro Hospitals. We tried to keep up our walks on the Headlands, and our meeting with friends. The family came down to the caravan I had bought and placed in the back garden of "Zansizzey", so Pat was rarely alone, and always had something and someone to occupy her mind. She continued with her needlework and over a period of eight years she made two sets of curtains for the bungalow, no mean feat, as the bay windows each had four curtains, plus a dozen others in other parts of the house, and a new set for the caravan. We never forgot our visit to tired old Dr. Cyriax and his foolish remark: "Go and find something to do." We made many friends in Trevone and entertained as much as we could. But the effects of the operations on the rest of Pat's body were growing and various painful internal examinations had to be made.

I tell all this not to harrow the reader or myself, but because it gives the background to my considered thoughts about pain, about euthanasia and about suicide.

When we returned to "Cedarwood" in 1987 some months after the biggest operation that Brice performed, Pat was very low and had a bad winter, spent mostly in bed. In February 1988 I noted in my diary, "Pat is very miserable, there is talk of suicide again." In consultation with Dr. Beech it was agreed that the depression was probably due to the after effects of the operations and the multitude of drugs which she had at one time or another taken over a long period - Tofranil, Bolvidon, Ativan, Aproxin, Amoxycillin, Obenin, Colefac, DF118, Velocef, lpral, Ciproxin, Fortral, Pyridoxine, Voltarol, Zantac, and several more. Pat agreed, though with reluctance, because she knew that she had become dependent on some of the pain-killers, to experiment with a complete withdrawal of all drugs over a period of three weeks. She knew what the symptoms of withdrawal would be and with incredible bravery she agreed to take only one drug, Ativan, an anti-depressant drug used to treat anxiety and insomnia. For several days she persevered but there followed long periods of vomiting and the experiment had to be abandoned. Beech went away for a few days and his colleague came to visit Pat and unbelievably, because he must have read her notes, he prescribed Valium (known as the doctor's "cure-all" for old and difficult patients) whose side effects are drowsiness, fatigue, ataxia or unsteady gait, and lots of others. The Valium made her sick again and I withdrew it. Slowly Pat was restored to something like normality, and we survived through into 1989 and 1990.

Jason Brice suggested that Pat should have a complete body scan with a new machine and as a result he agreed to perform a last operation. But he had a change of heart. I assume that he had sat down quietly to work out the pros and cons of the most major surgical operation which Pat would have to undergo and he decided that he could not perform it. It was also dangerous, as he would have to go into her back through her chest, and, in view of her age and all that she had gone through, he was not willing to take the risk. We visited him in his clinic and he explained the situation and his great regret.

The big operation which had been scheduled for March 5th 1990 was cancelled, and he told Pat that he could do nothing more for her, but that he would have no objection to her approaching other experts in pain control, nearer our home - Southampton was forty miles away - who would presumably get in touch with him before they decided on any treatment.

He did agree to do a repair of a previous operation, a laminectomy, and this took place on April 12th 1990. On April 19th the pain returned and Jason Brice told our GP that this was because Pat had left hospital too early. She always was anxious to get up as soon as possible and return home, probably because of the great expense we were being put to in the private hospitals, even though I assured her that the money must not be a priority. Again we struggled through the year, spending some months in Cornwall, and returned for yet another scan on September 28th, 1990. The results were not good. There was arthritis on pretty well the whole spine, and other growths which were obviously causing pressure and pain. Surgically the case was hopeless. Pat was told to get her drug intake down to the minimum, but this too was a hopeless injunction, since the pains were increasing, not diminishing.

On October 18th, 1990 Pat had arranged to see Dr. Beech at the Surgery in Lindford at 5:30 p.m. When she had not returned at 6:30 p.m. I became anxious and telephoned the surgery. "Yes, she left here half an hour ago." Had she gone to see a friend? She would surely have told me in advance. I suspected that she had taken her hosepipe with her and was going to drive into the country in the Maestro. I telephoned the Police and a search was instituted in places where she might have driven into a quiet country lane. At a quarter to ten I heard the sound of a car in the drive of "Cedarwood". Pat had returned. Her intention had been frustrated. She had driven in the dark up Fernden Lane a few miles away in the parish of Haslemere, not far from my old Church of St. Stephen's, Shottermill, a lane well known to us. But she had got herself bogged down in mud a few yards from the road and had been rescued by a father and his small son returning to their home at the end of the lane. They had towed her out of the mud and put her on her route home.

What an incredible wife I had! Abandoning her intention, she had engaged father and son in conversation, had elicited that the boy was aged about eight years old and was a dyslectic. The next morning we drove to their home with information about teachers who were able to cope with dyslexia, with the name of a school in Farnham, and she stayed with the boy's mother in earnest conversation for half an hour.

Little was said about this second failed attempt at suicide and life returned to whatever was normal. We shopped and went to Forest Lodge regularly for coffee. Pat loved clothes because she had always been poorly dressed by her mother who economised in every way possible. As a child she had had one best dress and one overcoat. Now she could indulge her admitted extravagance in shoes - when she died she had 13 pairs; in shirts, 23 of them; trousers, 11; and skirts, 6, plus all the accessories. She had little jewellery and rarely wore any. She did not even wear the engagement ring that I had bought her for a week's salary in 1943. Life went on for another year.

In early 1991, Jason Brice had not in fact "abandoned" Pat. Under pressure from me he agreed to send Pat to the Wessex Hospital for yet another MRI scan on another new machine, though he must have known what the result would be. Meanwhile we had made contact, with Brice's agreement, with the local neuro-surgeon in Farnham, who promised Pat that she would meet with his "pain-control" group of four or five specialists, in September. There were two bases of hope for her, one that the scan would reveal a state of affairs that could be controlled; and also that the group of doctors, including a pain-control expert, a physician, and a psychiatrist, would be able to help her. Her hopes were not to be realised. Jason Brice wrote a letter after examining the results of the final scan to say that the deterioration of the spine was continuing apace and that nothing more could be done for her. The Farnham surgeon omitted to make the appointment with his group for September and said that they would not be meeting again until January.

Another straw had failed her. The final blow came when, having received all the information from the specialists, Paul Beech came to see Pat. He explained the hopelessness of the situation as kindly as he could and said, "We will try to make you comfortable." She didn't want to he made comfortable. She wanted to be fit and well.

Pat's mother had died at ninety-two, her father at eighty-three, one aunt at ninety-four, another at eighty-six, and the whole of the Meredith family had been long lived. Pat knew that she would live just as long as they, because she was in good health apart from her spine and the effects that her pain had had upon her inner workings.

She knew that with increasing doses of morphine she would become an incontinent cabbage. She was already constrained to get up five times a night, and we were sleeping in separate rooms because my sleep was being constantly disturbed and I was in no fit state to look after her twenty-four hours a day.

Euthanasia, easy or quiet death, was illegal, so the only solution in Pat's mind was suicide. We discussed it fully and I had to tell her that assisting a suicide was against the law, and that though I could not help her because of that, and because of my own beliefs, I would not stand in her way if she made the decision in full possession of her own will and senses. I knew that she had an ample supply of sleeping tablets, and also I had discovered a small bottle of whisky in one of her drawers. I had destroyed one set of hosepipes and tapes but I suspected that she had another somewhere. Constantly she told me that it would be better for me if she were out of the way, but I assured her that this was not a consideration on my part. Not only had I promised love and loyalty to her in sickness and in health, so long as we both should live, but I believed that she still had so much to give to her friends and to her children. We spoke about the afterlife and the Christian hope, and she told me again that she prayed for us all daily. It seemed that she had made her great decision.

A great peace seemed to have descended on her life. From October 17th, 1991, we did everything together, had coffee and bought plants at Forest Lodge, went to tea with our neighbours, had them back to tea. She was her old, outgoing effervescent self. She talked to her children on the telephone and to her grandchildren, in the most normal way, not saying any goodbyes which could be misinterpreted. I continued with the usual treatments to her back, the heat lamp, the gentle message, the hot and cold compresses, the anti-pain spray. In the car, on her makeshift bed, we drove to Marley Down, Blackdown, Frensham Ponds and were closer together than ever before. A few months before, I had bought a new car with powered steering and automatic gears in the hope that Pat could drive it short distances to see her friends and so feel at least some independence from me, but she was never able to use it.

On the morning of November 2nd, 1991, I awoke at about 5.30 a.m. to see the reflection of the garage light. I went to the garage and found the car engine running, but Pat was lying on the cold cement of the garage floor, unconscious. I put her to bed and called Paul Beech who came later that morning when she had recovered. He gave her a stern but gentle lecture and explained that suicide was no real solution, certainly not to those who were left behind. It transpired that Pat had not mastered the new car's electric windows, so she could not get them shut in order to fill the car with the poisonous carbon monoxide fumes. "I always was rather dumb about mechanical things." It was a wry joke.

Beech told me that failed suicides always make a further attempt and that I must be on my guard. For two more days we had a peaceful time together. It even seemed that the pain lines which had become so marked on her face, where the cheeks had fallen away, had disappeared. I did not think that the fourth and final attempt would happen so soon, but on the morning of Tuesday November 5th, I again woke at about 6.30 a.m. to the light of the garage. I went out and found Pat slumped in the front of the car with the garage door closed, her face purple with the poison. She was dead and plainly had been for some hours as the engine of the car was still running and the hosepipe from the exhaust was still pumping the obnoxious gas into the car. I called Paul Beech and the Police and after they had gone I called my children who were naturally shocked and devastated. The kindliest of policeman came to spend time with me and take down all the information he needed to make a report. I said goodbye to my loved one of forty-eight years and she was taken away. I wrote to all our friends with a typed note that Pat had died and that the funeral would be a private one with no flowers. Donations in lieu of flowers might be sent to me for onward transmission to charities which were dedicated to the relief of pain, I received more than one hundred letters of sympathy and more than £500 in gifts, which I divided between St. Christopher's Hospice and the Back Pain Association.

I asked the Rector of Headley, Dick Woodger, who took the Cremation Service at Guildford, but who did not know Pat very well, to be brief and make the service one of joyful thanksgiving, which he did admirably. Pat's two brothers and their families came, along with Jill and her husband and our two grandchildren, Sam and Mimi, and Peter and Jeanette, and we all tried to give thanks that Pat's long years of suffering had come to an end, and we remembered her as she was, the joyous, fascinating, outgoing, lovely person that she had been to so many friends, teachers, children, parishioners, old ladies in nursing homes and hospitals. I remembered that my daughter Jill had said to me on the telephone on the morning of November 5th, "Daddy, that was the most unselfish thing that Mummy has ever done." I treasure that, and I know it was her motive.

The inquest was held at Alton and I was able to explain to the Coroner who was a very sympathetic man, that my wife had taken her own life in full cognisance of what she was doing, after long, rational thought and he agreed. There was not a breath of "while the balance of the mind was disturbed." He was particularly impressed with the beautiful letter which Pat had left. It said:

"Darling Boy, from Your Girl,

You said, 'don't write', but I couldn't leave you without a word. Thank you for being the most wonderful, caring, helpful husband anyone could ever have. I know I am being *very selfish* and I am very worried about the strain which will be put on you. If I felt I'd get better, even in six months or so, I'd stick it out, but I know this pain, (some days better than others) is with me to stay and I feel I'd live until well up into my nineties, as in all other health matters I am so very fit, so I think it best to get it over and give you a chance to make a life for yourself, not tied down to looking after me, and trying non-stop to make life bearable for me by endlessly bathing my back and rubbing it; and always putting on the TV and radio when there are things I want and foregoing things you like. I could write a book about all you do for me.

Please tell the children I am truly sorry and I do love them very much and am very proud of their successes and we've never had any drink or drug problems with them have we? I'm sorry too about my real friends who are always so caring and understanding and helpful. You know who they are.

If I have any money left and you don't need it, can it go principally to Mimi, as I expect Sacha would see Sam through. Once they've got 2 or 3 'A' levels they will be alright. I think there will be grants, and if not they will be able to borrow for their higher education.

As you know, the reason I get so het up about Mimi and Sam is:- I couldn't bear them to have such a broken secondary education as Michael and I had, and that is the reason I am sure we did so badly at 'O' level and didn't even attempt 'A' levels. I cried and cried and was utterly miserable for months at not being allowed to stay on in

New Zealand at Wanganui Girls' College. Michael couldn't cope with Enfield Grammar where he was sent, but I think he quite enjoyed St. John's, Leatherhead. He copes better with disappointments than me. You know all this, so it's silly to write it all again!

I expect Jill would get rid of all my clothes - I know how extravagant I have always been - or if it might be better not to worry Jill, perhaps Jeanette, would do it; she does, I think, feel part of the family. If Peter is half as good to her as you have always been to me, she is lucky. For I am sure he is and I am glad he has someone to share his life with. You have such a broad back!!! (This refers, even after a lifetime, to the first sermon that Pat heard me preach on "Having a Broad Back". SH) and an amazing ability to cope but I do know it will be lonely often - wouldn't you like to share with someone? (another little joke between us - I had always said I couldn't bear the thought of being married to anyone else. SH)

Thank you from the bottom of my heart for 48 or is it 49 (?) wonderful years,

Always your Girl.

Remembering how much listening to the records of the Welsh boy soprano Aled Jones had meant to Pat all through her illness, we played at the Cremation a tape of him singing "Come unto me, all that labour and are heavy laden, and I will give you rest," from Handel's *Messiah*. It seemed to be the most appropriate of all texts and of all music. Looking back on her letters, even those few I have quoted in this book, could anyone believe that Pat was not welcomed by our Lord? Can anyone believe that such a suicide, such a selfless person would, as the Church *used* to teach, be rejected at the "throne of grace"? (Don't preach, Stanley!)

I knew that many would be upset at the thought of Pat taking her own life, and even more that it should have been a parson's wife, so to a number of my friends and to the Doctors and Clergy, I sent an extract from a lecture I had given, many years before, in 1971, on *Some Modern Moral Problems*, which included a passage on suicide and one on euthanasia. I have been a supporter of voluntary euthanasia for most of my ministry, and I believe that if it had been legal on November 5th, 1991, with adequate safeguards, a painful suicide need not have taken place with all its attendant legal business, its pain and sadness and unpleasant undertones. I will not attempt to

360

re-write it for this book, but I append it exactly as it was written in 1971. No human being should be permitted to suffer what Pat suffered.

SUICIDE AND EUTHANASIA

These notes are extracts from a general lecture given in *March, 1971* on *Some Modern Moral Problems.* They are not exhaustive since the lecture covered six themes. I have not changed my views in 20 years, and the joyous task of caring for my wife in the last 12 years of a 48 year marriage when she was never without pain, has reinforced them.

Suicide

Until a few years ago suicide was felt to be the greatest of all sins against God and against self. The law of the land accepted what was then the Christian ethic. Now the law no longer charges a man with a crime if he fails in a suicide attempt. The Church used to bury suicides in unconsecrated ground to show its displeasure. This too no longer applies. The reason for this is obvious. What was once thought to be a sin, deliberately chosen (and this is what makes sin a terrible thing) can now be seen as an aberration for which a man may not be responsible. How much is society responsible? What is there in life that makes it so insupportable that a man will want to end it? How many suicides are due to physical causes - tumours or other brain damage? How many are due to personality defects, psychological blemishes and imperfections which cannot be overcome by an act of will? Anyway, what is suicide? Why does everyone think that Captain Oates' self-sacrifice was so marvellous when he went out into the snow in order to save companions from the burden of his presence? It was a naked suicide. And was not Jesus on one view a suicide? He could have saved himself. So could St. Paul, St. Peter and the other apostles, all of whom died of martyrdom. If human life is so important, then surely to deny in a form of words one's faith is not such a terrible thing! So the argument could run. It is said that astronauts carry cyanide pills or the equivalent for use if their return to earth is made impossible. Is that morally wrong? Few would say so if the alternative is a ghastly form of lingering death. You can see how difficult it is to say that suicide is and must be wrong in all cases, even if it can be argued that it is wrong in some cases.

Euthanasia

While we are in this field I should like to say something about euthanasia. I remember writing a paper condemning it more than a quarter of a century ago, in 1946, but a year ago, in 1970, my revered father-in-law died. He had been a faithful priest for nearly sixty years and when he died at 83 he had all his mental faculties in full. But he died of an internal cancer which was both very painful and very unpleasant, and which lasted several years, becoming progressively more distressing. I have emphasised that he retained his mental faculties because he became firmly convinced as he approached the last stages of life that nothing was being achieved by keeping him alive. He did not want to be a burden to his wife with whom he had lived for more than fifty-five years. He knew that the cost of nursing was diminishing the amount of money she would have to live on when the end came. He knew that it was distressing to the rest of his family to see him so emaciated and in such discomfort. And if the argument for euthanasia or voluntary death is strong is the case of a very old man, how much stronger it is in the case of a badly crippled child, or a mentally retarded child, or an adult made mindless and moronic by some terrible accident.

The Christian believes that our lives are not our own to do with as we will. They belong to God. That is why Christianity has always condemned suicide and murder. So it is argued, "What is euthanasia but both suicide and murder combined?" The doctor has his Hippocratic oath, which he does not in fact "take", and he places his skill and devotion at the service of his patient, but does that oath require him to keep that patient alive to the very last moment when dignity, beauty and meaning have vanished and when, if the patient were an animal he would be prosecuted for causing it unnecessary suffering? It is said, and the argument is a strong one, to be taken very seriously indeed, that only on the basis that the doctor will do his utmost to keep a man alive can we base any confidence at all. No doubt a doctor could with ease despatch a sufferer with drugs and no one but himself would know. What trust could we have in the medical profession if we always had in our minds that at any moment they could exercise a divine prerogative without us knowing? On the other side those who defend euthanasia say, would not the Hippocratic oath (itself deriving from a man born 460 years before Christ) be more humane if it emphasised rather "thou shalt not officiously strive to keep alive?"

What happens at the moment is that as the end in such painful cases as cancer approaches, the amount of pain-killing drugs is increased. This does in effect shorten life and hasten death, but, so the moral theologians will argue, there is all the difference in the world between giving a dose that will prove fatal merely to relieve unbearable pain, and giving deliberately a fatal dose which will end life there and then. But is not this not mere casuistry?

Into this problem in recent years, especially since the heart transplants began, has come the basic question "what is death?" *When* does a patient die? When the heart stops beating? But cases have been known of patients' hearts being kept going by mechanical and electrical means for years on end. Is this *life* if the functioning of the brain has already been impaired by injury and the patient is never actually conscious? If a doctor should switch off the machine in such a case is he *killing* the patient? By what possible devious argument can it be said that the sanctity of human life demands that it be prolonged?

And if it be added, as it often is, that the State cannot possibly condone the taking of human life what hypocrisy and muddled thinking is revealed! The average length of life for a young officer in the infantry in the 1914-1918 war was two days - the State sent them out to die by the thousands, these young soldiers. Doctors also end life quite legally if a mother's life is at stake during pregnancy, and the Abortion Act has allowed more than 60,000 (in 1970; 150,000 in 1990) embryos a year to be terminated. "Death should be left to God" some will say. But we do not leave birth to God. We prevent it, we space it, we arrange it. Often it happens as a result of a few moments uncontrolled passion.

Isn't part of the problem here that we have been taught that death is always an enemy, that the act of dying is always a tragedy? To the Christian it is neither. The Christian believes that life in another dimension will be immeasurably better than life here, so why should he fear to die? He knows that he is not going into the dark, not going to a place of shadowy extinction, but into the presence of God, where, purified and purged of the dross of sin and self he will enjoy God for ever. Death is not the end of a journey. It is a milestone on the way. It is a relatively unimportant element in God's plan for us.

Stringent safeguards would be necessary if voluntary euthanasia were to be legalised and it was on this that the last bill foundered in 1936, though it was supported by many Christian leaders, including the then Archbishop of Canterbury. This is not something which we ought to leave to the individual doctor. He needs the support of the law for what he already does in many cases. Suffering can be creative. No one is denying this and no one will deny that suffering is part of every man's life to some degree. The moral problem is to decide when suffering ceases to be creative, and when it becomes inhuman and wicked cruelty (itself a sin) to prolong it.

About the time of Pat's suicide Ludovic Kennedy, a leading advocate of voluntary euthanasia, had appeared on a TV programme and in my view had made some inadequate comments and conclusions, so I sent him a copy of the above. He replied and in a short subsequent correspondence wrote that he was "impressed by the memorandum. But the voluntary euthanasia I advocate can only be given at the patient's request and *must* be approved by another Doctor (as in Holland). Also, atheists have no fear of death either, as they believe this life is everything, and there is no other." He also wrote, "I agree that those who are not terminally ill should also be considered but I doubt if legislation could be introduced on that head until a bill to end the suffering of the terminally ill has first been passed. The Christian dimension is not one which concerns me personally, as I am not a Christian."

I, of course, had stated my own view that stringent safeguards *would* have to be applied and in a subsequent letter to him I emphasised that if the law were ever to be changed, in my view the twofold support of the Medical Profession and of the Church would be necessary. Plainly the support of the Roman Catholic Church would not be available, but the Church of England and the Free Churches had all in their time discussed it officially and progress might be possible in that area. As far as the medical profession is concerned they are divided. A minority is officially against euthanasia, but a majority admit that they would assist death in certain circumstances. Though 79% of British people would like to see the law changed and voluntary euthanasia made legal, the BMA in June 1993 voted that there be no change in the law.

The House of Bishops of the Church of England discussed the matter in 1992. They stated that in their view there are limits to human autonomy and thus to what human beings may do to themselves or ask others to do to them. They added that to justify a change in the law it would be necessary to show that such a change would remove greater evils than it would cause and that they, the Bishops, did not believe that such a justification could be given. So the debate continues.

In the series of Channel 4 programmes, *Talking Heads*, a programme headed by Ludovic Kennedy called *Consider the End* was broadcast in 1993, and a booklet was published containing, in the form of dialogues with Hippocrates (the so-called Father of Medicine, who lived and died between 460 and 357 BC and is the presumed author of the Hippocratic Oath) the arguments for and against, as understood by a Doctor, and Anglican Priest and an ethical Philosopher. Apart from a few snide remarks about there being more Anglican priests than parishioners (why are intelligent people so ignorant and prejudiced about the Anglican Church? It's our own fault I suppose), the arguments are fairly put, including the strict attitude of Dame Cicely Saunders of St. Christopher's Hospice, and the rather muddled view of the Roman Church's spokesman on that occasion, who said, "We are not masters of our lives," (which we plainly are!) and, "when I go to the dentist I take my mind off the pain by reflecting on Christ's Passion." (Tell that to a patient with terminal cancer.) The painful case of Dr. Cox who was tried and convicted of attempted murder when he gave a fatal dose of potassium chloride to a family friend suffering dreadful pains from arthritis, will be with us for a long time to come. After a year's suspension he was allowed to resume practice.

The following appeared as a news item in the Daily Telegraph in October, 1993:

"AWARD WINNING POLICE DOG SHOT TWICE IN FARM SIEGE DIES.

Kain, a police dog twice commended for bravery died yesterday after being seriously injured in an armed siege. The six year old dog was shot twice on Wednesday while trying to disarm a man who was later shot by a police marksman. Kain was taken by ambulance to a veterinary surgery. After a night of tests and treatment he was expected to make a full recovery. When he was found to have spondylosis, a spinal condition, which, together with his injuries, would have made walking extremely difficult, he was allowed to die under anaesthetic. Sgt. Ralph Blackburn, in charge of the Newton Abbot police dog section, added 'Kain was one of the family. Bob (the dog's handler PC Bob Smith) made the hardest decision of his life when he realised that there was nothing more that could be done. *In the end he had to put Kain's quality of life before his own emotions.* There was no way we were going to allow him to merely exist as a cripple.'"(my italics)

Comment is almost superfluous. Many who support the legalisation of voluntary euthanasia are often heard to say: "We wouldn't allow a dog to suffer like that." Kain was not allowed to suffer. Accepting that the cases of animals and humans may be different, it is a valid point not to be lightly dismissed, for Pat too had spondylosis!

The sentiments conveyed in the multitude of letters which I received after Pat's death moved me and still move me, deeply, and the memory of them keeps my own memory of Pat alive.

There was her hairdresser who wrote of "A very lovely lady", a phrase that was repeated more than once in other tributes. Her opposite number on the boy's side at Midhurst Secondary Modern School in the 1950's: "She was probably the most whole hearted and genuine school teacher that any of us have ever known." Pat was right to tell me in 1943 that her vocation was to teaching, and not to being a parson's wife!

One who was at College with her in the 1930s wrote: "She was always so full of life. Miff (her friends pet name for her - until she met me she was always called Myfanwy or Miff), Christine and I have known each other since we were eighteen and have kept in touch ever since. We enjoyed our College life and had lots of fun together. Miff was always so cheerful and kind and anxious to help everyone. Such a happy character!"

A girl whom she had taught in her first teaching post in Clacton in 1937 and whom we had met subsequently, remembered her. "I always remembered her coming to join the staff at the Grammar

School. So vivacious and so lively." A teacher whom she had helped when she was Deputy Head at Walderslade wrote, "When I was a young teacher Pat was always so kind to me, and when everything had been too much, she always had just the right thing to say to make everything seem in proportion." A fellow teacher at the Midhurst Grammar School was equally sincere, if more high flown; she was perceptive too: "Her great courage and selflessness shone out in that last act as they did through her life. As I was thinking about her these words came unbidden but compellingly into my mind: 'Put off thy shoes from off thy feet for the place whereon thou standest is holy ground.'" The tributes came twelve thousand miles from New Zealand, from fellow teachers and former pupils at Iona College, some of whom had not seen her for more than forty years, but on whom she had made such an indelible impression:

"Such a marvellous personality."

"Several of the wives of retired farmers here were old Iona girls who have vivid memories of her still."

"We have kept in touch over 40 years which shows what a dynamic person she was."

"She was so special with such a splendid spirit. She was always a giver."

And the one from New Zealand which I treasure most because it was so true:

"I remember her at Iona. She was so full of fun and vitality and always finding ways to help and encourage other people, not least the domestic staff down in the School laundry when someone there was in trouble."

One whom I had asked to sit with Pat from time to time when she was confined to a couch in White Friars at Rochester, told me:

"Thank you for inviting me to sit with Pat all those years ago. They were good times. Pat's kindness and friendship have left a lasting impression."

And that was when she was not well! When she was well she was irresistible:

"We have the fondest memories of Pat and many enjoyable fun-packed meals at White Friars."

This simple sentence from one of her dearest friends, Hilda Sutton, sums them all up: "It is impossible to imagine life without Pat. She was such a super person."

I was indeed the most fortunate of men to have had such a wife.

There were other letters which spoke more specifically of the way in which she coped with her illness.

"Her courage and fortitude during years of pain have been an inspiration to us all." Her childhood companion from Waganui who came to England and stayed to become Permanent Secretary of the Board of Trade, Max Brown, wrote, "What a brave girl she has been, and such a painful long illness for someone so naturally athletic to bear... and knowing that, after all your care for her, Miff has done her very best for you at the last." Another said, "Pat was marvellous the way she stood up to all the pain she had to bear. I shall always remember how welcome she made me and how cheerful she seemed to be about it all."

I wrote to all the Doctors who had been so kind to Pat and who had tried so hard, within their limited knowledge, to ease her pains. Dr. Paul Beech wrote:

"Dear Stanley,

Thank you very much for your letter and the TENS machine (technically transcutaneous electrical nerve stimulation. This was the electrical pulsating machine which had been useful only in the early days but which other patients might find helpful. SH) I deliberately waited until after the inquest before replying. I was disappointed that I was unable to help Pat more than I did. As you may know, David Gruebel Lee (the last surgeon whom we consulted in Farnham. SH) wrote to me and expressed surprise at the degree of her spinal problem and the difficulty of management.

Your wife was determined to be as active as possible, quite rightly. You did everything humanly possible to help her. I tried my best. It is very disheartening that despite everyone's good efforts she had so much continuing pain. Should you or your family have any questions I will be pleased to try to answer them.

Best Wishes, Paul."

The saddest man must have been Jason Brice. He had tried so hard and spent so much time and energy and surgical knowledge in

trying to help Pat, and I know that Pat felt she had let him down. I
had tried to explain to him that his efforts had *not* been in vain, and
that he had given Pat several years of a bearable life, enabled her to
see her grandchildren grow, and that she had been so grateful for his
care and friendship, but I guess he was so upset that he did not reply
to my letter.

When men of the intellectual calibre and spiritual depth of C.S.
Lewis, author of *The Problem of Pain* have been unable to explain it,
it is unlikely that I shall have any particularly valuable things to say
about pain. I hope I have made it clear that I do not hold the medical
profession responsible for being unable to work miracles. It is not
their province to do so, only to assist nature's own healing processes
until such time as nature itself says "Enough is enough. It is time to
go." We know a great deal about the human body, somewhat less
about the mind, but what we know is infinitesimal compared with
what we do not know. More and more doctors are willing to admit
their ignorance, and to allow that they sometimes make mistakes.
What is so sad is the development of the attitude that it is quite wrong
for doctors to make mistakes, with the sometimes implied belief that
they do so through carelessness or culpable ignorance and therefore
the patient has a right to financial recompense through the courts. Of
course there may be the occasional cases where this can be proved and
recompense is indicated, but I deplore the attitude of the person who
said to me after Pat's operation which caused her incontinence, "Why
don't you sue the surgeon? You could get quite a lot of money." The
surgeon had done his utmost with an operation of infinite complexity
and which he had warned us both could be highly dangerous. How
could one possibly accuse him of incompetence or negligence? He
was a friend!

If I have one caveat about medical practice in the control of pain,
it is in the prescription of drugs. As a layman in medical matters I
knew that there had been a vast increase in the number and availability
of drugs for two main purposes - medical and psychological or
narcotic. I had no quarrel with the use of the first category of drugs
in Pat's case - those tablets, injections, medicines which are intended
to fight and overcome living organisms in the human body, or which
were intended to create medical conditions in which safe surgery and
healing can take place. But it was when Pat became "hooked" on
painkillers like Equagesic, and DF118 that I began to have my doubts.

I had been Chaplain to a TB hospital, as I have already recounted, and as much as anyone I had seen how many patients had cause to be grateful to hospital researchers and the drugs industry, for their healing. In this century we have seen the disappearance (or virtual disappearance, though some are coming back) of leprosy, small pox, cholera, polio, TB, some forms of cancer, and we have seen the development of drugs of the corticosteroid variety, which have relieved the pains of millions. Many of these drugs are known to have "side effects" and great advances are being made in the control of those effects. In my view they are part of the divine provision for the relief of pain and the doctor should be regarded as the agent of divine healing, whether he himself acknowledges this or not.

Pat was prescribed two kinds of the drug which I have called narcotic, the type which deadens pain at the point of the pain, and the type which deadens that part of the brain which controls the feelings of pain. In general those are popularly known as "tranquillisers". It is reported that the proportion of people using tranquillisers in Britain is higher than in any other country, including the United States and in the opinion of some medical men their use has reached epidemic proportions. Certain it is that their availability to the young "on the street" has greatly increased the "drug problem" which sees the illness and eventual death of many teenagers every year.

It was easy for the doctors whom Pat saw, whatever their view of the cause of her pains, to reach for their prescription pads and to seek to alleviate her distress with Ativan, or Librium, or Valium, or Mogadon. It did not get to the root of the trouble and the relief was illusory and temporary. This is in no sense a criticism of the doctors. They were trying to relieve symptoms which they could not explain, and it is time we stopped regarding the doctors (as they would themselves ask us) as all-knowing gods. For the relief which they did give we were grateful.

So much of our human pain is caused by our own human folly or ignorance. There is no doubt that Pat's body had been overstrained, her spine asked to bear burdens which it was not designed to bear. It was discovered through various X-rays that she already had a scoliosis, a lateral curvature of the spine, though whether it was congenital or had developed through her physical activities could not be ascertained. Without doubt this was aggravated by her hairdressing and the carrying of the heavy hairdryer up stone staircases in

Victorian buildings. To that extent the pain was explicable and not attributable to an unknown cause or "act of God". It was "her own fault." There is no doubt either that mankind is responsible for many of the carcinomas; for silicosis, asbestosis and many forms of cancer and asthma; and that eczema can often be cured when the "nervous" cause of the disease is discovered and removed. We were not able to discover such causes in Pat's illness. She had no worries, financial or otherwise, she was fully occupied in work that she loved, she had a host of friends. To tell her that it "is all in the mind" was not only cruel, it was false.

It was interesting to me to observe a slight change of attitude in Jason Brice after he had recovered from a major back operation himself. He was leaving a football match in Southampton when he slipped and fell, injuring his back. For months, even after his operation, he was in acute pain, and his sympathy for his patient in similar case became more noticeable! How human we all are. It is a strange fact of human nature that when we ourselves are fit and well we tend to be lacking in sympathy to those who are apparently fit but are making "heavy weather" of life. We suspect, with the young lady of Deal in my Limerick at the head of this chapter that, "their pain isn't real," and are tempted to tell them, "Pull yourself together!"

Pain is real. In spite of the assertions of Mrs. Eddy the founder of Christian Science, that matter, pain, evil and death do not exist ("A boil simply manifests through inflammation and swelling, a belief in pain, and this pain is called a boil.") those who are in pain not only "dislike what they fancy they feel", they know that their whole personality is affected by it. The millions who suffer from back pain are not suffering illusions. Pain is a large part of the experience of all animal creation. Prehistoric animals, whose skeletons have been found with diseased bones, growths and swellings, were clearly subject to pain and disease. St. Paul wrote about this to the Romans, "it is plain to anyone with eyes to see that at the present time all created life groans in a sort of universal travail. It is plain too, that we who have a foretaste of the Spirit are in a state of painful tension, while we wait for that redemption of our bodies which will mean that at last we have realised our full sonship in Him." As usual Paul is combining the physical and the spiritual in his metaphors as he tries to tell his readers that mankind's hopes and aspirations will be one day fulfilled in the triumph of Christ. Christians believe that no pain is borne in vain, that all the pains of men have an eventual end..." no more mourning, no more crying, no more pain, no more death."

It is not easy for a priest to see any purpose or divine goal or reason in Pat's twelve years of pain. It is not easy to understand why all the prayers which had been offered did not bring any *physical* healing, though where those prayers were for me, there was an undoubted strengthening of my own capacity to carry on and survive. It is difficult to see any part in a "vast eternal plan", or to accept that "faith" would bring us through. In a case of organic disease or injury I had always taught that faith is best expressed in a willingness to use methods of healing which God has revealed to the medical profession, using that term in its widest sense, embracing "alternatives" where they had proved effective. Along with faith, however it is to be defined, there had to be hope and love. For twelve years we had experienced both of those cardinal virtues. Hope was kept alive in the various ways I have recalled, and we were surrounded always by love. Many of us who discussed it were almost primitive (basically human?) in our questioning: "Why should someone who had taken up a totally unselfish way of life to assist her fellow human beings, be punished in this way?" It was almost a reversal of "shall we do evil that good may come" - "why has evil come out of good?" To all of these questions there is no adequate or satisfying answer. We cannot know. We are thrown back upon that other element of faith which our critics call "pie in the sky when you die" - a conviction that "one day" all will be revealed, that whereas we now see in a mirror obscured, then we shall see plainly, face to face. I think it was, all unconsciously perhaps, because of this conviction, that Pat was not afraid to die.

CHAPTER 16

ENVOI

"'Envoy or Envoi'. A brief concluding stanza.
A postscript in other forms of verse or prose."
Collins New Concise Dictionary.

"For I am declin'd into the vale of years."
Shakespeare. Othello.

Shakespeare usually had a word for it. He did not say "vale of
tears", but of "years". This may not be a brief postscript, but, in any
self-revelation such as this, some final word is necessary. So much of
what has been written in the last part of these memories concerns Pat,
that I now have to write of myself, living alone, without her. Of
course that isn't true. She was so much part of my life from 1943
onwards that I am not me without her, even now. This house is full
of her personality. A wooden shield beating the arms of her school at
Midhurst hangs in the front hall below the arms of St. Edmund Hall,
Oxford, one of the prime influences of my own life. The furnishings
and the carpets and all else, we chose together. The curtains, all
twenty-six of them, she made with her own hands. On the
mantelpiece is a small snap in fading black and white from our
honeymoon, which shows a beaming young couple sitting on a
Cornish wall at the farmhouse at Morvah, near Pendeen, forgetting
the miseries of a wartime honeymoon, obviously taken on the only
fine day of the fortnight. Pat is in the regulation grey jersey of her
PE College and the regulation pleated grey skirt of that uniform. She
is hugging me tightly, with me in my regulation uniform of the
thirties, sports jacket and grey flannels. We look so happy, and it
didn't matter that these were almost the only clothes we had, that the
day before, Pat had walked from the Vicarage to the Church, to the
surprise of the waiting crowds, in a bright flowered dress and straw
hat, with my sister Enid as her bridesmaid in her more sombre dress,
to join the bridegroom in his crumpled (but sponged) four year old

suit, at the chancel steps. We still have the one official photo that was taken outside the Church to prove it.

There are other photographs, always of a smiling woman whom you would love to meet. One in her cook's hat, and overall, with spoon and mixing bowl, taken outside the Vicarage at Shottermill to show that she had passed her Domestic Science Diploma at a time when demonstrating jumps over a box and a buck had become too much for the gym mistress in her forties. The small "studio portrait" on the other side is lovely too, but it does not convey the natural beauty of the amateur snaps. There is the soft toy given to Pat by Mimi, then an affectionate four year old grandchild, with the words "This bear loves you" across his chest. Pat was at a low ebb when she was given that bear and it did help. There is even the musical box in the shape of a Swiss chalet brought back from one childhood holiday by Jill, or was it Peter? It is so long ago. Other snaps crowd the shelves and mantelpieces - grand-children, friends, parties in the garden, families playing clock golf on the lawn; other friends sitting on the patio steps, interiors of Christmas meals and parties, and sadly, as the years went by, the smile, though real, is more forced, as if the pain could hardly be pushed into the background of the mind. The cases of music tapes are still here with their memories of hours spent, in day and in night, using music as the only bearable therapy.

I am indeed "declined into a vale of years," years of memories. "We have been happy, in spite of everything, haven't we?" Pat would constantly ask me for this reassurance, in her last six months of life. "Oh, my dear love, we have, we have!" There was no other answer. In her last letter she had written, "I do know it will be lonely often," and it is, but not unbearably so. As I have remarked, Pat and I were such different characters. I am by nature a loner, and have been since the childhood I described. To one who, by the nature of his profession has spent his days and months and years, mornings, afternoons and evenings, in the company of others, visiting them, comforting them, marrying and burying them, in organising conferences, visiting schools and doing with others all the things that clergy have to do, a time apart alone is no great burden. Nor am I ashamed to admit that to live alone is now a relief, knowing that I no longer have to share Pat's suffering, watch her face agonise with pain, get up five times in the night for treatment of her back, to have to answer the constant question of her last years: "What shall we do today?" What *was* there to do? To be endlessly attempting to think of some activity which would fill a morning or an afternoon was a burdensome thing, and was part of the pain that I had to bear with the appearance of normality and patience when I felt like screaming, "We have done it all!" It was the fact that this vital, energetic and quick spirited person could no longer walk more than a few yards, that made me feel helpless and inadequate to help her. Her friends and mine have been very understanding. They know that in feeling a sense of relief that "it is all over". I am not being disloyal to Pat. They know that it is a very human reaction to long years of grief at another's misery which I could only look upon with impotence.

Loneliness is the lot of those who have no faith, no friends, no inner resources, no loving family, no hobby, no creative activity to pursue. I am so fortunate that my days are full, and that at seventy-seven years old parishes still want me to conduct services for them, that I can still read and write. Reading all the books I have wanted to read but haven't had the time to read, is a happy occupation. I have friends and family, and a lovely coast along which to walk daily. Writing these memories has in itself been a "remedial treatment" for loneliness. I have come also to realise more deeply what are the important things in life and religion. I become more and more impatient and frustrated with the trivial things that seem to occupy the minds of the so-called "Church Leaders." I become baffled that the Church newspapers have to carry so much copy about the bickering between the various sections of the Anglican Church, when the condemnation is clear in the correspondence which Paul had with the Corinthian Church - "How dare you say, I belong to Paul, or I belong to Apollos? What is Paul, what is Apollos? After all, they are servants. Apollos and I did the planting. It is God who made things grow!" I do not find the word "Churchmanship" in the New Testament Gospels. Nor do I find a pre-occupation with material things and with money or even with the Ministry. Rather the opposite. Perhaps an old man can say things about these matters which a young man cannot say to his congregation. I wish to be known as a Christian, not as an Anglican, not even as an "Evangelical Catholic", though I acknowledge with deep gratitude my debt to the Church into which I was born by baptism and which I still seek to serve. But I also owe a debt to many writers of other Churches, Methodist, Roman Catholic, Scottish Presbyterian, German,

American and to all those clergy and laity whom I have known in my various parishes and in the dioceses. I have been critical of those who have sought to educate me formally, but I must thank them for their patience and admit that I have undergone, not always willingly, a lifetime of learning from them and from others.

How much longer I have to stay on this earth and seek to help and serve others, I cannot know. The older I get the simpler becomes my faith. Even doggerel verses which I should have scorned in my more academic life mean much to me now. One such was sent to me by a fervent Baptist member of Pat's staff at Walderslade. She was a teacher of typewriting and office practice and had a terrible time with the girls, who despised her teaching methods and her religion. Pat had helped her and had made life bearable for her. I was pleased to receive it, because the same words had been framed as a picture on the wall of the bedroom where I slept in the house of a friend for several months before going to theological college, in January, 1940, and for years I had been trying to find a copy to give to simple folk who wanted simple help when they were passing through difficult times.

WHAT GOD HATH PROMISED

God hath not promised skies always blue,
flower-strewn pathways all our lives through:
God hath not promised sun without rain,
Joy without sorrow, peace without pain.
But God hath promised strength for the day,
rest from the labour, light for the way,
grace for the trials, help from above,
unfailing sympathy, undying love.

Simple doggerel, yes: even simpler theology, but does it matter if one believes it to be true? I believe it. Without such simple faith I could not have survived the years of trial.

But most of what I believe and teach I owe to the life I lived with Pat, who fifty years ago wrote to me that she wanted "a practical religion". In all those years I did not hear her utter a critical or cruel word, not even against those who had been critical and cruel towards her. In all those years never did she abandon a friend, or hesitate to put herself out for others. In one letter I have quoted she called herself "selfish". If there were times (with me, with no one else) when she could have been called "self-regarding" it was her illness alone that made her so, and who would not be in such circumstances? If I am slowly learning to be unselfish I learned it from her. If I am slowly learning what it means to be a friend to another human being, it was from her that I learned it, for not only did she have a "genius for enjoyment", but she had a genius for friendship. Of course she had her human faults and weaknesses, but, without making a formal show of her religion, she demonstrated all the gifts of the Spirit, love, joy, peace, patience, kindness, goodness, faithfulness, gentleness, self-control. Perhaps I am learning some of them now too.

In a bookshop the other day I came across another piece of writing which has helped me and which I hope to be able to live up to in my final years, however many they are:

> I live alone, dear Lord,
> Stay by my side.
> In all my daily needs,
> Be Thou my guide
> Grant me good health,
> For that indeed I pray
> To carry on my work
> From day to day.
> Keep pure my mind,
> My thoughts, my every deed.
> Let me be kind, unselfish
> In my neighbour's need.
> Spare me from fire, from flood,
> Malicious tongues,
> From thieves, from fear,
> And evil ones.
> If sickness or accident befall,
> Then humbly, Lord, I pray,
> Hear Thou my call.
> And when I'm feeling low,
> Or in despair,
> Lift up my heart
> And help me in my prayer.

I live alone dear Lord,
Yet have no fear
Because I feel Your presence
Ever near. Amen.

It would be praising it too much even to call it "poetry", but it speaks to the human condition, as many more literary prayers do not. Those who live alone need above all to know that someone cares, cares enough to know that something may be amiss if no light is seen, no milk taken in. Electronic and telephonic communication is now available for those who live on their own, but because we are spiritual, as well as material, beings, we need something more; we need the divine assurance that is simply defined in that prayer.

In a Maori quarter of a town in New Zealand where the first Christian missionaries had come, through the CMS from America, there is a marble headstone to one of the first women Maori converts in the mid-nineteenth century. She was no doubt illiterate, no doubt the mother of a large family of children and grand-children. She probably had little time for prayer or "Church work". I treasure the photograph I took of it. At first reading it is simple enough. It is a quotation from Mark 14:8. Look at it again and see how profound it is. It was true of Pat. I hope it will be true of me (gender changed!).

ERIHAPATA TE WHERO
Age 83 years
SHE DID WHAT SHE COULD

I did what I could with the talents God gave me. Have I come to any conclusions at the close of a long Ministry? Yes. I tried to put them in brief form in a sermon preached on the day of the Golden Jubilee or my ordination as Deacon, on June 30th 1991. To this long story I have nothing more to add. As is appropriate it is only an appendix, but it ends my story - so far.

APPENDIX

A Typical Lent Programme

ST. STEPHEN'S CHURCH
SHOTTERMILL
Lent and Easter 1962

You are invited to take part in the worship of your Parish Church this
Lent. Lent means "springtime" a time for growth and these services
and addresses have been arranged to help you and your family to grow
in the knowledge of God. A warm welcome always awaits you at St.
Stephen's.

ASH WEDNESDAY, March 7th.
        The first day of Lent
        Holy Communion 7, 8, and 10.30 a.m.
        Mattins and Litany 7.30 a.m.
        Children's Service 9 a.m.
        Evensong and Address 8 p.m.

PALM SUNDAY, April 15th.
        Palms will be distributed at 8 and 11 - 10 a.m.

HOLY WEEK, April 15th to 22nd.
        Holy Communion: Monday, Tuesday, Wednesday, 8 a.m.
            Maundy Thursday 8 and 10.30 a.m.
        Devotional Service each evening at 8 p.m.
        Thursdays service will be in preparation for Easter
Communion.

GOOD FRIDAY, April 20th.
        Mattins Litany and Ante-Communion 8.45 a.m.
        Family Service 10.30 a.m.
        "The Three Hours Devotion" 12 - 3 p.m.
            Conductor: The Rev. A. W. Mills, Vicar of Thursley.
        Stainer's "Crucifixion" at Haslemere Parish Church, at 8
p.m.

(Combined Choirs)

EASTER DAY, April 22nd.
　　Holy Communion 7 and 8 a.m.
　　Family Service 10.30 a.m.　Address 11.10 a.m.
　　SUNG EUCHARIST 11.25 a.m.
　　Festal Evensong and Procession 6.30 p.m.　Holy Communion
　　7.30 p.m.
　　("And note that every parishioner shall communicate at least
　　three times a year of which Easter to be one" - The Prayer
　　Book.)

WEDNESDAY EVENINGS at 8 p.m. from March 14th.
　　Devotional Service: "The Rejection of Jesus"
　　March 14th.　　"Cleansing our Temple"
　　　　21st.　　"To Jesus by Night"
　　　　28th.　　"Apathy at Bethesda"
　　April 4th.　　"The Fickleness of Crowds"
　　　　11th.　　"The Hatreds of Governments"

SUNDAY MORNINGS at 11.10 a.m. (the address comes at the end
of the Family Service and at the beginning of the Sung Eucharist.
Worshippers may enter the Church at 11.05 a.m.)

　　　　"Lessons from the Prophets"

　　March 11th.　Job - suffering.
　　　　18th.　Jonah - why be a missionary?
　　　　25th.　PARISH COMMUNION 9 a.m.
　　　　　　Jeremiah - living your faith.

　　April 1st.　MOTHERING SUNDAY
　　　　8th.　Isaiah - God and the Nation.
　　　　15th.　Isaiah (2) - man needs a Saviour.

SUNDAY EVENINGS at 6.30 p.m.

　　　　"What Jesus Longs To See"

March 11th.	In little children.
18th.	In boys and girls.
25th.	In lovers.
April 1st.	"Tongues of Fire Service No. 6"
8th.	In single folk.
15th.	In married people.
22nd.	In us all.

Friday Evenings at 8 p.m.
UNITED SERVICES and "ANY QUESTIONS"
Questions should be sent as soon as possible to the Vicar or any of the Clergy and Ministers

March 16th.	St. Christopher's Church.
23rd.	The Congregational Church.
30th.	St. Stephen's Shottermill.
April 6th.	At 7.30 p.m. in St. Christopher's Hall. Bible Society Evening with a "Monoplay" by Grace Benton.
April 13th.	The Methodist Church.
20th.	GOOD FRIDAY Stainer's "CRUCIFIXION" at St. Bartholomew's Church, with the combined choirs.

MOTHERING SUNDAY, April Ist.
The Family Service will be at 10.30 a.m. and it is hoped that all families will make a special effort to come to their Mother Church on that morning.

TUESDAY EVENINGS at 6 p.m.
"Mountaineers" - a series of special services for children from 7 to 14, followed by games etc. in the Church Room.

WEEKDAY COMMUNION. Wednesday at 8 and Fridays at 10.30 a.m.

(The Tuesday intercessions will be omitted during Lent.)

You and Your Children
(1959)

A Third Open Letter to all Parents in Shottermill
(the first two were sent in 1956 and 1957)

Dear Parents,

What are your reactions when you read headlines such as these:

"Girl of 12 picked up in Park Lane."
"Five boys questioned in murdered policeman case."
"Teenage riots in London streets."
"Youths held in 'dope' investigation."
"Juvenile Courts crowded."
"No room in Borstal institutions."
"Mother says, 'I go in fear of my life.' Attacked by son."

Do you say, "Well of course it couldn't happen in my family."? But it **does** happen in some families - and no doubt those parents thought it couldn't happen to them. It **could** happen to your children even in this quiet country parish.

Am I trying to scare you? By no means. Though we cannot escape the terrible facts about many young people to-day, the large majority will not get into trouble with the police, and will not go around flashing "flickknives". They will grow up into decent citizens, obeying the law of the land and not doing anyone any harm.

But is that all you want for your children? Are you content that they should grow up ignorant of the Christian faith? For make no mistake, it is because girls grow up without any guidance for living that they got picked up in Park Lane. It is because boys are no longer taught the commandment "Thou shalt not steal" that so many of them are caught thieving.

It seems that to-day very many parents just do not care. They do not know where their children are at night, they are constantly telling me that they have lost control of their teenage children, that they are horrified at their children's language, and behaviour. I am not surprised. In the present prosperous state of society we have begun to think that material things are all that matter. When a nation gets into that state, and history is full of tragic examples, it is a doomed nation.

Six years ago we had built up a Children's Church and Sunday School of 120 children in this parish. To-day, in every other department of Church life we have made great progress, but we who are concerned with the spiritual training of the children cannot conceal our apprehension at the fact that to-day only about half that number are receiving any religious instruction outside school hours.

Magistrates and judges, probation officers and heads of approved schools all testify that there is an undoubted connection between the frightening increase in juvenile crime and the lack of religious teaching in Church and Sunday School. We know some of the reasons for the nationwide decline in Sunday School attendance - the possession of a motor-car, widespread Sunday excursions, TV, etc., have all helped to draw children away from Church. But most of all it is because parents themselves have ceased to care.

Is that true of you? Do **you** really care that your child shall grow up knowing what is right and what is wrong? Do you want him to be Christian?

Christian leaders of all denominations are deeply concerned about the growing generation - so are we in this parish. But the Church can do nothing without the parents' co-operation, and it cannot teach spiritual truths to your children if they never come.

The Church building is there - the teachers are there, the time is arranged to suit your convenience - our great desire to help you and your children is there - we want nothing more than to serve Christ's whole family.

If your children were baptised in the Church of England it is your solemn duty to see that they are taught the Christian faith. If you do not, your responsibility before God is very grave indeed. **(But it's not much good if you do nothing about it yourself! We want you with your children.)**

If you do not belong to the Church of England this is **not** an attempt to draw you away from your own Church. If you have no children of your own, at least pray for us in our work with the children.

We are not concerned primarily with numbers or with counting heads - we are concerned to see that our Lord's command to bring the children to Him is obeyed, we are concerned to remind you of the terrible warning He gives to those who cause the little ones to stumble, either by wrong teaching or by preventing them from being taught. Lent is soon beginning. Will you do something about this absolutely vital matter by encouraging your children to take part in something suitable to their age this Lent. A list of what goes on at St. Stephen's is on the back page of this letter.

God bless you and your families, help you to bring up your children as God's children. That is the sincere prayer of

Your friend and Vicar,
STANLEY HOFFMAN.

Shottermill Vicarage,
Haslemere.
February, 1959.

FOR YOUR CHILDREN (of all ages)

1. Sunday School. Every Sunday in the Church Room at 10.30 a.m. Children from Woolmer Hill Estate are conveyed and taken back by car. Aged 3-4 onwards.

2 . Children's Church. Held in Church every Sunday at 10 a.m. for 7-8 years and upwards. These have graded instruction and then take part with adults in the first part of Morning Service at 10.30 a.m.

3. Young Pilgrims. Every Tuesday evening from 6-7.15 p.m. For 7-8's upwards. A period of games, stories, instruction, handiwork, simple drama, etc., which supplements what they learn on Sundays, and is greatly enjoyed by the many who come. In the Church Room.

4. Junior Fellowship. Tuesday evenings from 7.15 p.m. For Teenagers. A Youth Club with the usual programme. In the Church Room.

5. The Church Choir. Boys and girls with useful voices from 8 years and upwards. Practices are on Wednesday evenings, 6.15 p.m. for the younger ones, 6.45 p.m. for the older ones. There is nothing quite like membership of a Church Choir for training in the Christian life.

6. Confirmation Classes take place regularly each year for those over 12. (For details contact the Vicar or Deaconess.)

7. A Youth Service is held on the first Sunday of the month at 6.30 p.m. specially to help young people.

Why not encourage your children to come to one or more of these this week? A great welcome awaits them.

The Making of a Deaconess

By the Rev. Stanley Hoffman, MA

Sermon preached on October 11th, 1964, at the Ordination of Miss Mary Dee as Deaconess by the Bishop of Guildford in St. Stephen's Church, Shottermill, Surrey.

Philippians 2:6-8.

St. Paul says of Jesus "... he did not think to snatch at equality with God, but made himself nothing, assuming the nature of a slave. Bearing the human likeness, revealed in human shape he humbled himself and in obedience accepted even death - death on a cross."

A Hindu woman once said to a Christian missionary: "Your Bible must have been written by a woman." "Why?" asked the puzzled missionary. "Because it says so many kind things for women. Our pundits never refer to us but in reproach."

The second part of that statement is, I hope, no longer true in Modern India, but it is not so hard to see the reason behind the idea in the first half. It is one of the glories of our Christian faith that it "says so many kind things about women," that it gives them a high place and believes they have a high vocation. The Gospel record shows many women enjoying the closest friendship with our Lord, and not only did he use them as instruments of his good news as God had used a woman to be the instrument of redemption by being the Mother of the Saviour, but also he was ever ready to be seen with and to help, those women whom society in his day had abandoned or ostracised.

The women of the early Church

In the story of the growth of the early Church women have a place of honour. There was Phoebe (Romans 16:1) whom St. Paul commends as "a good friend to many, including myself." She held office as a deacon in the Church at Cenchreæ, where her work, like that of the men deacons, was primarily for the social and bodily needs of the Christian community. There was Priscilla (mentioned three times in the Acts and three times in the epistles, always in association with her husband, Aquila), who helped to teach the Christian faith to Apollos. There were Euodia and Syntyche (Phil. 4:2), who were doing work similar to Phoebe's in the Philippian Church, though they did not agree very well! There were Tryphena and Tryphosa (Romans 16:12) (heavenly twins!), there was Julia and the sister of Nereus (Romans 16). There was Dorcas the needlewoman (Acts 9), who filled her days with "acts of charity and kindness," and there was Rufus' mother, whom Paul "called mother, too" - l like that touch in Paul, whom we tend to think of as rather a woman-hater - even he needed mothering!

The list of the faithful women of the New Testament is too long to give fully, but bearing in mind the state of seclusion and subjection which was the normal lot of the women of the first century, it is clear that the Church was determined to give practical expression to the truth that "... there is no such thing as Jew and Greek, slave and freeman, male and female; for you are all one person in Christ Jesus." (Gal. 3:38).

We know that the office of a Deaconess was recognised in the early Church. It is also spoken of in the writings of the pagan consul, Pliny, to the Roman Emperor, Trajan, early in the second century. There were many Deaconesses, too, in the Eastern Church, where the separation and isolation of women made it necessary for them to be ministered to by their own sex, and they acted in every way as clergy except that they exercised none of the specific functions of the priesthood. As the centuries passed the Deaconess order became merged in the religious orders of nuns and it is only in the last hundred years or so that the ministry of women has come out of the convent into the world.

The emancipation of women
This was part of a greater movement - the movement towards the complete liberation of women which we associate with the names of the great ones - with Florence Nightingale, who laid the foundation of nursing; with Josephine Butler, who found a new approach to the problem of the victims of immorality; Eglantyne Jebb, who worked for the unwanted children; Sophia Jex-Blake, who battled for the right of women to enter the medical profession; Elizabeth Wordsworth, first principal of Lady Margaret Hall, Oxford, who contended for a

woman's right to be educated on an equality with men. One hundred and two years ago the Deaconess Order was revived when the Bishop of London set apart Elizabeth Ferrard by the laying on of hands for the work of a Deaconess. The name of Elizabeth Ferrard should be known to all who have the privilege of having a Deaconess working among then, for she was one of the first to recognise the need in the Church for women who would wholly dedicate their lives to the service of God and their fellows, not in a convent, but in a parish, working alongside the parish priest. Central authority in the Church is always slow to move, and the Church's own Parliament, the Convocations, did not canonically recognise the Order until 1923 (Convocation of Canterbury) and 1925 (Convocation of York).

Servant of the servants of God

This is a tiny part of the background of what we are doing today. You, Deaconess Mary, by the laying on of hands of the Bishop, have entered into a great and worthy inheritance reaching back into apostolic times. It is not a heritage of position or pride of place, rather of lowly service in which you are to be a follower of the Master servant himself. You, like the parish priest, like the Bishop, are to be in the ancient phrase (first used of himself by Gregory the Great, who was Pope from 590-604) "servus, servorum Dei...", "servant of the servants of God." Your ministry has been given to you by God. Your people, the people of this parish, have been given to you by God, and you are their servant because you are a follower of the Christ whom St. Paul tells us in my text, "assumed the nature of a slave. He did not snatch at equality with God, but bearing our likeness he humbled himself and was obedient..." The Deaconess, like the Deacon, like the Priest, like the Bishop, must pattern her life upon the example of Christ the humble servant of man. This patterning is, of course, quite impossible unless we ministers submit ourselves wholly to the ruling will of God.

Humility, Obedience - and Joy

Humility is not a natural virtue. It is a divine gift. Pray for it. Obedience is not a natural attitude, it is a divine grace. Pray for it. There are many things in parish life to make us think we are more important than we are - the position we hold in the Church and in local society, the authority which we undoubtedly wield over our people. Self-importance, desire for praise, undue regard for the high opinions of our people, these are the Devil's temptations to those who forget that they are called to be humble servants of God and his people. Humility and obedience, these are the Christ-like virtues we must have. In the Office of Deaconess you have already accepted the obligation of obedience to your Bishop, to your Vicar, in so far as he directs you in your work. Much more, your obedience is to God and this will involve for you the pains and tensions which all who are in any kind of ministry know very well. Because the obedience of Christ whom we follow, was an obedience unto death - even the death on the Cross, the servant of the servants of God will not expect ease or comfort or safety, she will not expect to grow rich, she will not even look for the rewards that the world offers, she may at times be lonely, at times sad and frustrated. Though this may seem a sombre picture that I paint for you, you already know that it is only half the truth. As a parish worker you have already experienced the great joy that lies within the ministry of service. It was so with Jesus too - "who for the sake of the joy that lay ahead of him endured the Cross, making light of its disgrace" (Hebrews 12:2). Christian joy springs not from external circumstance, but from your own firm interior faith, from the deep conviction that God guides you, God comforts you, God loves you. We shall pray for you today that you may have intense joy in your ministry as a Deaconess. You are known among us as a happy person and we pray that your happiness may be deepened in your future work for God and his people.

The responsibilities of the parish
     This is a great day for Mary, but it is also a great day for this parish. No minister, be he deacon or priest or Bishop, be she parish worker or Deaconess, can truly serve the servants of God, unless they desire to be served and are ready to be served. How then must a parish receive its Deaconess?
     First, by recognising what has been done here this morning. Deaconess Mary has dedicated herself to a life-long service in the Church of God. By the laying on of hands she has been given the Holy Spirit's grace and strength to perform that service, but because we are fellow workers with the Holy Spirit of God, the help that the members of a congregation can give to her in that life-long dedication is immeasurable. You have been wonderful in the welcome and love

and friendship that you have extended to all our parish workers - I beg you to ensure that this continues.

Second, I would urge that the parish and congregation recognise the work of a Deaconess as primarily spiritual. This does not mean that Deaconess Mary is now so exalted a person that she cannot be expected to iron a surplice or help with a stall at the Summer Fête any more. It does not mean that in future someone else must be found who will play rounders with the Young Pilgrims. But it does mean that you will give her time for her prayers and her spiritual life, her reading and her meditation. It does mean that you will be ready and anxious to listen to her as she speaks to you in your homes, in meetings, or in Church, of the things of God. For her primary task is to save souls and all the manifold activities of her life must be directed to this end. One of the problems of the pastoral life is persuading our people that our ministry to them is a whole ministry - to body, mind and soul. Body and mind, it seems, are easier to minister to than the soul. So do not be afraid to use your Deaconess, to bring to her your spiritual problems, and do not be scared if in her visiting she does speak to you of the things of God rather than of the weather - for this is what you really want, too, isn't it?

Third, I would ask you sincerely to pray for your new Deaconess. This is not just a customary pulpit appeal. Though Mary has this day been given additional grace for her work, the paradox is that she will need even more your help and prayers. The laity of the Church can help their ministers in so many ways, not least in daily prayer for them. As you see us go about our work, pray for us. Isn't it true that only as we pray earnestly and regularly for people do we learn to honour and love them?

You have heard in the Bishop's charge what are the duties of a Deaconess - to minister in temporal as well as spiritual things, to instruct and to teach, to assist the minister of the parish, to help and to advise and to pray, to visit, and perform the many other functions of her office. Mary has said that she will, with God's help, do all these things.

I now ask you, people of this parish and congregation, if you will help her - by your prayers, by your Christian love, by your friendship, by your help and co-operation. I shall say to you, "Will you help her to learn and to do all these things?" - Will you respond, if you are sincerely determined - "I will, the Lord being my helper."

Will you help her to learn and to do all these things?
I will, the Lord being my helper. Amen.

(Note: I have included this *thirty year old* sermon among my appendices to demonstrate

(a) that Women's ministry was recognised and accepted as a true ministry over a generation ago.

(b) that in the time scale of eternity God has taken only a short while to show His Church that in Christ there *must be* no male or female, bond or free.

Perhaps in another generation we shall be amazed that it has taken (in our own human scale) so *long* for us to see where God is trying to lead us!)

FAREWELL TO A WAIF AND STRAY

Address at funeral of Deaconess Jane Jefferies, 12.2.91.
Manormead Chapel

Have you ever wondered what it must be like to be an unwanted child? an orphan, a waif as we used to call them?

To have no parents to love and to care for you...

To have no grandparents to go and complain to when your own parents become intolerable... no one of your own to tuck you up in bed...

To have no brothers and sisters to play with and quarrel with, to visit and holiday with when you are grown up and they are married...

No cousins, no nieces, no nephews...

To have no one to send you presents at Christmas and on your birthday...?

Selina Jane Jefferies was one such - how she hated that name, Selina - and to know that explains much about her - her loneliness, her withdrawnness as she got old and frail, her occasional sharpness and sadness. It also explains the character of her dedication and ministry over many years. It *doesn't* explain the miracle of God that made that little waif into a Deaconess in the Church of God.

Many of you will only have known her as a shrunken little old lady, almost cowering from life in a huge armchair, as the one who tried to escape into the darkness when the storm clouds gathered. I don't know the origin of that fear. It probably goes back to some event in her childhood, or some terrifying experience of bombing when she was ministering in a south London parish.

But she was not always like that. I was her Vicar and colleague for 5½ years. The one who had never had a home of her own until she retired was a welcome member of my family, living at the Vicarage, and sharing much of our life. My children loved her because she was full of fun and never judgemental when they spoke or behaved badly - as Vicarage children often do. They called her Deaky and she loved it.

She was trained for the ministry as a Greylady in the Southwark diocese - and they trained them well in those days - in prayer and study and parish work, in visiting and the conduct of services; in Sunday School work and youth work. She did all that exceptionally well, and I know that there are many who are grateful to God for this little waif who became a bighearted friend and counsellor of old and young.

So my memories are not of the ageing and aged Jane. They are of the singlehearted Deaconess on her moped, driving around the parish with her grey veil flying in the wind; they are of the Friday afternoons in Holy Cross hospital when between us we would visit over a hundred people. The sad old dears in the geriatric ward loved her.

My memories are of her training Sunday School teachers to cope with the more than one hundred children we had in the Church room each Sunday morning. They are memories of her in the Youth Club, playing table tennis with those rather rough teenagers - they loved her too. My memories are of her devotion in Church as we said the daily offices and taking a full part in Sunday services, reading lessons and prayers, giving well thought-out addresses from time to time - that was a rare thing more than thirty years ago. So much more I could tell you as I remember her with affection. When she retired she did not give up her work with people, and I know that she was welcomed for her ministry in Wonersh and at Holy Trinity Guildford.

Life was never easy for the one who had no family, but obstacles are made to be overcome and Jane overcome them gloriously. I give thanks for the unknown person perhaps in the orphanage, who set her feet on the Christian path of service to God and her neighbour. Her faith was simple and her love greater than her body. That is why I read the lesson from St. John, and not the complicated theological speculations of St. Paul. In her Father's house are many resting places - she has been welcomed there. The resurrection faith overcomes our doubts and our hesitations. She knows now what she always taught, that Christ is the way, the truth and the life. We thank God for her and rejoice in the hope of her resurrection into a life where she will have a real family.

UKC DEGREE CONGREGATION
Canterbury Cathedral. 27.11.82

Honourable Chancellor... Ladies and Gentlemen,

I have been given six minutes.

Coming as you do, Chancellor, from north of the Border, you will appreciate that for any Minister to be confined to six minutes is nothing but pain and grief.

You will also know that no address delivered in the Kirk is worth paying attention to unless it has six points at least, well documented and illustrated.

However, being a man under authority I will attempt to restrain myself to six minutes, and to no more than two points. Was it also a man from north of the border who told his theological students:

> "Tell them what you are going to say,
> Say it.
> Tell them what you have said."

Good maxims I think, for clergymen, politicians, academics and teachers. So...

I am going to say "Thank You"

I am going to say "Fight on."

I say first, "Thank you" on behalf of *Dr*. Lawton, *Master* Polmear and myself, to the Senate and Council of the University of Kent at Canterbury, for the honour we have received, to Professor Simpson, and to you, Chancellor, for so graciously conferring the Degrees.

It was always a pleasure to be associated in matters of Education with *Alastair Lawton*, one of the most knowledgeable skilful and efficient Chairmen and education specialists I have known. It is of course known to all men that the Latin word Doctor means teacher! and Teacher Lawton has enlightened many people in many things, not least in how to be firm, and in how to oppose you without being rude.

I was pleased also to serve for several years with *Nicholas Polmear* on the Governing Body of Christ Church College and its Committees. He was for many years a Master of the Arts - of dealing with City and County Councils, managing and governing bodies and those hard-working and often misunderstood folk, the teachers. He wears his years lightly but none is listened to more keenly, for the voice of his experience carries immense weight.

We shall wear our hoods with pride but without presumption. As a preacher I shall perhaps wear mine more frequently than my colleagues. Indeed, I shall wear it tomorrow, putting aside that other, red, hood from a certain ancient city in the Isis valley. I shall be proud tomorrow to display it in the Chapel Royal of St. James' Palace, no less.

So the first thing I say is "Thank you!"

The *second* thing I would say, as a retired and ageing Director of Education who fought many battles in 15 years of traumatic and often ruthless educational upheaval, is "Fight On"! In those 15 years almost every school and college was at one time under threat of either radical change or closure. It even seemed that a college's own educational philosophy must be transmuted into something entirely different at the whim of the bureaucrats in London. I am delighted to have played a small part along with Alastair Lawton, Nicholas Polmear and many others - not least *Geoffrey Templeman* - in the fight for the survival, as an independent Church College, of Christ Church. Tribute must also be paid to those who carried on a similar but even more difficult fight for Nonington College.

Such battles can clearly be won if the cause is just and the territory worth defending.

Every part of the educational system is under stresses and strains which it has never had to bear hitherto. Hundreds of graduates will not find jobs commensurate with their abilities and training. The names of Aston and La Salle remind us that the end of the struggle is not yet.

Here in Kent *David* with his five small stones will have to fight and overcome the Goliath of the University Grants Committee and all other Philistines; Michael and all his angels must continue the struggles against the devil and all his angels (I will not identify!) and at Nonington the watchword must be "On, *Stanley* On" to maintain and develop what is a unique institution in its own field.

But no school, college or university is worth saving if it does not serve society and promote the high standards and inspiration which lead men and women to attain the unattainable goals.

To the university and its associated colleges the message must be - *Fight on*, for the highest standards of academic excellence, morality and public service. Fight on for the maximum of independence of government and bureaucracy. Struggle to be what a much respected Assistant Education Officer in this County, Bill Moore, speaking of Church Schools, called "Islands of divergence and varied freedom". I like that - UKC Christ Church and Nonington - "three islands of divergence and varied freedom."

What have I said? I have said "Thank your" on behalf of us all. I have said to you all: "Fight on."

And that, I hope, is about six minutes!

S.H. HOFFMAN

(Note: Jo Grimond, later Lord Grimond of Firth, was the Chancellor.

David (Ingram) was the Vice-Chancellor.

Michael (Berry) was Principal of Christ Church College.

Stanley (Beaumont) was Principal of Nonington College.

Alastair Lawton was given an Honorary Doctorate.

Nicholas Polmear was given an Honorary Masters Degree.

Geoffrey Templeman had been Vice-Chancellor.)

Padstow. Pentecost 6. June 30th, 1991
Fifty Years On. (A Sermon in reminiscent mood)

Last week I received the annual news letter from the theological college which sent me out into the world to be an ordained minister fifty years ago today. This is part of what it said:

"Currently there are fewer people training for Ordination in the Church of England than ever before. At least eighty places in the colleges have not been taken up... numbers of candidates for ordination have been dropping for the past four years and there is no sign of any change in this pattern. If this decline in the number of ordination candidates continues it will have very serious consequences for patterns of training in the Church. There will not be the people to maintain the patterns of Ministry as we now know them."

It was a long letter, sad and depressing to one like myself who entered the ministry at a time when six hundred men were being ordained each year as Deacons, when every parish however small, had its own parish priest; when congregations were large, the number of confirmation candidates were rising each year; when the Church in every parish was the centre of worship, learning and social activity.

Fifty years ago to this very day, I went as a newly made Deacon to my first parish of seven thousand souls; later that week I was sent to help at a Youth Club for three hundred adolescent boys and girls; to visit and take services in the local Hospital, every Sunday I took a Bible class for forty youngsters; a hundred members belonged to the Bible Reading Fellowship, half of whom met every month to study the set passages; every week I was expected to make at least thirty house visits; I taught every Friday in one or other of the four Church schools. I was one of three curates in that parish. Today it is two parishes combined, and there is *no* curate. No wonder the Warden of my theological college appeals for more vocations to the Ministry and for the money to pay them.

You can guess that on this day of all days I have been taking stock, looking back, and wondering. Taking stock of half a century of a marvellously varied and interesting ministry - thinking of the hundreds of babies I baptised, the several hundred boys and girls, men and women I prepared for Confirmation; the hundreds of couples I prepared for marriage; and I have been wondering what effect several thousand sermons may have had, God willing, on those who heard them. Looking back too, on many failures of ministry - days when the voice of God has told me to follow a certain line and I ignored that voice and sadness followed. Times when I had failed to follow up a bereavement regularly enough to help a widow who subsequently committed suicide. Times when I have not been loving enough, caring enough, helpful enough, prayerful enough, to help prevent the breakup of a family. Times when I forgot my ordination vows.

I have wondered much too, what help my sixteen years in Diocesan education may have been to the clergy and teachers in a hundred parishes with Church Schools, or the 150 men and women Readers God gave me to train, or the thousands of laypeople who attended the parish conferences I was privileged to lead over fifteen years.

Of course, there have been rewards, and as the world might judge, successes. Many confirmation candidates have remained faithful to their vows; many of those I have joined in matrimony have continued to love each other; the occasional sermon does seem to have helped; and I still get letters from parishes and schools where the Christian faith is being taught effectively and Jesus Christ is still alive.

But the fact remains, and the daily papers tell us so frequently, the Church of England seems to be in decline - or is it? Are there no signs of hope?

I have been making a sort of balance sheet of the Church as I knew it fifty years ago and as I know it today. On the positive side there are many changes of which I approve, and which have brought about a more Christian, more Biblical, more evangelistic, more lively Church. You may not think some of the examples I give are important, but they do indicate significant trends for the future.

First over these years I would put the *Humanisation of Bishops* and senior clergy. The Bishop who ordained me on Sunday June 29th, 1941 was a renowned theologian, with half a dozen scholarly books to his credit, but he had like most Bishops then, and regrettably many Bishops today, almost no parish experience. His only advice to me in the interview before he made me Deacon was to "Read the novels of Jane Austen once a year." His only word to me before my priesting was that I must not marry until I had been at least five years in Orders, and that he would not licence me to hear confessions until I was thirty. He had no authority, divine or otherwise, to make either of those prohibitions. I never spoke to him again, or indeed saw him again in the years I was in his diocese. Today Bishops are more human and more approachable and more helpful to their clergy. They are at last "Episcopoi", Shepherds.

Next I would put the development of *women's* ministry - fifty years ago Paul's injunction that women should keep quiet in Church was obeyed to the letter. Deaconesses and women workers were not even allowed to read the lessons, let alone the epistle, and certainly not preach. Today the Church's worship and ministry could not continue without the major contribution made by women Deacons, Deaconesses, women workers and women Readers. When we remember the part played by women in Jesus' own ministry and in the early Church the wonder is that we have taken so long to use women properly, and recognise their equal, if different, service to God. (Since this sermon was preached, women *have* been admitted to Priest's Orders. SH)

Allied with this over half a century is *the elevation of the laity*, the ordinary members of a congregation, to their rightful place as a royal priesthood, with again, equal though different, functions to those of the clergy. Why has it taken us so long to learn that the Church is made up of "all faithful people", not just the clergy, as people still so often say about a man being ordained "he is going into the Church" as if the Church equals the clergy.

When I think back fifty years and look at what we did, we clergy in reserving to ourselves every function except perhaps running the summer fête and the missionary jumble sale, I am appalled at how little we used the manifold *talents of the laity*. Today, as we learned from the letter from Lincoln, there are just not enough clergy to do the necessary work of the Church. So you and I are at last partners and equals, and the laity are not second class citizens of the Kingdom of God! There are dangers of course - I know of one parish where the congregation has taken over completely. They tell the Vicar what to do. They dominate the worship with their guitars and their dancing in the aisles. The theory is that this will attract the young. It does, but only one kind of young. It isn't the dignified worship of the Prayer Book, even the new Alternative book. What has happened is that the older members of the Church, who have maintained it, supported it and preserved it, have been driven away, the Vicar has left and what was meant to be a loving, worshipping community, joined in union with Christ at his altar, has become a divided unloving faction.

In the realm of *worship* I have no doubt whatsoever that the changes of the last few years, sensitively introduced with ample discussion and co-operation have been of great benefit to the Church. Although some have deplored the disappearance of Mattins as the main Sunday morning act of worship, at least in one Diocese known to me where over many years I shared morning worship in nearly two hundred churches, the lively congregations are those who share regularly in the Eucharist. And if we really do believe that we receive Christ himself in the bread and wine of our communion, surely that is to be expected and it is as it should be.

On the *other side of the balance* sheet there are items which make me sad.

First I would put the *decline in positive teaching* of the Faith and of Christian and moral values. This is partly due to the virtual end of the Sunday School - blame TV and the motor car if you will; but also, in my view, to the poor training of the clergy in theological colleges largely staffed by men with little parochial experience, so that many clergy are not able to communicate the basic truths of our Faith in words that you can understand, and in a way which makes you want to hear more. It is also partly due to the loss of thousands of Church schools since the war.

At a deeper level it is clear that the Church has suffered from the *ills and afflictions and the doubts of the society in which it is at work.* It is hard to proclaim a loving God when we contemplate daily on our TV sets, as we were not able to fifty years ago, the wars and revolutions, the floods and famines, the storms and destructive cyclones, the volcanic eruptions and the earthquakes which have destroyed whole communities and killed millions. Why does God allow it? Does He care? Can there even be a God when there seems to be so little evidence of his presence in our midst? The Church has not always helped people to face these great questions, so the people feel that it is increasingly irrelevant, unable to meet their deepest needs - whether it is coping with bereavement, with divorce in the family, painful illness, crime and the kind of society in which the unemployed receive a small handout and the rich get richer. "I went to Church last Sunday," someone said to me not long ago, "I was looking for some help, some encouragement, some strengthening, but all I got was hymns I couldn't sing and a sermon I couldn't understand."

There are a lot more changes I deplore but there isn't time to mention more than a few of them. I am sad at the disappearance of the *boys' choirs*, because so often that is where the seeds are sown which grow into vocations to the ministry. Perhaps girls' choirs will sow the seeds of future women's ministry!

There is no doubt that the Church has been pushed to the margin, the sidelines, for a historical reason - the state has taken over almost all the *social functions* of the Church. Fifty years ago in my parish we provided the entertainment, the youth work, the charity which kept poor families in clothes; the Vicar was the man folk came to when they were in trouble, and he was the man who took up the causes which needed to be publicised. Then too, very few women went to work, so their influence for good in their families was immense. They had the time.

I deplore too the *divisions in the Church* which have arisen in the last half century, highlighted in the General Synod between Evangelical and Catholic, fundamentalist and traditionalist, and I often wonder what Jesus would say if he were asked to speak in Synod. I grieve too at the increasing bureaucracy in the Church at every level, at the time we waste discussing the same things over and over again. Take *baptism* which the Synod will discuss at its next meeting - we were debating this in my theological college fifty years ago. It was the first subject on which I was asked to speak in a clergy Chapter in 1949. We are still talking about it. How sad. What we ought to be talking about is how to make more Christians, not how to alienate potential Christians.

You might think from all that that there is no hope for the Church, that depression has set in and the end of the Church is nigh. That is not what my faith teaches me. It teaches me that the Church is of God and if it is faithful to its calling the gates of hell cannot prevail against it. All Churches and all people go through troughs of despair as well as heights of elation. Never was the life of the Church at so low an ebb as in the 17th and early 18th centuries, but God raised up the Wesleys, and the men of the Evangelical and Catholic revivals of the Victorian age. He will do so again if we have faith. Even in fifty years we have seen stagnation and advance, black despair and high hopes.

My message to the Church would be to echo Paul's words to the Colossians which we heard just now...

"Above all, put on love, which binds everything together in perfect harmony. Let the peace of Christ rule in your hearts to which indeed you were called in one body. And be thankful." Love, peace, harmony. That is the antidote to the poison of depression and disunity. That is the secret of spiritual power. Love, peace, harmony. For the love of the Church which it has given me over half a century and for the love of so many church people, I am indeed thankful.

INDEX

HUSBANDS, Mrs. Infant
teacher, 89

HUTCHINSON, R. Latin
Master at RGS, 98

HUTCHINSON, The Rev. C.
(A priest's prayer to Jesus),
152

Hypnotism as therapy, 346

Ignorance, Sexual, 309

Illness, Pat's progressive,
C.15

Industrial Christian
Fellowship, 144, 175

Initiation, Christian (the
Report), 124, 276ff

Inspections of Schools, 220

Institution and Induction, C.9

Iona College, New Zealand,
171, 328

Ireland, village schools in, 89

JAMIESON. Bishop P., 213

JEFFERIES. Deaconess Jane,
212, Appendix

JOHN, J.E. English Master
RGS, 97

JOHNSON, Vera. Girl at
"The Swan", 44

JONES, Aled. Boy Soprano,
333, 359

JONES, P.L. Maths and
Careers Master RGS, 98

KARR, Alphonse (quotation),
133

KELLY, Dr. JND Tutor,
Chaplain, Vice-Principal &
Principal SEH, 123, 129

KENNEDY, Ludovic, 363ff

KING Edward, Bishop of
Lincoln, 144

King's College, London, 110

King's School, Rochester,
239ff, 331

KIRK, Kenneth, Bishop of
Oxford, 155, 167

Kitchen, at "The Homestead",
influence, 47

Knutsford, Clergy Training
College, 105

MACQUEEN, J.M. French
Master at RGS, 93, 98

MALLAM, Mary. Organist,
Chertsey, 181ff

Managers & Governors of
Schools, 261, 267

MARGARET, Princess,
HRH, 169, 299

MARGARET ROSE,
Princess. School in Windsor,
169, 299

Marriage, 172, C.13

MARY BEATRICE, Sister,
Holy Cross, 205

MARY, B. Virgin, 28

MARTI, M. French Master
at RGS, 98

MASCALL, Dr. Eric. Tutor,
Lincoln, 140

Mattins at Lincoln Cathedral,
143

Mattins at St. Stephen's, 198ff

Medway Towns (Chatham,
Rochester, Gillingham), 237

MEE, Arthur. Children's
Encyclopaedia, 102

Men's society, 201, 204

MEREDITH, Sir James (Pat's
grandfather), 160

MEREDITH, J.N.M.C. The
Rev. (Michael), 175, 316, 358

MEREDITH, Myfanwy, (Pat,
my wife), C.13 et passim

MEREDITH, R. Creed.
Vicar at Windsor, 150, 159,
189, C.8

MEREDITH, Richard (Pat's
Brother), 178, 313

MEREDITH, Sylvia (wife of
RCM) Pat's Mother, 172,
C.13

MEREDITH, a remarkable
family, 160

Midhurst Grammar School,
190, 193, 231, 234, 324, 372

MILBURN. Dean RMP at
Oxford, 125

MILLINGTON, E.C.
Chemistry Master RGS, 98

MILLS, Mrs. Landlady at
Oxford, 115

MILNER, Capt. J.C. History
Master RGS, 98, 102ff

MILTON, John, Poet, 67

Ministries, Specialist, 248

Misbourne, River, 78ff

Missions. Interest in, 189ff,
214ff

Money raising for Church
Hall, 182ff

Money, shortage of, 176, 192,
197

Montessori method of
teaching, 34

MONTGOMERY-
CAMPBELL, Henry, Bishop
of Guildford, 185, 194

MOORE, W. Deputy CEO,
Kent, 270, 395

Moral Rearmament (Oxford
Group), 129ff

MORGAN, Sam. Geography
Master RGS, 98ff, 104

MORRIS, The Rev. Peter,
284

MORTIMER, John &
Penelope, 309

MORTIMER, R.C., Bishop of
Exeter, 124

MOSLEY, Sir Oswald,
Fascist Leader, 120

Mother's Union, 105, 204,
318

Munich Crisis, 128

Murders in Denham, 71ff

Music as a therapy, 333, 339

Music at "The Homestead",
37

Music as taught at RGS, 100

Musicians as plagiarists, 295

Nannies, children's, 176ff

Napalm, use of, in Korean
War, 220

Napoleon, 17

NATFHE, Negotiations with
the Union, 247

National Hospital for Nervous
Diseases, 345

420

SIMPSON, Prof. D.C. at Oxford. Lectures, 124

Sin, original, 40, 61, 114

SOAR, Canon Reginald. My predecessor, 255

Social Security, cost of, 87

Social Work, the Church's, 161ff

Songs, father's favourite, 24

Southampton General Hospital, 351ff

SRAWLEY, Chancellor of Lincoln, lectures on Worship, 141

STARES family in Weston, 178, 320

Statistics, enjoyment of, 87

Steeple Claydon. Offered living of, 178

STEVENSON, R.L., 20

Stewardship campaigns, 182, 293

Steyning, Sussex, 134, 137ff

STIRLING, Darrel & Jane, 331

Stoke Poges, 67

STONE, H & A. Marriage Manual, 309

Study material for parishes, 273ff, 292ff

Suicide. Lecture. Pat's, C.15, 354, 357

Suicides at Chertsey in Thames, 189
at Oxford, 119ff

SUMPTER, D. PE Master at RGS, 97

Superstitions, Mother's, 41ff

SUTTON, Hilda, 331, 367

Swastikas at Windsor & Shottermill, 139, 164

Swimming as therapy, 333, 339

Synod, General, 275ff

Tailor, Journeyman. Grandfather, 17

TALBOT, Marianne. Quotation, 119

"Tales of Hoffman", 274, 295

424

WELLS, H.G. On social ranking, 33

WELSBY. Canon Paul, Rochester, 288

Wembley Exhibition1924/5, 24ff

Westcott House Theological College, Teaching Week, 141

Weston, Bath, parish of All Saints, 174ff, 319

"Whitefriars" House at Rochester, 233ff

WHITELEY, Roy. Stewardship Adviser, 293

WILD, Bishop Eric, of Reading, 252

WILLIAMS, Gavin. Organist, 330

WILLIAMS, May. Friend of Pat. Organist, 330

WILSON Elaine, 118

WILLS family. Walter, Doris, Frances, 137

Windsor, Curate of, 155ff

Wireless set. First, 50

Wives, Clergy, difficulties of, 190, 318ff

Women's Ministry, 196, 211ff, Appendix

Women Readers, 280, 286ff

Women Students at Oxford, 121ff

WOODGER, The Rev. Dick, Rector of Headley, 357

Woolmer Hill School in Shottermill, 218ff

WOOLNOUGH, Canon.F Sec. CACTM, 109, 289

Working Wives, Problems for, 190ff

Worship, forms of, 198ff

Year, the farming, 79

"Young Pilgrims", 203

Youth Clubs, 161

Youth Services at St. Stephen's, 204

"Zansizzey". House at Trevone, 329, 341ff